MODERN SALTWATER SPORT FISHING

BOOKS BY FRANK WOOLNER

Modern Saltwater Sport Fishing

Grouse and Grouse Hunting

Spearhead in the West

My New England

The Complete Book of Striped Bass Fishing
(with Henry Lyman)

The Complete Book of Weakfishing
(with Henry Lyman)

The Sportsman's Companion
(with Henry Lyman, E. C. Janes, and Clyde Ormond)

MODERN SALTWATER SPORT FISHING

by Frank Woolner

fully illustrated

Crown Publishers, Inc., New York

ACKNOWLEDGMENTS

I am indebted to a host of grand anglers from all corners of our watery world. They are the folk I have met, or have corresponded with, during a lifetime of fishing the sea. Each has taught me something of value. The erudite oceanographer, the chance acquaintance on a surf-lashed beach at midnight, the jungle guide who speaks little English — all have added to whatever intelligence of the craft I boast.

The great teachers are old seafarers, laconic and grumpy; commercial fishermen, suspicious of "sports," yet loquacious once you have gained their confidence; marine biologists and scientists and oceanographers who are afraid of lay writers because reporters so often warp words and meanings: most important — the rank-and-file angler who always offers a gem of truth that has escaped savants. I am fond of everyday fishermen: if you can speak their language and match cusswords, they provide facts that confound authorities. Invariably they are right.

My thanks go also to a wonderful group of saltwater outdoor writers and anglers, many of whom provided specialized information and photographs to illustrate this work. Credits are duly listed, but cold type cannot adequately express my appreciation. It is flattering to find so many able colleagues and craftsmen who are willing to share their particular expertise.

Special credits are due Henry "Hal" Lyman, publisher of *Salt Water Sportsman* Magazine, an authority with whom I have long collaborated in scribbling about marine angling. Hal was kind enough to read every chapter of this book in first draft, and he offered criticism where I suffered mental blocks or omitted important facts. Without his help I might have thrown some wondrous backlashes.

Edward F. ("Spider") Andresen, my associate editor at *Salt Water Sportsman,* helped with details about modern sport-fishing boats and the aerial spotting of fishes. Spider has been a charter skipper, a commercial swordfish harpooner, and an aviator. He is one of a new breed of anglers, who employ little, buzzing black boxes, sophisticated boats, and airplanes to bring great game fishes to hook.

Finally, I thank Nick Lyons of Crown Publishers, my editor in this venture. Nick is an angler, a superb writer, and a sensitive soul who is quite as appreciative of an opalescent dawn as a fine fish on a taut line. He loves inland trout, yet I think that he has been inoculated with the beneficent virus of sea sport. Nick also bedeviled me into a full year of labor in writing this book, and for that I do not know whether I should offer thanks or invite him to share an offshore fishing trip in a hurricane.

FRANK WOOLNER
Shrewsbury, Massachusetts

TABLE OF CONTENTS

Frank Woolner.

THE WORLD OCEAN ↱1

Playground for a Sea People

Not many years ago, I stood with a group of friends on the soft sand of a Cape Cod ocean beach while one of our first space satellites slid across a deep, blue-black zenith. It moved slowly, a miniature spark of fire, like a lazy cruiser threading a buoyage of stars.

Thoughtfully, we went back to our fishing, casting big surface plugs out into the dark Atlantic, seeking the cat-eyed striped bass that were prowling this rim of sea. Quite suddenly the earth was made smaller while the waves still rolled as though there were no lands beyond the hissing ground swells.

I knew better. To the left, had I glasses of sufficient power, it might have been possible to see the rising ground of Plymouth where the Pilgrims settled and starved and prayed and helped to build a nation. To the right? Three thousand miles of tumultuous ocean before Portugal's ancient seaports chinked the darkness with incandescent light. The sea's a very big thing.

Speeding in from outer space, our modern astronauts see a globe that grows steadily larger as their hurtling capsule devours the miles. It is a marbled sphere, glowing with faint blues and whites and irregular, scattered deeper tones, the shadowy, almost postscript shapes of land masses.

Blue predominates, for it is the color of the sea, and the sea covers almost three-quarters of our planet. Approximately 29.2 percent of the earth's surface rises above Homer's "wine dark and unvintageable ocean," so—whether we like it or not—we are all sea people. Evolutionists tell us that life originated in warm brine, and perhaps we are destined to go back to that medium in some undetermined future. Certainly the inscrutable ocean draws humankind. Men from the hinterlands annually rush to coastal resorts, hurry to the great beaches, and peer into an illimitable horizon. By God, it's the ocean! They stand there and gaze, enraptured, take pictures of themselves and their families with the sea as background. Herman Melville spoke of this in *Moby-Dick,* but you can see it enacted daily on any seashore, anywhere in the world.

Everyone knows that there are seven seas—and that is nonsense! There is a world ocean: it girdles and encompasses our globe; it shapes the continents and chews away or builds headlands as the surging currents and the tides and the winds pursue their inexorable courses. There are tornadic rivers in the sea, and continent-sized lakes so generally calm that they have imprisoned ancient mariners for weary months. There are quiet bays and landlocked harbors, vast flats and savage reefs. There are murderous tidal rips and benign coves and cold upwellings. The running tides sweep into estuaries and pulse through mangrove-bordered tidal creeks where the fiddler crabs duck into foxholes under rank marsh grasses. Nowhere is life more abundant, nowhere so diverse. We probe the outermost planets, but one of our last frontiers remains the enigmatic world ocean.

Surf casters find twilight a prime fishing period.

The seas are full of fishes, and until such time as we manage to destroy their nursery grounds or harry them into extinction by ill-advised commercial exploitation, they will remain a burgeoning renewable resource. Like the marbled globe seen by a returning astronaut, our world is small, no longer large enough to absorb all-out assault. We must practice conservation and management, else surely we will die.

This book is devoted to modern marine angling from a sportsman's viewpoint, but I have the greatest respect for commercial fishermen. These farmers of the sea are concerned; they employ erudite marine biologists and oceanographers to seek the truth. They desire a healthy renewable resource, a harvest well planned to ensure future wealth. Whether American, Russian, British, Japanese, Portuguese, or any of the other great sea peoples, these reapers of the ocean's largess are fully aware of the difficulties involved. Nobody plans suicide.

I note this at the very outset, for there is a certain small contingent of ill-advised sport fishermen who seek every opportunity to harpoon the commercial operator. Too often emotion overcomes reason and the angler blames a lack of fish on professionals who—as often as not—do not even seek the species that seems in short supply. There are, it must be admitted, occasional instances of transgression, opportunism, and unscrupulous exploitation—such as unlimited long-lining—but these are exceptions to prove a rule. Because their fortunes depend upon it, a majority of commercial fishermen practice good management.

Saltwater sport fishing is a relatively new development. Certainly men have always fished for fun, as well as sustenance, but marine angling for the sake of pure sport failed to become popular until the mid-1800s, and the big boom had to wait for the turn of the twentieth century. Indeed, it did not blossom into a mass preoccupation until two world wars and approximately fifty years had passed into history.

Of course, there were men who used sporting tackle in the 1800s. The split-bamboo rod came out of Great Britain about 1850, and very quickly became the choice of wealthy adventurers. Because these rods were expensive, they remained the tools of specialists for many years. Similarly, rods made of laminated woods enjoyed a lengthy heyday, again too costly for the average citizen to consider. Beautifully machined reels and carefully laid lines served a small minority of well-heeled sportsmen in those days.

At first, there were two groups of people who found sport in yanking fish out of the sea, and they were analogous because they lived right on the coast. One faction converted the ocean's largess into bread and butter through netting, trapping, and hand-lining, but they loved the work involved. What better labor than that which is also sport? A sunburned doryman's eyes always kindle with secret joy as he feels the writhing weight of a tremendous halibut oscillating up out of the depths. Undoubtedly, the ancient Incas, who fashioned stones as sinkers and lines from jungle fibers, glowed with pleasure as their arduous operations brought gleaming fish out of the brine.

And then it became true sport, perhaps first for old sailors who had swallowed the anchor and tried to convince their fellows that the sea no longer called; for schoolboys and gentle vicars and men of letters. Wielding crude tackle, or occasionally armed with the best available, they came down to the docks and caught conger or skate or striped bass. The fish varied, according to latitude and longitude, but they graced the tables of those long-gone sportsmen who cast a line for fun as well as sustenance.

Now I am going to make enemies among seadogs, and I couldn't care less, for there is no profit in useless legend. Advanced sport came to the ocean from far inland. It was the hinterlanders who came and conquered: landlubbers who couldn't conn a boat, chart a course, or read a compass—people whose eyes widened at the astonishing rise and fall of tides, the mathematically predictable current changes, seasonal winds, temperatures, upwellings, rips, and murderous offshore bars. They were innocents in chaos, but they had two things going for them—a new perspective and much intelligent curiosity.

This mass assault upon the sea as a new sporting arena began in the final years of the nineteenth century when a few mavericks blazed the way. They were pioneers and they took their lumps while writing a primer for the multitudes who would follow. In almost every case, the early birds were inlanders who possessed considerable wealth that enabled them to employ the best tackle available and to hire seafarers who knew the moods of the sea and could navigate precisely.

Wealth never emasculated these pioneers on the sea's sporting grounds. While that magic ingredient enabled them to indulge their fancies, they plumbed the unknown, often risking their lives to open up new areas. Their flesh was just as subject to sunburn and chill as the skippers and mates they employed; their muscles ached after a hard day on a loppy sea, and their hands also bled when taut lines and leaders sliced across skin painfully dried by the combination of salt and sun. They hardly needed this sort of punishment, but they were adventurers and they blazed new trails. Finally, they possessed intestinal fortitude. Neither the early birds nor their seafaring guides were ever found lacking in this commodity.

So they were inlanders who conquered the immortal sea with sporting tackle. They did so because they added a new measure of creativity and expertise to the blue-water sailor's ancient usages. Where old seamen stolidly accepted practices proved by their fathers and great-grandfathers, the new breed took nothing for granted—other than the awe-inspiring immensity of salt water. They learned how to cope with the often treacherous ocean, and they devised new weapons and new strategies to grapple with the giants of the sea. The teacher became the pupil as capable skippers bowed to the new logic of their patrons. Together, they posted tremendous advances in the art, yet none boasted mastery of all problems on the capricious ocean. Nobody will ever do that, nor will the angler ever close his book, supremely confident. The world ocean is vast, and many of its secrets still elude the grasp of man.

Prior to the cornucopia years of the late 1940s, marine sport remained the domain of a selected few. That rod and line had been enjoyed for a full century before that time is undisputed. Henry William Herbert, a transplanted Englishman who was one of America's foremost outdoor writers under the nom de plume of Frank Forester, was rhapsodizing about saltwater fishing prior to the mid-1800s. Much of Forester's information was faulty, but the interest was there. Genio C. Scott, a great scribbler of the 1870s, detailed angling with light tackle for such wonderful gamesters as the striped bass, bluefish, and weakfish; G. Brown Goode followed in the eighties with a learned book called *American Fishes.* While Forester's illustrations were ludicrous— one depicted a striped bass with an extra set of fins—Goode's were so generally excellent that some are still used by ichthyologists.

Before the turn of the century, marine angling had become a status thing. It was an era of tycoons, of big fortunes, and American imperialism. The best of the enthusiasts risked their lives, if not their cash, on a dream. They brought new ideas into saltwater fishing.

Some of these immortals succeeded, while many failed. In 1882, A. W. Dimock freighted an Indian canoe down from New York and caught big Florida tarpon at the mouth of the Homosassa River. Far ahead of his time, Dimock not only subdued these great, chrome-plated brutes, but managed to take a host of spectacular action photographs. He used relatively heavy tackle, but try to imagine playing a huge tarpon from a canoe!

Great game fish had been whipped prior to the late 1800s, but always on heavy gear or handlines. About 1871, a Nova Scotia schoolteacher named Thomas Patillo challenged giant bluefin tuna at Liverpool Harbor and succeeded in boating a 600-pounder. Tom used, according to Van Campen Heilner who related the tale, "thirty-two fathoms of ordinary codline" on "a swivel reel of some sort." While the Nova Scotia schoolmaster certainly hooked his quarry, evidently he played it via the keg-line method, with his banks dory the "keg." Since all authorities list Charles F. Holder's Catalina tuna as the first taken on rod and reel, there is some question whether the Canadian pioneer even employed a rod.

Holder's conquest of a 183-pound tuna off Catalina Island, California, in 1898 is well documented, and this catch launched big-game fishing as we know it today. Modern anglers consider a 183-pounder "just another baby," not quite heavy enough to be classed as a giant and easily subdued on lighter tackle than the rig used by Holder. The difference, of course, is the star-drag reel of today. Few moderns would care to challenge a full-blooded tuna of that size with a simple winch attached to a standard boat rod. Holder was a hero in his time slot, a conqueror of monsters. I suspect, in spite of his leather thumbstall, that he collected blisters.

Sailfish had been caught as early as 1901, and striped marlin shortly thereafter. Each catch was a headline event, and should have been, considering the tackle of the time. While it was easy enough to wrestle a featherweight or middleweight battler to beach or boat on a knuckle-buster reel, advantage passed to the quarry when its weight matched or surpassed that of the angler. Something had to be done in order to even the odds.

Shortly after the turn of the century, a handy California gentleman named William Boschen invented the first revolutionary saltwater reel. Bill was a fisherman who got pretty sick and tired of busting his hands every time a great gladiator took the bait and departed for far horizons. Moreover, he was enamored of the wonderful broadbill swordfish, a species he later sought to the near exclusion of all else.

Like all inventors, Boschen spent some years tinkering with his new adjustable drag reel. Sometime before World War I he got in touch with Julius vom Hofe of Brooklyn, and Joe Coxe, a pair of master mechanics and craftsmen. Boschen, who appears to have been a modest man, declined the honor of having this great advance named after him, and so Julius vom Hofe produced it as the "B-Ocean."

The reel made history. Initially, contemporaries scoffed, but William Boschen wasn't at all deterred. He took the new winch out and caught a 355-pound swordfish in 1913. *That* perked ears all over the world. There is nothing better than success to advertise the virtues of a new development.

With the successful conclusion of World War I, fortunes burgeoned in America and the wealthy began to bend their gaze on marine angling. It was still much too early for participation by rank-and-file citizens, especially those who lived inland. Coastal dwellers seldom used very sophisticated gear, sticking pretty much to handlines, heave-and-haul, or lures trolled from the pitching decks of catboats. There was a multitude of sport and game fish, so nobody felt underprivileged. The head boats sailed out of metropolitan ports and patrons collected everything from cod and haddock to blue-fish, weakfish, porgies, sea bass, and tautog. The tackle was crude, but effective, and coastal anglers began to derive much joy from the harvesting of various fishes.

Yet there was no boom in the years immediately following World War I. Surf casters still employed heavy heave-and-haul gear; they coiled linen or tarred cotton line on the beach, whirled drails above their heads and sent them arrowing far out over the breakers. Retrieved, hand over hand, drails accounted for surprising numbers of striped bass and bluefish. This is no easily mastered art and now it is all but for-gotten.

Far prior to the universal acceptance of Boschen's earthshaking star-drag reel, sophisticated anglers were using well-made knuckle-busters like the famous and beauti-fully machined Vom Hofe winches. These were favored at such elite watering places as the Cuttyhunk, Squibnocket, Pasque Island, and Cohasset Narrows clubs. The rods were split-bamboo or natural Burma cane, and the lines were the popular linen twist called Cuttyhunk. There was little casting with artificial lures, but much bottom bouncing with such baits as lobster tails. Striped bass were vectored in by copious chumming with marine delicacies, many of which—like the lobsters—would now be too expensive to use as chum or bait.

In those first years of the new century, aristocrats of the eastern cities congregated at the great striped bass fishing locations. They enjoyed plush living accommodations, such as those at Cuttyhunk; they employed a retinue of guides, chummers, and gillies. These zealots fished from skeletonized wooden and steel stands erected above the breakers, and they lacked no creature comfort. The old Cuttyhunk flag was adorned

Surf-casting platform at Squibnocket, Martha's Vineyard, now long gone.

with a rocking chair and three stars on a blue field—the stars of Hennessy brandy.

Zane Grey soon earned himself a niche as a saltwater fishing pioneer. While Grey was busily turning out potboilers like *Riders of the Purple Sage,* his heart was out on the sea with royal game fish. The author's western novels made him rich and famous, yet they are impossible junk compared to the magnificent accounts of fishermen against the sea that he turned out as labors of love. No big-game buff, to this day, can read his *The Case of the Hungry Swordfish* without a pursing of the lips and a surge of sympathy for the anglers who realized, after 11½ hours of gut-busting combat, that a great, well-hooked broadbill was tranquilly feeding on flying fish. After all these years, one can still share the pained, stunned silence after that line was parted.

Boschen's reel, unveiled in 1913, was the most important single contribution to saltwater angling in our galloping century. Crusty old sportsmen, as usual, were loathe to accept its virtues, and then, of course, there was a great war to be fought and won. Until the world returned to a semblance of normalcy in 1919, marine fishing languished, the sole concern of commercial operators and coastal dwellers.

Even with peace, there was no immediate rush to the sea. Grey was there, ranging the world ocean and making history with rod and reel. Off Catalina, the disciples of Holder were catching more marlin and tuna as they experimented with kites to skip baits. There was a stirring in the Deep South, where a scattering of sportsmen had "discovered" bonefish and tarpon. Bait-casting reels were most commonly used, although a few brave souls were already beginning to experiment with fly rods in the salt. The pioneers of this era are legion, and I will name none of them! Many of these old boys are still alive and kicking, and they kick like merry hell when you mention that any one of their contemporaries developed a specific method, opened up a fishing ground, or created a new fly type. All hands claim to be first! While I could make an educated guess, it would have to be just that. They were all great.

Meanwhile, far up along the North Atlantic Coast, squidders were beginning to replace heave-and-haul operators in the surf and it became fashionable for residents of coastal cities to book passage on head boats to catch a whole grab bag of sport fish. During this period of relative affluence in the late twenties, there was a glimmering of interest along every seaboard, but a majority of sportsmen still kept their attention riveted on inland species. Striped bass were not plentiful, thanks to the strange cycle of scarcity and abundance peculiar to that species, and big game had yet to interest wealthy playboys. Zane Grey, almost single-handed, ranged the oceans—and nobody really cared. His books on fishing are classics now, but they were greeted with faint praise at the time of publication.

Zane Grey and Captain Sid Boerstler. Grey was one of America's pioneer big-game fishermen and a grand writer. *Photo courtesy Captain Sid Boerstler*

All this changed immediately after President Franklin D. Roosevelt jolted old-line conservatives and yanked the nation out of an abysmal economic depression. Ocean fishing very suddenly became an in thing, and we owe much to those who were financially able and courageous enough—in the vernacular of the day—to try anything once.

On the North Atlantic seaboard, a small coterie of enthusiasts recalled Holder's conquest over bluefin tuna, and ruefully noted that Zane Grey had whipped a 758-pound tuna off Yarmouth, Nova Scotia, in August 1924. Bigger fish were there for the taking, and a grand assemblage of sportsmen conned private cruisers over the cold seas from the Maritime Provinces down through the Gulf of Maine to Block Island Sound and Montauk during the early and mid-thirties. Great names were made then: Michael Lerner and Ben Davis Crowninshield, Dr. Leon Storz, Tommy Gifford, Jimmy Whittall, and S. Kip Farrington, Jr. Other greats were pioneering tropical waters. H. W. Woodward and Ernest Hemingway conquered the great tuna and billfish of Bimini and Cuba. Farrington was both fisherman and Boswell, but his books were still to come.

While angling history was being made on blue-water grounds, marine angling generally simmered on a very low burner prior to the end of World War II. There was notable progress in the development of tackle, and more people sought sport in the surf and on the party boats. Yet, as it always had been, the proponents of classic salt-water fishing were either the wealthy or those of more moderate means who lived within a few miles of the coast. Inland anglers continued to concentrate on sweetwater species.

Salty literature remained scant. In addition to Genio C. Scott, Goode, and Forester, together with a host of scribblers who attempted to chronicle ocean angling (but had no firsthand information to offer), the cupboard was nearly bare.

Of course, Zane Grey's accounts of marine angling, first published in 1919, were like a fresh sea breeze, and he was followed by such titans as Van Campen Heilner, a grand fisherman and writer. Harlan Major's monumental *Salt Water Fishing Tackle* was published in 1939. It was a good book then and it was improved by a later updating; unfortunately, like so many of the truly fine works, it is now out of print.

In that thunderous, strife-stricken year of 1939 *Salt Water Sportsman* magazine came into being, but it was far from a national journal at that time. Hugh Grey, Oliver H. P. Rodman, and Horace G. Tapply pooled their slender resources and launched a weekly four- to eight-page tabloid-sized newssheet for marine anglers in New England. Because all three were accomplished fishermen and fine writers, Volume I, Number 1 was a very readable offering. It is a matter of record that the first issue nearly bankrupted the trio because Ollie's spaniel ate all the postage stamps that had been purchased to mail the masterpiece.

Zane Grey, Van Campen Heilner, and Harlan Major were the earliest of the modern authorities. Down south, L. S. ("Lou") Caine was producing fine material in the late thirties. His *Game Fish of the South,* published in 1935, is still good and accurate reading, marred only by the fact that it covers freshwater species as well as those found in the salt chuck.

Soon Ollie Rodman, a gracious Bostonian, was writing razor-edged copy. Together with Heilner, Raymond R. Camp, and Erl Roman, he must be listed among the first modern pooh-bahs of surf casting. What they wrote during the early forties survives the critical probing of time. These specialists zeroed in; they knew precisely what they were talking about and, if you have their books in your library, they will prove quite as valuable today as when new-minted. If the tackle is outmoded, as it certainly is, the methods and techniques are timeless.

S. Kip Farrington, an early chronicler of marine
angling, with two 617-pound swordfish he caught
off the coast of Peru in 1941.
Photo by S. Kip Farrington

S. Kip Farrington, Jr., the driving force behind Wedgeport's International Tuna Tournament, and later an enthusiastic tub-thumper for Cabo Blanco in Peru—a crusade that died through no fault of Kip's, but only because of a shift in ocean currents (Farrington steadfastly maintains that Japanese long-liners decimated the grounds)— offered many articles and two noteworthy books, *Fishing the Atlantic* and *Fishing the Pacific*. Both sounded as though they were dictated at shout level during a Force Five gale, and both offered much vital information, together with some lousy poetry by big-game enthusiasts who were far more zealous than literate. The books are musts in any marine angler's library.

Kip once called me when I was a fledgling editor of *Salt Water Sportsman* and gave me blue hell for extolling the fighting abilities of striped bass. In tones more nearly suited to oral communication in a typhoon, he advised me that "if you tied a 10-pound striper to the tail of a 5-pound roosterfish, the bass would be towed to death!"

At that time, back in 1950, I had yet to make the acquaintance of Pez Gallo, but I certainly respected the august Kip Farrington. Much later I learned that he had a point. The rooster is a tremendously strong battler, a fighter whose tactics include the dogged power of a jack with the acrobatics of a tarpon. And yet, after all these years, I think that Kip was wrong—because it is absolutely impossible to compare fishes. The one on your line at any given moment is always the greatest, and I think Kip would agree.

Well before World War II paralyzed sport fishing on all coasts, charter and party boatmen were operating wherever the trade warranted. Head boats predominated, because fees were within the reach of average citizens, yet there was a steady gravitation toward the more costly charters. In New Jersey, and later in Florida and the Caribbean, a tough and crusty young skipper named Tommy Gifford was walloping everything from bluefish and school tuna to sails and marlin. Like most of us then, Gifford interrupted his fishing to attend a war, and he served with distinction. In view of his later reputation as a stormy petrel, one wonders how Tommy ever managed to obey orders from higher authority; he must have been a difficult subordinate, but a man to trust when the chips were down. I met him only once, at his slip in a Key Largo, Florida, marina. He was extremely opinionated, but all of his pronouncements made sense. We got along well, all things considered, such as the fact that I was the jumped-up editor of a marine fishing magazine, long on surf casting at that time, but with no great knowledge of blue water.

The first great boom in saltwater sport fishing was a direct result of World War II. Perhaps nobody can sort out the chemicals of the time and determine precisely what happened. I would guess that an entirely logical chain of circumstances triggered this massive flush of interest. Certainly until 1946 the game had simmered along, the bailiwick of the indigent coaster and the wealthy adventurer. The prewar masses simply were not excited about great fish in the sea, nor had they the means to experiment.

Among the end products of war, in addition to fields of white crosses and sad memories, are other and happier developments. Because humankind is stretched to unbearable limits of inventiveness and innovation during such a global conflict, science prospers and men who might otherwise live out their three score and ten in somnolent villages suddenly find that the world is both wide and fruitful. The adventurers, those who have returned with medals and honors, cannot accept a humdrum existence; for them there must be sport with a spice of danger. Bugles in the storm, and all that sort of nonsense.

Of course, that doesn't explain the phenomenon. Part of it must be credited to a greater affluence, rapid transportation, and more leisure time. There is much to be said for the fact that inland waters, even by the end of World War II, were fast approaching a point of no return. Pollution and "progress" were destroying once immaculate trout streams and mountain lakes. Communications media clarioned the exploits of marine anglers and manufacturers created saltwater tackle well within the budgets of average citizens. Indeed, the war wizards had invented miraculous materials that, like the swords of antiquity, could be beaten into the plowshares of sporting tackle.

Quite suddenly, following that war, marine sport fishing was camp, and it was the game of the everyday citizen as well as the wealthy. Enthusiasts found that deep-sea fishing was really a figment of the imagination and that shoal waters offered a wide variety of wonderful gamesters that might be taken on all sorts of tackle combinations.

Inevitably, cults developed. There was the brotherhood of the high surf, people who would settle for nothing other than a striped bass, a bluefish, a channel bass, or a tide-runner weakfish. There were the offshore people who wanted tuna and sails and marlin; the bottom bouncers who took great delight in wrestling cod and haddock and snappers and groupers. They were a great and growing association of anglers, and most of them came from the hinterlands.

They came without prejudice or knowledge of the sea. They learned to respect the ocean, and many of them are buried in its depths because they dared too much. Because they were inlanders, these new arrivals scoffed at useless tradition and experimented with new methods. In many cases, they failed, and yet their astonishing successes completely revolutionized saltwater sport fishing as it was known prior to World War II. The old seafarers found themselves skipping very nimbly to keep up. In 1946, the world went fishing, and the world's people went to the sea.

Since that time the sport and the literature have prospered. A whole host of bright young men are currently producing books about marine angling, and some of them will be remembered ages hence. I have my favorites, but only time and the measured judgment of bookmen and saltwater fishermen can applaud the nonpareils. I make one exception.

In 1949, Henry ("Hal") Lyman bought *Salt Water Sportsman* magazine, lock, stock, and fish-finder. At that time Hal was a young guy of independent means whose biography was rather unique. Prior to World War II, he'd scorned the fact that he had a fortune at his command and went out to prove that a proper Bostonian could make his own way. As a youth, after graduating from the usual Ivy League prep school and Harvard complex with honors, Lyman went to work as a flunky on an inland daily newspaper. Then the big war came along and Hal characteristically enlisted in the U.S. Navy.

Lyman fought that war in destroyers. He was torpedoed once, shot and was shot at numerous times, and can claim an assist in sending a few German U-boats to the deep six. Now balding and twinkle-eyed, he seems a very mild person, and yet his nickname along some waterfronts was "Knife." Hal is a very velvet-glove type, but there is keen metal beneath the cosmopolitan surface.

Lyman enjoyed a few years of peace before he was called back into service as a reserve officer during the Korean conflict. In 1950, I assumed command as editor of *Salt Water Sportsman* while Hal fought that war, returning as a full commander. There were tongue-in-cheek reports that he had an angler's fighting chair installed on the fantail of his destroyer.

Like the aforementioned Tommy Gifford, I am a difficult subordinate, but I consider Hal Lyman one of the world's foremost authorities on marine sport fishing. Certainly there are areas in which he is weak, and he will not hate me for saying so, but he has more total grasp of the situation in all the world's oceans than any man now alive. That's why government and fishery agencies of many nations, including those of the Communist bloc, often seek his opinions in the fields of marine sport and commercial fishing. I don't know whether he will become immortal, but Lyman is one of today's final authorities.

The sea remains a tremendous challenge and a new frontier. We have just begun to fish around the edges, and our techniques—quite adequate now—may be passé within another couple of decades. The essense of life is change. Therefore, we will continue to learn and our studies will add to the joys of angling. We fish in a world ocean and the world grows smaller with each revolution of the earth.

Tomorrow, thanks to rapid transportation, greater affluence, and intelligence, sportsmen will thread this entire planet to seek great game fish. There will be a pressing need to study languages and cultures, to be at home wherever the great jets land. Sport fishermen, whatever their native lands, are kindred spirits, rarely affected by partisan politics.

The world ocean enfolds us. It is the last true frontier on this spinning sphere.

We are a sea people.

WEAPONRY - RODS AND REELS ~2

Basic Tools for Marine Angling

Only a great fisherman has the right to call a rod a "pole," and a fishing line a "string." Therefore, I am going to do neither in this discussion of primary weapons employed by modern marine anglers. Today's tackle is highly sophisticated and deserves much respect. We have witnessed a beneficent revolution during the twentieth century.

It started with the creation of split-bamboo rods sometime in the mid-1800s (1850 is the year usually cited) and continued with precisely machined reels, such as the classic Vom Hofe series that ushered in a new century. These were the tools used by such specialists as Charles F. Holder in 1898, and there was little change when Charles B. Church set a longtime record on striped bass in 1913. During that very year, Boschen and Vom Hofe introduced the star-drag reel, one of the greatest advances in marine fishing tackle.

An Englishman, Holden Illingworth, quietly produced another bombshell in 1920 when he invented the forefather of all modern spinning or fixed-spool reels. Perhaps "invented" is not the word to use, for Illingworth really developed an idea that goes back into antiquity. Aborigines had experimented with basketlike spools upon which line was wound by hand and then cast by turning the axis of the spool toward the target. A Scotsman, Peter Malloch of Perth, fashioned a fixed-spool reel in 1884, but it was a rather confused affair mounted on a sort of turntable, actually a bastard progeny of principles involved in both basic spinning and revolving spool theory.

Illingworth was first to put it all together, to introduce gearing, an enclosed housing, and a bail. He didn't invent the whole animal, but he surely made an ancient principle workable under practical conditions. Spinning first attained popularity in Europe, but it wasn't until 1935 that Bache Brown popularized it in the United States. Actually, because of initial sales resistance—and then a great war—spinning in America remained in the doldrums until 1946.

It should be noted that "spinning" is not always a reference to fixed-spool tackle. In Great Britain there is a light-tackle technique that makes use of a long, limber rod and a very simple single-action center-pin reel that is called spinning. Granted, this is primarily a freshwater outfit used on so-called coarse fish. Just to add a bit of confusion, fixed-spool, in England, may be called either thread-line or spinning.

In those somnolent years between great wars there was no rapid development of fishing tackle. A few saltwater anglers used braided silk lines, while a majority favored tarred cotton or the more efficient, if problem-plagued, linen twist called Cuttyhunk. The affluent boasted split-bamboo rods, sometimes double-built, but they still thought that one tiptop, plus some facing guides, was sufficient.

The explanation for facing guides is interesting. Our grandfathers knew that the Burma cane and split-bamboo rods of the time were prone to develop "sets." Therefore, it seemed reasonable to conclude that facing guides would solve the problem; when a stick began to warp, you simply turned it over and used the facing guide, thus warping it back in the right direction. No one appeared to realize that by the time a rod had acquired a "set" its wooden fibers were severely strained. Reversing the tip simply hastened crystallization and subsequent breakage. Golden memories aside, it was a strange season in which a busy surf caster did not shatter several rods, each in the midst of a glorious adventure.

Tubular fiber glass was a child of war, and it had its birth pangs. I well remember an occasion, shortly after Hitler's legions had been ground into the dust, when the representative of a famous American rodmaker attempted to demonstrate the power of his new glass stick. The patter was convincing, and the rod seemed a winner.

Then a colleague, applying pressure on a line that extended from the tiptop, used a bit too much muscle—and the rod exploded with a loud report and an accompanying cloud of dust. Viewers sadly went back to split bamboo and carefully wound Burma cane for surf casting. Neither were really ideal for saltwater work, but they remained the best bets. Similarly, big-game anglers placed their trust in laminated woods. Who needed a glass tube that might blow up, or even one of the new steel shafts that had been known to fracture and spear a fisherman right where he least needed spearing? At that time, I had a tubular-steel surf rod that worked like a charm until it parted in the midst of a power cast. Thanks to stresses generated, the tip section whipped back and carved a neat, bloody little hole just to the right of my belly button.

In those early days it took a certain amount of rampant optimism to experiment with new developments. Practically all of them had teething troubles, some serious enough to arouse doubts in the minds of their inventors. Julian Crandall, the autocratic old genius who was one of the first to experiment with braided nylon lines at his Ashaway Line & Twine emporium in Rhode Island, was heard to mutter about the excessive elasticity of his "damned fishing string." Shortly afterward, together with contemporaries, he solved the problem. So many intelligent people were solving problems then that fishing tackle advanced more rapidly during the forties and fifties than it had in the preceding hundred years.

In rapid succession, anglers were treated to tubular and solid fiber-glass rods, fine synthetic lines, highly sophisticated revolving-spool reels, and equally well-engineered spinning winches. Terminal tackle and lures maintained the pace so that, very suddenly, the marine fisherman found himself in a wonderful new era. In the forties and fifties we forged new weapons for a new frontier of sport.

The frontier was there, only vaguely recognized, yet practically all of today's great tackle combinations were either marketed or on the drawing boards prior to the sixties. Thereafter, progress was measured in the improvement of existing gear. This improvement will continue through the remainder of a racing century. However, we can detail weaponry that has been thoroughly field tested and found highly efficient.

We can also note, sometimes with a slightly raised eyebrow, that marine fishing is far from a muscleman's game; it is everything from the lightest in tackle and the ultimate in finesse to grunting and groaning over a Herculean rig while a sea monster bores into the depths or greyhounds five hundred yards from the transom.

Imprimis, be advised that you can catch saltwater game fish on almost anything in the way of tackle. You can employ a handline, stone sinker, and crude hook—as the ancient Incas did—or you can turn the trick with an astonishing variety of mechanical aids. Within reason there is no tackle too light, and really none too heavy. It depends upon the desire of the angler, the fish he seeks, the water and weather conditions that must be sumounted.

Having said this, I immediately seek refuge in the realm of specialization. Unless you're a wishful thinker, you do not seek giant tuna with a fly rod, nor do you hunt bonefish with a 14/0 130-pound-test outfit. Our world ocean offers a wide variety of game fish and fishing conditions. The well-informed angler employs tackle that is job-rated. There are nuances of technique, yet saltwater fishing methods are remarkably similar throughout the world. I covet the thought that a truly great sportsman should be quite as expert with a fly rod as he is with the various weights of spinning tackle, bait- and surf-casting rigs, light trolling, and big-game combinations. If he's a real fisherman, he'll also know how to take the nibblers with a basic bottom bouncing rig, and he'll enjoy every moment of the action. The great ones are incurable enthusiasts.

Once, off Islamorada, Florida, Charley Whitney and I fished with Joe Brooks, certainly one of America's modern marine fishing pioneers. Joe, who had taken most of the famous game fish, was already a legend. We were casting tiny bucktail lures to catch blue runners for sailfish bait, and Charley inadvertently cast across Joe's line while he was tied into one of these midgets.

Brooks, who is one of the gentlest guys in the world, suddenly became peevish. "My God, Charley," he wailed, "I've got a fish on, and you crossed my line!"

To Joe, who had fished around the world and set his hooks into a wide variety of spectacular gamesters, this minnow on his line was the most important fish in the sea. And he was entirely right!

The tackle is your choice, but make it modern and make it tough—unless you have some strange desire to emulate the trail blazers. Nowadays, fiber-glass rods practically dominate the field. They do so because they are far superior to laminated wood, split bamboo, steel, or any other material in the business of combating the drying, corroding, salt-wet destructive forces of brine. On an inland trout stream I am very fond of a perfectly balanced split-bamboo fly rod, but I would not subject so ethereal a wand to the fury of the open ocean. If I did, there is no doubt that the rod would perform beautifully, but the ocean is a killer. That's why our modern tackle is designed to be as nearly indestructible as our science allows.

Fiber glass, designed in wartime, is the ocean's rod material and it has proved more versatile than anything else. Almost nothing bothers glass (although it will fatigue slowly), and it is a reasonably cheap material. In anything but the very lightest of fly rods (and this is arguable) fiber glass boasts properties far in advance of any organic building blocks. There is no doubt about this, although traditionalists still maintain that split bamboo and the various laminated woods boast such virtues as craftsmanship in construction that ensures secret joy, beauty to provide hyacinths for the soul, and an indescribable "feel" they say is lacking in the vulgar, cheap, atomic age of glass.

I can sympathize with the traditionalists, for I too feel that craftsmanship is disappearing from this earth. Still, any reluctance to accept technical advances is a symptom of stupidity. The Kentucky rifle was a masterpiece, its customized fittings rarely equaled in this day, yet Dan Boone's flintlock is a sorry antique compared to the cheap, mass-produced big-game rifles of the seventies.

There are, roughly, two general rod blanks made of fiber glass: one is tubular, and therefore very light, while the other is solid. Both serve a multitude of purposes. While the tubular rod boasts light weight and fast action, it is never quite so tough and indestructible as the solid shaft. Invariably, you will find that the better marine fishing rods are tubular, while cheaper models are solid. This in no way indicts the solid fiber-glass rod as an inferior product; for certain operations it can be a very practical tool.

Think "solid" if you want a tough, practical stick for pier and bottom fishing, for medium trolling, or for the attention of youngsters who are prone to abuse delicate equipment. While guides and reel seats on a solid fiber-glass rod are just as subject to failure here, as on a more ethereal weapon, the stick is nearly indestructible.

By all means choose tubular fiber glass if you want the finest in balance and action. This applies all the way from ultralight spinning and featherweight fly rods on up the scale through bait casting, high surf, and light trolling to big-game sticks. While there are degrees of excellence in tubular fiber glass, you will be reasonably well satisfied if you purchase the products of any well-established tackle maker.

There is no all-purpose saltwater rod, and we'd better believe that at the very outset. The stick that is calibrated to handle a certain well-defined weight range in casting, or a specific level of stress in trolling, simply cannot be overloaded or undergunned if peak performance is desired. Similarly, rod action and length must be designed for a particular operation. No written word can narrow the choice down to one model, so a beginner's best bet is to query a local authority. Tell him precisely what you want to catch, where, and how; he will then be able to recommend a rod best suited to your needs.

Immediately the tyro will find that saltwater rods, unlike those manufactured for freshwater use, almost always are offered in one-piece *or* jointed versions. Theoretically, a one-piece rod is always superior in action. Because such a rod has a lesser number of dovetailed parts to invite trouble, a straight stick is both basic and practical. There are problems.

For example, a one-piece fly rod—and some have been produced—is a far superior weapon to the jointed article that is weakened by ferrules. Unfortunately, the fly rod is both limber and lengthy, so a one-piece wand is an abomination to carry. Unless you live right on the seacoast, or can transport rods on racks bolted on motor vehicles or boats, the breakdown version is a necessity.

Stowage and transportation, not efficiency on the sea front, are overriding considerations. I prefer one-piece surf-casting rods, yet they become liabilities when it is necessary to fly across a continent to some remote beach. Jointed surf rods can be made; indeed I have one, a magnificent tool produced by Fenwick. It is not now in production, due to limited demand and the high cost of manufacture, but may well figure in the future plans of world-ranging anglers. Airlines are understandably irked by passengers who desire to board jets with 10- to 14-foot fishing rods.

In addition to the surf stick, which is a stowage plague to metropolitan apartment dwellers who must utilize public transportation to and from beaches, there is much sense in the breaking down of lengthy spinning rods. Big-game tackle, because of the necessity of heavy, locking reel seats and hickory butts, invariably features two-piece rods with the tip in one section and the butt in another. This is proper and I see no other solution.

Perhaps, under certain conditions, there is logic in the more radical jointing of certain rods. Never a very diplomatic fellow, I once told Phil Clock, president of the Fenwick Tackle Company, that multiple-jointed rods were Mickey Mouse affairs and I wanted no part of them. Phil promptly sent me three of his Voyageur series, suitcase-sized sticks broken down into four pieces, and I took a one-handed spinning rod to

Central America. It worked like a dream of fair weapons and I had to eat my words.

If there is any moral, it is this: use one-piece rods whenever and wherever they pose no problems in stowage or transportation, but don't be afraid of the well-made jointed item.

Insist upon good hardware. It doesn't matter whether the rod is designed to cast a fly, a hunk of cut bait or a lure, to troll or to bounce bottom, the guides and the reel seat can make or break your fishing trip. In trolling, there is no substitute for fine tolerance roller guides, and the reel seat, particularly where big game is sought, must be ideally designed and tough enough to absorb Herculean stresses. There is little margin for error when a possible record gamester is heading for the bright horizon and you are sweating and straining while the mate anoints you with an occasional bucket of cool salt water.

Recalling marine corrosion, choose rust-resistant snake or ring guides for a fly rod. Be very certain that the rings on a spinning rod are equally tough and resistant to brine.

Ring guides are made of various metals and sometimes lined with ceramics. The poorest are thinly plated with chrome and soon groove. The best are solid carbaloy or may be fitted with a ceramic inner ring. Agate guides were the choice of a long-gone generation, and agate remains a magnificent guide liner; its only handicaps are expense and a tendency to fracture when subjected to any hard rap. Like the plebeian hook, fine guides are relatively cheap. Insist upon the very best and you will find that they pay their way.

Guide maintenance is imperative. Check them often and discard those that have been grooved or chipped. The slightest irregularity will fray lines and lose fish. Questionable rings can be inspected by running a woman's sheer nylon stocking through them. Any imperfection will become immediately apparent, and that guide should be discarded. You can go to work with fine sandpaper and crocus cloth, but the cost of replacement is so meager that repair is a waste of time—other than in an emergency.

Rollers enjoy greater longevity although the tiptop has a tendency to groove its bridges when wire line is jigged. The resulting jagged crease can bend wire at a sharp angle, and thus cause it to crystallize and break, or it can quickly cut any of the synthetic fibers. For this reason, some wire-line anglers who specialize in the jigging of lures always employ a ring guide at the tiptop, while the others are rollers. A major problem with a ring tiptop in wire-line fishing is the fact that it creates binding when a gamester dives straight down into the depths and must be pumped up. The sharp angle of the wire and the immovable surface of the ring ensure this sorry state of affairs. Of course, wire very rapidly grooves any ring, including the tough carbaloy type, so regular replacement is a necessity.

Your new saltwater rod, regardless of its type, should be fitted with enough guides to distribute the stresses generated in casting, trolling, and playing a fish. Today's trend is toward four to six guides, plus tiptop, in anything other than the light, very short boat stick, which may be adequately furnished with two rings and tiptop. Spinning rod guides should be rifled, that is, tapered in size from a large gathering guide that funnels the line spooling off the reel, down to a much smaller tiptop. The same principle applies, although never so drastically, in a squidding outfit. Where medium- to big-game tackle is used, the first roller guide should be positioned much higher on its bridge than those that succeed it in due process to the tiptop. This high-bridged first guide prevents a sharp angle from a large reel spool, an angle which, if acute, can cause dangerous friction.

There are exceptions to every rule, but these usually lie in the provinces of specialists. As an instance, some anglers who are expert in the live-lining of common mackerel to tempt big striped bass on inshore grounds often find that they require oversized ring guides. The reason for this has nothing to do with casting or the ordinary free flow of line; it is purely and simply a defense against weed growth and goglum in the water. If there is much weed and aquatic algae bloom, which tends to accumulate on a line, then the large guide is beneficial because it allows this gunk to flow through to a point where it can be picked off the line at the reel.

Rod length and action will vary according to the technique employed. Generally any trolling stick—and this includes those used on big game—will prove most practical if the tip measures 5 to 5½ feet long. Butts range from 14 to 18 inches on light to medium trolling rods, and up to 22 inches in the unlimited class. All should be fitted with gimbal nocks where a fighting chair will be used. Sportsmen who prefer to "stand up and fight him like a man" on light gear can get along with a rubber butt cap, although in this case a basic belt socket or cupped rod belt fastened around the angler's waist can save much wear and tear on the human frame.

Quite logically, boat rods are graduated from the very light to the heavy unlimited class. The last named is highly specialized and rarely needed on anything but such massive powerhouses as the giant tuna, the heftiest of the billfishes, swordfish, and huge sharks. Even with giant tuna, the classic unlimited rod requires much angler muscle and there is a definite trend toward somewhat more limber sticks coupled with 130-pound-test braid on 12/0 to 14/0 reels. Such Australian authorities as Peter Goadby frown on any combination bulkier than 80-pound test, but 130 continues to be a first choice for giants. Where the monsters are concerned, 80-pound test is light and 50 is no more than a stunt rig, successful only where the odd fish and the elements oblige.

Today's manufacturers increasingly tend to classify rods by the line tests best suited to complement them. Unfortunately, there is no industry-wide standard, so the 20-pound stick offered by one maker may be comparable to the 30- or 50-pound combination of another. I have a truly magnificent trolling rod sent to me for the express purpose of wrestling giant tuna from a small boat; it was touted as an unlimited stick, and it really is a great 30-pound-test rod. True unlimited (anything designed to complement 130-pound-test or heavier line) would make this rod look like a child's toy.

Since all manner of rods can be used in saltwater fishing, categorizing is difficult. Mitigating circumstances and special needs lead to the development of locally practical sticks. Assuming that line-test ratings can be used as a measure to designate ideal trolling rods (and they do not always apply), this particular tackle at least falls into a fairly precise length bracket—the 5- to 5½-foot tip and the 14- to 22-inch butt. No such easily applied measurements can be cited in bait casting, spinning, fly casting, and squidding. We can only recommend averages and state reasons why they are chosen.

Bait casting is all-American and it evolved in Kentucky with the famous Meek reel, designed to toss baits and lures into the hidey-holes of inland black bass. Nowadays, a minority of anglers use the light, revolving-spool outfit to catch a variety of marine fish. Invariably, the saltwater bait-casting rod is a beefed-up version of that used on such freshwater fish as black bass. The marine item is calibrated to heave lures in the ⅝- to 1½-ounce range, and it measures approximately 6½ to 7 feet from butt to tiptop. There are the usual variations, including the so-called popping rod, which is simply a lengthier (maybe 8-foot) and more powerful stick, a sort of connecting link

Claude Rogers of Virginia Beach plays a sea trout with a standard bait-casting outfit.

Frank Woolner and Curt Gowdy debate the merits of conventional and spinning rigs used for surf casting.

between bait-casting and surf-casting tackle. As a matter of fact, the popping rod quite subtly becomes a light surf-casting stick and the two are interchangeable. Originally used to cast shrimp-baited hooks preceded by a popping cork, this rig remains a very satisfying outfit for light, close-range work from beach or boat.

The true surf-casting rod is a much heavier tool, although it has been produced in all weights and actions to suit the needs of anglers. Now in partial eclipse, due to the ease of spinning, the classic squidding outfit will remain a weapon in the arsenal of marine anglers because its performance has yet to be topped by anything invented. For certain tasks, no other outfit is so practical. On the debit side, revolving spool requires a measure of expertise. You must educate the right thumb in casting, and the left thumb in laying line during a retrieve. Is it too much to ask supposedly intelligent anglers to train a couple of thumbs?

Surf rods, and I am now speaking of true squidding sticks, range from jetty jockey types of 8 feet, overall length, and weight-throwing capabilities of 2 to 4 ounces on up to the "Hatteras Heaver" of North Carolina's Outer Banks and the "Production Rod" of Cape Cod, either of which will measure 10½ to 11½ feet from butt to tiptop and will handle lures or bait-sinker combinations ranging from 3 to 8 ounces. These are big, tough sticks, meant to drop a lure or bait at a cool 100 yards. They are, primarily, casting instruments and not fish-fighting tools, and they are predicated on the assumption that you can't catch a fish unless you can reach him with a lure big enough to turn the trick, and you can't set the hook at maximum range unless the rod is planky enough to exert considerable pressure.

In the jetty jockey version, a squidding rod often is a cut-down version of the big high-surf stick. Usually it is lighter in weight, shorter (8 to 9 feet overall), and designed to cast lures in the 1½- to 3-ounce bracket. On rock jetties—and in open boats—snap casting is necessary, so butt length is diminished. Depending upon the individual angler's preference, measurement from butt cap to reel may be anywhere from 18 to 20 inches, where the shore caster's choice will be 25 to 30 inches.

There are further variations. On the Pacific Coast, where sportsmen cast very light sinker-bait combinations to surf perch, corvina, and flounders, and in the semitropics, where surf-running pompano feast on sand fleas and other minute delicacies, a very limber tip is highly desirable. Lengthy rods with soft tips serve a definite purpose on the charter boats of southern California, where featherweight anchovies must be cast to considerable distances. Sticks fabricated with this office in mind are long, limber-tipped, and feature power at midsection.

Quite similarly, surf casters who desire much power—plus the ease of fixed-spool—often choose long, limber-tipped rods designed to compete with the heavy squidding outfit. They push their luck and never quite succeed. However, if a shore caster refuses to master revolving-spool for heavy work, then he must go to a spinning rod that will measure 10½ to—in extreme cases—14½ feet. Such outfits never cast heavy lures or baits as well as the classic squidding combinations, and they are far too light of tip section to set a heavy wire hook at maximum range. Besides which, big bucket-sized spinning reels are clumsy. Thread-line, as a technique, only scales an angler's Olympus when it is dedicated to the casting of light lures.

Modern marine sport fishermen use three basic reel types, with a number of subtle variations. One is the revolving-spool multiplier, with and without internal braking, although practically all ocean-worthy models are so equipped. A second is fixed-spool or spinning, both open-faced and closed face. The latter remains questionable for saltwater use because its design forms pockets for corrosion to develop. Finally, there is single-action, the simple one-to-one ratio fly-casting instrument, now offered as a multiplier with built-in drag, but basically designed as a line-storing device.

With few exceptions, today's saltwater reels are highly sophisticated, beautifully designed and machined. You will discover dogs among them, usually those turned out by opportunists and quick-buck importers. Please note that I do not sound the usual chauvinistic "buy American." United States manufacturers produce quality products—and much junk. Europe and Asia do the same thing. If you're an American, choose foreign reels only when they are imported by reputable concerns whose service departments can provide spare parts and vital maintenance. Englishmen, Australians—and anglers all around our world ocean—had best employ the same yardstick: buy reputable merchandise that is backed by service.

Revolving-spool is far more diverse in types than any of the others. These range from the small, basic quadruple multiplying bait-casting reel, which was developed for freshwater angling and later adapted to marine use, on up through surf-casting and light-trolling instruments to the very specialized internal drag big-game reel.

While the prototype of all bait-casting reels was a direct drive model without any drag mechanism, free spool, line-laying device, antireverse lock or antibacklash feature, modern saltwater anglers demand all or most of these features. In order to cope with strong marine game fish, multipliers should be equipped with smoothly functioning adjustable drags and feature spools capable of storing a sufficient amount of line and backing. Quadruple multiplying gearing is retained in smaller reels, and many feel that linelaying devices are important, even though they handicap distance casting. Beginners like antibacklash gimmicks, but advanced anglers scorn them because, like the linelaying worm gear, they chop yards off a flawless cast.

Probably the first bait-casting drag used on salt water was the so-called "Cub-Handle" introduced by Pflueger in its classic Supreme reel. This was a fixed, sliding brake, preadjusted to the supposed ideal amount of tension before addressing any particular game fish. It was good, but it was a half measure and a poor attempt to bridge the gap between direct drive and the marine angler's need for a smooth, adjustable drag.

Old-fashioned knuckle-buster reel with leather
thumbstall, used until the star drag was introduced.

Pflueger and other manufacturers have now bowed to the necessity of free spool, antireverse locks, and silk-smooth adjustable drags. All are readily available on a host of beautifully designed and machined multipliers. In light-tackle fishing, line-laying devices are still in vogue, although many experts remove them. Antibacklash devices and worm gears are crutches, very important to the fumble-fingered but handicaps to the advanced angler who has spent many years educating his thumbs.

The finest of modern bait- and surf-casting reels feature light plastic or alloy spools to facilitate easy casting. Spools are fitted to a close tolerance for use with slim monofilament lines, yet they are quite as efficient when braid is chosen.

In conventional revolving-spool casting, there is a subtle progression from the one-handed outfit to that used in two-handed high-surf heaving. The reel is basically similar, although it now features a wider spool, and the line-laying mechanism is discarded. Many reputable firms have experimented with line-leveling gadgets on surf reels, and all have been defeated. The absolute necessity to heave lures to maximum range, plus the particles of sand in any breaking wave, make an angler's thumb supreme.

A true squidding reel, like all specialized instruments, must be tailored to requirements. Perhaps the Penn Model 140 Squidder comes closest to overall perfection; it is a reasonably old design, and yet it remains very nearly ultimate. Any fine squidding reel must be wide-spooled, fitted with a smoothly functioning star-drag braking device, and an antireverse lock. It must be light in weight and small in size, yet boast an indestructible spool that features sufficient line capacity—say 200 yards of 36-pound-test braid or an equal amount of 30-pound mono. The reel must be fast and rugged, and its spool must be light enough to resist overrun. A heavy metal spool always utilizes centrifugal force to defeat the caster. Such a reel should also feature rapid takedown for on-the-spot cleaning and changing of spools.

Checking the drag tension on a squidding reel.

It doesn't really matter whether you employ braid or monofilament on a squidding reel; the balance will be so critical that it will perform well with either, although there will be a necessity for angler expertise in using the various weights and types of lines. Some specialists prefer braids at night and monofilament by day, but there is a steady gravitation toward mono for all uses. In high-surf squidding, 36-pound-test linen, and then braided nylon, used to be classic; nowadays, a majority of surfmen prefer 30-pound-test mono.

It should be noted that monofilaments can be treacherous because they possess a thing called "memory." Unless a reel's spool is built to withstand the pressure of this inherent elasticity it may explode under pressure. To combat the threat, manufacturers now offer plastic or light-alloy spools that have been beefed up to absorb the tremendous pressures generated.

All the better casting reels are multipliers, with gearing rating from 3-to-1 up to 4-to-1. Since speed of retrieve is an admirable virtue in light-casting winches, these ratios are fine compromises. Progressing to medium and heavy trolling reels, the retrieve ratio is sharply diminished to ensure greater power and control in playing a monster. There, 2-to-1 is just about standard.

Every well-made big-game reel features a one-piece machined spool designed to absorb murderous stresses. There are, roughly, two types of drag mechanisms employed—the multiple-disk star arrangement, best exemplified by the time-honored Penn Senator, and the finely adjusted lever-operated single-disk type, featured by the justly famed Fin-Nor. In big-game fishing, there is a trend toward the latter, but star drag is still employed by a majority of blue-water anglers.

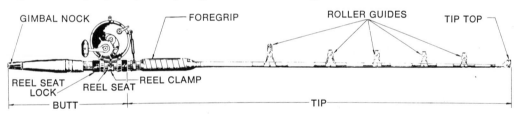

Schematic drawing of a big-game rod and reel.

All big-game reels are fitted with harness lugs welded or machined into the tops of the end plates. The use of shoulder or kidney harnesses is absolutely necessary in the playing of sea monsters, and a light shoulder harness can be most comforting even when the quarry is a relative lightweight of 50 to 100 pounds and the angler fights from a standing position. For that reason, harness lugs decorate most offshore reels from 4/0 on up.

On Bermuda's Challenger Banks, a few years ago, I hooked a yellowfin tuna on a 4/0 30-pound-test outfit. For some reason that critter wrung me out and, after about 30 minutes of give-and-take stand-up battle, I was relieved by the addition of a light shoulder harness. The fish weighed only 57 pounds but, like all yellowfins, it was a sounder and a looper. The harness gave me an opportunity to use my back and my shoulders, with an occasional pause to flex cramped fingers.

Whatever the reel, a smoothly operating drag is essential. That which binds and jerks is a potential loser, and this applies on sheltered waters as well as offshore. Whether your reel is a saltwater single-action fly-casting model, a conventional squidder, any of the bay, offshore, or big-game types, or fixed-spool, the drag must be smooth and readily adjustable, else it becomes a liability when the chips are down.

Gary Bennett of Cocoa, Florida, finds light spinning tackle ideal for sea-trout fishing.

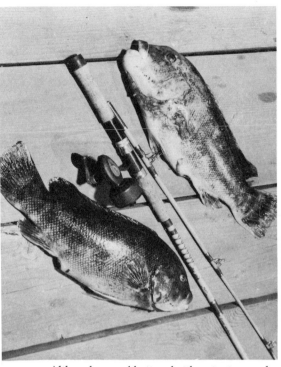

Although rugged bottom battlers, tautog can be bested with light spinning gear.

Medium spinning tackle catches big bluefish for Karl Osborne, a Vero Beach, Florida, outdoor writer.

A good drag must endure hours of screaming punishment without overheating and consequent binding. There is no excuse for a poor drag.

We have, in our new arena, a wide variety of excellent spinning reels. All the better models are open-faced, and the best feature freely revolving line rollers to defeat line chafe, plus smoothly functioning, easily adjusted brakes and antireverse locks. Bails may be spring-activated or manual, and those who employ fixed-spool on big fish often prefer the latter, because it has less parts to tempt Murphy's Law.

Any marine spinning reel worth its salt should be fabricated of metals resistant to corrosion and rust. It is heresy to expose a fine freshwater reel to the murderous elements of the sea. Unless you thoroughly wash, dry, and lubricate such a reel immediately after a trip to the briny, you can be sure that your trout-stream jewel will be reduced to a lump of immovable junk. With one exception—and this is questionable—the saltwater reel bears only superficial resemblance to its sweet-water cousin.

The exception is the single-action fly-casting type. Here a light-tackle sportsman can get along with certain inland versions that boast sufficient line capacity. Pflueger's standard Medalist probably has conquered more marine gamesters than all other single-action reels combined. Although never designed for the ravages of the world ocean, this is a well-engineered and constructed instrument that, with proper maintenance, is quite up to tangling with a host of small- to medium-sized marine game fish.

Hal Lyman uses a fly rod to catch dolphin off Stuart, Florida.

There are two sharply divided schools of thought in fly casting, and we shall get into these in another chapter. Briefly, one minority faction agrees with Lee Wulff—who happens to be an all-time great—in arguing that any sophisticated braking arrangement is excess baggage on a fly-casting reel. Lee has subdued some eyebrow-raising fish, including striped marlin, with a basic single-action winch, so his opinion is valuable.

However, a majority of great feather merchants prefer fly-casting reels that not only boast smoothly functioning internal drag mechanisms, but in some cases feature 2-to-1 gearing to facilitate retrieve, plus free-spooling so that the winding handle doesn't pummel knuckles during swift give-and-take battle. Until very recently, all the truly great saltwater fly-casting reels were expensive ($100 to $150), but these prices have been just about halved by a few manufacturers. Criteria still include the lovely Fin-Nor series, the hand-built Seamaster, the Taurus, and the Bogdan.

Drag and gearing aside, any marine fly-casting reel must boast twin virtues—the strength to absorb tremendous punishment without exploding, and a spool large enough to accommodate a considerable amount of backing. On the sea you will want *as much backing as possible,* which usually boils down to an absolute minimum of 150 yards of Dacron braid attached to the fly line, and about twice as much if you seek the great game fishes of the sea. Remember, unless you employ a stout fly rod and a heavy leader tippet, a 12-pound striped bass will always go into the backing. Obviously, a 100- to 150-pound tarpon or marlin will stream a great deal of this precious commodity. Think tough construction, smooth operation, and maximum line capacity.

A minority of anglers always seek shortcuts. It would be delightful to employ a rod with the resilience to cast a light lure or bait far out over the sea, together with the planky power to set a hook at long range and to muscle a heavyweight to boat. No one has yet offered a fisherman's version of the swing-wing fighter plane, which extends or retracts its wings at the push of a button, but this is possible. Whether such a development would be welcomed by a majority of anglers is arguable. The average advanced sportsman wants to give his quarry a fighting chance.

Some years ago California's Fenwick Rod Company unveiled a fly rod that attempted to solve the problem. No electronic push-button affair, the rod was simply a tubular fiber-glass blank calibrated to cast a fly with ease. Having hooked a fish, the angler then inserted a glass stiffener into the hollow butt of the rod and was then able to play his quarry with a much more lethal weapon. I dubbed this stiffener "the purple shaft" and questioned its legality because the thing made it possible to hook a fish on one outfit and play it on an entirely different combination. That the "purple shaft" works is undisputed, that it is sporting is another ball game.

Similarly, magazine advertisements now extol the virtues of battery-powered "automatic" reels that, at the pressing of a button, take all the labor out of retrieving a game fish. Some of these, I think, are ideally suited for use by handicapped people who have only one arm to work with, or by unfortunate folk who must live with a heart condition. I take a very dim view of their use when the "sportsman" is healthy and endowed with the usual complement of arms and hands, and I doubt that they will ever become very popular. Certainly such reels will never be accepted in world record applications, nor will they be recognized in tournament competition. They are the tools of the handicapped and the meat fisherman, a boon to the former and no great credit to the latter.

Some sterling characters defeat serious infirmity to challenge those of us who are physically whole. The late Freddy Harris, a great Cape Cod angler and charter skipper, operated with one arm, the other a stub amputated below the shoulder. He used standard tackle and often made the rest of us look like duffers; he required no mechanical or electronic advantages.

People like Harris are eyebrow-raisers on all salt-sea coasts. They prove that we don't need unfair advantages to catch fish, that basic tackle is sufficient and, indeed, that such gear offers a maximum in sport.

There are far deadlier methods than rod and line—if the end product is fish flesh—but we, as anglers, will continue to resist unsporting tactics. The tackle improves, but who wants a sure thing?

WEAPONRY - LINES, LEADERS, AND CONNECTIONS ～3

Linkage to Ensure a Fast Fish

Never in history have fishing lines been more efficient than they are now. Together, users and manufacturers have insisted upon and created a healthy family of braids, monofilaments, and metal strands that leave little to be desired—yet will be improved with each passing year.

This search for perfection began long before "sport" was an important word. For thousands of years all fishing lines were fabricated from such organic materials as tough plant fibers, animal sinew, horsehair, and silk. Twisted fiber lines, together with stone sinkers and crude hooks, have been retrieved from the middens of the ancient Incas. There is little doubt that similar lines were employed long before the South American sun gods were adored.

By the time considerable numbers of people were angling for sport as well as sustenance, marine fishing lines were made of silk, twisted linen, and well-tarred cotton. All these continue to see limited use, but all possess crippling faults. Cotton lines are large in diameter commensurate with pound test and are highly vulnerable to rot and mildew. Silk was never a good choice on the sea, thanks to the ravaging attack of brine, and it was used by a small minority of Asiatics and transplanted inlanders until such time as they learned better—and better strands became available.

Well before the turn of this century, linen—especially the hard twist now generically referred to as Cuttyhunk (it was first developed by old Captain Crandall for Ashaway Line & Twine Company's trade on the Massachusetts island of that name)—became the premier saltwater fishing line. Admittedly, it *was* the best for several generations of pioneering anglers, but it has been phased out by modern synthetics. Today's advanced angler uses linen only to lash baits or to seize a rope end. The old-timers' charge that good Cuttyhunk had a special "feel" is quite accurate. A sow's ear never felt like a silk purse.

Since a few contemporary writers, prone to research in musty old accounts, still recommend linen line, Cuttyhunk's benefits and handicaps should be listed. The stuff is stronger when wet than when dry; it resists fraying, and it enjoys a dearth of elasticity and a good knot factor. Against these virtues, linen easily succumbs to rot and mildew; it swells like a poisoned pup when wetted; it is highly abrasive to the angler's thumb and, in casting, it ensures a shower bath with each heave. Cuttyhunk's diameter, per pound test, is considerably larger than the new synthetics, so you can pack less of a given strength on a reel's spool. Almost nobody uses linen line in modern, sophisticated marine angling.

There were precisely three revolutionary developments in saltwater fishing tackle during the first half of the twentieth century. One, as aforementioned, was Boschen's star-drag reel, and another was the fiber-glass rod. The third was the creation of synthetic fibers and extrusions that have lent themselves so admirably to fishing lines.

Nit-pickers may cite important advances in lure design and ancillary equipment, ranging from outriggers to fighting chairs and big-game harnesses, but you go into battle with a rod, a reel, and a line. All else, with the exception of the plebeian hook, adds up to basic improvement on ancient inventions. Even the hook, a vital component, has changed little over the years; we have better metal to serve our needs, but little innovation in design. Lines, on the contrary, jumped light years ahead immediately after the conclusion of World War II.

All the best are synthetics, a chemist's brew of elements that are only slightly affected by the ravages of heat, sunlight, moisture, salt, and bacteria. I think it irrelevant to dwell on the scientific breakthroughs and the molecular structures of modern fishing lines. These things are well documented and of major importance only to laboratory technicians who forever seek something better. They understand the problems that plague their technology and, inch by inch, they answer apparently impossible questions. Improvement, during the past thirty years, has been so rapid that we can only applaud those alchemists who have synthetized basic elements to give us magical strands to fish in the sea.

Nylon, a derivative of coal tar, came first—and the first nylon lines were about the worst connections you could envision—they were terribly elastic and unstable. Without the absolute dedication of manufacturers who would not admit defeat, we'd still be fishing with tarred cotton and linen. Indeed, many of the anglers who experimented with nylon braids immediately after World War II were convinced that the new synthetics might be impervious to rot and mildew, but that they'd never take the place of time-honored Cuttyhunk.

All the manufacturers persevered, and very shortly they offered braids that featured controlled elasticity, great strength, and fine diameter. Suddenly nylon braid was the only line to use in surf casting. By 1947, only the diehards continued to use Cuttyhunk, and they weren't very happy when contemporaries achieved longer casts without burned thumbs and demonstrated the rot-resistant nature of the new synthetic.

Dacron soon entered the lists. Another synthetic fiber, this one featured much less elasticity than nylon, a benefit that also introduced the handicap of inferior knot factor. Early Dacrons ensured a finer strand per rated pound test, but they were "hot" lines, hard on the educated thumbs of a caster. For a few years these failings could be cited, and then the nameless, tireless laboratory technicians made changes. Dacron is still "hotter" than nylon, so far as the caster is concerned, but nothing is currently better than a good Dacron braid for medium- and big-game trolling.

Other polyesters may soon challenge the top-runners. Cortland Line Company is now marketing Micron, a silk-smooth synthetic braid that casts beautifully and features controlled elasticity. Micron has been touted as a spinning line, something I cannot yet swallow, but I have used it for heavy surf casting on a revolving-spool reel. The line casts well, is not hot, suffers no excessive fraying, and is smaller in diameter than either nylon or Dacron braid. Since Micron is still new, a few years will be needed to place it in its proper niche.

Nylon monofilament arrived almost simultaneously with braid. Mono is an extruded filament, and the first offerings were terribly elastic. Anglers delighted in the fine diameter and transparency of these new strands, but they cursed its tendency to stretch, its unstable properties, and an insidious thing called "memory." Mono then, and to a certain extent now, will stretch, but very shortly resumes its former dimensions. If a reel's spool is not rugged enough to contain this expansion—*bang!*

Back in 1964, fishing Costa Rica's Colorado River for tarpon, I watched as a neighboring angler screwed his drag tight while a great sabalo went rocketing down toward the sea. There was a tortuous moment or two while the rod became a perfect arc and the breeze harped on taut mono. Then, incredulously, the fisherman's apparently stout bay reel blew up. He was left with a mare's nest of tangled line and a winch that had been completely destroyed.

Shortly afterward the same thing happened to me, far northward. I was loose-leaf "spinning" for big bluefish on Massachusetts' Cape Cod Canal, using a fly rod and a single-action reel loaded with 10-pound-test monofilament stripped into a waist-level basket. This is an effective technique when using small baits on a fly rod because the coils of loose mono, confined in the basket, shoot well.

A 7- or 8-pound chopper had taken the sperling bait I presented and had driven far out into the big ditch. The memory factor of that reasonably light line was enough, under pressure, to explode a fine single-action fly-casting reel.

To a major extent, this problem has been licked—first by controlling the elasticity of monofilament, and second by the development of reels that feature almost indestructible spools. It is, however, a problem to keep in mind and possibly to guard against by employing a judicious amount of soft-braided backing as a cushion.

In spite of the slow phasing out of linen and tarred cotton lines, both of which are still sometimes used, the present variety of fishing lines is ample. Included are nylon braids, Dacron braids, the new Micron braid, nylon monofilament, single-strand wire, braided and twisted wire, and nylon braid with lead core. Add also fly lines designed for saltwater work. Why so many different types? Specialization!

Nylon monofilament undoubtedly serves more general purposes than any other modern line material, and it will dominate the future. Mono is smooth, tough, fine in diameter, and offers the benefit of partial transparency. It is produced in a variety of colors and neutral shades, together with fluorescent tints—usually blue or yellow—which certainly aid the angler and may provide a measure of underwater camouflage. In many cases, one of monofilament's greatest boasts is its meager cost. Price is one reason why the single-strand extrusion often is employed in areas beyond its present capability.

Initially, nylon monofilament seemed made to order only for fixed-spool casting, a method that has never lent itself to the use of braids. Mono remains ideal in spinning, far better than anything else, but it has also successfully invaded the fields of revolving-spool casting and trolling. There are cutoff points, at which the single strand begins to labor, yet mono is certainly most efficient when combined with certain light rod-reel combinations. Even in fly casting it finds an important place as light shooting line. The key word is "light."

In spinning, it is generally conceded that 20-pound test is just about maximum. Beyond that, the heft and the stiffness of the line becomes a definite handicap to casting. Actually, 20-pound test is quite sufficient on any fixed-spool outfit that is used wisely.

There is, in addition, a massive switch to monofilament in middleweight bait casting, surf casting, and trolling. Part of this is due to the minimum cost of the line, but one cannot disregard its obvious benefits. While a conventional caster must develop new control techniques, fine-diameter mono ensures longer heaves, the stuff boasts less water resistance than braid—a boon to surfmen who fish the bottom—its translucence is a plus factor and, in cases where soft-mouthed fishes are sought, leaders may be discarded.

For high-surf casting, 30-pound-test monofilament is now displacing the old classic 36-pound-test braid. Beyond that weight, the single-strand extrusion becomes progressively unmanageable. Therefore, advanced surfmen who need 45-pound test for work with big fish continue to favor nylon or Dacron (or possibly Micron) braids. It should be noted that these specialists are members of a very small group. Rarely, in shore casting, is there any need for lines testing more than 30 pounds. We will see a rapid phasing out of braids for this work.

The same reasoning applies to middleweight bait casting, where mono has proved most efficient. Curiously, very light conventional bait casters are still best served by braids, primarily because these are less tangle prone and more stretch resistant in the minimum diameters favored.

It is in the field of trolling that monofilament becomes most controversial. That it is widely used and increasingly popular is indisputable. That it is the best choice for all "dragging" is arguable. Too often individual anglers and charter skippers vote for mono because the stuff is cheap and easily replaced; they brainwash themselves into extolling it as most efficient.

Actually, mono serves very well in light to medium trolling; it comes a cropper only in the heavier tests. There, excessive elasticity, memory, and a dangerous stress point at which the line becomes brittle discourage big-game anglers. Up to approximately 50-pound test, monofilament lines used in trolling appear to be highly efficient. Beyond 50, problems arise. Giant tuna anglers of the North Atlantic, together with those who seek huge billfish, are convinced that Dacron is a far better choice when one must go to 80- or 130-pound test. These specialists will have nothing to do with heavy monofilament leaders, maintaining that they never perform as well as steel wire or cable and invariably result in break-offs after long and arduous battles.

Admittedly, a growing number of big-game buffs, including most of the monster hunters of Australia and New Zealand, are enamored of mono in the heavier tests. It is instructive to note that these Down Under professionals also scorn anything heavier than 80-pound test, counting 130 as unnecessary. On most of the world ocean, where giant tuna records have now soared over the 1,000-pound mark and huge billfish are targets, 80 is considered light tackle and nobody apoolgizes for the use of 130.

Perhaps 80 is adequate on any game fish other than the full-blooded giant tuna, the great billfishes and broadbills. Any of these may be taken on such light gear when the fish, the sea, and the elements oblige, but there are occasions when a huge bluefin enjoys adequate depth in which to sound. Regal billfish often come clear time and again, thus burning their energy at a tremendous rate, yet they also can plunge into the abyss and require brute strength to bring them up. By comparison, huge sharks are sluggish.

Dacron braids remain most efficient in the heavy line tests, with mono coming into its own from 50 on down. Choose round mono for all uses. Some years ago there was a flurry of interest in flat or ribbon extrusions designed for casting. They were great—for that office alone—and I erred in acclaiming them during the first flush of use. Flat monos lay well on a conventional reel's spool and they cast beautifully, but the damned things are subject to much twist. Obviously, no flat mono should ever be used on a fixed-spool reel, for trolling or for live-lining.

Nylon braids, really the first triumphs of the new synthetics, are now entering an eclipse phase. This is partially due to the increased use of monofilament and partially to the properties of Dacron, which is better suited to trolling and which has been improved so rapidly that it now challenges mono in light-tackle casting.

The nylon braid has always been smoother and "cooler" than its blood-brother Dacron. That's because nylon absorbs a bit more water, which acts as a lubricant, and because the fibers are naturally softer in texture. A good flat braided nylon line is soft, stretch-controlled, and possesses an excellent knot factor. Because it is manageable, backlashes (called "overruns" by experts) are easily picked out—even under the wan light of the stars. For this reason, nylon braid is still favored by a minority of nighttime surf casters who, as often as not, prefer 30-pound-test mono when the sun is shining. In some big-fish areas, and particularly at night, 45-pound-test nylon braid is chosen because it can take a measure of fraying—hard to detect in the dark—and still tests out at better than 30.

Nylon braids may be flat or hollow. Some are cored, but this type currently finds favor with a very few bait-casting types. The flat or hollow-braided nylon is generally favored by modern bait and surf casters.

Dacron asserts its mastery in medium- to big-game work. You can use mono very successfully up to, approximately, the 50-pound-test class. Thereafter, until technicians perform new miracles, Dacron braid reigns supreme. Its fine diameter and lack of elasticity, its stability and toughness, copper the bets of blue-water trollers. Nothing is better in the 80 to unlimited tests, and there are many who maintain that nothing is better for any surface trolling when you progress beyond the 30-pound class. In this arena, Dacron's sole black mark is greater cost than ubiquitous mono. Whether in racing automobiles, high-performance airplanes, or fishing lines, ultimate performance is expensive.

There is in America, and soon will be throughout the world, increasing interest in the use of metal fishing lines for trolling. There are three basic types, plus the usual variations: single-strand stainless steel or a Monel alloy, metal braids, and nylon-sheathed lead core. All require a certain measure of expertise in use, and all are deadly when it is necessary to troll a lure or bait at intermediate to maximum depths.

Single-strand wire is most difficult to use, and also most effective in most cases. Because this stainless steel or Monel strand is fine in diameter and heavy in sectional density, it slices down very quickly. Unfortunately, the stuff usually is springy and requires much angler control in streaming. Beginners invariably find themselves overrunning or backlashing, and a wire-line backlash is just about the most exasperating mess known to man. There are occasions where as much as 200 yards of 25- to 40-pound single-strand must be streamed; more often it will be enough to drag 100 feet of wire in a rip. In either case, the proper length of line must be marked, and there will be an overriding necessity to control it with an educated thumb. Quite naturally, only revolving-spool reels lend themselves to this operation.

Braided or twisted metal lines are easier to control, but they never sink as rapidly and—in some cases—are subject to fraying and stretching. The latter results in streamed coils that assume the shape of a long spring and prevent the immediate setting of a hook. Almost always this handicap becomes apparent after repeated use, so braided wire is most efficient when it is new. After a few big fish, replacement is good sense.

Lead-core lines, actually a thin core of soft lead held within a braided nylon sleeve, are easiest of all deepgoing strands to handle. Thanks to bulk, they never plumb the depths as rapidly as single-strand does, but they can be very effective on relatively shoal grounds. Lead core is both soft and manageable. The horrendous, springy backlashes of single-strand are seldom encountered, so tyros who lack educated thumbs can fish in peace. Lead core, in addition, usually is well marked in bright colors; therefore, a fisherman can gauge his depth and length of line by the number of colors streamed. One handicap is the fact that a lead-core line, allowed to settle on the bottom, will automatically mold itself around every boulder and obstruction in its path. Having bottom-fouled a lure, it is wise to maintain a very tight line while backing down, else one may break off a lot of expensive lead core.

There are lead-core shooting heads for fly lines, sheathed in soft plastic and intended to take feather lures away down into the dining halls of various marine fishes. They cast like sacks of beans and they are highly specialized. Moreover, they are rather farfetched attempts to make a fly rod all-purpose. I think they only prove that you can bastardize a fine outfit and thus catch fish. Like the business of trolling a fly, nothing is really achieved, other than the hollow boast of a zealot who has invaded a field that properly belongs in the bailiwick of another tackle combination.

Practical fly lines are another thing. There is no doubt that the long wand has invaded salt water, and this is healthy. Major manufacturers have produced specialized torpedo or forward tapers that are ideally adapted to casting on the sea front. These are nylon and Dacron braids ideally balanced to certain weights of rods and coated with plastics that defeat the attrition of the sea. You can purchase floating, slow-sinking, rapid-sinking, and floating with sinking tip lines, plus shooting heads, which fulfill all present needs. To go beyond these types really defeats the art of fly casting.

There remain linen and cotton, with or without the tar of old seafarers. Linen is still used on many seacoasts; it is tough and effective when properly maintained. To keep such a line at peak performance it must be washed and dried after each outing— else rot and mildew will destroy it. Cotton, tarred or untreated, is similarly ravaged by natural deterioration; it can be used for rough bottom fishing but, like linen, will never again be the choice of the scientific saltwater angler.

In tournament fishing, or when IGFA records are coveted, line test becomes very important. It is worth noting that lines do not always test out as advertised. In 1960, a young woman named Rosa Webb caught a 64½-pound striped bass that fractured the existing IGFA women's all-tackle record. At the time she was using a mono touted as 40-pound test, but which proved to part at something below 30. Happily, Rosa collected certificates for all-tackle *and* for 30. Too often the denouement is less pleasing.

One afternoon it was rather hard for me to retain a poker face when a zealous manufacturer's rep donated a line that he extolled as "the strongest 10-pound-test line in the world." It was. In fact, it parted at precisely 17 pounds when submitted to laboratory analysis.

This gentle deception is very common. Too many line manufacturers understate tests so that the user will indeed think that he has "the strongest" 10-pound test, 15, 20, or whatever. The exception is a line purposely braided or extruded for record fishing. These are always prominently labeled "IGFA Specification," and they will always break somewhere within a precise 5 percent *under* the rated test. Such lines are, of course, preferred by advanced anglers.

Reels should be filled to the utmost capacity, a measure that not only assures enough line for any given task within the outfit's capabilities, but also simplifies casting. Where fly lines or metal strands are employed, there will be an additional necessity to use backing. Duffers often conclude that any ancient and thus questionable braid or mono is sufficient for this office, but the exact opposite is true. Backing should be as carefully selected as the lead-off line, for it will absorb tremendous stresses. Pressure always builds as a fish goes rocketing out into the blue, hauling more and more line behind him.

Almost always, backing should be heavier than the primary line and leader. The exception is fly casting, where a monofilament tippet will test well under the line itself, and therefore below the backing. Even here there is a need for strength far greater than the leader's breaking point. Marine feather merchants choose Dacron braids from 14 pounds on up to 30, the latter where great offshore gamesters are sought. Eighteen to 20-pound test is just about standard for all-around work with a saltwater fly rod.

Backing is quite as essential where wire line is used. In many cases, the hank of metal will be no longer than 100 to 150 feet, although there are techniques that require as much as 200 yards. In any event all, or practically all, the metal will be streamed. Obviously, a big fish will go far into the backing and, at this point, an angler appreciates perfection and cannot settle for less.

Never use monofilament for backing! Memory makes it unacceptable for this work. Dacron braid is best; it's tough, fine in diameter—so that you can pack more of it on the spool—and is the least elastic of any line on the market. Backing should never be taken for granted, because it's a last reserve. Employ new line and use as much as possible. Be very professional in the matter of connections. A nail knot or a spliced loop, carefully seized, will do on the fly-casting reel. Some trollers like a small swivel to connect wire and braid, not only because it is solid, but because it clicks an announcement in passing through the guides at night. Others favor a slim Key Loop knot for light tackle. If a swivel is chosen, be sure that it is small enough to pass through the guides, whether ring or roller. Backing is life insurance for an angler, the final toss of the dice when a great game fish wages all-out war.

In America, we discuss leaders; elsewhere, fishermen speak of "traces." A leader (or a trace) is the connection between line and lure. It is most important and is often both misunderstood and abused. Too often a heavy leader is employed where it is not only unnecessary but a distinct liability. Fishermen are forever prone to load for bear when they seek rabbits.

Since monofilament line is now favored for light to medium work, the worth of a metal leader in saltwater angling has become specialized. So has the need for interminable swivels, bead chains, snap fasteners, and leather thongs. Most of these have an important place in the scheme of things marine, but it is stupid to defeat our own purposes by employing too much hardware.

Necessity is the key word. If one seeks a soft-mouthed species that lacks abrasive gill plates and sandpaper skin, there may be no need for a leader tipping a monofilament line. Swivels, snaps, and other hardware may only increase the difficulty. In many cases, with mono, it is both intelligent and logical to bend the hook or the lure directly to the bitter end of a running line. Hardware may be, and often is, a necessary evil. If you can operate without it, do so.

Saltwater leaders accomplish two basic purposes, and one of these is most important. With the single exception of fly casting, where a properly designed and tapered leader ensures a good cast and fools the fish by its terminal transparency, leaders offer insurance against sharp teeth, razor-edged gill covers, abrasive bodies, and equally thorny caudal fins. A majority of marine game fish disregard the opaque nature of a leader, but can be spooked by the turbulence created by swivels and other hardware, another reason to keep such ironmongering to an absolute minimum.

Presently, the better leaders are made of cable-laid steel wire, steel cable with a smooth nylon outer coating, properly chosen lengths of heavy monofilament, and single-strand stainless-steel wire. In many cases, bronze-colored wire is preferred over the nickel or chrome-plated article, because this hue seems to afford a measure of camouflage. Single-strand stainless, the "piano wire" of a passing generation, is both light and tough; it lends itself to rapid rigging via the haywire twist, yet it possesses one Achilles' heel—a tendency to kink and to part at the kink. This fault is cited by those who prefer cable, especially for big game, yet single-strand champions stick to their guns, holding that the fine wire's advantages even the score.

Almost always—and fly casting is a single exception—a leader's strength is roughly twice that of the line it graces. Indeed, in heavy fly casting for such hard-mouthed brutes as giant tarpon and billfish, the flycaster uses a 12-inch tippet of 80-pound-test mono blood-knotted to the end of his 12-pound primary leader. One good rule of thumb, obviously impossible in fly casting, holds that a leader should always be slightly longer than the length of the fish sought. Thus, IGFA rules specify that leaders may be no longer than 30 feet in big-game fishing, and no more than 15 feet in any line-test category below 50. Other than offshore, where a sportsman seeks true sea monsters, lengths are considerably diminished, geared to the size-of-fish theory.

Wire or cable is recommended for use on sharp-toothed species (bluefish, for example), or those with cutting gill plates (such as snook), or abrasive bodies (sharks). Monofilament serves the purpose where gamesters are soft-mouthed and lack any particular armament on their bodies, but are still thorny enough to part a light line. Striped bass boast no sharp teeth, but their jaws are abrasive. If a fight is both long and strenuous, a heavy mono leader is good insurance.

Wherever possible, monofilament leaders are best chosen for light casting, while cable or single-strand wire is supreme in trolling. There are the usual exceptions. Obviously, any caster who seeks saber-toothed prey, regardless of the gamester's size, is benefited by wire, and there are blue-water sportsmen who feel that heavy mono is ideal on the acrobatic, smaller billfishes. As mentioned, giant tuna buffs of the North Atlantic find no substitute for cable or wire, and those who seek trophy blue marlin, black marlin, and broadbill swordfish are similarly inclined.

The light-tackle angler often finds it expedient to use a very short leader—something in the 4- to 6-inch bracket—or just enough to keep the line's bitter end out of the chomping jaws of a toothy fish. Trolling leaders are longer than those used by heavers, if only because they are streamed in the wake of a boat and not cast. Usually, in casting, the overhang is slight and a lengthy trace becomes an abomination—unless it also serves as a mono shock line extended well back into the reel and secured via a blood knot or some other slim, smooth connection.

The shock line, or shock leader, is just that. In casting, it absorbs all the brutal stresses in starting a lure or a bait-sinker combination on the way, while a line of much lighter test then follows. Some casters rely on a doubled line that is lengthy enough to provide adequate overhang and then go back to the reel's spool. Others prefer a true shock, either heavy mono or stout braid. In either case, the shock line should be long enough so that several turns may be made around the reel's spool prior to casting. There is a problem, of course—the connection.

If the shock line is heavy braid attached to a lighter braid, it is feasible to use a smooth splice. Mono, attached to braid or even to lighter monofilament, requires a knot, and knots are hard on educated right thumbs. The user of a shock line therefore learns to lay line very carefully during each retrieve, so that the connecting knot is well over toward the right side of the reel's bell housing and will not lacerate a thumb during the next cast.

Almost always (but not always) a wire leader requires some sort of a barrel-swivel connection, plus a snap fastener. Most barrel swivels really amount to connecting links, not devices that defeat line twist. Indeed, few standard barrel swivels really accomplish the task for which they are touted. Ball-bearing types, such as the fine Sampo, are most efficient, yet anglers who troll erratic lures that spin and loop usually find it quite necessary to employ a keel device of some kind, in addition to swivels. Make note of the fact that a lure that spins either is poorly designed or has been damaged. Naturally this does not apply to the few that actually spin by design, and these are the types that require keels, planers, and the most sophisticated of ball-bearing swivels. There remains the necessity to attach line to leader with a minimum of fuss and bulk.

Wire or cable usually requires a swivel, and this is best attached with a crimped bronze sleeve in the case of cable, or with a haywire twist when wire is used. Light cable can be tied in with a Key Loop knot and so can mono, whether or not a connecing swivel is employed. The crimped sleeve is neat, slim in profile, and strong. It may be the best choice for any cable, including those that are plastic-coated. However, an angler must use the exact sleeve size for the wire to be crimped. If the sleeve is too large, the crimp may not hold and will certainly be bulky. If too small, it may cut strands of cable. A good crimping tool is essential; pliers will not do the job.

Where single-strand wire is employed as a leader, nothing tops the time-honored haywire twist: it is neat, slim, and workmanlike. Be sure to finish it off by twisting the bitter end of the wire back and forth so that it ultimately crystallizes and breaks flush against the standing part. This is important, unless you are fond of picking up sea lettuce and lacerating your fingers.

If a leader is light in weight, made of mono, single strand or braided metal, it may be quite feasible to attach lure or hook directly to the bitter end of such a leader. More likely, you will find some sort of a snap fastening logical. Make it light and strong.

A great many snap fastenings are currently available, and the most common—a basic safety-pin design—is just about the worst hunk of junk ever invented. It invariably fails under pressure, and its conformation presents angles that hamper lure action and aid ultimate destruction. Always choose a stainless-steel rounded snap with a locking feature. There are cases where a snap-swivel is recommended (usually in trolling), but the caster will be better served by a simple, well-made snap that boasts no swivel, but is attached directly to the running line or the terminal end of the leader. Its light weight does not materially hamper the action of a lure, yet it facilitates the quick changing of artificials.

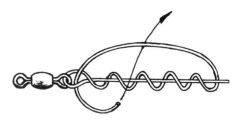

Improved Clinch Knot.
Knots, courtesy Du Pont Stren

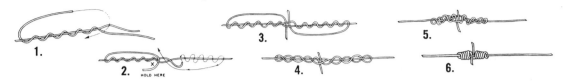

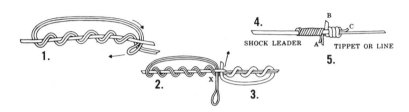

Blood Knot.

Stu Apte Improved Blood Knot.

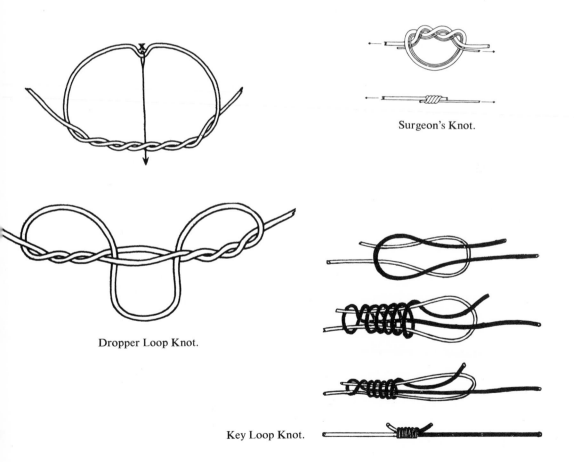

Surgeon's Knot.

Dropper Loop Knot.

Key Loop Knot.

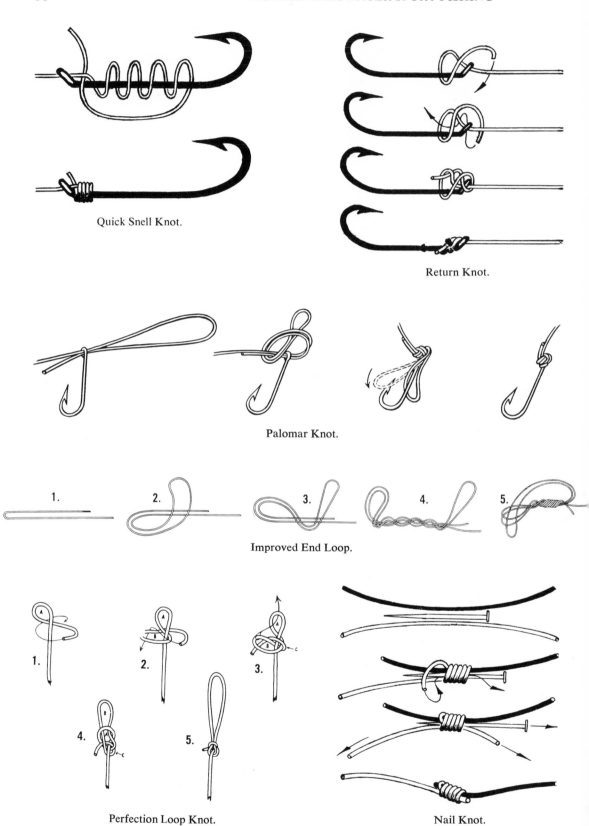

Quick Snell Knot.

Return Knot.

Palomar Knot.

1.   2.   3.   4.   5.

Improved End Loop.

1.   2.   3.   4.   5.

Perfection Loop Knot.   Nail Knot.

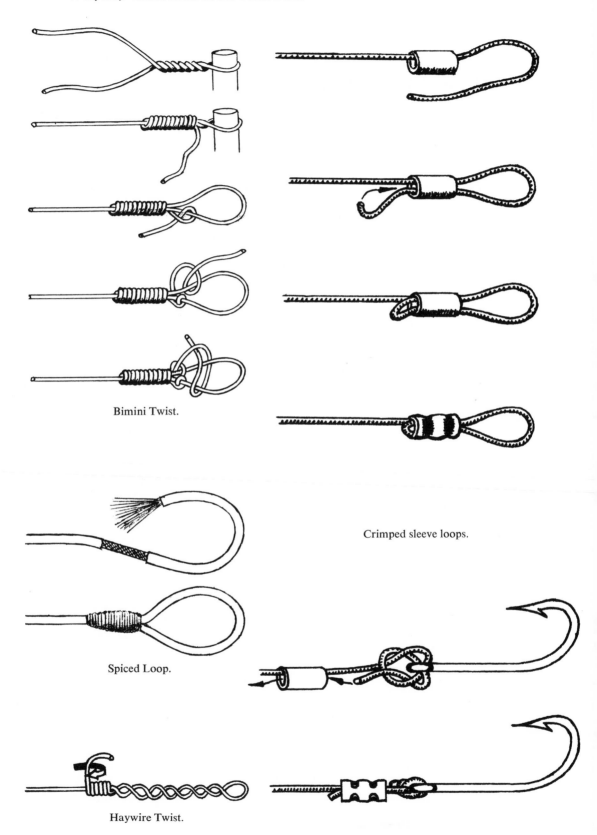

Bimini Twist.

Crimped sleeve loops.

Spiced Loop.

Haywire Twist.

In trolling, the snap-swivel connector almost always is best placed *between the line and the leader,* not at the terminal end of the leader. This facilitates the rapid changing of leaders and baits that have already been prepared and iced. Offshore it is a mistake to place this connection between leader and hook or lure, for it serves no purpose in that position.

Today's great saltwater anglers have evolved a whole series of knots and splices, some of them guaranteed (dubiously) to provide 100 percent efficiency. Obviously, those who seek records require every iota of possible strength from their connections, yet there is no necessity for the beginner to master each intricate knot, jam, and splice prior to a saltwater fishing trip. A few are imperative, and they are simply tied. All of the more important connections are progressively illustrated in this book, and therefore I offer no lengthy descriptions.

Practically all of us who fish in salt water are fully conversant, or should be, with a few basic connections. These seem elementary, yet it always amazes me when a tyro first attempts to tie so simple a bend as the plebeian Improved Clinch. How do you explain the Bimini Twist to a scholarly gentleman who finds a simple Clinch an exercise in frustration?

Actually, the everyday marine angler can get along with a minimum of basic connections. First, I think, is the Improved Clinch. It is ridiculously easy to tie, sausage-fingered newcomers notwithstanding. In execution, you pass the bitter end of the line (or monofilament leader) through the hook's ring or the lure's eye; loop it back and make five turns around the standing part of the line; bring the bitter end back to pass through the loop next to the ring, and then bring this end back again to pass through the standing loop that has been created at the apex of the five turns. Snug up smoothly, using a bit of saliva for lubrication. *Voilà*—the Improved Clinch, one of angling's most important knots. Learn to tie it, because you'll need it.

Second in importance, in my opinion, is the Blood Knot—in two versions. A simple Blood Knot is the angler's traditional connection for hanks of leader materials or lines, such as line to backing. It is small, neat, and strong; it is easy to tie and yet it is regularly muffed by beginners.

In tying, you simply lap the ends of two strands, allowing a considerable length of line on each end. Spiral one end of line around the standing part of the other—at least five turns. Next, bend the bitter end of the spiraled line back over the wraps and pinch it in place with your fingers at that point where the wrap begins. Now spiral the second end of line in the opposite direction and return it in the same manner, passing the bitter end through the central loop from the side opposite that which has been pierced by the first strand. Pull on both ends and snug up slowly, smoothly. Again, a bit of saliva will ensure lubrication. Once tightly snugged, the two ends of mono can be clipped flush to the knot.

In the Stu Apte Improved Blood Knot, "improved" only because it is used to connect radically different sizes of monofilament, the same technique is employed, but the smaller line is doubled to achieve more bulk. This one is more difficult to tie neatly, and the angler may have to use his fingernails to push the loops together as the fastening is snugged up. Stu Apte's innovation is valuable when a very heavy short hank of mono must be attached to a much finer skein of synthetic, as in fly-rod fishing for tarpon where the leader is tapered down to 12-pound test and then tipped with an abrasion-resistant foot of 80-pound-test material.

Another connection that serves to join strands of different sizes is the Key Loop, also known as the Albright Special. While it never rates so high in strength as the

Stu Apte Improved Blood Knot, the Key Loop is effective, indeed superior where a light, coated wire or fine cable is joined to monofilament or braid without benefit of swivel.

In recent years much has been made of the Nail Knot, a neat, slim connection to join a fly line and leader butt, or to attach any relatively hard line to a softer braid. Some accomplished anglers create this fastening with no tool at all, but a nail or a finely tapered steel shaft helps. The object is a tight jam, with no crossing loops that might threaten a cutting edge.

A lot of flycasters prefer spliced loops, if only because they permit the immediate changing of lines. Either connection is strong and smooth, but the loop takes a bit more time to prepare. Some specialists favor a loop to connect line and backing, and a Nail Knot, which is more streamlined, to join line and leader butt.

There are multitudes of specialized connections, such as dropper loops, employed by bottom fishermen in salt water, and fine snells to connect leaders and hooks used in bait fishing. The more important of these are illustrated.

Offshore anglers who seek big game dote on knots and splices to secure doubled lines. One of the favorites is the Bimini Twist, also called the Hundred Percent Knot. It isn't the easiest of fastenings to prepare and is best created by two people—or by one, with the aid of a post to hold the initial loop. A Bimini Twist is spiraled at least twenty times, and then snugged up to the head of the loop so that twists are packed and neatly aligned but never crossed. The bitter end is then half hitched around one side, and then the other side of the loop. Finally, a half hitch is whipped around the entire base of the loop.

Those who splice feel that their connection is both smooth and truly 100 percent. In many cases, the perfectionists use dental floss to whip-finish the connections and to provide ultrasmooth passage through the rod guides. Wraps, incidentally, are also used by light-tackle anglers who desire the very slickest of connections. Nylon thread may be used for seizing, and the finished splice anointed with a flexible gum rubber or plastic coating. A marine flycaster's shooting line and backing often are connected in this manner, unless the spliced loop is used.

In surf casting, and particularly where braids are used, an ordinary double overhand knot may be quite sufficient to secure a double line. In this case, the loops should be drawn up carefully so that they do not overlap, and the bitter end then cut off short and melted to prevent fraying. Such a connection will not measure up to the splice or the Bimini Twist, but it will be so close that the difference is minor—and it is easily created. A double overhand knot, for practical use where line tests are not critical and records are not sought, is quite adequate.

Most synthetic lines are flammable; they melt under heat, and this is a fringe benefit. After tying a regulation knot, the bitter end of such a line can be touched with a glowing cigarette end or a lighted match; it will promptly melt and then solidify as a ball of hard material. Fraying is thus defeated and the resulting hard ball keeps the knot secure.

One of these fine days, probably before the end of the century, we are going to find it possible to fuse line and leader, or leader and lure, or line and backing with some electronic gadget that will connect a light strand with a much heavier one. Until that time it will be wise to study the basic connections, and then learn how to create the more sophisticated knots and splices. Good connections, in angling and in life, are important.

WEAPONRY-THE BUSINESS END ~4

Terminal Tackle

When marine anglers speak of terminal tackle they mean anything beyond the line's bitter end, including the leader, possibly a sinker or planing device, swivels or other hardware—and a hook or lure. A "terminal rig" subtly alters the definition: it is a carefully contrived blend of components such as a sliding sinker or fish-finder (a "leger" if you're British) together with a hook or hooks properly positioned to accomplish best results when angling for a specific sport or game fish. Terminal rigs are legion, but most of them stem from a few basic patterns.

In fishing, there is nothing quite so terminal as the ubiquitous hook, or the artificial lure armed with one or more hooks. Curiously, a majority of anglers seem willing to spend many hours of research, plus more cash on rods, reels, lines, fast boats, and sundry backup equipment, yet neglect an equally vital selection of hooks that will make or break a glorious adventure. If a barb fails because it is ill chosen for the task at hand, no otherwise sophisticated tackle combination will remedy the error. Even the best of hooks are inexpensive, so there is little excuse for choosing the cheapies and the bends designed for some task other than that immediately called for.

Rarely will any freshwater hook prove reliable in salt water. Those that are blued, japanned, or lacquered (bronzed) invariably rust and corrode on a first outing and turn into such much junk before they have done their job. Seagoers require barbs fashioned from corrosion-resistant metals, or well plated with tin, cadmium, nickel, or gold. Well-tempered tinned steel remains best, although stainless steel appears to be the hook material of the future. There have been experiments with alloys containing much nickel, but these never approach the strength of steel and therefore must be drawn from heavier wires. Moreover, the predominantly nickel hook never holds a sharp point.

Stainless steel may well triumph before the end of this century, and some present-day anglers are satisfied with the current product. I prefer standard high-carbon steel, well plated and nicely tempered.

Generally speaking, the smaller marine fishhooks are drawn from steel wire, bent, cut, and fashioned into the required shapes and sizes. They are then tempered and plated with care, in order to assure a quality product. Obviously, attention to detail and craftsmanship is important. The better manufacturers seek perfection, so you can rely on hooks offered by well-known makers such as Mustad or Wright & McGill.

Larger marine hooks are forged, not simply bent into the required shape and tempered. In this operation, the hook's wire is hammered along part of the shank and through the bend. Usually the point is triangulated or diamond ground, and the eye brazed to ensure the utmost in strength. Heavy plating follows a meticulous tempering process.

There are exceptions. Some very large shark hooks are bereft of forging, bent from heavy wire or bar stock. They'd be stronger if forged, so such a barb sacrifices some measure of performance, relying on mass, rather than well-understood, technology.

Size designations always confuse a newcomer, and sometimes stymie experts as well. That's because manufacturers often create their own standards. There are guidelines, followed fairly accurately, but rarely comparable within fractions of an inch and, at certain points, changing without rhyme or reason. There is, for example, no adequate measurement of gap, size being determined by shank length.

Saltwater anglers are unlikely to find much practical use for the tiniest of hooks, although some specialists who seek tiny coral fish on tropical reefs might make good use of the miniatures. With small hooks the numerical designation *decreases* as the product becomes larger. Thus, a Number 7 will be one-sixteenth of an inch longer than a Number 8, and so on up (or down) the scale. Just to confuse things, that one-sixteenth of an inch progression changes to one-eighth after you reach Number 3, to continue through Numbers 2 and 1.

Thereafter, we have a whole new can of worms, with numerical designations increasing through the "O" or Ocean series. From 1/0 to 5/0, half-inch steps apply. The higher the number, accompanied by a diagonal line and an "O," the larger the hook. And that isn't all.

Freshwater anglers usually are spared the task of choosing specific wire sizes, although these will vary with the size and type of hook. In marine angling, one must take special cognizance of light, heavy, and successively heavier wires. These are indicated by the letter "X." In practice, X is standard steel wire, while XX is somewhat heavier and stronger. These designations go on up to a present maximum of 6X, seldom encountered.

The length of a hook's shank is also designated by an X, but with the word "long" or "short" added. Naturally, shank length affects the barb's performance. Either the very short or the very long create problems of one kind, while they solve others. Theoretically, when a hook is suspended from its point and allowed to hang freely, that which balances with spear and angle of line pull exactly parallel will penetrate most efficiently. There are numerous ifs and buts, so I prefer to judge a barb on its proven capabilities in the field. Academic anglers catch few fish.

It should certainly be apparent, but evidently is not, that the diameter of a hook's wire is important. There are rules of thumb, subject to argument, yet we find it necessary to choose a barb that is ideal for use on a fish sought, and with the tackle employed. That's why there are so many different sizes, bends, and variables.

Rule One: you cannot adequately sink a heavy wire hook with an elastic line and a limber rod tip. Therefore, with light-spinning, bait-casting, or fly-casting tackle, one is forced to use light wire and a sharp, finely tapered spear point. Utmost strength must be sacrificed to ensure efficient hooking. Fortunately, bull strength is not a factor with featherweight gear, because the tackle will be resilient enough to prevent disaster. Initially, it is necessary to drive a barb home, and I have had my own comeuppances.

One unforgettable night on the striped-bass fishing grounds of Cape Cod, trophy bass were straightening the standard 7/0 barbs that armed my rigged eels. I do not know how a striper does this, but on heavy tackle they sometimes manage to destroy a formidable hook with the greatest of ease. Mine came back as straight as pencils, and I vowed to cure that failure. Accordingly, I rigged a few eels with 8/0 Sobeys, forged big-game hooks in the 3X-strength category, for use on the following night.

Again, bass in the 30- to 40-pound bracket were walloping rigged eels. I lost six fish in a row, because the heavier points of the big Sobeys would not penetrate their jaws. Finally, I went back to standard 7/0 O'Shaughnessy singles and came up with a respectable catch. Lesson: the lighter the tackle, the lighter the wire diameter of hooks and the sharper the points to be employed. There are no shortcuts.

On any saltwater front a variety of bends serves specialists. Each is job-rated for a separate task and there is no all-purpose hook, although the O'Shaughnessy style probably comes closest to cosmopolitan efficiency. In round wire or forged versions, this bend serves many purposes. O'Shaughnessy can be straight, kirbed, or reversed, depending upon the whim or the conviction of the user. In long- or short-shanked versions it is a very practical fishhook.

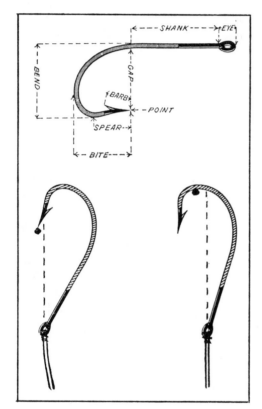

Top: basic parts of a hook. Bottom: hook shape determines penetration and holding potential ensured by line of pull.

Basic hook types include, top to bottom: needle-eye Sobey and Martu for big game; O'Shaughnessy, Siwash, turned-up and turned-down eye claws, including sliced-shank bait-saver and short-shank; long-shanked and kirbed flounder hook.

Wherever anglers use bait, the claw hook has become a primary challenger. Offset, and with its needle point sharply bent in, this is a very effective barb, possibly the most efficient of all for light to medium bait fishing. In America, Wright & McGill's Eagle Claw has become so successful that the trade name is a generic term. Overseas, the fine British Sealy enjoys similar acclaim, and there are Americans who demand Sealy hooks for tough work in the surf. Mustad offers models that cannot be faulted.

All the claw hooks are roughly similar in design, although there are differences in quality control that place one brand above another. These instant grapnels are ideally suited to use with bait, but their balance does not lend itself so well to use with artificial lures. Similarly, the kirbed or reversed point, quite possibly an aid in hooking a game fish on bait, is bad news where artificials are used and precise balance is necessary. There the straight hook, although inferior in the matter of instant pene-tration, may be better chosen.

Many of the bends used in saltwater fishing are refugees from the hinterlands, while a few are old seafarers that boast no virtue other than questionable traditions. In too many cases obscure styles are touted as ideal for use on certain fishes, only because they once appealed to anglers. There is an unfortunate tendency, among writers, to substitute research in a library for observation on the scene of action. Hence we still find supposedly erudite advisers recommending linen line for saltwater use and hook types that should have been phased out with the hoop skirt.

Sneck, Sproat, and Aberdeen have largely been replaced by claw types. Even the Carlisle, long considered ideal for winter flounder fishing, would be hard pressed to match the efficiency of a long-shanked claw. I'd choose the claw every time, yet I freely admit that there are good reasons for bends other than the claw and the hard-working O'Shaughnessy. Nothing has yet topped the Siwash or Pacific Salmon for use on jumping fishes with soft mouths. The Siwash features a deep bite and a long, gradually tapered needle point. It holds well, providing that it can be driven home. Because the point is slim and therefore subject to blunting, it is best used on such soft-mouthed acrobats as salmon and bluefish, and it can be an abomination on hard-mouthed species.

Some bait fishermen like sliced shanks, hooks designed to hold a bait in position. One should note that the tiny barbs on such a shank also discourage removal of a tired bait, and can shred the fingers of a careless angler. Bait hooks with a single pin, either soldered or tied in close to the eye, have been offered and are often prepared in home workshops. They do the job, but a sea worm or other slippery bait can be held quite as securely by slipping it up over the knotted monofilament that joins hook to leader.

There are points designed like a porcupine's quill, with a series of tiny, backward pointing edges. They are feasible, but you still find difficulty in removing an unwanted bait. Nothing has proved better than the time-honored barb, although some sportsmen feel that barbless is better—they simply flatten the point. It doesn't make much differ-ence, so long as you keep a tight line, and a barbless hook certainly goes home faster than any of the gripping types.

Hooks used on big game are necessarily heavier than those employed to snag light and middleweight battlers. They are always forged, with brazed eyes, or often needle-eyed, to facilitate the neat rigging of baits. There are two very popular bends, the Sobey, which is well rounded and features a slightly turned-in point, and the Martu, similarly constructed, but with more open bite. Both are straight, precisely balanced, and armed with razor-sharp triangulated or diamond points.

Assuming that strength is adequate for a given task, that weight and size are con-sistent with requirements, the shank length of a saltwater hook may be quite as important as bend. A short-shanked hook is more easily hidden within a small bait and will thus be swallowed quickly; therefore, the small, short shank is preferred when fish are prone to reject anything that feels or looks strange.

Problems arise when you must take a sharp-toothed species that will chomp leaders after the hook has been swallowed. There may be no redress, other than a steel leader, or a long-shanked, and therefore more visible, hook. Some gamesters, like the small-mouthed winter flounder, are remarkably stupid, so the obvious solution is a long shank that does the job and permits easy unhooking. The old Carlisle was designed with this in mind and it is a good hook. A long-shanked claw is better.

Regardless of bend, size, or shank length, to be really effective any hook must be razor sharp. There is no excuse for dull hooks, for any angler in his right mind will carry either a hone for the tiny barbs, or a file for larger points. Usually, in salt water, the file is preferred; it touches up points with a couple of swipes and in a minimum of time. A hook should always be so sharp that, in the words of old rod and line commercial Arnold Laine: "You can't touch it without having it stick into your finger!"

For some obscure reason, the angler of America's Atlantic seaboard usually chooses hooks that are too large for the job at hand. Pacific sportsmen make better use of barb sizes, and sometimes go too far in the other direction. Both groups have good and logical reasons. The West Coast angler often finds it necessary to use very small baits, such as the native anchovy, which would be burdened by a large hook, while the Atlantic craftsman finds his quarry feeding on relatively huge herring, menhaden, and mackerel. A tiny barb would be lost in the bulk of such a bait. So it really boils down to necessity. Ideally, a hook should be just large enough to do its work, and not one millimeter larger. There are, naturally, strength requirements when you get into heavy tackle where stresses escalate.

It might be possible to addend a series of charts, with hook sizes and types specified for each game fish, and such a chart would be nothing but an educated guess, plagued by the usual qualifications. Many of the glamour species are to be had in size ranges from very small on up to trophy class, so hook type, in addition to other requirements, would have to depend on the size of fish expected. Types would vary quite as widely, since the bend that is right for use with a chunk bait is not necessarily best for a live bait, a skip bait, or to arm an artificial lure. Advanced anglers study each type and size, with due attention to the fish sought and the method decided upon. In any event, choose the very best of hooks; they are relatively inexpensive and bargain shopping in this field is the best way to ensure crushing defeat.

Hooks, unless they are trebles that adorn a host of artificial lures such as plugs, jigs, and spoons, usually are employed in company with sinkers and leaders that have been graced by dropper loops, simple or three-way swivels and, possibly, floats. These terminal rigs are vital to success on offshore and inshore grounds and, although variations are endless, basic rigs are few. They include the sliding sinker, called fish-finder in America and leger elsewhere; the deep-sea, the hi-lo, and the simple weight coupled with a hook on a short leader. There are trolling sinkers, and these will be examined later.

Each of the variations is dependent upon sinker types, hence it may be well to examine weights prior to discussing rigs. There are really two basic types, the sharp-edged and the rounded, the first to dig into soft or sandy bottom, and the other to hold—without fouling—in rocky or rubbly ground. Of course, the pyramid sinker best exemplifies the edged weight, and the dipsey the rounded. Egg sinkers, usually pierced so that they also serve as sliding sinkers, are widely used. There are many sinker variations—diamond shapes, plows, scalers, and so on. Cotton "Bull Durham" tobacco sacks filled with pebbles are still used on many coasts. Iron nuts and bolts serve the purpose where more sophisticated articles are not available, and ordinary beach stones remain quite as efficient as they were when the Incas dredged fish out of the sea.

The fish-finder, leger, or sliding-sinker rig is preferred by a majority of the world's surf casters. In theory, this contrivance permits a gamester to take the bait and move off without feeling sinker weight. In practice it often fails, because tidal currents and line resistance defeat the initial hypothesis. Under ideal conditions there is no doubt that it works—and it inspires confidence—so the fish-finder enjoys tremendous popularity.

You can purchase a patented fish-finder device, which is no more than an eyed safety-pin snap. The eyed end slips over the running line while the snap secures a practical sinker. An ordinary snap-swivel is quite as effective, and less expensive. To assemble, thread running line through the eye of the snap, attach a leader of proper length via a barrel swivel that is large enough to resist passage through the snap-swivel's eye; attach a sinker, a proper length of leader, hook, and bait. You're in business.

If currents are not very strong, or if it is desired that the bait roll along the sea floor, then an egg sinker may turn the trick and dispense with fish-finder or snap-swivel. The egg sinker is very popular in the tropics, and it is hard to argue with success. Egg sinkers are versatile; they can be used in trolling, as well as in still-fishing or drifting.

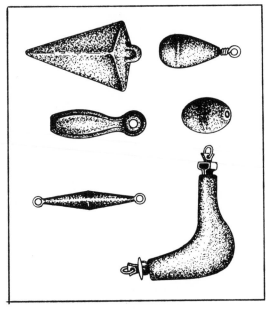

Sinker types, pyramid, dipsey, bank; pierced egg, diamond, deep sea drail.

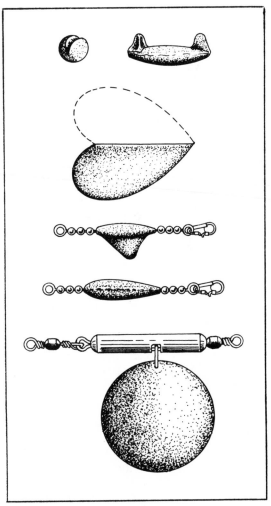

Sinker types, from top: split shot, pinch-on, flat keel, keeled trolling, standard trolling, cannonball with quick-release swivel.

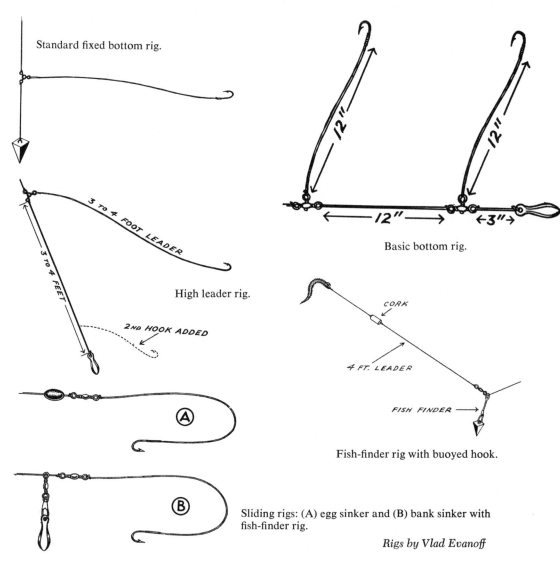

Standard fixed bottom rig.

Basic bottom rig.

3 TO 4 FOOT LEADER

3 TO 4 FEET

High leader rig.

2ND HOOK ADDED

Ⓐ

CORK

4 FT. LEADER

FISH FINDER →

Fish-finder rig with buoyed hook.

Ⓑ

Sliding rigs: (A) egg sinker and (B) bank sinker with fish-finder rig.

Rigs by Vlad Evanoff

Some highly accomplished anglers scorn the fish-finder theory and feel that a game fish will always feel the weight that anchors a baited hook. Therefore, these rebels prefer a static weight, either pyramid or dipsey, depending on bottom conformation, positioned ahead of or behind a leader of adequate length. I don't agree—although with some bold species, they have a point.

"Adequate length" of leader cannot be ideally defined, because it varies with the fish sought and the ideal depth at which a bait should be presented. In some cases, 12 to 18 inches of leader is deemed sufficient, and the leader is designed so that the tempter will be on, or very close to, bottom. There are times when a somewhat longer leader is buoyed up with small cork-barrel floats, so that the baited hook will drift well above bottom and thus escape the attention of deep-down scavengers. Much depends on the fish sought; some feed right on the deck, others cruise a few feet over the heads of crabs and other bottom scroungers.

The hi-lo rig is aptly named. It is ideally chosen when two species of fish are sought, one right on the bottom and another at a higher level, for example, cod and pollock, or porgies and weakfish. A sinker is attached to the bitter end of the leader, with

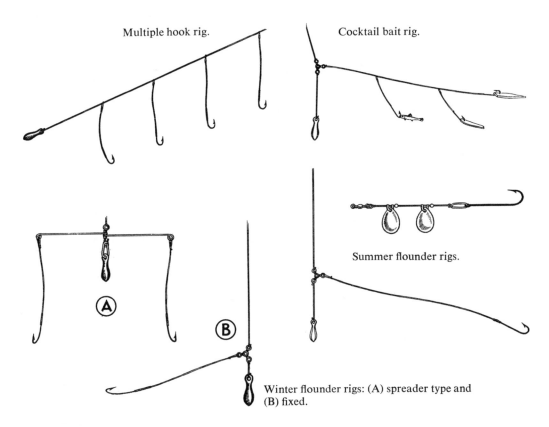

Multiple hook rig.

Cocktail bait rig.

Summer flounder rigs.

(A)

(B)

Winter flounder rigs: (A) spreader type and (B) fixed.

dropper hooks positioned at proper intervals above. Usually two hooks are used, although more may be employed. The idea is to offer baits at different levels. There are, of course, many specialized rigs that employ three-way swivels and other hardware.

In addition to dipseys, light pyramids, and egg sinkers, the light-tackle angler often requires something more subtle, and here the split shot (BB or buckshot) can provide just enough weight to take a bait into payoff territory. Patented clinch-on sinkers also serve a purpose and these should be included in any marine angler's ditty bag. Ordinary lead strip is another secret weapon, for it can be cut to proper length and wrapped around line or leader at any point deemed logical. Strip lead also adds weight where needed on artificial lures, usually wrapped around hooks at the balance.

"Deep-sea rigs" is a misleading phrase, because there is no such thing as "deep-sea sport fishing." Anglers, whether rod and line jockeys or commercial draggers, operate in the shallows that extend out from any coast to the edge of the continental shelf. While true blue water offers sport with pelagic gamesters such as the great marlins, swordfish, albacore, and tuna, nobody other than starry-eyed oceanographers probe the abyss.

Actually, the deep-sea rig is a bait-sinker combination very closely allied to the basic static weight, leader, and hook. The classic weight is a kidney-shaped drail that plummets into the depths and carries with it a short length of dropper-hooked leader armed with one or usually two single hooks. Deception is minimized, for the deep dwellers are something less than fastidious. Object is the presentation of a bait at an optimum depth, usually something between 100 and 300 feet. The deep-sea drail is ideal, yet far from popular, probably because dipseys of comparable weight are easier to procure and are cheaper.

The trend toward artificial lures in salt water seems to be very modern, and yet some types were originated by seafarers of antiquity. Of these, Aelian's Macedonian tuna lure, fashioned of crimson wool and sea-gull feathers, dates back to A.D. 3. Flies were described at about the same time, and it is quite possible that aborigines of the Polynesian Islands were far ahead of the Macedonians with a trolling jig called the "pearl." Finally, nobody knows how long the American Indians had been catching fish on thorn or bone hooks lashed to carrot-shaped pieces of wood. May we describe these as the first plugs?

Quite certainly the South Pacific pearl, still in use among those paradisiacal islands, antedates a whole family of modern trolling lures and bucktail jigs. It was, and is, a streamlined natural-shell artificial armed with a single hook of soft metal—soft, so that it will bend or break before a line is parted, and will thus prevent the loss of a treasured pearl!

Dressing of these lures varies. In many cases, the hook is adorned with hair—pig bristles tied at right angles to the hook. This configuration astonishes modern anglers, who invariably stream any dressing parallel to a hook's shank, yet it may impart action to the crude shell lure. Perhaps there is a lesson for moderns to ponder.

Harlan Major, in his great book *Salt Water Fishing Tackle,* describes the almost religious regard in which a Polynesian angler's pearl is held. "To its owner the pearl represents security, and its loss is a calamity, for it takes the place of a bank account and security." Therefore, if a man's pearl lure fails to take fish, he requires his wife to sleep with it and cherish it, in order to break an obvious hex. Are there present-day wives who will agree to sleep with, and to cherish, a treble-hooked plug in order to assure its potency?

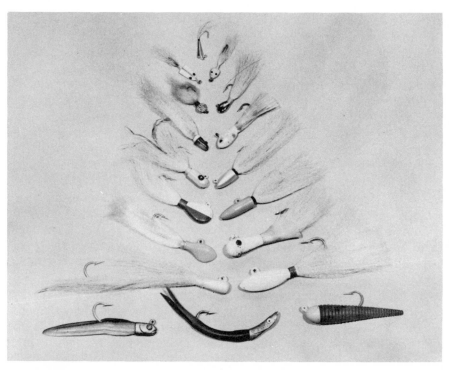

Lead-head jig types, including rubber and soft
plastic types.

Not likely, yet I hold that all of today's lead-head jigs, variously called bugeyes, bucktails (regardless of dressing used), bait tails, and so on, are really descendants of the old pearl. So are the various Japanese feathers that are employed all over the world. These are the deadliest of all artificial lures used in saltwater fishing.

That's a strong statement, yet if I had to choose a single basic lure, it would have to be the basic bucktail because it will do just about everything and it tempts practically every sport and game fish in the sea. You can cast it, troll it, or jig it over a deep reef. It can be produced in a variety of weights and sizes, tipped with pork rind or strips of natural bait. It can be used at all levels and it is equally efficient on night or day tides. Bucktails range all the way from the horizontally flattened Phillips Wiggle Jig, designed to swim over air-clear tropical flats, to bullet-headed bombers that plummet into the depths.

During World War II, when airmen and naval personnel were often set adrift on a hostile ocean, Bill and Morrie Upperman of Atlantic City, New Jersey, produced millions of bucktail jigs to grace survival kits. For once the bureaucrats chose an ideal lure to keep a starving castaway in fresh fish.

Nothing said here will induce a massive switch to bucktail jigs as artificial lures, if only because this classic usually requires a full measure of expertise in handling. Unlike spoons, which need only be trolled, and plugs which are designed to swim when dragged or retrieved, the bucktail must be manipulated by rod action. It can be bounced along the bottom, undulated through a rip, jigged above a productive reef, trolled and periodically jigged, or cast and brought back with variations of the "Florida Whip," a fast rod action that, with a bucktail, simulates the action of a scurrying shrimp or baitfish. The bucktail jig is, truly, the wet fly of the ocean. Because of its design, it rides hook point up, thus preventing undue fouling. You will find too many illustrations, in otherwise delightful angling books, showing the bucktail with hook down. Old seafarers can only shake their heads and pity chairborne editors. If, in this book, any bucktail's hook is pictured point down, I will cheerfully bend over and submit to a swift kick in the transom.

Practically all the lead-head types are armed with a single hook, although some make use of "stingers," also singles. The stinger can be embedded in a pork-rind strip, a thing I dislike, because it tends to foul on a cast. Admittedly, the rig sometimes accounts for short strikers. Only one close relation of the lead-head bucktail sports treble hooks, and this is the so-called clothespin plug, or Seahawk; it is a fish-shaped little lure of pure lead, with no feather or hair dressing, and it is armed with one or two trebles. The Seahawk has long been popular on the central and southern Atlantic coasts. Maybe it deserves a separate category.

It is said that the spoon was designed when somebody actually used the bowl of a tablespoon, drilled at both ends, as a fishing lure. This sounds logical, although today's models are pretty sophisticated, sized anywhere from miniature teasers used on ultra-light tackle on up to monsters like the famous Jersey Bunker Spoon, which measures a full 10 inches in length and 4 inches in width, armed with a big treble or two single hooks positioned ice-tong fashion.

Spoons are trolling lures. The best are entirely stable; they never spin, but they rock and swim with a maximum of flash and action. Such lures can be deadly at all levels, from a few feet below the surface to the utmost depths on wire line. Almost always they are employed in full daylight, and they require no great amount of rod manipulation. Again, as with the more difficult to handle bucktail jigs, spoons are killers on almost every sport and game fish that swims in the sea.

Splasher and following lead-head jig account for
pollock. The angler is Jim Kissell of Worcester,
Massachusetts.

The attraction is flash and action. Hooks occasionally are dressed, but this is lagniappe. If there are important prototypes, look to the famous Eppinger Dardevl series, the Tony Acetta designs, and the Pflueger Chum Spoon. There are hosts of variations and all suffice so long as they provide action and flash without the bugaboo of line-spinning twist.

Well-engineered spoons can be used close to the surface or away down deep. Since the tendency of such a lure is to plane upward, those used in the depths must be forced down there with metal lines, trolling sinkers, or planers. They are used on all coasts, around the entire world, and they are an important weapons system in any troller's arsenal.

The come-hither flash is also exhibited by revolving spinners that are used to attract fish. In salt water, the spinner is almost always a light-tackle component, at its best in shoal-water trolling or drifting. Several types are favored, chief among them the time-honored Colorado and the willow leaf. As an attractor, the spinner rides 3 to 6 feet ahead of a baited hook, or in some cases no more than 3 to 6 inches ahead of the tempter. This can be a productive combination in river or estuary angling, and it does quite as well when the angler seeks fluke while drifting across a coastal bay. In this use, a simple Colorado spinner flashes a few feet ahead of a trailing hook that is baited with a mummichog (killie), a slice of squid, or a strip of belly flesh and skin cut from another flounder.

Herring Dodgers, a trade-named type manufactured by the Pacific Coast's Les Davis, serve the same purpose, but in a slightly different way. The flasher is an oblong slice of chromed or painted metal that precedes a trolled bait and so entices salmon. Such flashers might serve well in other seaways but, to date, have never proved very popular outside the American Pacific Northwest. Better communication and an expanding marine literature are now making inroads on provincialism. Increasingly, successful techniques are migrating to new grounds.

It was inevitable that surf casters who had seen the efficiency of trolled spoons would attempt to simulate these lures and adapt them to casting. Therefore, back in the early days of the sport, tinclads or metal squids were evolved. They began with the drail, a crude, heave-and-haul device that is now practically extinct, and evolved into a whole series of wonderful lures that are heavy enough to cast, yet swim enticingly when retrieved. Quite suddenly the "squidder" became the royalty of surf casters, the purist of the twenties and the thirties. He had a great family of lures and, strangely, his vast selection has now dwindled to a very few standards.

A "squid" or a "tinclad" is a metal lure that swims like a spoon, yet is bulky enough to cast with ease. Initially, all were constructed of block tin, a metal that boasts a soft, translucent glow, but which proved too expensive for use on a production-line basis.

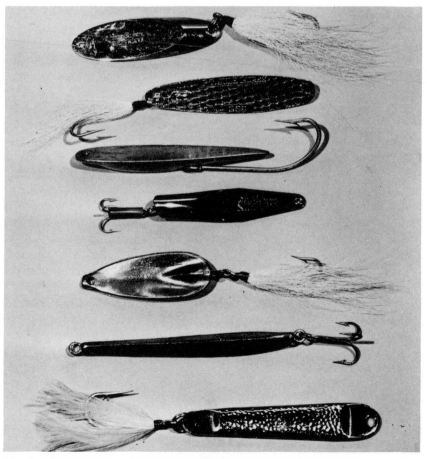

Metal squid variations favored by surf casters.

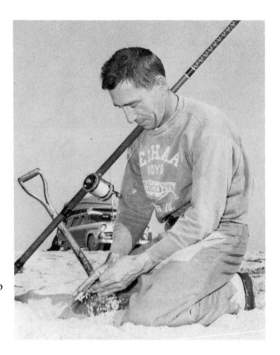

Surf caster George Geddry uses beach sand to
polish a block tin squid.

In the halcyon days there were a host of types, ranging from the bent sand eel through the magnificently designed Ferron and Johnston jigs to the Point Judith Wobbler, which was the nearest thing to a casting spoon ever devised for salt water. Each squid was designed for a specific task, and practically all have been phased out of popular existence. Today there are roughly two standards: the stainless-steel, hammered Hopkins Jig and the sharply sliced Acme Kastmaster, a descendant of the early Eda Splune. Both are great lures, yet there is much need for a return to earlier designs for specialized work.

Actually, the emergence of the plugger as a purist hastened the demise of metal squids. For approximately twenty years a tinclad was the chosen weapon of specialists, and those who employed it looked down their patrician noses at brothers who worked with natural bait or any other lure. Then, very suddenly, the plug came on strong, another instance of the inland angler's impact upon sea sport. Things change.

Modern plugging evolved in the American midlands, where revolutionary sportsmen began to experiment with wooden lures developed for use in fresh water. These innovators scorned ancient tradition, pioneered a new weapons system, and invaded the salt chuck. Marine plugs were first employed on tarpon and snook and sea trout. James Heddon is generally credited with creating and popularizing the modern plug, yet the American Indians were really first. When much later adventurers threw these lures at saltwater battlers, the plug was already established inland.

It was, for too many years, a maverick—scorned because of its treble-hooked armament. That's why the aristocratic International Game Fish Association relegated it to outer darkness as "an unsporting lure" over a period of more than thirty years, relenting only in 1971.

In all fairness to IGFA, no prejudice was involved. This organization has, from its inception, sought to create rules of fair conduct and sportsmanship that apply to all men and all methods; it is to be commended for proceeding slowly and for weighing every argument before jumping to a conclusion. IGFA seeks only a fair evaluation of record claims. While I have argued against certain of the association's standards, I cannot fault its caution in recognizing new methods.

But plugs came on, and they were sporting—first in the South, where people created tougher versions of the freshwater lures to take the more energetic of salt-chuck battlers, and then up along the North Atlantic seaboard. By the first years of World War II, a few inspired characters were experimenting with wooden artificials to take striped bass. Nobody really believed that they could do it, but the mavericks persisted.

On Massachusetts' Cape Cod Canal, a few harmless nuts in foul-weather gear began to use a Creek Chub Pikie Minnow plug designed to take muskellunge. It was a subsurface swimmer, but the addicts bent its wobble plate straight down so that it became a surface commotion type. The thing was too light to cast well on the tackle then available, but it was pretty deadly and the regulars called it the "Blue Plug." Soon the "harmless nuts" were being praised as pioneers of a new sport.

Shortly afterward some genius came up with the "broomstick." This was all that its name implies—a short length of wood cut from a broomstick, with a slanted cut at the head to ensure commotion during a retrieve. Stan Gibbs of Buzzards Bay, Massachusetts, patterned his famous Castalure after this prototype. The Castalure throws like a lead weight and creates enough surface commotion to excite game fish. To this day every North Atlantic old-timer calls a slim, surface commotion popper a "broomstick."

At that time Bob Pond, a young guy with a lot of curly blond hair and an absolute dedication to saltwater angling, came up with a plug he called the "Striper Atom." It was big—so damned big that most people felt it impossible as a fishing lure—yet it succeeded so well that, very suddenly, this was the criterion. A whole host of lure makers offered king-sized artificials during the springtime of 1946 and the years that followed.

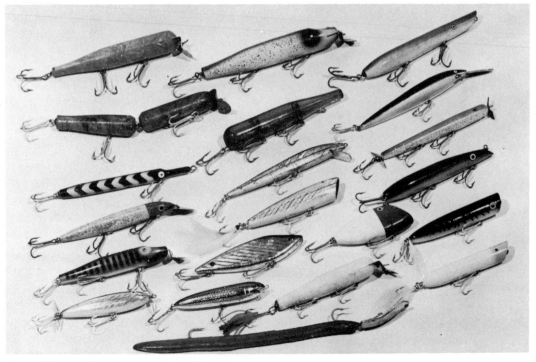

Some of the popular plug types favored by casters,
plus one soft plastic eel.

Dozens of small plugs are available for the light-tackle caster.

Modern hard plastic plugs take punishment in stride. This Rebel lure was fouled on bottom long enough for steel hooks to rust off and barnacles to accumulate, but the bait's plastic body and stainless fastenings have not deteriorated.

There evolved a few basic types, plus a great number of variations, and these basics have yet to be dislodged as standards; most of them had been presented on inland grounds years before, so they only required stouter rigging and greater size to challenge the sea. Wherever you fish, plugs will break down into approximately seven types, all very deadly under certain conditions, and all subject to much variation. There are, to pursue the matter in depth, the following:

Surface Poppers—a family that includes all the modernized broomstick types with their notched heads, together with a host of cup-headed models. All pop or otherwise create a noisy disturbance right on the surface. They employ sound waves as well as turbulent action to entice game fish.

Surface Commotion Plugs—serve much the same purpose in a different way. The commotion types feature propellers at head or tail (or both), or may utilize a fluttering spoon or "flaptail" aft.

Surface Sliders—sometimes called "stick-baits," rely on rod action rather than any built-in performance. In most cases, they are highly streamlined lures, without any added attractions such as wobble plates, spinners, or feather dressing.

Surface Swimmers—comprise a big family that features a host of variations. All are designed to swim or wriggle seductively on the surface, or just below the surface film.

Subsurface Swimmers—swim or wriggle at various depths, but always under water. They are highly successful, perhaps the most successful of all plug types.

Darting Plugs—Creek Chub Bait Company has patented the trade name "Darter," else I'd use this word to categorize all the many types. Darting plugs are subsurface tempters, but their action, as the word implies, is erratic rather than steady.

Torpedo Plugs—are the subsurface versions of sliders in that they invariably require rod action, rather than a simple retrieve, to tempt game fish. They are streamlined, lack wobble plates or other devices, and may be slab-sided. Some are mirror-finished and, like the subsurface swimmers, have been produced in many weights and sizes for efficient operation at different depth levels.

Critics will, of course, cite the popular Finnish minnow designs based on Rapala as instances of a separate category. Such lures are highly effective but they are, after all, variations of the subsurface swimmer. Similarly, we have whole new families of hard plastic and soft plastic plugs, the latter interesting because their pneumatic bodies may convince a striking fish that it has grabbed something temptingly soft and there-fore alive, thus preventing an immediate spit out.

The makers of soft plastic lures once spent too much time toying with the idea of exact duplication of forage creatures, and too little gray matter exploring natural action through design. They failed gloriously until such time as field testing proved that a lure must act, as well as look like something to eat. Having surmounted this ob-stacle, the makers of soft plastic lures quickly emulated their predecessors in creating basic designs—and succeeded. Most successful of all, to date, is the Alou Eel, a metal and plastic copy of the old natural rigged eel and "whistle" wobble plate.

Basic plug types are very few, but subtle changes in design, and thus action, often result in a new killer. There is always room for improvement.

Variation of existing lures is dictated by sea-fishing conditions—always to the extent of beefing up the hooks and rigging, and even to altering types, as in the case of saltwater flies and popping bugs. The mountain man's dry fly is almost unknown on any seacoast; its place is taken by the popping bug, which is seldom the furry, hairy, or rubber-legged creation cast on an inland lake.

Marine flycasters have to get it away out there and achieve distance without a lot of false casting. Therefore, feather lures are designed to cast, as well as to catch fish. The popping bug is streamlined, almost always featuring sparse dressing tied on the hook shank, but no wind-resistant wings or other goodies such as floppy rubber legs. Streamer flies are similarly compact, built to convey the impression of large size and bulk without actual bulk to retard a long cast. Marine feather merchants may prate

Never underestimate the power of a saltwater game fish. This plug has been shattered and its heavy hooks twisted.

This white marlin fell for a soft plastic eel rigged with a single hook and fitted with a bright orange plastic skirt at the nose.

about pattern, but they know in their secret hearts that there are very few. Here, where tides rise and fall, fly types and basic color schemes seem more important than the precise marrying of exotic feathers, fur, and tinsel.

Basic saltwater flies are simply constructed, at least by comparison with the tradition-bound and intricately fashioned artificials used on inland trout and Atlantic salmon. Like all other marine lures, they are beefed up with somewhat heavier hooks, although one of the major faults of the saltwater flycaster lies in the use of overheavy hooks. Let's pursue this in another chapter.

Trollers, in spite of the old Polynesian pearl, have always relied on natural baits or strips, carefully rigged. Such edible offerings are still deservedly popular and efficient, yet there is an eyebrow-raising switch to artificials on blue-water grounds. The oldest types are Japanese feathers, no more than streamlined lead heads dressed with variously colored feathers. These lures, including modern versions dressed with nylon fibers, are universally popular; they can be used, with or without sweeteners of fish flesh or pork-rind strips, close to the surface or in the depths, and in various sizes they will take everything from the smallest of marine battlers to the largest.

One variation of the Japanese feather is the nylon eel, best represented by Tony Acetta's Jigit-Eel, which is frequently used in the depths on wire line. Tony also introduced a variation, commonly referred to as "The Ragmop," a lead-headed, chain-linked creation dressed with a lot of nylon thread tied at right angles to the chain. Shades of the Polynesian pearl!

Soft plastic-trolling baits have become very important during the past decade. Again, as in plug types, these lures originated as look-alikes, but were not taught to swim. Nowadays, the plastic eels and squids offered by reputable makers not only simulate the natural forage species, but resemble them in action. Pseudo eels, squids, balaos, and strips so far appear most successful. However, with such soft artificials, it is usually necessary to set the hook immediately when a fish crashes the bait. Dropback, with a plastic tempter, may be successful, but usually is not. Scent again?

Big-game fishermen still rely on natural baits, very carefully rigged, but blue-water anglers of the Pacific Coast have found the so-called "Hawaiian Lure," or Knucklehead, effective on marlin and other great gamesters. This offering is a true product of our atomic age, a clear plastic, scoop-headed lure of considerable size that is dressed with glittering Mylar and soft plastic strips of various colors. It closely resembles the "teaser" that is used on many coasts, but unlike a teaser it is fully armed. The lure succeeds, and that is sufficient to mark it as an important development in the family of artificials.

Teasers, of course, are decoys used to toll up big game fish in the wake of a cruiser. Usually, they are much larger than the armed baits, often work close to the transom, and are yanked out of the water after a great gladiator has zeroed in and can be diverted to one of the hooked baits. Often a billfish crashes the teaser, and then anglers execute that well-known Chinese fire drill in rushing to stations and manipulating armed baits.

Big-game fishermen rarely use multiple baits, other than strings of teasers such as the famous Nova Scotia "grapevine" and similar strings of herring, mackerel, or squid with tail-end Charley armed. In light to medium game fishing, however, multiple lures have been employed for many years. Some hold them unsporting, but scoffers must remember that trout and salmon anglers have always employed dropper flies, a rigging fully capable of taking more than one fish at a time.

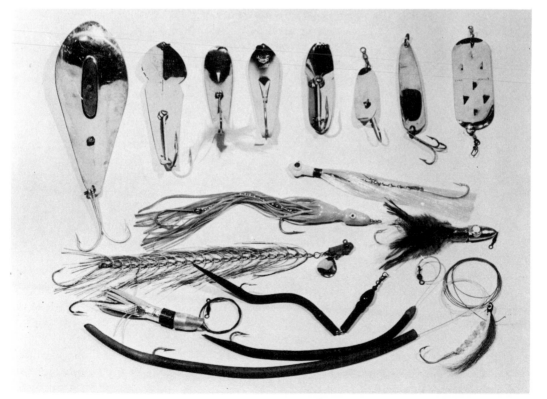

Trolling lures that serve anglers on many coasts.

In salt water, multiples have ranged from two or more baited hooks on a terminal bottom rig on up through trolling devices that make use of a plug and a bucktail jig, separated by two hanks of monofilament and a three-way swivel, to spreaders originally trolled in the Chesapeake Bay and armed with four to six spoons, or bucktail jigs brought down to a killing level with a sash weight.

In the late sixties, some inventive character in the Montauk, New York, area produced a variation that was immediately dubbed the "Coathanger," then the "Christmas Tree" or the "Umbrella." All are multiple lure rigs that stream clusters of lures and are capable of taking two, three, or more fish at a time. The increased use of metal line ensured the deadliness of the combination for, with metal, it could be dragged in the depths.

A modern trolling umbrella is a four-armed contraption that may stream as many as four, eight, or even sixteen artificial lures. Plastic surgical tubes have proved very effective, and some have reported great success with such tempters as bucktail-dressed spinners or plugs. Obviously, a completely equipped umbrella is a fairly expensive contraption; therefore, it is trolled on heavy wire line to minimize loss by bottom fouling or fish action.

Whether such multiple lure rigs are sporting is arguable, if only because "sport" is a word that must be defined by each in his own way. These are meat-fishermen's in-

Al Reinfelder of New York exhibits a multiple
spreader "umbrella rig."

struments; they are dangerous because so many armed hooks are flying when a multiple catch is winched aboard. There are charges that fish damage themselves by fighting each other and the rig, and it is very certain that heavy tackle must be used to crank in two, three, or more gamesters at a time.

Such rigs should be banned in any sport-fishing tournament and, of course, no catch on such a contraption should be recognized for honors. This is a far cry from the trout fisherman's dropper, or the plugger's lure with an armed fly or pork-rind strip riding ahead. Ideally, any sporting weapon should be designed to catch one fish at a time.

This feeling of mine should not be construed as an argument against commercial fishing, no matter how it is done. If a citizen chooses to make a dollar with rod and line, rather than with gill net or trawl— so long as the law smiles on the practice—I cannot complain. Indeed, I will champion the right of the fisherman to harvest a legal, renewable resource. But I will not regard such a practitioner as a sportsman, and I will not honor any catch he makes as a rod and line record. The trick lies in taking them one at a time, honorably, with tackle that provides a challenge. Otherwise, we'd better forget about fine rods, sophisticated reels, carefully prepared baits, and nicely designed artificial lures. If we speak of sport, we must give the quarry a clean chance to escape.

Killing is easy. We can long-line or harpoon the great billfishes, shoot sharks, seine schooling tuna, and drag a bottom clean of cod and haddock. Within reason, some of these things may be necessary to feed the world. I offer no argument, other than a plea that commercials farm well and take no more than a safe, renewable harvest. The weaponry is both extensive and lethal. As sportsmen, we'd best seek a limit to the arrows in our quiver.

And we'd better pay attention to any selection of end tackle. That's where the game begins—and that's where it ends with a trophy or bleak disappointment.

LIGHT TACKLE ~5

Relativity in a Choice of Equipment

A well-educated angler knows that designations ranging from ultralight, through light, medium, and heavy are valid only as they relate to fish sought and gear employed. A giant tuna buff goes very light when he seeks monsters on 50-pound test. An ultralight enthusiast who relies on 6-pound mono to capture a 20-pound fish is well muscled by comparison.

There is a healthy trend toward the use of lighter, and therefore more sporting, gear on all the world's seacoasts. In many cases, particularly in the hands of skilled anglers, such equipment ensures better catches. Unfortunately, a larcenous minority views ultralight simply as a status symbol, using featherweight gear for work far beyond the capabilities of the equipment. We then drift into the bailiwick of stunt fishing, a rather senseless search for fame that is predicated on the capture of some unusually large fish on tackle best suited to lightweights. Such an entrepreneur rarely admits that he broke off a majority of battlers before the lucky placement of a hook, skilled boat handling, shoal water, or herding—or perhaps all in unholy concert—succeeded in reducing an eyebrow-raising specimen to possession.

There is always the tale, perhaps apocryphal, of the famous "no line-test record," in which a skipper demonstrated that through skilled boat handling he could herd and ultimately exhaust a fairly large bluefish tuna to the point where a gaff might be driven home. No rod, no reel, and no line—simply a logical chain of circumstances that involved shoal water, a frightened fish, a clever skipper, and a highly maneuverable boat.

Practical light-tackle fishermen have developed fine-line angling to a high art and their techniques are well worth studious examination. As always, where professionals are concerned with practical measures, tackle is job-rated and entirely suitable—even superior—for the task at hand. Light tackle is ideally used where it is most effective, both to catch a fish cleanly and honorably and to ensure the utmost in sport.

Although light tackle is a relative term, extending through the entire range of gear from the miniature ultralight spinning rod with its spider-web monofilament line on up to big-game weapons that rely on 50-pound test to challenge fish that may scale 500 to 1,000 pounds or more, most of us define the term by referring to light spinning, bait casting, and fly casting. In all of these, I persist in noting that one can go fine—or very heavy.

With the exception of trolling, light-tackle angling is a short-range business that stresses accuracy in presentation of lure or bait, plus the subtleties of a light line or leader that is tipped with a very small bait or a miniature artificial lure. The advantages are many, and the handicaps are only those associated with improper use.

Spinning gear is light-casting tackle, period. It was designed for and it works best with light lines and small lures. Fixed-spool cannot challenge revolving-spool above 20-pound test; it is far from ideal for trolling or bottom fishing, yet it is one of the world's most delightful tackle combinations when used within its wide, yet limited, sphere of efficiency.

Light tackle? If the kids had actually caught a
finback whale, beached on Cape Cod, they'd have
had reason to boast.

In the world of lightweight marine angling, spinning may well be a pacesetter. It
can do just about anything, although often less practically than a bait-casting or fly-
casting combination of comparable weight and action. With a few exceptions, I prefer
fixed-spool for close-range operations with miniature lures or baits. Indeed, if I had to
be limited to a single light-casting outfit, it would have to be a 6½- to 7-foot one-
handed spinning rod calibrated to handle lures in the ⅛- to 1-ounce bracket on lines
testing between 6 and 10 pounds. The reel would be a finely engineered open-faced
model with a smooth drag and line capacity in the 200- to 300-yard range. Most of
the time 100 yards of line are sufficient; the remainder is insurance.

With such an outfit, bolstered by extra spools of line in the various practical tests,
a man can successfully challenge bonefish on tropical flats—using tiny skimmer jigs in
the ⅛- to ¼-ounce range—or go to somewhat heavier jigs, spoons, and plugs with the
confidence that they'll take redfish in the Gulf of Mexico, stripers wherever they are
found, bluefish, ladyfish, snook, sea trout, baby tarpon, and a whole host of other light
to middleweight battlers found in bays, estuaries, and inshore surf. Ten-pound-test
line, in the hands of a capable angler who isn't prone to panic, can take some very big
fish—say those well into the 50- to 100-pound bracket.

Joe Brooks, with Stu Apte guiding, jumps a
46-pound tarpon on a plug-casting outfit.
Photo by Joe Brooks

Hal Lyman, right, caught this quapote on light
spinning tackle in the Colorado River, Costa Rica.

Summer flounder (fluke) will take bait or lures
fished close to bottom.

Carlos Barrantes plays a Colorado River tarpon.

Line tests are critical. Great saltwater anglers have whipped creditable fish on every-thing from 2-pound test on up. International Game Fish Association's current 6-pound-test minimum category is very practical on a host of shoal-water species, although it becomes questionable offshore. Eight may be nearer a light-tackle norm, with 10 moving into the heavy category for one-handed spinning. There is a logical need for stouter lines when fish must be tweaked out of a mangrove jungle. In this case, one must often overpower the quarry at the very outset, else risk disaster. There is a vast difference between playing a fish under goldfish-bowl conditions and maneuvering a stubborn scrapper out of a brush pile.

Very light lines, say 6- to 8-pound test—or lighter if you're an adventurer—facilitate casting and accuracy with featherweight lures or baits. It is possible to go very light on a clean bonefish flat where a gray ghost may streak off with 100 yards of mono, yet finds no sea fans or turtle grass in which to tangle and cut the strand. One simply keeps the rod tip high and trusts a smooth drag. The high tip in flats fishing is a defensive maneuver. There, one tries to keep running line out of the water and hence out of contact with weed growth or bottom obstructions. After that sizzling first run, you can lower your aching arms, try to control a trembling upper lip, and fight it out on old-fashioned terms.

Things change when it is necessary to drop a miniature jig, spoon, or plug into a tiny pocket away back under the mangrove roots that harbor snook and baby tarpon. There, a strike will require immediate pressure to yank a determined battler out of cover and ensure against its rocketing through a maze of submerged jungle growth. It is very spectacular to see a silvery, junior-grade tarpon come looping out of a black, shaded pool to deposit a plug in the mangroves some 4 to 6 feet above the surface, but it gets wearing when a tackle box is denuded of plugs. Solution: somewhat heavier line in order to upend that acrobatic little brute and get him out into open water where the odds are more nearly equal.

In gentle surf, estuaries, or bays, there is less difficulty. There, the major handicaps of light tackle are encompassed by limited casting range and the size of lures that must be used. Benefits are legion. Nothing is better suited to the capture of school stripers, puppy drum, sea trout, and practically all the small- to medium-sized trophies found on all coasts. If you can reach these gladiators with a proper lure or bait, light one-handed spinning tackle will outfish the muscleman outfits and provide more fun in the process. There is a joyous delicacy involved, a sense of ultimate finesse, and a happy lessening of fatigue.

As a man goes lighter, he finds that every atom of strength in the tackle chain must be utilized. That's why pros become fanatics about knots and jams that approach the utopian 100 percent factor. There is a necessity to employ new monos that have not been fatigued. A lot of sharpies replace a line after a single day's angling, and there are admitted record-seekers who will do this after the capture of any husky specimen. Everyday sportsmen need not adopt so rigid a practice, but it is common sense to cut back a few feet prior to any fresh adventure, and to be most vigilant in the detection of wearing or fraying. Watch a fine light-tackle angler in action, and you will note that regularly, almost subconsciously, he runs thumb and forefinger across the bitter end of his line after a cast. If there's the slightest fray, nick, or other imperfection, he cuts back.

Even the finest of monofilaments are inexpensive, so there is no excuse for using ancient strands that have become slightly weakened by stretching or exposure to sunlight over a period of time. (Mono should always be stored in a cool, dry, and shaded place.) Natural deterioration, admittedly slight, is less threatening than a grooved or chipped guide ring, a bail roller that does not roll, or a supposedly smooth drag that becomes jerky or difficult to adjust when a lot of line is streaming into the wide blue yonder. With light tackle, the margin for error is sharply diminished. Tactics and equipment must be flawless.

At the very least, start each season, or each long-awaited fishing trip, with new line, and then carry extra spools filled to ideal capacity. Be sure that reels are clean and properly oiled, that worn drag disks have been replaced, and that bail rollers are doing precisely what they're supposed to do. It is always wise for a spin caster to carry extra bail springs; for some reason, these never break close to home, but always when you're somewhere back in the jungle with fish practically attacking the boat. The best tackle is none too good, for even the best can go awry. Think perfection, and be prepared to make repairs on location.

On the tactical side, too many beginners panic when a powerful game fish runs off a great hank of light mono. The tendency is to screw the drag tighter, and this is precisely the moment when a drag should be backed off! Seagoing spinning reels pack lots of line, but drag pressure increases as spool diameter decreases. Given enough line, together with a drag set at, say, half the breaking test of the line, a long run will increase pressure to a point where the mono must part of its own weight, water resistance, and the drag-buildup that is guaranteed by the diminishing diameter of the spool. If you want to be sticky about it, a line without any drag at all *must part* at some point after a sufficient yardage is streamed. So sock it to them up close, but ease off when they get away out there.

Light-tackle buffs employ a few rules of thumb. First, drags are preset to hooking tension, never more than one-half the line's tested strength, and usually no more than one-third. In most cases, this will be sufficient to play a fish, but the pro will be forever ready to back off as a long run develops, or to tighten when the quarry is weary.

Great anglers never give a fish one split second of rest, but neither do they tempt the fates. You can't stop them in their tracks when they are green, and you're a patsy to allow a battler any rest period.

Of course, some happy enthusiasts tempt the wrathful gods of the sea. I have lounged around too many smoke-filled motel suites, glass in hand, while theory-stuffed warriors tested knots and drag settings with spring scales, seeking precise braking pressures that will belabor a fish without parting the line. Those who trust the last fraction of strength in such tests ask for later frustration on the sea, because close-range calculations undergo all sorts of nasty changes as line streams behind a rampaging speed merchant, or bellies in tidal currents when the quarry curves right or left. Whether ultralight or unlimited, there is no way to revoke the laws of physics. Praying won't help.

Spinning never approaches the accuracy of revolving-spool tackle, but top hands attain near perfection; they do this by feathering the coils of mono as they spiral off a fixed spool. An extended index finger does the job, subtly guiding and ultimately stopping a lure as it arcs out to target. Of course, the cast must be fairly exact to begin with: the feathering index finger simply steers a lure, as does the bait caster's educated thumb. Ideally, the bait descends on target, but may have to be slightly checked, so that it will drop right on the bull's-eye with a minimum of splash. All fine anglers, regardless of casting tackle used, learn to do this, and the practice becomes subconscious.

You don't cant a spinning outfit in casting. Line up the target and deliver on an almost vertical plane from straight overhead, or slightly to one side. Don't side cast, unless this is necessary to flip a lure under an overhanging shore cover. Some grand anglers, graduates of bait casting, always twist the wrist during a cast, so that the reel is sharply canted. In plug casting the technique cannot be faulted, because it allows the spool to ride on a smooth bearing. No such center-pin bearing is involved in spinning.

It has been said that "anybody can learn to spin in ten minutes," and this is true if one simply means an ability to cast without backlashing or otherwise aborting a heave. There is, of course, no such thing as a backlash in spinning, but there is a horrendous thing called "line slough." This occurs when a reel's spool is filled to a point where it becomes uncontrollable, or when the angler has broken one cardinal rule of thread-line operation—reeling against the drag. When this happens, the line is rapidly twisted and becomes absolutely unmanageable. On the next cast a great tangle emerges to foul the gathering guide or, very often, to jam so suddenly that the lure goes sailing horizonward without benefit of line. A serious line slough makes a backlash look like no sweat. Cut it off and forget it. You'll only run a fever trying to untangle the mess.

My friends in the tackle industry may hate me for saying so, but one of modern spinning's worst faults is that tendency to twist a line. Theoretically, the line always twists during a cast, but reverses on the retrieve, so that you wind up with a perfectly pristine strand. Twist is introduced, not when a powerful game fish is screaming off against the drag, but when an excited angler turns the reel's handle while line is still departing. Twist is multiplied with each turn of the handle, and trouble follows as surely as dawn follows deep night.

The trick, obviously, is to cease reeling while any gamester is ripping line off the spool against a drag, and to resume only when pumping makes it possible to deposit mono on the spool with each revolution of the bail. Unfortunately, some twist is always incorporated, because no craftsman finds it possible to gauge the exact moment when a weakening fish suddenly revives and starts a new run. This sort of thing doesn't happen with revolving-spool, but then a conventional reel seldom possesses the delicacy to present a midget lure on target with the fish-fooling gossamer mono-filaments that have revolutionized sport fishing. We pay a price for performance, and I mention this difficulty only to prove how smart I am, and as a sad memorial to the many line sloughs I have created through inept reel handling.

Within the capabilities of the tackle used, it is possible to put a great deal of strain on a game fish with very light gear. Experienced operators seem to defy physics when they lean into a willow-switch rod to punish a powerful adversary. However, they know exactly how much pressure can be exerted and when it is necessary to beat a hasty retreat by slacking off. In the hands of an expert, ultralight becomes high art.

Fixed-spool continues to be a light-tackle weapons system when you get into two-handed work, either for boat casting or for use in the surf. Line tests go up, but so do the stresses that must be managed. If fish weights are comparable, say in the 1 x 5 ratio or more, then the same niceties of handling will be necessary, and the same credits and debits accrue. Whether fixed-spool or conventional, we always strike a balance. The lighter the line, the easier it will be to cast a bait or lure, assuming that initial casting stresses can be overcome by a shock leader or a very limber tip. There will be a necessity to set a proper hook, a thing that becomes progressively more difficult at long range when the rod is limber and the line elastic. You simply cannot use a planky rod—which is ideal to set a heavy hook at the 100-yard mark—with a spinning reel. This statement will infuriate a host of spin casters, but it is true.

Karl Osborne of Vero Beach, Florida, collects an average cobia on spinning tackle.
Photo by Karl Osborne

Jim Rizzuto, a Hawaiian outdoor writer, collects a
small ulua on a spinning rod.
Photo by Jim Rizzuto

Spinning begins to phase out at approximately the 20-pound-test bracket. Fifteen
or 18-pound test is standard "heavy," and it does well within reason. Beyond 20—a
mono test that is used only with the heaviest and most awkward of fixed-spool gear—
you get into difficulty with casting. Lure weight can lacerate the right index finger, and
the friction of such heavy line pouring off a spinning-reel's spool is considerable.

Of course, much more friction is suffered with fixed-spool than with conventional—
in all size ranges. There is the very matter of line issuing in a cone, which must then
funnel down through a large gathering guide and through progressively smaller rings
to the tiptop. There is much line slap and consequent slowdown. During a long cast,
the deep, slotted spool of a spinning reel ensures rapidly increasing friction as the
line loops out. Empirical proof is offered to any angler who desires to replace the
mono on such a spool; as it diminishes, pressure becomes evident, to a point where,
when the last few hundred feet must be removed, it may be necessary to unwind
manually, rather than to stream out over the spool's lip.

Spinning is a light-tackle system and should never challenge the prerogatives of heavier revolving spool; it *can* be used in trolling or bottom fishing, and it *can* whip some of the medium-heavy game species, but out of its chosen sphere—which is casting—it becomes trouble prone and clumsy. The man who goes heavy with fixed-spool tacitly admits that he is too inexperienced to handle an outfit that does the job better.

American bait casting, the lightest revolving-spool method, is now in decline and employed only by a minority of specialists and studiously ignored by a host of Johnny-come-lately anglers who are too inept to train a pair of thumbs in casting and retriev-ing. The bait-casting combination will see a renaissance, because nothing has proved better for certain tasks, and because the average angler progresses with each year of his apprenticeship. Spinning has brought millions of new sportsmen to the sea and in so doing has generated interest in the more sophisticated arts of revolving spool and fly casting. No man of imagination can long resist a challenge.

The seagoing bait-casting rig is a direct outgrowth of gear used on black bass. Usually beefed up, it seldom equals ultralight spinning where there is a necessity to flip midget lures, yet it reigns supreme in a sort of in-between niche where lines are neither spider web or hawser, and where tack-hole casting accuracy is demanded, plus instant control at the strike and during the playing of a game fish.

Nowadays, almost all marine bait-casting reels are equipped with free spool, a smoothly adjustable star drag, an antireverse lock, and sufficient spool capacity to cope with saltwater game fish. Most of the better instruments are fitted with line-leveling devices, which are immediately removed by advanced anglers because such gimmicks ensure a measure of friction and thus handicap distance casting. For the same reason, antibacklash devices are the province of the beginner, not the regular, on fishing grounds.

Unlike spinning, very light bait casting is best served by nylon or Dacron braided lines because they are more manageable under the thumb, while monofilament is used in the midtests, say 10 and 12. A short leader is used, mono for soft-mouthed fishes, and wire for those with teeth like timber wolves. A whole host of lures complement the outfit, and bait casters use everything from lead-head jigs and spoons on up through a variety of plugs. The edge is measured in control, both in casting accuracy and the subsequent playing of a game fish.

Common mackerel are wonderful light-tackle battlers.

Larry Green finds bait-casting gear adequate for
lingcod near San Francisco. *Photo by Larry Green*

Long ago I had this in mind when I asked the late Amelio DeStefano of Boston to build me a plug-casting rod calibrated to handle ⅛- and ¼-ounce lures. I'd taken bonefish on spinning tackle, and wanted to emulate J. Lee Cuddy of Miami, a fine fisherman who had proved the worth of modern plug-casting gear on the flats. For a reel, I chose the fine little Garcia Ambassadeur 5000, and for line the 10-pound-test monofilament. This, to me, seemed an ideal rig to drop a tiny bucktail precisely where I wanted it—not a foot over, or a foot to right or left, but smack on target.

It worked beautifully, but my first bloodletting was a surprise. Claude Rogers of Virginia was with me, and Claude has always been an exponent of revolving spool, so he was easy to convince. Up to that time, and it's years ago, Claude had yet to tangle with a bone, so I offered advice.

"These things will take a lure and *always* run about 100 yards. Keep the tip up high and the drag light." Every bonefish I had hooked in the past had done this, so I was an instant expert. Very shortly I learned that one never says always.

It was a miserable day for flats fishing, cloudy with too much wind. A bonefisherman is a hunter as well as a fisher; you see the quarry before you cast, and our famous white fox is a flitting shadow at best. We waded the coral sand and marl of Sombrero Beach at Marathon, Florida—Claude, Hal Lyman, Jimmy Mays, and I. For an hour nobody saw a fish or even spooked one.

Then, incredibly lucky, I saw a slight flash of reflected light from the flank of a bone rooting in the marl. It was too choppy and cloudy to see more, but I flipped a quick cast to the spot and my ¼-ounce Wiggle Jig was taken immediately. Claude was close by and I hoped to show him that astonishing initial run of a hooked bonefish.

No such thing! The confounded critter sizzled around me in tight circles, never taking more than 30 yards of mono off the reel. We kept that one, a 7-pounder, for pictures (the curse of the man who writes about angling), and Claude was polite, although I knew he wondered about that 100-yard run. Soon he learned that I was right—most of the time—and I learned that a light plug-casting rig could be very gratifying on a bonefish flat and that one should *never* make positive statements about anything!

Now I doubt that I proved anything very conclusive. Spinning would have fared as well under the circumstances, and although I prefer plugging for many tasks, I doubt that I will ever again challenge bones with anything other than a fly rod or a fixed-spool combination. These two are ideal on wide-open ocean flats, so perhaps I was guilty of the eternal amateur's sin, the desire to prove a personal point against common logic.

However, nothing tops the expertise of a seasoned plug caster when it comes to dropping a lure precisely on target, a major advantage when game fish are lurking in tiny pockets of water rimmed by water hyacinths or tucked under overhanging shoreside brush. A good practitioner is quite capable of hitting a 2-inch bull's-eye at 50 feet, overhand or sidecast, and then initiating an immediate retrieve. This is most important when you comb a jungle-bordered waterway or sharply indented sod bank where success depends upon exact placement, subtle lure action, and split-second control after a strike.

Light-line-bait casting is lovely, provided that an angler has the opportunity to use a smoothly adjusted drag in a goldfish-bowl area. Things get sticky when a game fish must be steered out of a jungle, or right through it. Inland black bass fishermen, specialists in their own right, long ago discovered that the heaviest bronzeback in the sweetwater world could be had with lines testing 2 to 10 pounds, *unless* said bass were in the usual canopy of lily pads and aquatic brush piles that they favor. In this case, even a 9- to 10-pound-test line will part when pad-wrapped by a much smaller fish. The canny regulars went to 12- or 15-pound braids—and succeeded.

Marine plug casters must also battle shoreline brush. A snook has the disconcerting habit of arrowing right through a maze of mangrove roots unless he is tipped off balance and hauled out of cover right at strike. Baby tarpon aren't so likely to thread the brush piles, but they rocket out to zoom through overhead tangles and leave plugs dangling forlornly 4 to 6 feet above the surface, firmly stuck into the leather-textured mangrove leaves.

Plug casting can be magnificent in the open ocean, or on clashing rips where pelagic gamesters are taking small bait. Benefits are encompassed in the accuracy of presentation, direct contact, and enough clout to discourage immediate dives into floating weed or anchored kelp. There is a nice balance here that is lacking in the pendulous spinning rig. Enthusiasts believe that with a light revolving-spool outfit they are better able to "feel" the changing moods of a fighting fish and thus apply more or less pressure with drag or thumb. For whatever it is worth, I believe that this is so.

However, some artificials are ideally tailored to use with a plug-casting rig, and others do better on spinning gear. Usually, popping plugs work better on a bait-casting stick than on the more limber spinning rod. Some of the sliders simply cannot be given

Charles F. Waterman whips an Everglades snook with a plug-casting combination. *Photo by Charles F. Waterman*

A lot of back-country anglers like plug rods for tarpon on the fringes of the Florida Everglades. *Photo by Charles F. Waterman*

proper action with fixed-spool and, unless a fast whip retrieve is intended, bucktails also fare best with plugging gear. I always prefer plug-casting tackle when a lead-head's retrieve must be slowed down after dark, or where fish are logy enough to go for the slow bring-back. Control is better, both in casting, retrieving, and in playing a fish. The rig is superbly balanced.

It may be proper to include popping rods in the light-tackle category, for many of them are connecting links between true-bait casting and high-surf weapons. Unfortunately, the popping rod is a vanishing American, now subtly merging into a big family of sticks used to cast from boats or jetties. It is, really, an extension of the plug rod, somewhat lengthier and with lines upgraded. Initially, "popping" was a southern technique, the combination of a fairly long and limber rod, a revolving-spool reel—usually a Service Reel or one of that type—a float or "cork" to provide commotion, and a following bait, usually a shrimp or a shore minnow. The basic rig is still used throughout the world, although the popping cork and bait are often replaced by a small plug or metal lure. Specialists in the Gulf of Mexico are not convinced. They still boat or beach quantities of sea trout and redfish on the traditional cork and shrimp. The only concession made is a trend toward the use of medium spinning outfits.

Light tackle also encompasses trolling on offshore and inshore grounds where the same requirements apply—featherweight lines, together with rods and reels capable of handling the sought-after fish, while providing a high measure of sport. In some cases, this is overdone, yet that always depends upon an angler's dedication and desire. If a fish caught on light tackle is a much more satisfactory prize than one brought to gaff or net on heavier gear, that is enough to answer the question. A point of order: light tackle may delight the user, but what about companions who are working with heavier gear?

There is a time and a place for all things, but there is little to be said for the light-line zealot who boards a party boat where colleagues must fish shoulder to shoulder, nor for a similar mismatching in a picket line of surf casters armed with heavier equipment. The result is inevitable: tangled lines and stormy tempers. Light tackle is not always the most sporting of weapons, and sometimes its proponents have reason to wonder.

I remember a day off Islamorada, Florida, with Joe Brooks and Charley Whitney. We had agreed to go light, so no one boasted lines testing over 12 pounds. Joe and I each caught a half-dozen small dolphin that were delights on the slim wands. Then I hooked one a bit larger, say 10 pounds, and it provided a hearty scrap.

After the manner of dolphin, another of the species followed my hooked fish; it was much larger, and Charley Whitney very carefully steered his light-strip bait into the strike zone. In no time at all he was hooked up and enjoying a series of twisting, technicolor jumps. Joe and I boated our miniatures and relaxed while Charley continued to lean into a 12-pound-test rod that was strained to the limit.

Thereafter, for an unconscionably long time, Charley was a sole performer. The rest of us sat back, nibbled our fingernails, offered endless advice, and wondered whether he'd ever break off or land the fish. Somehow the line had been frayed, so it had become less than 12-pound test.

We lost a lot of precious fishing time while the skipper jockeyed his boat and Whitney pumped with joy that finally deteriorated into a grim slugging match. Before it was ended, Charley was thoroughly sick of that dolphin holding a fathom or so under the transom and making short runs against a drag that, considering the frayed line, was screwed up to near-disaster tension.

Charley was fisherman enough to resist locking up or hurrying his quarry, so he took his time as we all must do in light-tackle angling. It seemed an eternity before a 29-pound, thoroughly beaten bull was hoisted over the gunwale. Whitney thought he'd have had more fun with a stouter rig, which might have permitted a real wrestling match and resulted in releasing the fish while it was still green; his dolphin had broken its heart against the light, steady pressure and couldn't be returned to the sea. There were more of these brilliant acrobats as the afternoon lengthened and that strange emerald edging appeared under the shoreside cumulus. Finally a sail came up to investigate, but he didn't like our strips, and time had run out.

In trolling, as elsewhere, featherweight gear scores when it is needed to draw strikes. There are occasions in bay and estuary angling (and sometimes away out in the blue) where you will go light or you will not catch fish. Then the very fine rig is fully justified. In other cases, it merely serves as a sop to the angler's vanity, not a necessity, or it is a well-planned operation to break an existing record. No argument there—I respect the true record hunter, so long as he does not spoil the sport of others.

Worth recording is the fact that a long battle on light gear, if successful, will more thoroughly exhaust, and often kill, a game fish than a much shorter dogfight on stouter gear, after which the quarry may be released, still bright of eye and hard of muscle, to fight again.

Think about relativity. A 50-pound-test big-game outfit versus an 80-pound rig might well be compared to a 10-pound versus a 30-pound combination inshore. Both 50 and 80 are light on the grounds where true monsters are found. With 50-pound test, stout on most of the middleweights, you must have a lucky rabbit's foot in your pocket to whip a 500-pound giant tuna. In order to do so, the elements, as well as angler skill and good boat handling, must be in your favor. If a giant tuna persists in diving—or dies in the depths—you will not plane him up with 50.

Indeed, 80-pound test may be insufficient when a man tangles with game fish weighing 800 to 1,000 pounds or more. That it can be done is quite well documented; that it can be done regularly introduces the usual "ifs" and "buts." With practical line tests, those best suited to a particular task, you are able to control the fish and, where necessary, to plane him.

Charley Whitney of Provincetown admires a 29-pound Florida dolphin he caught on 12-pound-test line.

Lee Wulff with a great light-tackle catch, a
597-pound tuna boated on 50-pound-test line.
Photo by Lee Wulff

While 50-pound test is ultralight for giant bluefin tuna and the largest of marlin and swordfish, it is tremendously heavy for Atlantic and Pacific sailfish. Unfortunately, this is the test most often used on spindlebeaks that weigh between 40 and 70 pounds on the East Coast of the United States, and about twice as heavy in the Pacific. Nobody really needs anything with more clout than 30-pound test on sails and white marlin. Gradually, modern marine anglers are learning to arm for a species sought.

This reasoning certainly applies to fly casting, where the typical marine combination possesses more brute strength than 90 percent of the one-handed spinning and bait-casting rigs employed by everyday citizens. Fly casting sounds like the ultimate in delicacy, but it can be very hard hat and rough. If you harbor a doubt, be my guest on some fine September morning when Cape Cod's school stripers are walloping sand eels and bluebacks right in the wash. There is always much muttering and incredulous raising of eyebrows when I hook a 5- or 6-pound bass and proceed to yank him out of the suds in split seconds. The spin casters shake their heads, yet few seem to understand that my heavy rig's weakest link is a 15-pound-test mono tippet, while they are armed with 8- to 10-pound-test lines and less resilient rods to absorb sudden stresses. I am really working with an outfit fully capable of taming a 150-pound tarpon!

A very few experts, like Charley Waterman of DeLand, Florida, a grand outdoor writer, an ex-professor of English literature, and a fisherman par excellence, point out that a medium 8-foot rod and well-tapered leader will take many of the great inshore game fish. Any fly rod will do on the salt chuck, including the lightest of wands, so long as you job rate them to the task at hand. Charley thinks that we generally go too heavy, and I feel he is entirely right; we only succeed in inducing unnecessary angler fatigue and invading fields that rightly belong to another system. The fly rod is truly light tackle only when it measures up to that criterion.

There are, unfortunately, a few questionably honorable publicity seekers who parlay the long rod into fame and fortune by using it as it never was intended to be used. They are the folk who will stream a feather lure behind a bounding charter cruiser and then claim a fly-rod catch, although the technique was trolling. Some use live baits on fly lines, suitably tipped with leaders that test well over the accepted norms, and again speak of fly "casting." There are the specialists who employ lead-core shooting heads to get a fly into the depths, after which it is jigged to entice a bottom feeder like a rockfish or grouper.

Fly casting is light tackle only when a feather lure is *cast,* and when no boat motion or chasing is allowed to tip the balance. At present, the Salt Water Fly Rodders of America keep the best records, each application carefully examined to determine tackle, technique, and the strength of leader tippet employed.

In America, we generally regard 12-pound test as maximum tippet strength in salt water. If heavier leaders must be used to defeat sharp-toothed fishes, or those with abrasive hides or cutting gill plates, then an additional 12 inches of heavy mono or wire is allowed *beyond the specified tippet*. This is both fair and equitable, and so is the Fly Rodders' acceptance of unlimited tippet catches, so long as these are specified and the quarry is brought to hook by casting from shore or from a boat lying dead in the water. It may be quite impossible to detect all spurious claims, but the desire is there. The trouble with fly rods is that they can be truly light, or very heavy, and it takes minute examinations of components to reach any worthwhile conclusion.

Light tackle is always a very relative thing, no matter what weapons system is employed. All the various outfits can range from featherweight to overpowering. In too many cases "very light" is improperly associated with status, with little regard to effectiveness. This is a state of affairs that leads to cheating, long-line releases, and actual falsification of affidavits documenting tackle and methods. No honor accrues to him who injures fish after fish because his tackle is insufficient, even when such an operator manages to land a noteworthy gamester that is defeated through a lucky combination of shallow water, outside help, or illegal bait-lure combinations. Plaudits are due the highly competent who use tackle wisely and well.

Saltwater sport fishing needs light tackle, within reason, and the trend is toward the healthy use of practical gear. The fakers will be eliminated, as they always have been in the pursuance of any game.

A bluefish splashes as it tries to overpower a resilient fly rod. *Photo by Kib Bramhall*

THE FEATHER MERCHANTS ⌁6

The Science of Fly Casting in Salt Water

Saltwater fly-rodding, for some psychotic reason, is forever categorized as ultra-light angling. It may well be, for a marine feather merchant can operate with gossamer gear. He can also use a rig stout enough to yank an ox out of a mudhole. Please be advised that a fly rod, per se, does not always mean delicacy, finely tapered leaders, and ultimate finesse. On the world ocean you can use this tackle like a brain surgeon's scalpel, or with a hard hand and much muscle.

Actually, the standard saltwater fly-casting weapons system is reasonably light. Therefore, the angler who operates honestly and within certain sharply defined limitations that are imposed by the tackle itself is sharply challenged. Of course, he can fool observers by winning laurels with a rig that looks gentle, but is really barroom tough. There are always those limitations.

Any fly-casting outfit is a short-range tool. The best of craftsmen can grunt and groan and heave a big streamer or popping bug slightly better than 100 feet. Most of us settle for 50 or 60, which happens to be the best killing range anyhow. While experts swear that it is quite as easy to set a hook at 100 feet as at 50, elementary physics proves them wrong. Some tournament casters have the disconcerting habit, while fishing, of casting well over 100 feet, after which they retrieve just far enough to pick the whole thing up and make another laudatory cast. They're not really fishing—they're casting. The exhibition creates a lot of deep breathing (angler and audience alike), but it doesn't catch many fish.

Granting that occasionally it is necessary to throw a heroic length of line in order to reach feeding game, the ability to heave simply assures easy, faultless delivery at the optimum ranges of 50 to 60 feet. Strive for distance as an exercise in control. Like Aunt Samantha's elderberry wine, it can't hurt—and it may help.

In addition to limited range, two other factors plague the marine flycaster: he can't offer feather lures large enough to interest certain game fish, and he can't move any fly fast enough to intrigue others. It is quite useless to present a 3- or 4-inch artificial to a critter intent on eating herring, mackerel, or mullet that measure 12 to 14 inches. A feather or hair-dressed fly of that size is impossible to cast any appreciable distance, although it can be lobbed far enough to tease some easily approached species.

On the Atlantic seaboard, trophy striped bass ordinarily feed on big baits, hence they are not unduly fevered by a small artificial. The fly-rod angler must wait for a moment when the huge bass become selective and take to gobbling small stuff like sand eels and spearing. Enthusiasts of the Pacific Coast are not so thoroughly handicapped, for the forage fishes of that seaboard are generally small. Flies can simulate anchovies measuring 4 to 5 inches.

Speed of retrieve hurts fly-rodders all over the ocean. Many game fish are used to attacking relatively fast-moving baits, so they are turned off by a lure that moves slowly. Unfortunately, there is no way to strip a fly fast enough to con the swiftest of the predators under normal conditions. You can troll, but this is not fly casting. Solution?

A fast strip, with the rod held low, still brings that fly along in a dreamlike sequence of 2- or 3-foot darts, with pauses between strips. You can sweep the rod forward, ensuring a charitable 6 feet of fly speed, after which there is a deadly dull pause while slack line is retrieved. If you utilize a boat's forward motion to create suitable lure velocity, then—again—you're not fly casting; you're trolling, and this can be done better with other outfits.

Often a popping bug will turn the trick, not because it moves rapidly, but because its very nature creates commotion on the surface. A bluefish, for example, may crash an actively worked popper when it will scorn a streamer fly zipped along at top speed. Canny flycasters sometimes tease fish that are attracted to a slow-moving fly and then dismayed by its slow progress. The trick is to take that fly or bug away the moment a fish shows interest. Then cast back and repeat the process. Some of the speediest of strikers get so mad at the constantly disappearing fly that they finally rush it at touchdown.

Marine fly-rodders are plagued by wind, and usually blessed by a lack of jungle vegetation to snag a low, poorly executed back cast. There are the usual exceptions, where fish are sought in tropical creeks and bays. There, the mangroves are always primed to frustrate an otherwise fine delivery.

Generally speaking, the open-water fly-rodder can be a sloppy practitioner; he rarely has to worry about the height of his back cast and the subtle taper of a leader. His prime requisites are adequate range and a measure of accuracy, both achieved with a fly that is huge by comparison with the offerings of inland regulars. Much expertise is involved, but for a duffer the going is pretty easy.

At a Salt Water Fly Rodders of America panel discussion some years ago, an ardent young angler declared that he'd enjoyed considerable success with striped bass along the Jersey coast, but had been frustrated on an inland trout stream while his companions caught fish. What was he doing wrong?

Those who manned the panel were fully conversant with fresh water and salt—but how do you tell a beginner, diplomatically, to learn his trade? As I recall, the panel bumbled along with suggestions about leader tippets and fly presentation. The lad couldn't follow this reasoning to begin with; he'd been slapping a big hair fly into salt water and he'd been catching bass, so he felt that the same aboriginal techniques should work on trout. There are parallels, yet there are vast differences between trout fishing and the roaring, hell-for-leather marine approach.

It is, simply, a new discipline. For example, almost nobody uses a double-tapered or level fly line on the sea. You employ a forward taper (torpedo-head) line and, if you are a true addict, you will insist upon the relatively new saltwater forward taper that is very heavy up front to permit the instant shooting of line without excessive false casting. An educated marine feather merchant works with approximately 30 feet of forward taper and running line, plus another 30 or 40 feet coiled neatly on a boat's unobstructed deck, in a plastic tub or in a basket tied to his waist. There is little false casting, for the saltwater taper is heavy enough to turn the trick in one or two well-coordinated motions.

A good deal of timing and "feel" is involved. Once mastered, this seems elementary. You simply load the rod with that short head of heavy taper, and then shoot running line. The heavers invariably use a double haul, but for practical fishing a single or half haul is quite adequate and involves less arm waving. Most beginners only confuse themselves when they essay the double haul prior to mastering the mechanics of basic casting. It is worth noting that an educated flycaster, like the great Lefty Kreh of Miami, can throw 100 feet of line without any haul at all. And with nothing but the tip section of a fly rod, if you really want to be impressed!

Granting that a wide variety of fly rods and components are possible and even efficient on the sea front, you will want a pretty authoritative stick for all around fishing—say something measuring 8½ to 9 feet, calibrated to handle lines in the 9- to 10-size bracket. A few enthusiasts go to 11 and still think themselves undergunned.

Several of the larger freshwater reels, chief among them the wonderful Pflueger Medalist, will do for small- to medium-sized fish, but these inland winches are somewhat outclassed when you covet heavyweights. There, a more ruggedly built instrument, preferably one with a smooth adjustable drag and lots of line capacity, will prevent undue cursing and help to catch powerful game fish.

If I belabor the point, forgive me—but it is important. You will want all the backing you can comfortably pack behind a standard fly line. This means 150 to 200 yards or more of braided Dacron or Micron, never monofilament! The backing should test 18 to 20 pounds if you seek the middleweights, on up to 27- or 30-pound test if you stalk trophy tarpon or billfish. Backing is insurance, and you'd better believe that marine fish require a tight rein. All knots and fastenings should be well tied and snugged up with care.

Saltwater battlers, with a few notable exceptions, pay little attention to leader diameters. Many will take a streamer fly or a popping bug that is whacked down with all the subtlety of a thrown brick. Unlike trout and salmon, they seldom examine the intricacies of fly pattern, and they are likely to crash anything that remotely simulates the general size, color, and action of a natural oceanic bait. This, of course, does not excuse an improperly tapered leader that is physically incapable of turning a fly over to provide a neat touchdown.

Any leader should be tapered from a heavy butt down to a fine tippet, even where the fish are unselective. Unless the leader is gradually tapered, it will not perform; it will fail to overpower the fly, and a cast will seldom arrive on target without loops and kinks and wind knots. One way is to use a heavy, knotless salmon leader that is extruded from, 40-pound test at the butt down to 10 to 15 pounds at the bitter end. You can always add tippets.

It is, of course, quite practical to make your own leaders from 18-inch hanks of rather stiff monofilament, again tapering down from a heavy butt to the prescribed tippet—say 30, 20, 15, 12—with each section neatly blood-knotted. If a short (12-inch) length of stout mono or wire is required, this can be added to the tippet with a Stu Apte Improved Blood Knot (with mono) or with a key loop with light cable wire. The classicists hold 12-pound test to be right as a saltwater tippet, but lots of folk go higher, tapering down to a husky 15. Better go heavy in the beginning, and tempt the fates after you've learned to handle a saltwater fly line. Really 12 is enough—it can take a surprising amount of punishment.

The truth is, you can taper down to 6 and be a hero, or you can taper to 20 and nobody will know the difference. A lot of joyous marine fly-rodders do that, swallow their conscience, and smile modestly as they receive plaques for fish caught on a "delicate" little fly rod. An honor system is involved.

Leader length is never so important here as it is in a clean mountain torrent. The norm is about 9 feet, but a lot of specialists think "9" when they really mean 12 or 14.

That's because the usual hank of heavy mono, tied into the bitter end of the fly line via a nail knot, really becomes a part of the leader. A subtle taper-down can be important on such spooky feeders as bonefish and permit. There, the fine end-tackle not only ensures a measure of camouflage, it imparts a more fluid action to the fly. Generally, though, make it short and manageable.

Sweet-water fly-rodders rarely stream all the fly line during a battle with a trout and, in most cases, they are able to control the ebb and flow of that line with the thumb and forefinger of the left hand. This technique simply will not work on the big salt chuck, no more than it works on a great northern river where Atlantic salmon test an angler's skill. In the ocean, you must always assume that a fish will go into the backing, and you must expect that he will do this very rapidly. Certain operational tactics immediately become important.

In saltwater fly casting you shoot a lot of line and often find great coils lying about your feet at the moment that a game fish strikes. Any dolt knows that a fly line has a perverse mind of its own; it will slither under the soles of a man's tennis shoes, loop around a handy gas can, an outboard motor's operating handle, or any other readily available obstruction. Therefore, the first requirement is a reasonably clean, clear space in which to store free line. This may be an uncluttered boat deck, a basket strapped around the angler's waist, or even a plastic garbage can strategically placed to receive those wicked loops of free line. Some enthusiasts swear by artistically draped tarpaulins, and others by carefully stretched fishnets. The object is an immediately controlled, yet rapid, flow of loose line, so that the angler can come up solid and play his fish right off the reel. Discipline is pertinent. Things happen very rapidly when a big one takes a fly.

Famed angler Stu Apte poles the boat while master
flycaster Ray Donnersberger of Chicago searches
for flats-roving tarpon.

This fish may cartwheel on the surface, or simply turn and bore away with the speed of a torpedo. The run will be irresistible and, without any doubt, will go into the backing. Meanwhile, the angler stands flat-footed, with anywhere from a few yards to 30 or 40 feet of line coiled underfoot. His first and most important mission is to get that loose line fed smoothly through the guides, so that he can play the fish off the reel. For the moment, after a good hookup, everything else pales in significance. You may hop around like a tourist on a Pakistani bed of hot coals, but you'll form a loop with the thumb and forefinger of the left hand, exerting just enough pressure to control, yet not to snub up, and you will pray that the last of that loose line will whip through the guides. If it doesn't, you'll wind up making the usual time-worn excuses.

Once loose line is out, you should be under control, playing a fish right off the reel. Then the battle to conquer a strong gamester on fly tackle is very similar to that with any other outfit. You apply maximum pressure, within the capabilities of the rig, never letting the fish get a moment of rest to recharge its batteries. You pump and reel, but never try to perform both operations at the same time. There is one thing in your favor—the resilience of the long rod. Only a lowered tip and a sudden confrontation between irresistible force and immovable object can write kaput.

This happens if you fail to bow when a monster goes rocketing into the air. They call it "bowing" because an angler actually seems to perform that rite when he lurches forward to throw slack line. If this is not done, there is a distinct possibility that a jumping fish's body weight will part the leader upon reentry. The practice began with Atlantic salmon, but is even more important with the huge game fish of the sea.

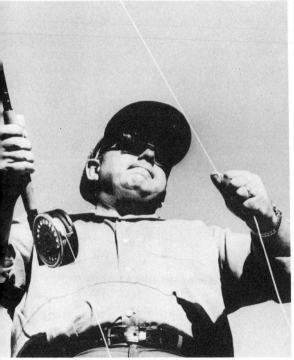

Leon Martuch, Scientific Anglers chief, sets the hook with a combined lift of the rod and a grip on the running line. *Photo by Mark Sosin*

Leon Martuch lunges forward in "bowing" to a big fish as it jumps. *Photo by Mark Sosin*

Spurts of high speed, together with jumps, will tire the quarry very rapidly. This is the best thing that can happen to a fisherman, so long as he manages to second-guess his fish and prevent any sudden strain caused by a low rod tip, a tight drag, or a very human tendency to "stop him in his tracks." Throw slack when they jump, and never try to snub up a strong runner. On the other hand, never give any hooked fish a moment of respite; the instant he hesitates or shows any sign of weakening, sock it to him.

An inland flycaster—and most of us started there—will grasp his rod firmly, right fist on the grip, index finger and thumb of his left hand guiding the line. That's about it, from strike to landing net. The reel is no more than a storage bin for line.

Things change in the salt where it is virtually certain that every challenger will go into the backing, will be played off the reel, and must be hard-handled. Now the rod's butt is tucked up against one's floating ribs; the right hand alternately grips the butt and manipulates the reel. In playing a heavy fish, the angler's left arm is extended so that he can grasp the rod's shaft just below the gathering guide. This position guarantees a maximum of leverage and control.

Some marine fly-rodders prefer a short extension butt, certainly an aid in playing a strong fish, but a handicap in casting. Loops of line invariably foul that extension, no matter how short it is. In American waters the English two-handed fly rod is rarely seen; while such a rod would simplify the playing of a big fish, its shortcomings as a casting instrument are obvious.

Extension butts can be, and often are, removable. In theory, you cast and hook up without benefit of the extension, and then plug it in for the ensuing battle. In practice, things happen so rapidly that the effort seems hardly worthwhile and and—an eon or so later—you wind up with a great game fish to release and a sore spot just northeast of the belly button.

Stiffeners are still used by some fishermen, but they are not considered sporting because their use entails hooking a fish on one outfit and playing it on an entirely different combination. Briefly, a hollow glass rod is beefed up after the strike by inserting a second glass shaft into the tube of the first. Among other things, the IGFA and the Salt Water Fly Rodders of America frown on this sort of thing.

While a great variety of marine game fish can be taken with the long wand, some species stretch the capabilities of the outfit. There is always an Alice-in-Wonderland aspect about enthusiasts who wade into the high surf to challenge fish slashing into bait about 50 yards beyond their most laudatory heaves. It is quite as illuminating to watch a self-professed master of the fly trying to match the successes of bottom fishermen armed with good revolving-spool tackle. To establish an impossible thesis—that a fly rod is all-purpose—a few overzealous workmen use shots of lead core to get a streamer down to bottom feeders, troll a fly behind a boat, or even live-line a wriggling bait pierced by a large, single hook. All of these things can be done with moderate success, but they can be done better with other outfits.

The most appropriate fly-rod fish is one that feeds on or close to the surface. The ideal gamester is one that can be approached, so that a cast of less than 100 feet is sufficient. The outfit is very versatile, within its sharply limited sphere of efficiency. Although a majority of experts prefer to cast from a boat with a clean, uncluttered casting platform, a fly man can work the banks of brackish streams and estuaries, shimmering tropical flats while wading thigh deep in clear, warm water, big northern sand beaches, rocky breakwaters, and even fishing piers.

Only incurable zealots push a fly rod in the high surf, yet there are occasions when it will outperform spinning and revolving spool in this big arena. That's when striped bass, particularly, are chasing small bait right in the wash. There isn't enough water to work a plug or a bucktail jig with any authority, but a big streamer or a popping bug needs little more than a heavy dew to float. Moreover, these buoyant little lures adequately simulate frantic small bait in the suds.

In this case, short casts are more effective, with payoff at less than 50 feet. If you're a commercial rod-and-liner—and I have been through that school—a big 9-foot rod with a number 10 line and a leader tapered down to 13- or 15-pound test will snake schoolies out of the wash so fast that colleagues can't believe their eyes. A trophy bass will still give you fits and, of course, you can always taper down and have much fun with the rambunctious 5- to 10-pounders.

In a coastal stream, or when casting across a strong current, a variation of inland wet-fly fishing technique is most effective. Cast up and across the flow, so that your tempter will swing in a wide arc. Any fly will swim close to the surface when a floating line is used and—in a strong tidal current—no fly will travel very deep, even with a quick-sinking line. A majority of enthusiasts prefer the floating line, if only because it is easier to handle, to pick off the water at any logical point and to get into action again with a minimum of false casts. The floater with a sinking tip is very effective when streamer flies are used, although it poses certain difficulties with a popping bug.

Sinking lines are valuable on the salt chuck, yet beginners expect more performance than can be delivered. In a strong tidal current it will prove very difficult, if not impossible, to get any sinking line down, say more than 4 feet under the surface. The flow simply buoys that strand along, bellying it and thrusting it closer to the surface as the cast arcs down in its predestined swing. In relatively quiet waters the sinking line really comes into its own and can be the difference between succcess and failure. If you want to get down, always choose a quick-sinking line; the slow sinker may be fine on an inland trout stream, but it is a mite too puny for the big, pulsing ocean.

Earlier I noted that a saltwater flycaster can be a rather sloppy performer and, usually, can get away with it. That "usually" is a sneaky way to turn the arrows of critics who think in terms of bonefish, permit, snook, and other specialized game. As a matter of fact, each species presents particular problems that must be solved if the angler wants to be a hero.

A bonefish is eternally spooky because he feeds in very thin water and is constantly worried about predatory fishes and birds and men. The white fox progresses nervously, flitting from one patch of weed to another, crossing the white, sandy patches quickly, and changing direction so frequently that he may be likened to a butterfly aimlessly sampling the blossoms in a field of clover. Any bonefish will get the hell out of there if the slightest shadow crosses his window, if any sound seems menacing, if any movement, flash of light, or color indicates the possibility of danger. The thinner the water, the spookier the bone.

Therefore, in fly casting for the famous white fox, one never false casts *over* the quarry. That split-second image of a line in the air, or possibly the thin shadow it prints on a brilliant bottom, will be enough to trigger immediate flight. If there must be false casting to lengthen a line prior to shooting, make it off to one side. This is a first hurdle.

Next—accuracy. In fly-rod fishing for bonefish there is a compelling necessity to drop the fly lightly and precisely on target. This dosen't mean hitting a cruising bone on the nose, for any such familiarity will send him into the deep blue at near supersonic speed. You lead him carefully, hopefully second-guessing the direction of his erratic,

Grubbing bonefish produce "muds," which are
spotted by alert anglers.

butterfly progress across a flat. Water depth will determine the amount of lead, for the
white fox becomes progressively chicken-hearted as the bottom shelves up.

Drop the fly lightly, say 4 to 10 feet in front of this jittery, questioning bundle of
nerves. This, in itself, can be a very traumatic experience for anyone who is making
a first acquaintance with the fox. All sorts of untoward things happen, most of them
caused by old-fashioned buck fever, but some by perverse little puffs of wind. No man
ever gets so blasé that he goes in coolly and calmly. When your eyes suddenly register
on that flitting, ghostlike form and you know that the slightest fluff can mean immediate disaster, the old heart begins to pound and otherwise steely reflexes turns to jelly.
The feeling is much the same as that when a rocking-chair buck bursts into view, or
the heart-clutching moment when a high-speed motor car hits a slick of oil or ice and
slides sickeningly.

It is suddenly necessary to be all craftsman, to be right on target, to get that fly
down with a minimum of fuss, and then let it sink to a point just above the marl or
grass. Retrieve will depend upon the course of the fish and its obvious interest, or lack
of interest. Usually, slow twitches are in order; yet, if the bone seems intrigued, one
may even find it profitable to stop the fly dead, and then move it forward teasingly.

Permit, the fish that advanced anglers seek after they have become reasonably
proficient on bones, require similar tactics—only more so! These great, saucer-shaped
pompanos have been taken on fly rods, but the list of anglers who have turned the
trick is a very select roster. Those who succeed automatically achieve a sort of hero
status among the best fly-rodders in the world.

Joe Brooks may well have taken the first permit on a fly. It happened back in 1951 at Content Key, Florida, and the fish weighed 12 pounds 8 ounces. One of Joe's books quotes 11 pounds 8 ounces, but that was a typographical error. The previous year he took one that scaled 5 pounds 10 ounces, also at Content on a fly rod, but this fish was hooked on a Johnson Golden Spoon; a nice catch, but not truly on a fly. Later, in 1960, Brooks caught a 23-pounder at Bimini, a scrapper that held the fly-rod record for a few years before it was shot down in flames by Chuck Walton's 30-pound 2-ounce monster at Sugarloaf Key in 1970.

Guide Bonnie Smith and Joe Brooks with the first permit ever taken on a true fly. The permit weighed 12 pounds 8 ounces, and was caught at Content Key, Florida, in May 1951. *Photo by Joe Brooks*

With either bone or permit, the cautious approach is mandatory. You combine the arts of hunting and fishing and you stress accurate, delicate presentation. There is no room for the thrown brick technique, and rarely any fisherman's luck. You make your own luck, and you'd best be highly skilled. You'd also be wise to think about low angler silhouette and clothing that blends into the surroundings.

Actually, in any close-range casting for spooky fish, an angler's clothing should be neutral in color. White or bright-colored shirts can be handicaps. Even the gleam of a highly polished fly rod flashing in the sun during the execution of a cast can spook these forever nervous flats feeders. The best practitioners dress like Apaches reconnoitering a wagon train, and they stoop over like camels in labor on that final approach. Where thin-water game fish are concerned, no camouflage, subterfuge, or skill in stalking is wasted. To ensure odds, you always wear polarized glasses to defeat surface glare, and you must learn to look *through* the water, not *at* it. Whether wading or poling a shallow draft boat, go in with the sun at your back, like a fighter pilot stalking a hostile formation. If possible, conspire to have that ever-present sea breeze at your back also. And be quiet! Shoal-water feeders won't mind normal conversation above the ripples, but they get edgy when some clod kicks a gas can in the boat, thumps his feet on the deck, or otherwise sends threatening vibrations in all directions.

"Bonefish Sam" Ellis of Bimini nets a 23-pound permit taken on a fly by Joe Brooks. That's Don McCarthy looking on. *Photo by Joe Brooks*

Having hooked one of these hair-trigger powder kegs of energy, a fisherman's joyous troubles are just beginning. It is now necessary to clear loose line quickly, to stand up, and to extend the fly rod's tip as high as possible while line screams off the reel in an alarming number of rpm's. The high tip offers a measure of protection against turtle grass and sea fans, assorted coral growth and mangrove shoots, which usually dot a tropical flat. The object is to keep every possible inch of running line above the surface.

The first run of a bonefish is unbelievable to a newcomer. The fish doesn't take with a crash—indeed, he often seems to mill around for a moment after the hook has been set. But then he's off, and the only parallel is a naval torpedo streaking across the flats. Most of the respectable ones will travel 100 yards at full throttle, and the big boys may go half again as far—all in the proverbial wink of an eye. They're fast, and they're powerful, yet they kill themselves with that tremendous burst of energy. After a bonefish has completed his first explosive run he is not too formidable a foe, although he may well make shorter, determined runs after being pumped and reeled back to the starting point.

A permit is much tougher, calling upon hidden reserves of stamina to make run after run, pitting his broad sides against the strength-sapping pressure of rod and line. Lots of permit are caught on the usual crab, conch, or shrimp-baited hooks, but relatively few fall to fly-rodders using feather artificials. This may well be the toughest of all great game fish to take on a long wand.

Snook snatchers will disagree, if only because the snook usually hides in a brush pile, far under the clutching mangroves. In this case, a fly-rodder's accuracy must be akin to that of the target shooter who drives nails at 50 feet. A snook frequently takes station in a tropical pothole well back in the brush, with angled roots surrounding him and a canopy of leather-textured mangroves overhead. He won't come out to take a fly or a popping bug, but he sure as hell attacks a lure that drops right into his hidey-hole, or is studiously bounced in there.

Little lantern jaws can be coaxed at close range, but the old stagers get edgy about a boat that swings in too close and makes waves. So, in order to be successful, you drift something like 60 to 70 feet off a shoreline that looks like a rain-forest jungle, and you throw flies or popping bugs into miniature natural potholes where an error of scant inches, port, starboard, or vertical, will get you a hang-up in some of the world's most exasperating natural barbed wire.

In addition to the need for tack-hole accuracy in casting, there is another thing about snook. Once hooked, well back under the overhang, they must be muscled out of there—fast. If this is not done, a respectable snook counts it his mission in life to rocket through the nearest maze of vines and mangrove roots, a thing that contributes to his life expectancy, but doesn't please anglers with parted lines and leaders.

Therefore, unless you're a light-tackle buff who counts one triumph more important than ten break-offs, it is best to go a mite heavy on tippet strength. You will want to hit this mule over the head with a two-by-four, not only to get his attention, but to yank him out of his home-grown bunker before he can get his tail curved around enough water to make you look like a clown. In the boondocks, a snook is bad news; he's at a distinct disadvantage when you muscle him into open water where the odds are more nearly even.

Similar tactics apply in the quest for baby tarpon, which so often cruise in the same quarters. It is very thrilling to hook a small silver king—and tropical anglers are wont to call anything under 20 pounds a baby—some 6 inches from the fiddler-crab-riddled banks under a screen of mangroves. Somewhere in a tarpon's immortal printed circuit there is a blob that says—jump! A tarpon almost always does this, even if he's hooked in the most impenetrable jungle. He'll come up like a berserk rocket, right through the saw grass and mangroves, and he will then submit to the law of gravity, leaving your fly, popping bug, and leader tippet well hung in leathery foliage. Solution? Power him out at strike, so that he has to fight on even terms and jump in open water. You're going to release him anyway, so there's no skulduggery involved.

Really big tarpon, the kind that Stu Apte has made famous on the remote keys of Florida, are another thing. They cruise the flats like somnolent torpedoes and are very susceptible to well-placed streamer flies. Again, accuracy is all-important. You must drop that fly a few feet ahead of a cruiser, and then move it slowly. Most of us get buck fever when a fish as long as the boat is sighted and must be cast to. There is always a nagging suspicion that this trip is not only unnecessary—but impossible!

Yet if mind overcomes muscle and the cast is truly consummated, dropping lightly some 4 to 6 feet ahead of the cruising behemoth, there is good reason to believe that the goggle-eyed warrior will vector in and take. A tarpon strikes like a sleepwaker, extending those great, telescoping jaws and sucking the fly in. Good guides can tell you just when to strike, after the fish closes his trap and begins to turn. You hit him—hard—with rod tip low, and the world suddenly erupts in a natural grand finale of briny fireworks.

Stu Apte's 154-pound tarpon became a world's
record on a 12-pound-test tippet. *Photo by Stu Apte*

There are several moments of complete pandemonium while the guide shouts instructions and you frantically clear all running line. The hissing, plastic-coated braid rattles through the guides like a herd of snakes while you hop and jump like a sinner exposed to first hot coals, and finally it is all out there while the reel's drag takes command and an unbelievably big, chromium-plated fish soars out of the water like a tormented missile.

Bow quickly, or face disaster! You are plagued by a 12-pound-test tippet, and the weight of this tremendous fish will be ten times that figure. Unless you provide slack line at the climactic moment of reentry, the tarpon will almost certainly part the leader and be gone in split seconds. You will learn to throw slack at every jump—or you'll be a loser. You will also learn to apply a maximum amount of pressure between jumps, so that the fish must burn energy at a lethal rate. The more often he jumps, the more certain you are of victory. If a tarpon could reason, he'd never jump but would simply bore off in one sustained run after another. A very few do this; you won't soon forget them.

But the jumper is soon brought to boat. The one to worry about is the runner, either foul-hooked or so snaffled that he can come out in clean, greyhounding leaps, mouth closed. *That* fish is bad news, because he is not overly bothered by a lack of oxygen. He can clean you or he can decamp to deep water. Exult when a silver king jumps. Get worried when he runs and seeks the depths.

Master fly-rodder Lefty Kreh caught this 38-pound barracuda on the Florida Keys. *Photo by Lefty Kreh*

A great many saltwater fly-rodders have now taken billfish on big streamers and popping bugs. This is a challenging game because there are so many handicaps. The difficulties are legion. Initially, billfish just aren't found in numbers, so there is the necessity to cruise endlessly in the best waters, to make the most of any opportunity, and to enjoy the services of a skipper and crew who know exactly what to do when the chips are down.

So far, conquests are limited to sailfish, both Atlantic and Pacific, and striped marlin. Without any doubt, anglers will come up with small specimens of swordfish, blue marlin, white marlin, and black marlin. Logically, the white should be first to fall, if only because he is a small customer and reasonably plentiful. Excepting sailfish and striped marlin, major difficulties lie not in the size of fish, within reason, but in methods of fly presentation.

For one thing, many of these great, pelagic spindlebeaks are acutely aware of the trolling boat's engine beat, and they can be spooked by any change in tempo. Since the flycaster is committed to casting for his fish from a boat lying dead in the water, problems multiply. A few opportunists, with larceny in their hearts, simply troll big flies in the wake of a cruiser, hook billfish that have been raised with teasers, and then claim fly-rod catches. The better craftsmen will not do this, hence they deserve medals for hooking, playing, and landing the monsters from boats lying dead in the water.

Mark Sosin with a fly-rod yellowfin tuna. Pete Perinchief of Bermuda is at right. *Photo by Mark Sosin*

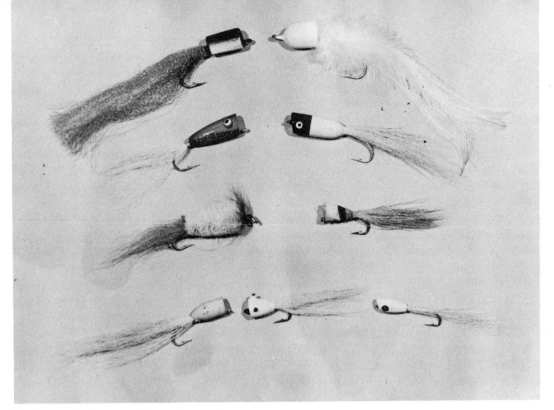

Typical popping bugs used in modern marine
fishing. Bulky types, top, are used on sailfish.

Forget about giant tuna. Perhaps they can be hooked on a huge fly, but they run off
so much line that no fly-rod combination yet devised is likely to conquer them. It
should be possible to take bluefins of 100 to 150 pounds on the long wand, but unless
you're an incurable optimist, don't tangle with those 500-pound-plus brutes.

Mark Sosin with sailfish taken on a fly rod.
Photo by Mark Sosin

Once again, in seeking out big fishes, the fly-rodder is plagued by a need for big flies or popping bugs. These simply cannot be cast to any considerable distance, not only because they are bulky, but because their air characteristics are impossible. The big fly is a very short-range lure; it can be flipped 40 to 50 feet in a fair wind, but it is almost always unwieldy, You just don't haul off and throw an 8-inch hunk of balsa wood and feathers, armed with a 7/0 hook, to any appreciable distance. The killing range must be minimal.

I have caught a lot of dolphin on flies. Indeed, that color-conscious gladiator of southern seas is a real patsy for feathers, so long as the fly is trolled in a cruiser's wake. That's the way it is done—90 percent of the time. However, you can murder school dolphin—and occasionally a big one—after they have been trolled in by successive hookups. Other hues may serve, but combinations of yellow and red hair or feathers seem irresistible to a charging dolphin. Get them coming after trolled **strip** baits or feathers, then kill the engines and drift to enjoy wonderful offshore fly casting.

Back in the jungles of Central and South America the fly rod can be a most satisfactory weapon. Hal Lyman and I, visiting Costa Rica's wonderful Colorado River one spring, ran into a solid week of heavy rainfall. The river ran like a flood of well-creamed coffee, and the huge silver sabalo were hard to find. We simply outboarded up into the big feeder streams where a host of familiar and exotic gamesters were ready and willing to take flies.

There were snook, old friends on so many warm seacoasts, characteristically ensconced in the brushy pockets, and machaca and majarra—the former a powerful, spectacular, high-jumping look-alike of the shad with a formidable array of sharp teeth, and the latter a marine version of the northern bluegill. Both proved fond of small streamer patterns. We caught some respectable jacks, plus some wonderful antediluvian-looking quapote, and we prospered, although thoroughly soaked by warm, tropical rain.

Quite naturally, the great game fishes inspire more newsprint than those bread-and-butter species found close to home and available in astronomical numbers. The northern weakfish—called squeteague in New England, weakfish or weakie through New York and New Jersey, and gray trout in Mason-Dixon country—is a grand fly-rod fish. He likes the shrimp variations and will also wallop big, gaudy streamer patterns worked in a chum slick.

Southward on the American East Coast and through the Gulf of Mexico, fly-rodders enjoy the southern spotted weakfish, or sea trout. Like his Yankee cousin, he's a patsy for a well-presented fly, whether it be a shrimp type or a streamer.

An enthusiastic feather merchant can become ecstatic over mangrove snappers and ladyfish, jacks of various types, and a whole host of species that are freewheeling enough to feast on moving targets. Puppy drum or redfish, the small channel bass of the southland, often declare war on slow-moving flies worked deep with sinking lines. On many occasions they'll rise to take a high-riding streamer or popping bug on the surface.

A veritable cornucopia of Pacific surf perch, kelp bass, rockfish, and lingcod will take flies properly presented. The West Coast halibut is a customer in shoal waters, and Atlantic flatfishes—although seldom the great Atlantic halibut—gobble feathers. Common mackerel can be coaxed to a fly of the most nondescript type, and it is worth noting that, ounce for ounce, the mackerel is a tougher battler than any inland trout. Small- to medium-sized sharks adore flies. The list is almost endless, limited only when a species feeds so deep that it cannot be reached with an unweighted fly.

Pacific halibut also take flies. Larry Green exhibits a big flattie. *Photo by Larry Green*

David Townsend with New England bluefish caught on fly-casting tackle. *Photo by Kay Townsend*

One of a very few trophy channel bass ever caught on a fly. Claude Rogers of Virginia Beach with his Eastern Shore catch, a 37-pounder. *Photo by Claude Rogers*

In the salt chuck, true fly patterns are scarce. There is none of the romance and tradition of centuries, the intricate marrying of feathers and tinsel and fur to create a specific artificial, nor is there any apparent need for so subtle an offering. Basic simulation in shape and general color seems sufficient, for we match forage fishes and free-swimming crustaceans rather than the insects and insect larvae so beloved of inland fishes. Some anglers find it difficult to bridge the gap and forever equate the wild, wide-open sea with a placid trout stream.

Until some genius proves otherwise, we have three basic fly types in the salt. One is a streamer fly that may be large or small; another is the studied imitation of a shrimp; and the third is a very streamlined surface popping bug or slider. I emphasize the word "type," rather than "pattern," and I think this very important.

Small hair or feather flies, hopefully intended to simulate tiny minnows, crustaceans, or shrimp, are effective on such flats feeders as bonefish and permit. Shrimp flies can be equally deadly on striped bass in a coastal estuary, or on weakfish in a sheltered bay or cove. The shrimp is a delicacy on any marine fish's banquet table, so there is good reason to copy it. Colors may range from neutral blond through brown, shades of blue and green, to the hot pink that has been so successful in recent years.

Elongated, with feather or hair dressing, the fly becomes a slim streamer pattern—a minnow in disguise. Mark the word, "slim." In order to cast a fly to any appreciable distance, the lure's air characteristics must be good. This cancels out the bushy inland offering, not only because it is air resistant, but because it does not represent natural forage in the sea.

The big problem here, unless you seek fish that are enamored of the tiny minnow, shrimp, or crab imitations, is a lure that appears to have considerable slim bulk, yet will cast easily. There is little room for air-resistant hackles, flaring feathers, or bushy bucktails. The trick is to make it look big while, in reality, it is a very sparse hunk of ordnance. Sparsely tied flies catch fish, while the bushy ones catch fishermen.

There is, naturally, a common ground. Hackle forward is used, and the reversed hackle streamer—which breathes in the water and thus ensures built-in action—has much to recommend it. These features must be incorporated in such a way that they will tempt game fish, but will not handicap the distance casting so necessary on salt water.

A vital need to throw has affected the design of popping and sliding bugs in this arena. You won't find many of these treasures equipped with furry hackles and squirmy, air-resistant rubber legs. They're streamlined, usually with a slim jet of feathers or hair dressing a single hook. They are usually poppers or bullet-headed sliders, and color schemes are prosaic. White, yellow, red and white, green, or blue and white dominate. Solid black is a good choice at night. The marine popping bug should simulate a forage fish struggling on the surface of the water.

Pattern, so far as saltwater flies are concerned, is arguable. There is absolutely no ironclad tradition, and there is much controversy about so-called pattern. We have a few streamer flies, such as the old Palmer-Diller, a couple of old-timers invented by Harold Gibbs and Frank Gibbs of Rhode Island to take striped bass; the Blonde series, popularized by Joe Brooks—really important in that they feature fore-and-aft bucktail dressing with a bit of tinsel in between; the Pacific Candlefish series, again erratic because there are so many color combinations, and a whole host of new departures that are questionable because no one, other than their originators, feels them indispensable. I have one of my own, and I won't bore you with a description.

When you get right down to basics, the saltwater streamer fly is a rather crude facsimile of a baitfish or a free-swimming crustacean; it is never very intricately designed or dressed, and it relies on overall color, size, action, and buoyancy—positive or negative—to be effective. Pattern is still something to natter about over an evening drink. The fish aren't overly concerned, nor are anglers impressed by colleagues who announce "patterns" that they have created. True pattern must be proved over a great span of years, and marine fly casting is a very new business. Don't hold your breath.

In many cases, a simple white or yellow bucktail is most effective. There are occasions when red, black, or other colors and combinations of colors work best. Some competent marine fly-rodders now feel that Mylar strips impart a special magic. The man-made glitter may well intrigue certain fish, yet this is no cure-all. Similarly, those who swear by maribou dressing have a point: the soft, slithery feathers of this African stork (or the look-alikes of an American turkey) can be very seductive, although short-lived. Maribou is fragile, hence its quivering action in the water. At its best in the construction of small inland streamer flies, the material is equally deadly on finicky feeders and spooky customers in salt water. Good stuff, but not very durable.

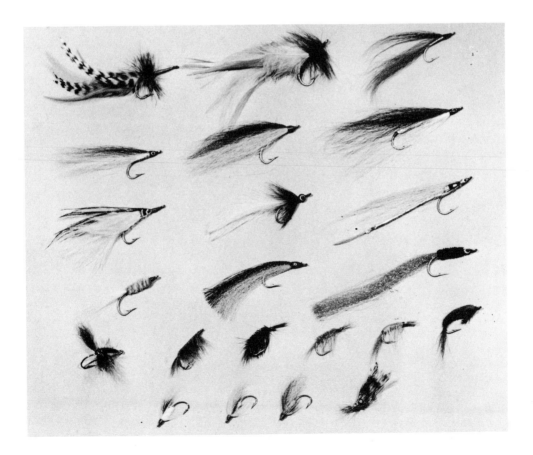

Effective feather and hair fly types for all-around angling.

In fly casting, the fact that a rod is limber makes it virtually impossible to sock a heavy hook home with great power. Therefore, the point must be very sharp. There is no excuse for a dull hook in any angling, yet a blunt point in fly casting borders on idiocy. The point must be slim and it must be razor sharp, else all other disciplines fail. Too many marine fly-rodders feel that hooks must be large and drawn from heavy wire. The exact opposite is true. Since the tackle is light and resilient, the hook should be small and finely honed.

There is a great and growing place for the long wand in salt water. It can be delicate or heavy; it can be a combination to take lightweights inshore, middleweights on offshore grounds, or even the most cooperative of billfish. No fly rod is equal to a struggle with really big game, but a lot of grand battlers can be subdued with feathers. The challenge is supreme, and it's all yours.

BAIT UP! ~7

The Role of Natural Baits in Saltwater Angling

Too many purists on today's saltwater sport-fishing grounds sneer at blood brothers who adorn hooks with natural sea creatures, and then strive to ignore the fact that live bait specialists worship at the shrine of a deadly art. Nothing, if we are willing to admit the truth, is quite so tempting to a predator as the forage he is accustomed to eat. While the artificial look-alike is spectacular and often effective, scholarly presentation of the real thing bows to no method yet invented. A well-educated manipulator of fresh baits is a true craftsman and he will generally outfish hidebound purists.

In this arena, there is a curious situation that both confirms and denies the arguments of self-appointed experts who swear by artificials. Since bait seems the royal road to success where beginners are concerned, they almost universally ignore so-called higher arts to place their trust in sea worms, shrimp, chunked mullet, or whatever is locally deemed most effective. Operating on faith, without any appreciable leavening of skill, they collect a few sport and game fishes, usually harvesting the least desirable and most plentiful varieties in any given area. Beginners always outnumber experts by a wide margin, so there is a natural tendency to regard bait fishing as the province of the unschooled. The exact opposite is true.

Masters of the art are likely to be veterans who have been through the whole schmeer from high surf to big game and back to fly casting. They have studied their quarry and have developed a sixth sense with regard to the movement of bait and the effect of tidal currents, bottom conformation, and weather conditions. Many of these classicists are equally adept with artificial lures, but common sense dictates a measure of versatility. Such men, and occasional women, are the deadliest reivers on the sea because they are not crippled by an allegiance to any one method; they are all-around performers.

Specialists use all manner of tackle, from the very lightest to tempt tiny, brilliantly colored coral dwellers of the tropics, on up to unlimited big-game rigs where monsters of the sea like their victuals bona fide and fresh. You can dump a huge chunk of flesh, impaled on an impossibly large hook, over the side to intrigue a white shark, or fritter your time away in delightful bouts with savory butterfish that measure 6 inches from blunt snout to forked tail and will only take the tiniest of offerings. There is a bait for just about everything that swims, and the presentation of said bait can be high adventure. Sometimes it borders on the exotic.

I recall a quest for sawfish in Costa Rica. These big cousins of the skates aren't universal favorites among anglers, but they can provide hair-raising sport. There is a place near the mouth of the Colorado River, right up against the border of Nicaragua, where heroes sally forth at night, anchor, and present cut chunks of local forage fish to trophy saws. It is a pretty weird operation, often lighted by a blazing flambeau that turns the surrounding jungle river into a flickering, half-seen, and murmurous aquatic version of Dante's Inferno. Heavy gear is necessary, because a full-blooded sawfish may be large enough to swamp a small craft. One always has an apprehensive ear tuned to the night sounds—harsh-voiced tropical birds, the sinister chuckle of the black, fire-tinted river, and the gargantuan swirls that might well be caused by those ferocious bull sharks of Central America. It is an experience, heightened by the soft patter of Spanish uttered by native guides and the feel of a heavy rod with a 6/0 reel propped against a handy gunwale.

Bait covers a tremendous variety of sea creatures that provide forage for sport and game fish, therefore selection is important and presentation should be flawless. You can be an abject duffer and succeed after a fashion, just as the country boy with a coarse hook and a clumsily strung night crawler will land an occasional trophy. But to be consistent, finesse is quite as necessary here as it is with the finely tapered leader and the dragless float of a dry fly presented to a wary brown trout in a quiet pool. In marine bait fishing, more so than in any other coastal technique, an angler actually "matches the hatch."

There are, it must be admitted, instances in which exotic baitfishes have been flown into great angling grounds and have scored notable successes. Almost always, if you read the fine print, these are tempters in the wakes of charter cruisers where the gamester has little opportunity to scent, taste, or examine before striking. **Action** triggers the attack, and an artificial lure might have been quite as potent. Native forage species always get the nod where a fish must be coaxed with a bait that looks, acts, and smells like a resident hors d'oeuvre.

Also admitted, some baits succeed in waters where resident fish have never seen or tasted them. Maine clam worms, whisked across the United States to California and Oregon, are much appreciated by bottom feeders of the Pacific. Once, a long time ago when nobody had experimented with eastern sea worms in the West, Frank Hammond of Wiscasset, Maine, shipped a flat of Nereis—air express—to me in San Francisco. I might have become a hero by coaxing Golden Gate stripers with those squirmers, but Murphy's Law prevailed. On the day that my clam worms arrived, some psychopath bombed the airline's freight depot, and I imagine my bait was plastered across the ceiling.

In spite of exceptions, it is generally agreed that most of our predatory fishes can be extremely selective. When they are feeding on sea worms they may ignore a succulent squid or a chunk of cut herring. If shrimp are spinning down on the tide, making their annual journey to the open sea, game fishes often will ignore any other bait to feast on the free-swimming legions. Great tuna regularly gobble mackerel, or herring, or squid—to the exclusion of all else. It is the educated angler's task to divine which of many offerings is currently desired, and to present that tidbit in a natural way.

The fare varies with each game fish, and very often there is a great choice. It is all very well to know that certain gladiators are almost omnivorous, devouring a marine smorgasbord that ranges from mollusks through free-swimming crustaceans to a whole host of vertebrates, but virtuosity is only attained by the fisherman who can decide which bait is currently favored. The masters do this with eyebrow-raising frequency, yet no black magic is involved.

All things under the sun enjoy seasons of abundance, including bait. If mackerel are swarming along any particular seaboard, then odds favor their destruction by larger game fish. A spring run of alewives usually means success for anglers who use branch herring as bait. Any massive influx of forage, such as squid, sand eels, menhaden, true eels, mullet, anchovies, flying fish or balao (ballyhoo), will trigger a massive onslaught upon that particular delicacy. A clever bait fisherman first hunts *bait*, and then zeroes in on the main chance.

There are regional favorites, important because they are resident, plentiful, and highly palatable to game fish in the immediate vicinity. A West Coast surf-perch addict chops so-called pile worms out of barnacled rock piles, or digs ghost shrimp out of the mud and sand. Shrimp are universal favorites, ranging from the tiny grass shrimp of northern seas to the big prawns of the tropics. Sea worms often get the nod in the North Atlantic, and plebeian clam flesh can be highly effective. Chunked or cut baits—again local favorites—often ensure success, and a whole army of crabs used whole, or cut into pieces, hoax bottom feeders.

Such bait can be used alive, fresh-dead, or cut into bite-sized chunks. There are hooking techniques that ensure success with each, and angling methods that are quite as important. Perhaps the first hurdle, and the most vital, is an educated guess that pinpoints a most desired bait at any specific time. Familiarity with the fish sought, its habits and habitat, together with a knowledge of bait and the conditions created by seasons and sea conditions, must be fed into a mental computer to arrive at a correct solution. Every great saltwater angler is an unabashed opportunist, forever ready to switch tactics in order to master nature's whims. In this vast cockpit there is no room for the inflexible zealot who cannot adapt.

Off southern California, yellowtail usually dote on anchovies, but frequently they become selective and desire small squid. The angler who is stubborn may stick with anchovies, but his successful colleague will see the light immediately and bait with a squid. When fish are selective it is idiocy to tempt them with goodies they cannot stomach.

Similarly, North Atlantic striped bass may lose their minds over anything from sea worms to squid or herring, yet they often go into ecstasies over other forage. The striper is a perfect example, since he is extremely selective, often feeding on one bait to the exclusion of all others and then—perhaps within the course of a single tide—switching to something else. The clues are always there.

In the Chesapeake Bay, when soft-shelled crabs are paddling their way down the tide, they may be the deadliest of all baits for rockfish (southern for striped bass). Up North, from New Jersey throughout New England, there are occasions when hard line storms strew the beaches with skimmer clams. A hot sun then kills the bivalves; they open, and the next tide wafts a great grist of clam flesh out to sea, thus setting up a natural chum slick. For another tide or two, stripers may be suckers for clam-baited hooks and they will ignore other natural baits or artificial lures. Whatever the game fish, any natural concentration or massive kill of a forage species is likely to trigger a feeding spree that will be advantageous to the observant angler. This, of course, is hardly enough.

Beginners seldom evaluate end tackle, so they pin a tempter improperly, often on a hook that is ill chosen and with a sinker that is inadequate. Luck is no lady, and success only crowns the brows of those who have learned a trade. A proper combination of hook, leader, sinker, and bottom rig is essential. You'd better plan each operation.

Offshore bottom fishing in deep water is far removed from baiting in the shallows. There, an enthusiast will have to drop his hook anywhere from 100 to 300 or more feet into a current-swept abyss. Depending on the strength of currents, sinkers may range from 6 to 16 or more ounces, so lines must be fairly stout. Monofilament works well in most cases. Wire is better, because it offers less resistance to the bellying tides, but wire doesn't spool rapidly enough to get down fast, and that is necessary. A skilled angler can use metal, but the beginner is always flummoxed.

Light tackle can be frustrating in this arena because the bait, literally, may never get down to payoff territory. Lacking sufficient end-tackle weight, a tempter may be buoyed up by currents and actually stream far downtide and well above bottom. You can stream line all day and never feel that solid bump that indicates touchdown. Better think in terms of 40- to 60-pound-test mono at the least, plus lots of weight. Even with this, or with heavier tackle, a big cod, grouper, or sea bass will feel like an engine block with a wiggle!

If you take dead aim at cod, haddock, halibut, or Pacific rockfish away down in the depths, an old-fashioned deep-sea drail is a good sinker type to employ. Dipseys are nearly as efficient, and the dipsey is more readily available so it is most often used. Sliding sinkers are rarely employed on the offshore grounds, nor do they seem very necessary; the bottom tribes are not very sensitive or wary—they disregard dragging weights, gulp a bait, and then move away with all the ponderous power of cruising submarines.

End tackle, for this work, usually consists of a two-hooked rig with a sinker attached a couple of feet ahead. You'll want it right on, or just above, the bottom so there are no floats or fish-finders. The ideal is a reasonably tight connection from rod tip to sinker and bait, so that a bite is immediately apparent as the rod is regularly raised and lowered. A rather stout rod, comparable to IGFA's 30-pound trolling stick, is favored, and the reel should always be a revolving-spool model in the 4/0- to 6/0- size bracket. Baits, usually, will be provided by the party boat involved, although some anglers insist upon toting their own favorites. Generally, that provided by the skipper will be adequate, although far from exotic.

Pacific Coast bottom bouncers often favor gangions, a whole string of baited hooks above an anchoring sinker. This rig is deadly on rockfish of various species, and it is not unusual to collect four or five at a time. Some decry this as sport, but it is mighty effective meat-fishing. On the Atlantic Coast, thousands of mackerel fishermen swear by a string of diamond jigs or plastic worms that, industriously worked, will harvest a half-dozen macs at a time.

There are occasions in party-boat angling where more than one species is expected, and the two swim at different levels. Then a hi-lo rig is featured, with one hook right on the bottom and another attached to a loop knot several feet higher up on the leader. Sportsmen who seek cod and pollock often use this combination to good advantage over rubbled ground or in the vicinity of a wreck. Cod browse right on the bottom, so a low-lying hook succeeds. Pollock, cruising at higher levels, find the dropper tidbit attractive. Hi-lo rigs are effective in the shallows too. Scup (porgies) and weakfish often frequent the same grounds; the former will be taken on the bottom hook, while weakies attack that which is higher. There are many variations, often with three hooks fastened to dropper loops, and as many as six when smelt are sought. Note that hook size and pattern is always tailored to the species in attendance.

Fish-finders seem most important in surf casting, and they are used on every sea-board in the world; tropical Americans aren't even cognizant of the fact that a pierced egg sinker is, actually, a form of fish-finder. There are channel bass specialists who feel that such rigs are unnecessary, citing the fact that tidal currents partially defeat the theory of a sliding weight. There is, however, no doubt that a fish-finder aids in the hoaxing of wary game! it is neat, versatile, and easily adapted to a variety of sea

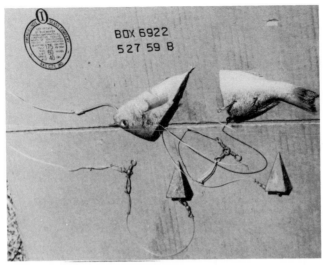

Spot head and tail sections, plus rigs used to catch
big channel bass. *Photo by Claude Rogers*

conditions. The leader may be very short or fairly long or adorned with one or two
hooks. Floats, to keep a bait a couple of feet over a bottom populated by trash fish,
can be added. In some cases, small barrel floats painted in brilliant colors seem to
draw strikes.

An angler's art in "reading the beach" will help him to catch fish. Surfmen who
frequent any shore will have faith in particular hot spots, but the regulars are uncanny
in spotting the edge of a bar, a breakthrough that serves as a marine freeway on a
flooding tide, or a slough where predators gather to dine on bait at certain stages of
flood or ebb. The idea, of course, is to set the table and bring on the entrée.

Each stage of tide—so long as some current is stirring to ensure live water—is
profitable. Rules change with species, but there are universal truisms. First, enough
water! This may seem elementary, yet it is most important. On an outer beach or on a
wide, tropical flat, some stage of the tide invariably promises more success than low
ebb. Bonefish probe the flats as tides flood, and warily move seaward as water levels
drop. Inshore anglers often feel that "two hours before and two hours after" the flood
are most productive. The exception will be an inlet or river mouth where an ebb will
send billions of tiny baitfishes and crustaceans swirling down into the sea. Regardless
of tide, live water is most important. You won't fill fish boxes at dead low or high
slack. Learn the precise time of current changes in areas you plan to fish, noting that
there is often a radical difference between tides and currents. Both are amply documented in U.S. Coast & Geodetic Survey Tide and Current Tables, available at any
good marine chandler's shop at low cost.

Some offshore fishermen believe that tidal changes and currents have little effect on
bottom fishing or baiting in general, and they are in error. Canny skippers always
figure the bait-tumbling commotion ensured by live water, and they also realize that
a change of tidal current can create spectacular change. Often fish that have been
loafing will strike viciously immediately after a change of tide, or launch a hunger
strike immediately after a wild spree. Look, also, for possible switches in weather with

high slack or dead low. At either of these moments the sea pauses, catches its breath, and reverses a process that has taken some 6 hours to develop.

In the surf, or offshore, the man who holds his rod has a far better chance to score than he who trusts a sand spike or a gunwale holder. Often, admittedly, action is so slow that it is prudent to use a holder, so these serve a good purpose. Still, a fisherman who can feel each slight, questing tap, and then either free-spools line or sets the hook at a proper time is most likely to be lucky. A sand spike should be fitted with a long, anchoring spike so that it can't be dislodged. Thousands of fine rod and reel combinations have been lost to powerful surf fishes, often the result of too tight a drag, in addition to an improperly designed and anchored spike.

Sand spikes help, but a surfman who uses bait must
tend his rod.

The use of lights by night fishermen is argued on all coasts. Sharpshooters are convinced that lights are bad news and they will go so far as to turn their backs on the surf while employing a tiny penlight to make some tackle adjustment. On the other hand, a lot of successful bottom bouncers use gasoline or propane lanterns for illumination, and see no harm in doing so. Common logic indicates that lights can be a debit or a credit, depending on how they are used.

A light that is constant never dismays a night-feeding game fish, while one that is erratic may spook them right over the horizon. Therefore, after it has been in position for a while, the gasoline or propane lantern works no ill, and it may even attract bait that, in turn, intrigues predatory game. Fixed lights, such as those at marine slips, always draw bait—and predators. The regular, intermittent sweep of a powerful beam from a coastal lighthouse serves no hardship, for resident fish become accustomed to it. Indeed, there are occasions when such artificial light helps, because it defeats "fire in the water," the angry sparking of dinoflagellates. Brilliant moonlight does the same thing.

Obviously, much depends on the species sought. A great many night-feeders will be frightened out of their skins by flashing lights. Others swarm into the peripheries of any illumination that concentrates bait. Weakfish, southern and northern, are patsies for a good baitman who works a brilliantly lighted dock area and casts his offering into the shadows just beyond the cone of light.

Since it is necessary to arm for a given task, many tackle combinations are practical. Spinning gear can be effective in light-tackle bottom fishing, although it is inferior to revolving spool for heavy work. The use of sinkers ranging over 3 ounces, plus heavy baits, together with the need for a solid connection between rod tip and hook make this so. Spinning is best chosen when the entire rig is light, effective up to about 15-pound test, with sinkers and end tackle calibrated to that weight of line. Lots of enthusiasts go heavier, but they defeat their own ends. I intend no slur on light spinning with bait, because I do a lot of it. The one-handed fixed-spool rig is a joy when sand flounders, blackbacks, or fluke are hooked on bits of clam flesh, sea worms, sand eels, or mummichogs. A light, two-handed spinning stick can pay big dividends where bait and sinker combinations add up to no more than 3 ounces. Beyond that, revolving spool is better.

Among bait-fishing techniques often ignored—and an exception to the belief that a fly rod is one of the worst sticks to use in bait fishing—is loose-leaf spinning with a long wand. The method entails the use of a standard saltwater fly rod and a single-action reel filled with monofilament in the 8- to 10-pound-test class. A single, light hook is bent to the end of the mono, or to a short length of wire where sharp-toothed fishes are probable, and a bait such as a spearing, sea worm, sand eel, or shrimp is attached to the hook. Pierce a baitfish through the nose or the eyes, a shrimp just ahead of the brain in the transparent horn. A worm should be strung so that it will stream on a slow retrieve.

It is quite possible to lob such an offering to a surprising distance if enough mono-filament is spooled off the reel as shooting line. Some sort of a basket may be necessary to hold loose loops of mono that otherwise might be tangled and braided by the wind. Various firms offer patent baskets, or you can make one from a featherweight plastic sink liner, strapping it round your waist.

There is one major threat in loose-leaf spinning, and that is the use of monofilament line on a single-action reel. Nothing else will do, and yet mono is forever treacherous. Unless you are very careful in the matter of pumping and reeling, it is very likely that "memory" will lead to an exploded winch. A cushion of soft braid, as backing, will help. I have exploded two reels in this way, with bluefish the parties of the second part.

Spinning tackle can be most effective in weakfishing—indeed, I feel that no tackle is more effective on this species, north or south. Many years ago southern anglers invented the popping-cork routine, and it is deadly to this day. Originally, the classicists used popping rods, a sort of transition between bait casting and high-surf sticks, together with Service Reels. Today the choice is light to medium spinning gear, and it is a good choice. In action, a float, or cork, is positioned ahead of a single, hooked bait such as a shrimp, a shore minnow, or a strip. The splashing of the cork attracts weakies and they then take the bait.

Curiously, this method has always been most effective on the southern spotted weakfish or sea trout, and the Gulf redfish. Up in Yankeeland, knowledgeable anglers vary the basic rig to take pollock on spring tides, and it has worked well on school stripers. The variation consists of a hardwood dowel that serves as both casting weight and floating splasher, together with a trailing bucktail lure or spoon to entice strikes. The rig, therefore, becomes a multiple artificial.

Light-tackle baiting also involves floats that do not splash, but which simply keep a morsel at an intermediate level. Nowadays a plastic bubble is most often used, pinched to a monofilament line at the required position. Below, a shrimp, sea worm, or shore minnow is properly impaled on a single or treble hook. Very small trebles are excellent with shrimp, sometimes better hookers than the time-honored singles. They're particularly good on big sea trout.

Shore casters find it profitable to drift baits, particularly where a strong outgoing current, at an inlet, provides motion and buoyancy. There, a streamed tidbit may work very well, effective as it tumbles down in the grip of the flow or, properly hooked at the head, when it is retrieved. The addition of a couple of split shots, depending on current strength, often helps to place such an offering in a strike zone.

Generally, though, drift-fishing a natural bait is best accomplished with the aid of a boat. This is a very deadly technique where flounders or fluke are sought, and it can be quite as effective on weakfish or other bay-feeding species. Motor dead, a boat drifts like a shadow, propelled only by wind and current. There is nothing to frighten the fish, hence they are entranced by a bait that tumbles or swims. In some cases, the addition of spinners can help, since they impart a come-hither flash.

This is particularly true in angling for fluke. These flatfish are far from sedentary; they hug bottom, but will race up to engulf any forage swimming at intermediate levels. The drill consists of a single hook adorned with a minnow, such as a mummichog, or a strip bait cut from the belly of another flounder. Pork rind can be quite as attractive. The come-hither flash is assured by a single or double Colorado spinner, or perhaps a willow-leaf type. Often a dipsey sinker is needed to take the bait down and keep it bumping along just over a clay, mud, or sand bottom.

Practical application consists of drifting across a known ground and streaming lines in the wake. Each pass is made with careful attention to ranges, so that new bottom is progressively covered. A well-designed sinker creates puffs of "smoke" which, together with a flashing spinner, is an attractor. Rig the dipsey some 4 to 6 feet ahead of the trailing hook or hook-spinner combination. Almost always, monofilament line is best for this task, and revolving-spool tackle is far superior to spinning gear.

Live, dead, or cut baits are tremendously important in trolling, a matter to be discussed in another chapter, a game that bridges the gap between true baiting and the manipulation of natural tempters that owe much of their success to visual attraction. There are arguments, pro and con, each worthy of study. Sometimes it is difficult to draw a line between basic natural bait and a pseudonatural that owes much of its success to seductive action.

Live mackerel, hooked lightly just ahead of the dorsal fin, are great baits for striped bass and bluefish.

Rosa Webb of Shrewsbury, Massachusetts, with her women's all-tackle world record striped bass, a 64½-pounder caught on a live mackerel at North Truro, Cape Cod.

Live-lining is all bait fishing, and it is true art. Practically all the ocean's sport and game fish can be taken in this manner, and in some cases it is the deadliest method on the sea. One might well note that live and wriggling baits presented in the wake of a trolling boat, suspended by kites; the struggling menhaden, mullet, herring, or mackerel streamed by an anchored small-boat fisherman; the sea worm drifted into an aquatic dining hall without sinker or float, all fit the pattern. Live-lining is the presentation of a forage fish, sea worm, crustacean, or other marine tidbit without casting and without the benefit of lure-inhibiting weight. Never sell it short, because it is devastatingly successful, effective on everything from the smallest predator or vegetarian in the sea to the largest.

In operation, one strives to make a bait look alive, yet somehow crippled. Game fish always look for the laggards, the wounded or sickly members of a forage school. Nature culls her misfits that way, so we simulate a very natural phenomena. The infinitesimal weight of a hook and the drag of a following line will be enough to cause a given bait to struggle, to flash distress signals, and, in some cases, actually to emit plaintive sounds that encourage attack.

In tropical waters, snook fishermen use pigfish for bait. The little forage species is fin-clipped, so that its progress is handicapped. More important, the pigfish so mutilated emits continual grunts of pain and terror which draw snook in search of an easy meal. Marine biologists have proved that most fishes sound off in one way or another, so who is to say that other live-lined baits do not broadcast their predicament and thus ensure speedy attack by predators?

That live-lining works is indisputable. A giant tuna can be vectored in by a mackerel, a whiting, a herring, a pollock, or some other locally plentiful offering. Huge striped bass are mesmerized by live-lined herring, menhaden, mackerel, and eels, while schoolies dote on squirming sea worms. Cobia relish live baits, as do albacore, yellowtail, and a host of other much-sought-after game fish.

In live-lining—and there are exceptions—a fresh and kicking bait is offered on a very light leader, without any confining sinker or float. We try to simulate nature in the raw, and the more lively the bait, the better. There are two basic hooking arrangements, depending upon the bait, the feeding of the game fish sought, and its power. In any event, the tempter must be so pinned that it will remain alive and struggling over a considerable period of time.

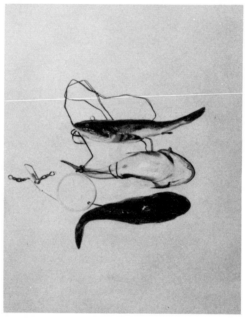

Bullheads, members of the Pacific sculpin family, are rigged as bottom baits.

Hook them lightly. With finfish baits, one popular technique calls for passing a barb through the skin, just ahead of the dorsal fin, never deep enough to pierce the backbone and so kill the offering. Occasionally, where short-strikers make life a misery, there is need for a "stinger," a single or treble hook attached to a short length of mono or wire and pinned ahead of a bait's caudal fin.

A live eel can be hooked through the lips or through the jaws and out the eye socket. (Carry a towel with you, for an eel is just about the slimiest, slipperiest creature in the sea.) Live shrimp are pinned ahead of the dark brain mass in the horn, or through the fleshy tail. Sea worms, if fresh, will survive for a suitable time when strung through the forward portion of the body.

Exceptions, mentioned above, are worth noting. Sometimes a lively bait·is best presented on a short tether. You can do this with an ordinary fish-finder rig and sinker, but the hooking arrangement changes. Instead of pinning the bait behind the dorsal fin, pass the barb through the solid flesh below the gills and ahead of the pectoral fin. That way, it will ride on a reasonably even keel in the current above the bottom. Maybe this is not a true live-lined bait, but it is a close comrade and it works.

Similarly, in big-game fishing, a live bait drifted back in a chum slick usually will be buoyed up by a float of some kind—a bit of cork, a hunk of Styrofoam, or a rubber balloon. Floats are also used in medium-game fishing where a live eel or a forage fish such as a mackerel, herring, or mullet must be kept out of bottom weeds. These are bothers, but sometimes necessary. Cork, or spheres of Styrofoam, with patent clips or simple pins to secure them at a desired spot on the line, are favored. Ideally, a clip or pin should be easily disengaged so that the float will slide down the line as a fish is played back to boat.

Usually, in live-lining, a fish will take a bait on the run, but will not always immediately swallow the offering. You'll feel the frantic effort of the bait as it attempts to avoid the rush of a predator—then a solid bump, which signals a strike. Be calm. Free-spool line with a thumb positioned to prevent overrun. Let the critter move out in an initial rush. Usually he'll halt, at which time he is engaged in turning the bait in his mouth and swallowing it. Strike when he initiates a second run after the pause.

This technique is far from foolproof, and an angler learns to gauge strike time by feel. Occasionally one can actually see a game fish engulf the bait and, if it is obvious that the offering has been well taken, an immediate setback is logical. Use of a treble hook helps on some species and, usually with a treble, you can hit sooner. Each angling area and each species poses problems, and no written word can convey the feeling you must master in order to ensure consistent success. Timing is all important, and timing is an art, taught by hours of trial and error.

With the single exception of big-game fishing, where braided Dacron in the un-limited test bracket is advisable to play a huge gladiator, live-lining is best accomplished with monofilament line and a revolving-spool reel. There is a need to spool line rapidly while a bait is being chased, and to allow further rapid flow after the fish has taken hold and is making its first run. If a rod is in a holder, there should be no tension other than that afforded by a good click ratchet. Those who handhold prefer thumb pressure to avoid backlashing during a sizzling run. It is then a simple matter to throw the clutch into gear and to come up solid. These things can be done with spinning tackle, either by backing off the drag or by handholding and feathering the reel's spool with an index finger as mono slips out. Problems are multiplied with fixed-spool and no real benefits accrue.

Variations in tackle always follow the fish. In the event that algae bloom (goglum) or other free-floating weed handicaps operations, one solution is the fitting of over-sized ring guides on a rod. This permits a lump of goglum to stream through to a point where it can be picked off by hand at the reel. Neat, "rifled" guides are likely to be so solidly packed with "dirt" that no retrieve is possible and you wind up hand-lining or, worse, parting a tight line just when success seems assured. Oversized rings may look strange, but they are very practical on any stick used in the business of live-lining.

Fiddler crabs are wonderful fare for a whole host of gamesters, including the tautog of North Atlantic waters and the sheepshead of the Deep South. Almost always a live fiddler is rigged for action by breaking off the big fiddle claw and passing a hook through the resulting orifice to emerge somewhere in the back. Fiddlers are great tempters for tautog when the season is advanced and trash fish make soft baits impossible. They are superb on sheepshead, although that barred warrior of Dixie is a master thief. To be entirely successful, according to all tidewater philosophers, you have to set the hook "just before a sheepshead bites." That's the usual scoop, but actually there is a tremor that can be felt by a specialist. Don't be frustrated if sheepshead clean you time and again; in due course you'll learn how to anticipate their gentle nibbling.

Local names are forever confusing, hence the importance of Latin. On the Pacific Coast a sheep-head is an entirely different fish, one that any Floridian would consider a member of the parrot family. He's quite a fine a gamester and is taken on a variety of baits. Sand crabs probably rank first in importance, although West Coast sheephead will also grab squid, anchovies, and chunks of abalone and lobster. Never so hard to hook as the eastern species, this gamester attains much larger size and is far better table fare.

Diced crabs are effective on many species, striped bass and channel bass included. Chunks of green crab are very deadly on midseason tautog. Black drum will take a whole hard crab, or will mash a large clam with a single hook concealed in its flesh. Usually the crab, if it is large, will be quartered. The hook is inserted through a leg joint and brought out through the carapace. Soft-shell crabs are another thing—some use a woman's hairnet to keep them from disintegrating, and the hook may be attached with a rubber band.

Sea worms are best presented in a lifelike way, streamed from a single hook, but don't be dazzled by tradition. Sometimes two sea worms, one rigged over the other, are better than one, and sometimes a bunched gob is even better. Where tautog or flounders are the quarry, a short length of worm—just enough to cover the hook—is much better than a whole squirmer. Profligate baiting ensures short strikes and lost flatties.

Crab bait and double bank sinkers accounted for this tautog. *Photo by Jerry Kissell*

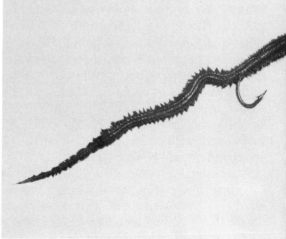

For best results a sea worm or clam worm is best streamed.

Over the years we have been taught that a natural bait should always be fresh, and this is good advice—but not always. Certainly a tempter that streams natural juices down into the currents should be better than one that is tired and literally bled white.

Score one for channel bass fishermen and others who systematically replace spot heads, mullet chunks, or diced crabs that have been scoured by the sea and are no more than tasteless shells. We need the oils and blood and juices that are exuded from the various baits. Often appearance of the offering is quite as important. On the other hand, a lot of sport and game fish are scavengers, hence the obviously dead and sometimes smelly tidbit is worth consideration. Northeastern surf casters have always felt that a rigged eel should be rather "high" in order to tempt striped bass. Catfish are notable carrion feeders, and cod will scoop up anything that is very thoroughly dead. Sometimes, and for no logical reason, spoiled baits fare better than fresh-dead on lively and supposedly fastidious feeders.

I don't know whether anyone has noted this phenomenon in the past, but sea worms that smell to high heaven and are practically turning to liquid occasionally please game fish. Spoiled squid—and if anything smells worse than a decaying squid I don't want to hear about it—can be killers. Some years ago a colleague informed me that he'd had no luck with sea-worm baits until an obliging dog sprinkled them. This "tip of the month" was not printed in *Salt Water Sportsman* because I thought it a little far out. One swallow never makes a spring but maybe I should have recorded the event. It happened.

Outdoor writers are forever delighted by reports of unorthodox baits, such as hot dogs (a perennial favorite), popcorn, doughballs, corn kernels, and green peas right out of the Green Giant's horde. Any meat product will draw an occasional strike, as will chunks of bread or doughballs, the latter favored by specialists who hunt mullet with light tackle. Corn kernels, for some inescapable reason, intrigue a few bottom fish, and green peas are great on such vegetarians as the Pacific opaleye, a species that also delights in chomping on small wads of green seaweed. Cagey mangrove snappers around tropical docks also fall for soft-boiled peas. Catfish, inland, or in the salt chuck, are patsies for smelly garbage, although some of them are more fastidious and will wallop fresh baits or artificial lures.

Nobody has made a strong pitch for cigar butts as fish bait, yet there is always a tale about the monster that rose to a casually tossed stinker. It happens, possibly due to reflex action, just as cod are found with false teeth (human) and assorted items of jewelry in their stomachs. Lots of fish swallow stones and seaweed while ingesting more palatable substances, but this dosen't trigger any massive switch to pebbles or kelp as bait.

Old-timers sometimes declare that a tautog swallows broken clamshells only to keep its vent open. That's nonsense, but a tautog's chute usually is bloody, thanks to the discharge of sharp-edged shells. Give them another million years of evolution and they'll find a way to avoid this discomfort.

Generally, the exotic offerings are important only as news items.

Bait fishing hooks depend on the fish sought. It is an exercise in frustration to use anything but a well-forged Sobey, Martu, or similar type on big game. Single, well-sharpened O'Shaughnessy bends in the 6/0- to 8/0-size range fare well with middleweights. I happen to be a staunch advocate of modern clawed hooks, such as the Eagle Claw and Sealy, for bait fishing. This bend is ideally suited to the task—with one exception. I hold it superior in long- and short-shanked versions to anything else, and my only reservation is the employment of a claw hook in a bait that is bulky. In this case, the sharply kirbed, turned-in point too often buries itself in the tempter and thus prevents a solid hookup. Use claws with soft baits, and stick with straight O'Shaughnessy, Sobey, Martu, or Siwash bends where the offering is big and hard. Most of the

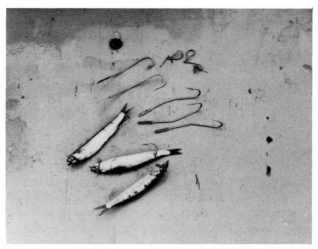

Small bait and long-shanked hooks used in trolling
for Pacific salmon.

other bends are nit-picking in the sea. I will be scored for this observation, but I worship at the shrine of efficiency, not tradition.

Increasingly, bait fishermen use trebles. They are most efficient when employed with live bait worked well above weed or bottom. There is a strong case for the miniature three-pronged barb, say a No. 6 arming a live, drifted shrimp, and a somewhat stouter gang—perhaps 1/0 or 2/0 on healthy mackerel, herring, or menhaden live-lined into a known hot spot. With such a hook, an immediate setback is more likely to be successful than that with a single because, if the bait is within the mouth of the game fish, one of those three prongs is likely to contact solid flesh. Small singles tend to straighten when they are driven into hard jaws, but the tiny treble that is secured well within the mouth or back in the gullet holds tenaciously.

Hook sizes are, of course, dictated by the bait as well as the fish sought. It is rather ridiculous to impale a grass shrimp on a 4/0 O'Shaughnessy. These little kickers, when used in a chum slick, should be threaded on something very small, say a true No. 2 or No. 4 barb—or a 1/0 at maximum. The shank and barb should be covered by using three or four of the little, transparent shrimp. Ghost shrimp, in Pacific waters, should also be strung on hooks small enough to present them naturally.

The angler faces a problem when he uses the flesh of clams, mussels, or abalones. Often these baits are dead-aimed at rather large bottom fish, so a reasonably large hook is desired. Fortunately, most of the big bottom dwellers are less than fastidious, so camouflage is not too important. Clams, mussels, or abalone should be well bunched, draped over the point. Where a whole clam is used, in fishing for such species as the black drum, the shell of the bivalve should be cracked and the hook inserted so that it can bite immediately after a pickup.

Chumming is practiced all over the world ocean and it often means the difference between success and failure. In Great Britain, chum is called "rubby-dubby," a much more expressive term than ours. Wherever the stuff is ladled overboard, much pithier terms have been used to describe its aroma. A soup of ground menhaden, clams, herring, or a combination of deceased sea creatures must be smelled to be appreciated. The fragrance lingers in the minds of landlubbers, especially those whose stomachs are affected by the motion of the sea.

Of course, chum need not be a gruel of soupy blood and guts. You will, depending upon the game fish sought, use such relatively inoffensive tibits as canned cat food, cheap sardines, whole kernel corn, fresh clams, mussels, or crabs—the last three bashed with a hammer so that their juices will flow. On America's Pacific Coast, live anchovies, mackerel, and squid are scattered astern to coax schools of yellowtail, albacore, or other predatory game fish. While this live-bait chumming is rarely done on the Atlantic seaboard, an eastern sportsman works the same dodge with tiny grass shrimp.

Chum, or "rubby-dubby," simply baits a ground and sets up a tasty, olfactory slick that intrigues game fish downtide of an anchored or drifting boat. The object is to provide just enough to tantalize, but not to glut, following gamesters, so that when their feeding colors are blazing they will find hooked baits ready and waiting. It works with everything from the smallest windowpane flounder on up to the royalty of bluefin tuna, and the only major handicap is a tendency to vector in trash fishes on the same grounds.

The come-on is tossed overboard or may be lowered in a chum pot that discharges its contents upon the jerk of a confining line. A very simple chum pot is an ordinary paper bag with a stone in its bottom and a proper freight of whatever tempter is deemed useful. This sack is lowered to the bottom, after which a sharp jerk on the line tears the water-softened bottom of the bag, thus releasing the goodies. Some like mesh bags or onion sacks, which allow tidbits and oily residues to seep out.

Be very sure that the free meal is not overdone, else the quarry may load up and depart without sampling a baited hook. Ideally, chum should be a taster—an apéritif—with the main course to follow. For the same reason that a before-dinner cocktail is far removed from the entrée, it is often wise to use a bait that differs from the come-on. Chunked butterfish is very likely to score when streamed in a soup of ground menhaden, and sea worms may draw strikes while grass shrimp are dribbling down the tide. Chum is window-dressing, a scent in the water, a promise, together with a small amount of actual food. Any bait then looms up as a reward. Indeed, scratching a muddy bottom with an oar, a push pole, or by the purposeful dragging of an anchor can help, because sea creatures are thereby dislodged and the smoke of suspended mud actually intrigues a host of bottom-feeding fishes.

Often a given bait, such as grass shrimp, can be augmented by cat food, or even by ordinary rolled oats. Where the shrimp are alive, some should be released unhurt and others pinched so that they will sink slowly. In Bermuda, much success attends chumming with a mixture of sand and hog-mouthed fry, a little baitfish. Sand contains some flavor of the mixed-in bait as it sinks, and wonderful scrappers rise right out of the abyss to enjoy a feast that isn't really there.

While the chum used by bluefishermen is a mixture of menhaden or some other oily forage species, and the bait invariably consists of cut butterfish or other chunked fish flesh, whole fish baits are favored by folk who seek the giants. A mackerel, herring, whiting, pollock, or some other locally plentiful variety is used to tempt the big sharks, giant tuna, and other heavyweights. Lots of giant tuna fishermen haunt the offshore traps or dragging grounds and look for action with horse mackerel when trappers or draggers make a haul. This is chumming on a grand scale and it has been successful in many areas, including famed Wedgeport, Nova Scotia. Ever since the Soviet Union began fishing off our Atlantic Coast, a percentage of canny skippers have been out there using the trash disposal as chum, and catching some big bluefins. It is worth noting that the Russians usually applaud such effort and that there is friendly fraternization between the foreign commercials and American sportsmen. Cold wars seldom are waged by fishermen.

The same general technique applies in the Gulf of Mexico, where shrimpers over prime grounds sort trash from a more valuable cargo. A considerable number of Gulf anglers look for shrimpers first, and then concentrate on the game fish these commercial operators have vectored in. It is common practice to obtain chum from such a boat, and then to drop baited lines in her wake. Sometimes coin of the realm is exchanged; more often a six-pack of cold hop-juice ensures never-ending friendship between sport and commercial.

Chumming methods seem to depend on tradition. Possibly the West Coast method, in which live baitfishes are used, is most practical, but it requires an abundance of forage. Live fishlets are not harvested in carload lots in the Atlantic, nor are party boats equipped with the necessary aerated deck wells to keep them healthy. Very little ground chum is used in the West, so possibly both groups are missing something very worthwhile.

In addition to fish and crustaceans, animal flesh and blood have been utilized, usually to bring sharks to hook. IGFA frowns upon the latter practice, so it should not be used where record applications are considered. While widely practiced, there is much room for experimentation in chumming. This is a magnificent aid to bait fishing, and it can be quite as effective in drawing predacious gamesters into the operational range of those who swear by artificial lures.

Purists, and that is a rather stuffy word, often sneer at those who use bait. Actually, the clever bait fishermen is a master of saltwater angling. He presents a tidbit that fish ordinarily feed upon, and he offers it so subtly that the quarry never suspects any deception until it is hooked and fighting for its life.

Duffers use bait, and duffers also beat the water to a froth with ill-handled artificial lures. Great anglers know how to employ everything from an immaculately dressed fly through plugs, tin squids, Jap feathers, and scientifically cut strips to the real thing, alive and kicking, yet harboring a hook. I hereby lose friends among the purists, but I declare that no man achieves the heights as an angler until he has learned the secrets of fishing with well-presented natural baits.

THE RAILBIRDS ✎ 8

Bridge, Pier, and Jetty Fishing

As far as a man could see in the wan light of a sickle moon, tarpon were churning the surface under Spanish Harbor Bridge eastward of Florida's Big Pine Key. It was midnight and, aside from occasional motor cars and buses that streaked down the Overseas Highway like scrambling jets, we had this bonanza all to ourselves. Charley Whitney, Ed Louys, and I were throwing ⅝-ounce plugs with one-handed spinnning tackle. Only one thing was wrong—we were running out of plugs!

That's an occupational hazard for people who challenge big fish, particularly tarpon, in the shadows cast by a bridge. We'd caught a few "babies" of 10 to 15 pounds, plus a scattering of snook, but there was a spectacular sameness about most of the action: a quick cast from bridge abutment or overhead railing, a few moments while the plug wriggled along, drawn swiftly into the shadow line by the burgeoning current, and then the strike, followed by a heart-clutching explosion of white water and an impossibly big, silvery form making a case for levitation.

A tarpon has a mouth like a cement curbstone, so a majority will throw artificial lures within two or three jumps. Those unlucky enough to get a barb securely fastened in some fissure of their bony mouths have other trumps to play, they simply turn and go rocketing through the bridge span, quickly parting a light line on rough, barnacle-encrusted pilings. You lose a lot of plugs this way, but sport is something out of a blood-and-thunder chiller.

Logically, in order to counter this dash into the pilings, one always ponders the thought of plugging downcurrent, so that a hooked fish will be more likely to race away with the current into unobstructed waters. It doesn't work, simply because many game fish, including tarpon, face into the current and lie right in the uptide shadow line where they wait for marine goodies to come tumbling down with the flow.

Roy Martin of Panama City, Florida, partially solved this problem with a rather bizarre method he invented to thwart the maneuver. Roy simply tosses rod and reel overboard immediately after a strike! First, though, he ties a stout line to the rod's butt, so that it can be retrieved with a snatch hook on the other side of the bridge. I've never been brave enough to try that stunt with a valued hunk of equipment. In addition to wear and tear on tackle from contact with abrasive pilings and rocky bottoms, brine must soak into every reel bearing and gear. Finally, such tactics might be unhealthy on a well-traveled bridge. On Florida's Overseas Highway, one often flattens oneself against the railing and hangs on for life itself as a bus rockets by and creates a coattail-flapping suction.

Of course, Florida discourages all rail fishing on this high-speed artery, and officials in most of our states post similar bans, yet anglers invariably break the rule. No season ever passes without a few tragedies in which the excitement generated by a strike causes the victim to lurch backward, directly into the path of a truck, motor car, or bus making knots.

Bridge pilings offer cover and food for a variety
of game fish.

The obvious solution is a catwalk for fishermen, and thousands of these are installed
by progressive states. Unfortunately, fish being perverse critters, feeding stations then
develop in bridge areas where there is no catwalk. Tidal currents shift channel beds,
so the walkway built over a promising spot this year may loom over a shallow and
unproductive flat a season hence.

In spite of dangers and laws prohibiting anglers from fishing bridge sections, the
hungries get fevered when there is any prospect of success. In metropolitan New York
and Long Island, striped bass addicts go to such lengths as blacking their faces with
charcoal, dressing in funereal garb, and hopping right over the railings to hang like

Karl Osborne lands a good snook from a northern
Florida pier. *Photo by Karl Osborne*

Al Reinfelder of New York coaxes bass from the
shadow line of a metropolitan bridge.

spiders as police cars roll by. I have a sneaking suspicion that Al Reinfelder, one of Garcia's bright young men in lure development, grew his beard to ensure a measure of nighttime camouflage. That brush, combined with a dark woolen stocking cap pulled down over ears and eyebrows, black pants, coat—and a black glass rod—blend into the shadows. The ability to spot an approaching police cruiser is valuable.

Bridges are ideal marine-fishing locations because they provide shade, shelter, pilings upon which succulent sea creatures grow, and funnels for racing tidal currents. It doesn't matter whether the span is ancient, constructed of moldering wooden pilings, or a product of advanced steel and cement architecture, fish will find and use it to good advantage. This being so, anglers also gravitate to bridges, and there are specialists who have learned every secret of this sometimes dangerous, always exacting and productive, business. Enormously adding to the thin ranks of experts, thousands of beginners simply drop well-weighted baits into the shadows cast by a multitude of spans.

In addition to space-age bridges that serve high-speed traffic, there are thousands of little-used back-country structures that provide fine sport and no mortal peril, unless a drunk falls over a railing and is swept away to some watery Valhalla.

Some bridges are bombastically christened "fishing piers," because they no longer serve an original purpose, but have been converted to angling alone. In Florida's Panhandle, old Pensacola Bay Bridge—which now parallels a modern traffic artery—has been preserved for the attention of anglers. There are access ramps, so that you can drive right out on the old road and park. No charge: it's all as free as the warm southern air. Pensacolans call it "the longest fishing pier in the world," and maybe they're right, if you subtly warp the definition of a pier.

Who cares? Bottom fishermen frequent this still solid roadway by the thousands. During the course of each year enthusiasts catch tons of fish, ranging from croakers and sea trout up to more exotic battlers. The only current handicap is the fact that Pensacola's "longest pier" is just a few yards from a new bridge over which traffic flows at considerable speed. Automobile accidents proliferate because it is difficult for a hairy-chested driver to concentrate on the road while he also ogles a curvaceous southern belle hauling a silvery sea trout out of the water to starboard. There have been suggestions that the "pier" be hidden behind a lengthy fence. It's a grand tourist attraction, so fender-bending is likely to continue.

Remote and miniature spans present no such problems. There are thousands of them, often known only to a handful of regulars who visit on the proper tides and strive to keep their hot spots out of the news. Some are worth only a half-dozen probing casts, to see whether fish are there, after which the prospectors move on to try another bridge or, perhaps, a local beach.

Wherever men fish bridges, the drill is similar. Certainly some fishes, usually bottom-grubbers, will be found on the downtide side, but the payoff location is that upcurrent shadow line. In broad daylight, fish will retreat into the dead spots created by current as it swirls around pilings at the edges of channels. At night, they move up to the shadow line and, wherever the water is reasonably clear, you can see them lying there like streamlined logs, or occasionally exploding into action to engulf bait. You fish the uptide sector because, as Willie Sutton said when some innocent asked him why he robbed banks, "That's where the money is!"

Techniques are tied to tackle. Those who cast from a bridge railing, or from an abutment—always a great place, providing you can reach a good lie—assiduously work the shadow line. A tarpon, striped bass, or snook may well dart out to snatch a plug or bucktail jig before it reaches his dark hidey-hole, yet he is most likely to take just as the artificial swings into deep shadow. Tactics therefore require a cast up and across the tidal flow, with lure manipulation from touchdown to that point where a quick retrieve is necessary to prevent fouling a piling. Plugs work well, and bucktail jigs or weighted plastic worm types may be even better. The Alou Bait-Tail, primarily a rubber eel tail attached to a lead-head jig, is deadly. Swimming plugs, darting types, and mirror-sided creations, such as the fine L. & S. Mirrolure, all coax strikes. While deepgoing artificials often work at night, the norm is a bait that travels no more than a foot or so under the ripples. There are, of course, exceptions. Subsurface plugs and jigs are far more attractive in broad daylight, and sometimes it is necessary to really dredge the bottom. This is a ticklish business, because it entails considerable skill in feeling the lure sweep along to the precise point where it must be retrieved or lost to the fangs of pilings.

Flies and popping bugs can be very effective lures, but you will lose a hatful on any night when tarpon are belting shrimp. Big streamer patterns seem most effective. Many years ago, when Stu Apte had just signed out of the Naval Air Force, where he piloted jet fighters, he, Ed Louys, and Bill Curtiss (another then tyro who, like Apte, went on to become a living legend among great flats guides) enriched flytiers by losing dozens of feathered offerings to Florida Keys tarpon on night tides. At that time few anglers used flies from bridge railings. Few essay the task to this day, because it is quite as hard on gear as it is thrilling.

Some tarpon, obviously bereft of good sense, will rush out into the uptide goldfish bowl to fight. In this case, the angler has a better chance to succeed, unless hooks pull out. A majority of silver kings make a spectacular jump or two, and then arrow back under the bridge, if they have not already thrown the lure back at your head. Almost no spinning or plugging tackle will hold the big ones. Charley Whitney and I once toted New England high-surf gear to the Florida Keys, determined to muscle those chrome-plated bruisers out of cover with 45-pound-test braided lines and big plugs fitted with 5/0 treble hooks. We lost a lot of plugs.

Snook also tend to double back and seek any jungle, whether natural or constructed of steel and cement. The southern lineside doesn't have the overpowering weight of a respectable tarpon, so an average specimen can be beaten with tackle in the 10- to 15-pound-test class. No finesse on most bridges—just a pulling match, with certain disaster for the fish or fisherman who yields. Any snook, regardless of size, is a bundle of energy with a short fuse.

Big striped bass may dart back into the meat-grinding pilings, but a surprising number of them steam uptide, where they can be wearied and then led to the nearest abutment for gaffing or release. Sea trout haven't the power to take a lot of line, but their mouths are soft, so you run into the problem of torn-out or keyholed hooks. Bluefish are gentlemen; usually they race uptide, thrash all over the ocean, beat the sea to a froth just before you gaff or beach them, and then endeavor to bite your hand off.

There are other ways to succeed. Bridge trolling is an ancient and honorable art wherever the span is not cursed with high velocity motor vehicles and is situated a mere few feet over the water. Specialists use fairly heavy tackle, rods in the 9- to 10-foot-length range, usually revolving spool. Swimming plugs, bucktail jigs, and a variety of local baits are favored. When currents are not too strong, night or day, these gladiators stroll back and forth along the railings, dragging lures on relatively short lines. The southern sportsman seeks snook, sea trout, and redfish. Ladyfish, jacks, snappers, and a host of other species manage to make life interesting, and the bridge troller—often intent on table fish rather than kicks—loses a lot of lures and does a lot of cussing when tarpon muscle into the act. Bridge trolling has never become very popular in the North Atlantic or in the Far West, but it could be effective in either place.

And then, of course, mention must be made of zealots who seek snook with poles and very short lengths of heavy cod line or wire bent to sizable hooks upon which are impaled large, live shrimp or pigfish. This is a deadly method on night-roving snook and it is spectacular, if questionably sporting. The pole is a powerful length of natural bamboo cane, 14 to 20 feet long, and there is no reel, the line being wound around the tip, just as inland youngsters rigged for perch and bullheads in an age long gone.

No quarter is asked, and none given. When a snook strikes, maximum pressure is applied by the rodsman, even to levering his aptly named "pole" over a bridge railing. There is a tremendous explosion of white water down below, and that snook goes *nowhere* unless he manages to tear free of the big barb. As quickly as possible, a bridge grapnel is attached to the cod line or wire via a split ring and is sent plummeting down in the darkness to, hopefully, impale the thrashing prize. Among other hot spots, the bridge over the Saint Lucie inlet at Stuart, Florida, is a famous location for this operation. On many a humid night I have consorted with the regulars who cluster there, exulting over big snook, or cursing the gaff-topsail catfish that sometimes take baits.

Perhaps this method has no place in any account of sport fishing, but it is done by people who are enthralled by the process—and it is effective. A close parallel is West Coast poke-poling, in which similar gear is used to present gobs of bait to hefty rockfish in kelp-filled tidal pools. Pacific anglers come up with a surprising variety, including lingcod of eye-popping dimensions. They look like prehistoric monsters and their flesh may be purple or green, yet the lingcod cooks into a white-flaked delight. Someday, if only to complete my education, I plan to try both methods.

All sorts of baits are used from bridges and all of them ensure success. In most cases tackle is heavy, with revolving spool taking precedence over spinning among the pros. Boat rods in the 20- to 30-pound-test bracket see much service, although experts often prefer a longer rod in order to steer fish away from the pilings. Lines usually test 30 to 40 pounds, or much heavier where such mammoths as king-sized groupers and jewfish are targets. Heavy sinkers are necessary, with pyramids favored in sand, mud, or clay, and the rounded dipsey over rocks or coral.

Light spinning tackle is employed, but it suffers because many catches must be winched right over the railings. Bridge gaffs or umbrella nets help to collect trophies. These may be lowered on free lines, or attached to the angler's fast line, so that they can be guided to the right spot with a minimum of effort. Usually the grapnel is so attached, while the flying net, or umbrella, is used as an unattached tool. Ordinary long-handled nets or gaffs are preferred where an abutment or a low bridge permits their use.

A lot of fine sport fish can be taken from the downtide side of a bridge. Flounders, white perch, smelt, groupers, snappers, and sheepshead are among the obliging species, and there are many more. Striped bass sometimes cavort in the current as they feed on small bait, although the positioned striper will always be on the shadow line. A winter-flounder specialist almost invariably employs a spreader rig baited with sea worms or clam flesh, a centrally mounted sinker, and small, long-shanked hooks. Red or fluorescent orange beads, plus garishly painted red, yellow, or orange sinkers, often help to draw strikes from flatties. The rig is periodically moved to stir enticing puffs of mud or sand.

A light-tackle angler who is not handicapped by colleagues using much heavier gear may score and enjoy more sport, but he will never collect the poundage of fillets racked up by his heavy-tackle companions. There are light spreaders, and there is no law against a simple, single-hooked bottom rig with just enough weight to keep it on the deck where it belongs. With light tackle, the problem may be compounded by the strength of tidal currents funneling through a bridge.

This, if the question ever arises, is one of the major differences between inland angling and saltwater sport. A rodsman who is familiar with fish in quiet hinterland ponds often underestimates the power of tidal currents, and further scorns the superior strength of marine game fish. Any sea-run gamester will pull about twice as hard as its inland counterpart.

Boats and bridges are compatible, either in trolling, live-lining, casting, or bottom fishing. It is always profitable to anchor just above a productive span and to cast or live-line baits into a promising shadow line. In the event of a solid strike, the anchor rode should be dropped on a buoy, so that the boat can follow a rampaging fish right through the dangerous pilings and into the downtide area beyond.

Bridge trolling from a boat demands much expertise on the part of skipper or helmsman, for he must know precisely how to crab into the current in order to present lures within inches of jagged pilings, and he must be prepared to gun the engine and get out into deep water immediately after a bait or lure is taken, or, conversely, to steam through the span to follow a green and angry gladiator.

Almost annually, I make a pilgrimage to Virginia Beach in late November or early December to sample the great striped bass fishing that occurs along the Chesapeake Bay Bridge. Trolling usually pays dividends, with everything from sizable bucktail jigs and plastic eels to subsurface swimming plugs the best attractors. Captain John Pierce, with whom I have fished on several occasions, is a master on the flying bridge. He cruises those pilings on the bias, ensuring that lures swim close enough to insult the barnacles and weed growth festooning cement supports, but just a foot or so this side of fouling. Each solid strike triggers two immediate responses: the angler exerts all possible pressure to yank his quarry out of dangerous territory, and the skipper guns his craft into open water. There are big fish here, and I never fail to lose plugs to critters that won't be snubbed up.

Bridges are ideally suited to live-lining for any game fish that delights in chomping on a free-swimming tidbit streamed from a boat anchored or using power to hold it in a tidal current. You can pursue this art in a craft of any size, from cartop skiffs to offshore cruisers, always providing that sea conditions are favorable. It's often necessary, if anchored, to employ an easy cast-off anchor rope with a buoy to prevent its loss.

It's far easier to hook a tarpon on live bait than on an artificial lure, yet there's little difference in the struggle that follows. Indeed, since a baited silver king often has more depth of water in which to work, he may expend less energy in jumping and more in powerful, driving runs. June Jordan of Marathon, Florida, used a fresh and lively mullet to tempt her women's all-tackle world record, a 203-pound bundle of chrome-plated scales and fury back in 1961. She was fishing from her husband's boat at Seven Mile Bridge, and Bob Jordan had to cast off quickly in order to follow the trophy through a dangerous span. It took precisely 100 minutes to conquer this monster, and June's victory was a testimonial to the effectiveness of live bait.

The encrusted marine growth and the shadows
under bridges keep game fish in residence.

Vlad Evanoff collects a striped bass from a Rhode
Island rock pile. *Photo by Vlad Evanoff*

Of course, any bridge is a platform for a shore-based angler. So is a dock or fishing pier. The former is seldom intended as a fisherman's roost, but conditions often thwart intentions. Fishing piers, on the other hand, are designed for that purpose alone and they can be very profitable spots to wet a line and teach a bait how to swim.

Lots of docks and boat basins are frequented by regulars, particularly during the quiet night hours when cruisers are tied up and stationary lights draw bait that, in turn, attracts game fish. There may be no better spot to rack up a bragging haul of northern or southern weakfish, bluefish, or striped bass. In the Gulf of Mexico, legions of anglers repair to coastal docks immediately after sunset to enjoy fast action with sea trout and redfish. In Massachusetts, I have enjoyed great sport with blues while loose-leaf spinning from the decks of draggers and other commercial craft tied up in boat basins. We were trespassing, but we wrought no harm and we caught choppers all night long until our arms ached and the dawn's light was almost painful in its intensity.

Commercial docks are prime territory in all harbors, and they will continue to please until such time as too many anglers invade the hallowed grounds. Multitudes always seem to include a few spoilers who cannot exist without committing acts of vandalism. When this happens, commercial skippers rightly demand police protection, plus gates and fences to defeat trespassers.

During daylight hours a commercial dock invariably sees too much traffic for good sport fishing, Nonetheless, such areas are kind to youngsters and beginners of all ages who want nothing more than the occasional snapper blue, harbor pollock, jack crevalle, or flounder. The true hungries arrive long after dark to seek out big blues, stripers, weakfish, white sea bass on the Pacific Coast, and a whole host of other questing, sociable game fishes.

Commercial sport-fishing piers are quite another thing. They cater to the rank-and-file angler, together with a fine leavening of advanced operators, charging each a minimal fee for the right to dangle a line from a platform that extends a considerable distance over the sea. Almost always the better piers include a tackle shop and a bait-dealer's emporium where the most effective of local tempters, alive or iced, are available at fair prices. Fish-cleaning benches, with running water, are there—and snack bars cater to patrons. All the premier operators are keen students of the sea, and a telephone call to any one of them will elicit information about weather, tides, wind direction, the most abundant species, and the bait or tackle that is currently succeeding. Only a few ill-advised pier operators embrace the chamber-of-commerce approach that holds that "fish are always biting." Of course, it doesn't take long for serious anglers to learn which operators are reputable.

Seasons, weather conditions, and optimum tidal phases are just as important in pier fishing as elsewhere, hence it is wise to make inquiry prior to any visit. All sport and game species observe certain times of scarcity and abundance, and all are affected by wind, water temperature, and tide. There is no rule of thumb that fits all cases, because seasons overlap and a fair wind in one quarter will be foul in another. The same applies to tidal phases; on some piers a flood may be most profitable, while another will see more activity during an ebb. Moreover, fish delight in upsetting all logic; sometimes they feed at times considered highly unusual. Larry Green of San Francisco —a fine angler and outdoor writer— claims that rainbow perch bite like snakes during a steady downpour. Often, where a species is "in season," any weather front or change in barometric pressure seems to influence sport. Some fish feed avidly just before, and just after, a major storm.

Live or iced baits used from piers will naturally depend on local forage and the desires of attendant game fishes. Almost always, bait shops will offer regional favorites, which may be any of several sea worms and pile worms, mullet, sardines, anchovies, squid, shrimp, or crabs. Shrimp rank first in southern waters of the Atlantic Coast and they are tremendously important. As you travel northward on this seaboard the sea worm assumes greater importance, with clam flesh second in demand. Live and dead minnows are employed everywhere, as are cut baits and strips.

On the Pacific seaboard, ghost shrimp are extolled as great baits for a whole host of inshore game fish. Unfortunately, these are not always available from commercial outlets, so the angler has to dig his own or, better, suck them out of the sand and mud with a "slurp gun," a hand-operated suction pump. There's always a fairly wide range of choice in the matter of bait, yet it is worth remembering that fish caught from a pier can be just as selective as their cousins finning over a remote slough or offshore rip. Here, as elsewhere, a master angler studies his quarry and the forage it covets— then presents the right tempter in the right location. It's easy to say, and not so easy to implement. That's why advanced anglers come up with most of the trophies on any platform.

On a pier, as elsewhere, you'll want a tackle box crammed with everything necessary to take advantage of prevailing conditions. A selection of hooks in different styles and sizes is imperative. Swivels, leader material, sinkers, floats, and fish-finders are equally important. If artificial lures are to be used, stock an ample supply. One enterprising Pacific Coast specialist converted an ordinary supermarket grocery cart into a highly efficient "pier buggy." He had rod holders welded into strategic locations, and then altered the carrier so that it boasted racks for a tackle box, a live-bait well, and an icebox, plus an extended seat that eased his tired carcass when things were slow. This enterprising lad even rigged a beach umbrella to ward off hot sunlight, and he probably relished construction of the buggy as much as the catching of fish.

It is unfortunately fashionable to dismiss the pier fisherman as a beginner, and indeed most of those who seek the long, T-headed platforms are tyros. Nonetheless, it is immediately apparent that a small percentage of the throngs on any given pier will take 90 percent of the fish decked. So we have specialists here, as elsewhere. On any structure you will find tackle ranging from ultralight on up to big-game rigs designed to conquer huge sharks. There is a surprising degree of specialization and, although some practitioners operate without conscious planning, many take dead aim at a species they know to be present. The disciplines are just as important here as they are in any other angling field.

Initially, a pier is nothing but a platform extending into the ocean. It affords shelter and shade to certain sport and game fish; its supports concentrate bait that, in turn, vector in a variety of game fish. A pier is quite as subject to tides and currents as any natural headland or bottom and, depending on depth off the midsection or T-head, the surrounding water will boast an equal share of resident or migrating fish.

Unless you specialize, the most practical pier-fishing tackle would have to be a medium popping or light surf-casting rod with reel and line to match, together with a selection of hooks calibrated to the species in attendance, plus sinkers best designed to hold bottom in that particular area. Floats, either cork, Styrofoam, or the plastic-bubble types, are well chosen when a bait must be suspended at intermediate levels. The long rod, say something measuring 9 feet overall, helps to keep bait away from the pilings and also helps to keep a determined fish from getting in there and cutting the line.

Conventional revolving spools are best for all-around work, and lines must be fairly heavy because—in most cases—it will be necessary to winch a fish out of the water and up over a railing. Occasionally, with a monster, you will have to play the fish shoreward and, if possible, get off the pier to land it on an adjacent beach. Most of the better commercial sport-fishing piers have bridge grapnels and nets available, or you may prefer to tote your own.

Some pier operators discourage casting, because of the danger involved. Others specify casting areas, such as the T-head, where those who want to flip lures seaward are accommodated. Common sense dictates tactics, for casting can be dangerous on a crowded platform, yet entirely within the bounds of reason on days when the structure is lightly used. Ultralight tackle is similarly discouraged in a crowd, for a self-appointed sportsman can disrupt the even tenor of his colleagues' operations. Go very light only when angling with birds of a feather, or as a lone wolf. There is no place for the spider-web outfit on a crowded pier or a party boat.

The disciplines remain. Game fish will face into a tidal flow and they will seek the shade of any structure. While roving predators may arrive from any point of the compass, chasing bait, residents are likely to hold in specific lies close to the pilings, heading into the current. Therefore, the most successful angler is likely to be one who presents a bait close to cover and is then prepared to curb the first, furious rushes of a fish that is determined to dart into the barnacle-studded pilings.

Fish-finder and hi-lo rigs do well on a pier, but there is a definite place for the float with a suspended live bait such as a shrimp, sea worm, or shore minnow. In some areas of the Atlantic Coast, from Virginia southward, good catches of king mackerel are made this way. Live-lining is practiced too, but this is reserved for days when a structure is far from crowded with patrons.

Casting metal lures or plugs can be productive on everything from small bluefish and Spanish mackerel on up to huge channel bass, migrating striped bass, and cobia. Almost always this is done from the T-head, where flingers will not interfere with bait bouncers along inshore rails. Along the Gulf of Mexico, from southwest Florida north and west, springtime surf casters enjoy a Roman holiday with big cobia migrating close to shore. Regulars often stand right on the rails in order to gain a height advantage in spotting cruisers with the aid of polarized glasses. In this case, heavy surf rods are used and the rain of heavy, lead-head jigs is spectacular when a pod of cobia is sighted.

Spinning with midget lures is quite as effective on a pier, but only when the sport does not handicap colleagues. Light tackle always raises the problem of landing a fish that weighs as much, or more, than the line test used. You can't winch the thing skyward. Bridge gaffs or flying nets are not always available for run-of-the-mill trophies, and it can be quite a chore to "walk" a struggling minor gamester all the way back to the beach.

Commercial sport-fishing piers are well built and periodically inspected for safety, yet there are ancient and rotting structures here and there—dangerous, but appealing to anglers. Generally these man-traps are posted with no-trespassing signs, yet they see lots of use by adventurers. Most of them ultimately go up in flames, fired by some careless sport who drops a lighted cigarette butt between cracks in the creosote-soaked planking, or are leveled by winter storms. Certainly the tumbling piles of a condemned pier offer cover for game fish. Such wrecks are best combed by casters or trollers operating from small boats. They can be great fishing locations, but no fish is worth a gamble in which accident or death is the reverse of success.

Anglers who frequent jetties also live dangerously, but at least the barnacled rocks under their feet are securely anchored. The peril, in this case, is occasioned by treacherous seas or a forgotten turn of tide. It is too easy to postpone a return to higher ground when fish are taking bait, so there are annual reports of jetty jockeys who have had to remain on far-out rock piles through an entire flood and ebb, or who have been swept off their aeries by slamming ground swells.

Jetties are productive locations, hence they will be fished. Specialists seldom suffer harm because they arm for the task and keep a close watch on tidal rise and fall. Ordinary boot-foot waders or hip boots are never sufficient for this work, because the rocks are slippery with accumulated slime and seaweed. Ice creepers or steel hobnails are required. Studded sandals are available to strap over boots, and some of the hungries wear golfing shoes with metal spikes in each heel and sole. One of the latest tricks is to have tungsten-metal studs, ordinarily used in snow tires, punched into new rubber boot-foot wader. There are kits for the do-it-yourselfer, but anglers in the frigid zones can always find a helpful garage owner or tire merchant who will install studs at low cost, or perhaps gratis if you're a regular customer. Felts, favored by lots of inland trout and salmon fishermen, will not do; you need bite in the big, roaring salt chuck.

Any rock jetty is a natural haven for bait, and therefore a target for game fish—and fishermen. Large and small crabs, spiny crayfish, and lobsters scuttle in and out of current-lashed interstices in the rock. Barnacles attach themselves to the granite, and seaweed lodges there. The habitat is favorable to everything from the tiniest of plankton and minute animal life to game fishes that prey on the shrimp, crabs, minnows, and mussels that devour the midgets. Clean, unobstructed bottoms are biological deserts; marine life burgeons in rock piles and weeds.

This being so, all rock jetties are popular sport-fishing locations; they harbor a resident population of game fish, plus migrants during a proper season. There is ample opportunity for employment of every basic casting and bottom-fishing technique, so long as the angler observes a measure of caution. Those who disregard danger signals often wind up on the obituary pages, rather than in the sports section with well-deserved trophies.

If there are rules of thumb, they might be stated thus: prepare for jetty fishing by wearing foul-weather gear and footwear that will bite through slime and weed; always know the local tidal phases and never overstay a visit to any distant outcropping; keep an eye peeled for unusual changes in the weather that may handicap a journey back to dry land, and use tackle designed for the task at hand. It is a rather good idea, in addition, to institute the buddy system in this dangerous work.

Some jetties are large, flat-topped, and relatively safe. These become natural fishing platforms for bottom bouncers who seek the deep feeders. Other harbor barriers are slim and jagged, with sections that can never be negotiated dry-shod. These, of course, are the man-killers, and they also yield grand catches of fish. Techniques, albeit altered by hordes of beginners who catch a fair share of common gamesters, while spooking the prized customers, are similar on all rock piles.

Hot corners are located close to the rocks, not away out in the glimmering, surrounding sea. Bottom feeders will be close in, nibbling away at crabs, worms, and darting shrimp. Small bait will also be close to the rubble, chasing plankton and minute sea creatures, or simply hiding from their enemies. Larger gamesters will herd smaller forage species and will establish lies in pockets where the recurring ground swells surge over deep holes. These are the spots to drop a bait or lure.

A squidder who works such water with skill and imagination will cover the length of the rock pile, starting at the beach and progressing seaward. While strikes are most likely right up against the riprap, game fish may be finning anywhere within casting range. Short heaves usually suffice; indeed, the typical northern jetty rod is a cut-down surf stick that is best suited to snap-casting and handling powerful battlers that slam baits a few yards off the tiptop. This, admitedly, is a specialized tool, but so are other weapons chosen by experts.

Having catfooted out to a vantage point, the angler must be prepared to land any game fish he is skillful enough to hook. Where the quarry is too heavy to be bodily winched out of the suds, a long-handled gaff is a necessity. Paint it white, and add a couple of fluorescent red or orange strips for visibility in the blue light of dawn or dusk. Tote a suitable priest and belt-attached stringer. There's no room for fancy footwork when rocks are sharp and slippery with weed, when waves are regularly slamming over them, threatening to dump you into the very cold and current-swept ocean. Any tumble can be bad news; a fall that does not result in treading water invariably leaves a scrabbling fisherman with lacerations inflicted by sharp-edged coral or barnacles.

Although lights are often viewed with alarm by night fishermen, you'll want one out on a wave-lashed jetty. A lot of rock-hoppers swear by the miner's head lamp, and it is a fine choice—usually worn draped around the neck rather than pinned on a hard (or soft) hat. A light under the chin is more easily trained on rod and reel, or aimed in whatever direction the beam is needed. Ordinary flashlights are prone to tumble out of a pocket and get lost, or they are shorted out by spray. Penlights with clips to attach them to an inner shirt pocket, are great to remove hooks from the jaws of fish—or backlashes from reel spools—and they are small enough to be held between the angler's teeth while he uses both hands in some nighttime chicanery. However, penlights are often too feeble to guide a tired surfman's way back to the beach. A jagged and broken rock pile can be dangerous terrain, especially at night. Never underestimate the peril involved in the careless negotiation of a lonely jetty.

Expertise? A case might be made for the superior skill of a clever jetty fisherman. The best of them seem half mountain goat and half student of the sea. They know precisely what they're doing, or they don't last very long.

But expertise is never simply a marriage of agility and education. The supposedly easy sport on any bridge, dock, commercial fishing pier, or other platform above the water always calls for a full measure of skill. That's why a small minority of anglers seem to be lucky.

Come on, now! They're not lucky. They know their business.

THE HIGH SURF ↲9

Classic Surf-Casting Techniques

Now *there* is a chapter heading that must be defined! The high surf is a wide-open sea rim where the ocean gets a long running start before it assaults the shore; it is not a tranquil bay or cove frequented by shore casters who lack the imagination and the plain, old-fashioned guts to challenge our last frontier. One must be suitably impressed by the elemental fury of a great ocean beach, the irresistible power of surging ground swells and the towering combers that smash home with a recurrent roar that is strange to the ears of summer people sleeping in their cottages a mile back of the dunes. There are men who feel that nobody ever attains virtuosity in saltwater angling without learning to fish the high surf.

There is something almost mystic about it, regardless of the fish sought, a sense of puny mankind pitted against a raging ocean, the ever-recurring tides and the winds. Somehow, fishing an open ocean beach, you stand on a border between civilization and a misty, savage no-man's-land that has never knuckled under. Adventure is there, coupled with the lure of joyous success and the spice of danger.

Once, years ago, my brother Dick and I came down to a North Atlantic beach in the deep night. The combers were piling ashore, booming like heavy artillery as they hit the dunes, the brine then rattling and hissing in undertow. Under dim starlight I waded into the swirling suds and sent a plug arrowing out into the void. A moment later the whole off-black horizon was blotted out by a tremendous wave, and the next thing I knew I was hurled 40 feet up on the beach, scrabbling for my life against the clutching backwash.

Wet, bedraggled, and with a hopelessly sand-packed reel, I went to find Dick. The same wave had toppled him, and we spent an uncomfortable hour cleaning tackle and yarning about what might have happened. Alone, in the dark and with no help, we might well have perished had the wave and the undertow caught us just right, No year ever passes without surfmen listed among those lost at sea. But we were young then, and reasonably tough, having just returned from a war. We shrugged it off. We cleaned our gear and went back into the suds. Before dawn we had a fine catch of striped bass to prove our mastery over the venomous surf.

Again, fishing with rod and line commercial Arnold Laine, a great practitioner who disregarded all elemental fury, I fished through a vicious electrical storm at night and, wonder of wonders, saw a 30-pound striped bass hit a plug and cartwheel on the surface during a brilliant flash of lightning. I wouldn't try it again, and shouldn't have at the time, but it was a novel experience.

There was another shrieking day when, during the eye of a hurricane, that astonishing hiatus between tornadic winds, I caught a striper, and very quickly got the hell out of there as the wind veered around to scream out of another quarter.

These experiences are typical of surf fishing, a game in which fury is not only taken for granted, but is vicariously enjoyed and sometimes put to good account. One must be a shameless opportunist, a slave to the running tides, forever searching for the evidence of an imminent blitz. One must prospect at all hours of the day and night, at dawn, at dusk, in broiling sunshine and driving rain, under the moon and when only stars chink a dark zenith.

Surf casting really owes its tradition to four great travelers of the inshore suds: striped bass, channel bass, bluefish, and weakfish. Of this quartet, the striper and red drum definitely rank first and second, with no order implied. Each is a power in its own right and each boasts a legion of champions. These are the fish that spurred the development of surf-casting tackle, and they remain the major prizes of happy beach-combers with long rods.

Every newcomer wants to know which is the best fish and, in this case, there is no ready answer because the two are totally unalike. Striped bass are active at all levels; they will take a bait presented on the bottom, or loop up to smash a surface plug. The striper is very aggressive, prone to much furious cartwheeling on the surface after a strike and given to swift, powerful runs. *Roccus saxatilis* is traditionally unpredictable, hence triumph becomes sweeter for the angler who has grown stubbly of beard and red of eye waiting out the long tides.

It is generally assumed that the channel bass always feeds on or close to the bottom, and this is a libel on the great red drum. He is usually caught on bait, yet there are times when he is a sucker for a metal squid or even a subsurface plug. Sometimes a trophy channel bass will take a surface offering, but this is the exception to prove a rule. The species is cursed with an inferior mouth, ideally engineered to scoop goodies off the bottom, or to take bait at intermediate levels.

Curiously, smaller channel bass, those called puppy drum or simply redfish, can be lured to a wide variety of surface swimmers, chuggers, and poppers. They aren't very spooky and you can practically hit them on the head with a lure when they're rooting on a shell bar. The big ones, pretty much confined to a section of the Atlantic Coast from the Virginia Capes down through North Carolina's Outer Banks, usually feed at mid-depths or right on the bottom. In spring and fall, I should add, casters often find them cruising very close to the surface, usually schooled-up and visible as a moving patch of red-orange color. When this happens, an accurate man with a big tin squid, such as the Hopkins Lure, may score smashing strikes.

Those who favor striped bass hate to admit it, but the channel bass is a far more formidable foe on a tight line. Once hooked and running, a big red seldom grandstands with surface acrobatics and swift runs, but he exhibits a lot of brute power. He goes away from there majestically and with increasing speed. Never very fast off the mark, he seems to gain strength with every yard of line streamed, and his stamina is far greater than that of the striped gladiator.

Any striped bass, even a trophy specimen, wages a swift, dogged battle, but he'll be tired when an angler's relentless pump-and-reel technique brings him close to the beach. Invariably, after one or two passes, he can be planed ashore on a ground swell. The bronzed Rebel of the southland is rarely so accommodating. He also runs hard and grudges every inch of line retrieved. At the end of it he resists the usual plane-ashore on a wave. Always a big red drum finds some last reservoir of strength to get his head down, curl his massive tail around a wave, and make a last ditch stand. Channel bass are not as spectacular as stripers, but they exhibit far greater bull strength and stamina.

One of the world's great surf trophies, a 60-pound channel bass. The angler is Claude Rogers, a Virginian famed for his skill in this discipline.
Photo by Claude Rogers

Charley Whitney of Provincetown lugs a 36-pound North Carolina channel bass back to his Jeep.

Both striped bass and channel bass are frequenters of the inshore surf and suds. Neither seems to mind suspended sand in the water, a thing that will turn away bluefish, but not weakies. The heavenly twins of the roaring breakers are powerful enough to slice through the advancing combers and to live in an environment that is all powerful motion and gritty particles of sand. Only occasionally will you see one caught by a racing ground swell to be hurled up on the shingle.

Blues prefer cleaner pastures; they are most likely to raid inshore grounds when the water is clear and a drop-off close. The chopper will head for offshore depths when inshore suds are roiled. Weakfish of all four subspecies seem undismayed by murky surf; they forage in sloughs and channels in calm or storm, and they can be taken on light tackle with either baits or lures.

While it all began with stripers and channel bass, today's surfman takes a wide variety of sport and game fish, and his tackle progresses from the impossibly light to the outrageously heavy. A man can coax delicious little sand fluke on an ultralight freshwater spinning rod, or stalk hulking sharks with a big-game combination (in which case the bait is either floated seaward under a balloon or occasionally transported via a radio-controlled model boat). A little guy named Herb Goodman, down in Florida, has perfected this technique, and many of the monsters he lands weigh four or five times as much as he does.

While fly rods sometimes prove valuable in a mild surf, big sticks traditionally conquer the suds. The squidding combination, although it is endlessly varied to improve the odds on specialized fishes, is a heaver and not a fighting instrument. Therefore, the surfman who seeks dinner-plate-sized pompano or surf perch may find it necessary to employ a "telephone pole," albeit with a limber tip. He has to reach 'em, or all bets are off.

Spinning tackle has become popular in the surf. Al Reinfelder, Lou Palma, and Nim Marsh work a Long Island beach.

There are two reasons why a surf rod is lengthy, say 9 feet at minimum, probably averaging 10½, and progressing to 12 and 14 feet. First, the big stick is a powerful tosser; second, its long tip keeps the running line high enough to defeat towering combers. These requirements apply, whether the reel is conventional revolving spool or coffee-grinder. Spinning, it should be noted, is favored by a great majority of modern surfers, although a select group of specialists keep revolving spool alive and may even be laying the foundations for a massive renaissance. Either combination can be effective and each boasts wide spheres of efficiency. Advanced anglers simply use that which is tailored to a specific task.

To any beginner, the pounding surf is an exercise in frustration. There is an endless sea, topped by the white horses of creaming breakers. Occasional sentinel rocks, draped in streaming kelp, seem to rise out of the depths to reveal their crowns and be lost to sight as a new ground swell surges shoreward. The very vastness of the open ocean is awe-inspiring, until such time as you learn to read its secrets. The clues are there.

All erudite surfmen learn to "read the beach," and they do this phlegmatically, almost as a matter of course. While prime hours of study are those of low tide, when bottom conformation and reefs or bars are easiest to spot, a practiced eye will always detect hints that reveal the banquet tables of cruising gamesters.

Easiest of all is to seek a height during a low course tide and to scan the surf line with binoculars. Note each bar and slough, each mussel bed or grass patch. See how outer bars are pierced by channels that lead into the sloughs or holes within casting range of the beach. When tides are building and the brine pours through these openings, surf fish will use them as highways to inshore banquet tables. Grass patches and mussel beds are excellent feeding ground. The turbulent water around a rocky outcrop is very likely to intrigue game fish, seeking lesser forage species, as the tidal currents build. Any point of land is worth investigation, for such fingers of sand, shale, or coral outcrop will create rips as the tide swirls in rising or falling. There will be a definite drop-off, a place where bait will be tumbled and game fish will congregate to collect an easy meal. Polarized glasses often help to spot these highways and dining rooms of the shallows.

Generally speaking, surf fish prefer to feed in live water, which means a tidal current either rising or falling. Dead low slack and static flood offer least promise, because there is no motion to keep the sea creatures tumbling and swimming for their lives. Even in areas where there is little rise and fall of tide, this situation obtains; hunters are most alert and active when currents deliver a constant supply of befuddled bait.

Usually, surfmen like a building flood—"two hours before and two hours after the top of the tide." Good reasoning triggers this observation, but it can be erroneous. For example, fine sport often rewards the angler who fishes the mouth of an inlet or coastal creek during all of the ebb. In this case, the falling waters disgorge great hosts of baitfish and crustaceans sucked up into the creek at flood. At ebb they come spinning down, caught in swift tidal currents, and predators accordingly line up, just outside the mouth of an inlet, to feast.

Similarly, where hulking battlers like the tarpon, big snook, and wide-shouldered channel bass find a season admirably suited to moving into inland waters, the mouth of a river or creek can be a very profitable spot to fish. In tropical seas, big jacks also move into river mouths during each spring season. One must study the quarry in order to be completely successful.

Surf casters often find it necessary to wade well out
where the ground swells are treacherous.

Surf casters are alerted by gulls feeding on small
bait driven to the surface by game fish.

There are subtle clues, often discernible only to surfmen who are students of the sea. An offshore bar, even at half tide, will be marked by a winking line of white caps. If there is a break—a stretch of agitated, yet far from rough, water—then that is a channel or opening, and it will be the highroad of game fish moving in from offshore depths. More than likely there will be a slough or hole between the offshore bar and the beach itself. As currents change and tides build, fish will be there.

Sometimes, and striped bass immediately come to mind, the edges of any offshore bar are prime producers. Because there is turbulence and a corresponding tumbling of bait, stripers line up at the edge of a bar. They may be outside the line of breakers, or just inside, so it is the business of the caster to drop lure or bait in a proper spot. Often this business of "fishing the bar" is most productive at half tide, rising, before predators have enough covering water to move inside and approach the suds and sloughs. Long casts may be necessary.

There are so many clues! A smart surfman always watches the action of such sea birds as gulls and terns. Both serve as the light cavalry of the beachcomber. A herring gull may laze on the dunes, head into the wind and to all intents completely somnolent, but let one stick of bait twinkle on the offshore waters, or one game fish batter the surface, and that gull will be off to prospect the chance of a free meal. Any concentration of gulls wheeling, dipping, and obviously excited, indicates the presence of action below. (It may be the garbage dumped by a passing cruiser, but more likely it is Murder Incorporated—with game fish belting the loving hell out of bait.)

Often gulls are spotted placidly floating on the surface. They may have been driven out there by beach traffic, but they may also be waiting for a feeding spree to resume. Bob Robbins, a Taunton, Massachusetts, squidding addict, makes a good point when he says that "goosey gulls" are worth watching. The bird that simply floats at rest is a poor barometer; the one that swims a bit, cranes its head to peer into the depths, and acts, as Bob says, "goosey," anticipates rewards.

Terns are quite as valuable in the fish-finding department. These graceful fliers trade back and forth, searching for small bait. If predators drive forage to the surface, there will be an immediate concentration. It is an angler's prerogative to drive a lure right into the midst of any frantic, whirling gaggle of birds. Odds are better than even that a game fish will be waiting.

Even where a single-questing tern, sweeping over the water in graceful flight, suddenly checks its swift course to turn and circle, one may rightly assume that the bird has seen something very interesting. Perhaps a big fish is there, well under the surface, but cruising in search of something to fill its insatiable belly. The right lure, properly presented, is likely to be engulfed. Birds, whether they are gulls, terns wheeling like fighter planes, or pelicans going in like suicidal dive bombers, are superb spotters. Be a bird watcher in the surf; it always pays off.

There are less obvious clues, and some of them cannot be mastered by any other than advanced students. A surf caster, quietly plodding through the dunes, keeps his eye peeled for bait thrown up on the shingle. A few kicking sand eels, squid, spearing or blueback herring means that something out there has forced the bait ashore. Baitfish and gasping squid do not commit suicide by racing ashore—unless there is great danger out in the suds. Whenever windrows of goodies dot the beach, look for action just beyond the first wave.

Moreover, once an ear is attuned, you can hear this mayhem of natural attrition on a night when the stars are dim. To a practiced ear, the thresh of driven bait becomes audible over the boom of breakers and the tinkling rush of sand and gravel as a wave rushes back down the shingle. The popping sound of game fish feeding on the surface, and sometimes the slap of broad tails, is distinctive. You can even smell the quarry at times.

Beginners find it difficult, but like those who essay ice skating, suddenly they achieve the impossible. Often I have advised a pilgrim that I have smelled fish, and seen the "you damned liar look," only to wallop striped bass or blues moments later.

I don't know the origins of these aromas but, fresh out of water and still vibrantly alive, each fish has a fragrance of its own, a distinctive scent that disappears as the creature dies. Thereafter—and very rapidly—the perfume degenerates into that well-known attar of dead fish. This is a thing worth pondering because nature has a reason for everything, no matter how obscure.

Not all game fish, alive or dead, appeal to the human olfactory; in some cases an odor is pleasant, and in others it is repugnant. A just-landed barracuda smells like a well-ripened garbage dump. Croakers and, to a lesser extent, channel bass, boast a strong and distinctive scent, somewhat chemical and variously regarded as disagreeable or borderline at best. Striped bass smell like thyme, and bluefish exude a clean odor of cut melons. Smelt are deliciously aromatic. All fresh-caught fishes waft scent into the air around them and, whatever the impact upon humankind, that scent is never the stereotyped blend of seafood in a market's tray.

Scientists, all over the world, agree that finfish use the sense of smell to locate food. Sharks are cited as practical examples, because they will vector in on a trace of blood and locate its source over a considerable distance. Laboratory tests have proved that some species confined in tanks can be stimulated by injecting small amounts of water—in which preferred baits have been harbored—into the aquarium. The scent is there and captive predators respond by active searching and the development of feeding colors. Chumming undoubtedly owes its effectiveness to this principle.

Evolution always favors physical attributes that help a given species to compete, to capture its prey or, conversely, to escape from larger predators. It seems logical to assume that the aroma a living fish exudes is a purposeful thing, designed either to establish territorial rights and kinship, to attract, to repel, to seek out forage, or to afford a measure of olfactory camouflage.

The great difficulty we must overcome, as human beings, is Disneyism—that wonderful nonsense called anthropomorphism in which all lesser creatures think, act, and respond to the higher emotions of Homo sapiens. Gentle souls cannot understand that, in the wilderness or the sea, death is a way of life. The well-balanced biological eco-system is one in which a food chain is complete, from the tiniest of bacteria and plankton on up to the grandest of living animals. When a gray whale dies its body returns to the basic elements and, in so doing, feeds uncounted billions of bacteria, plankton, small fishes, crustaceans, sharks, and—very often when washed ashore—carnivorous animals and scavenging birds. Many of these diners are tolled in by scent.

It is too easy to forget that the whale has its own body odor when alive and healthy. Nantucket's old sea hunters scented their quarry from afar. Similarly, on a much smaller scale, sport fishermen smell bluefish and striped bass before any surface action discloses the beast. This is very good news for an advanced angler, but not so fortunate for fish. Why do they exude scent?

A Caroling wren is not wooing his mate; he is telling other wrens, sparrows, and what-have-you to stay out of his territory. Owls hoot to startle prey species so that they will disclose their positions, and hawks scream for the same reason. There are courtship melodies, of course, and some of them serve a dual purpose. The "singing" woodcock both attracts a mate and defends a territory against other males of his species.

What has all this to do with fish? Simply that human beings often misunderstand or misinterpret the reasons for natural phenomena—such as scent. *We* decide what smells nice—and what stinks! Wild creatures and fish may not agree. That's obvious when scavengers delight in the aroma of something long dead. To them, the supposedly repulsive stench is incredibly lovely.

That which repels one recipient is likely to attract another. There are aromas guaranteed to whet the taste buds, and others to turn them off. There is the smell of danger and, an exact opposite, the olfactory sense of well-being and comfort. Obviously, scent is important and it affects a surprising number of emotions and functions, almost certainly more in the world of so-called lesser creatures than in man's. The wild thing's nose is far superior to ours; even though domesticated, a bloodhound can track an individual man. Perhaps fish are correspondingly superior.

What about fish? They all possess that nasty old BO, and each species is individually anointed. The big question is—why? Lesser posers are involved with how it works. We know that scent is there and yet, strangely, no scientist appears to have plunged into the subject. I hereby urge some bright young postgraduate to earn his doctorate by probing the various perfumes of sea dwellers. Certainly these aromas are functional, and one day they'll be fully explained.

For openers, and I admit to being a better poker player than marine biologist, let's lead with a hypothesis.

A healthy, living fish exudes a characteristic scent that establishes it as one of its own kind, therefore a member of a school, not to be harried, eaten, or driven into outer darkness. Scent serves the ends of communication and contributes to a sense of well-being.

Marine biologists have proved that sea-ranging salmon use the twin senses of taste and smell to scent out a natal river. Is it not quite as logical to assume that predators may literally "follow the scent track of bait" with their noses?

A fish uses scent to repel its enemies, having—through millions of evolutionary years—developed a "perfume" that resembles some danger signal or, possibly, a similarity to the aroma of a poisonous or otherwise inedible species.

A given predatory fish uses scent as an attractor, not only sexually, but possibly an aroma that resembles that of the bait he seeks, or even the tidbits that lesser forage species covet.

Fishes that reside in a particular niche of the marine environment, such as coral outcrops or seaweed, develop the scent of their surroundings so that they cannot so easily be ferreted out by wolves of the deep.

Are there sudden changes? If man, the highest form of animal, involuntarily creates new scents with emotions ranging from passion to abject fear, might not a fish do the same? A domestic dog, nose sampling air currents, always knows when a human being is afraid. Men in combat comment on the smell of fear.

Might not a fish be as physically unable to control the emission of scent? Perhaps the sweet wave of thyme, when stripers are feeding, is involuntary. Bluefish do not always cloy the air with an extract of cut melons.

There is much to think about and more to discover. I only know that certain forces are working and that the smell of fish (alive and healthy) has yet to be adequately researched. Any student who tees off on this quest, and succeeds, will please clip a small portion off his triumphant sheepskin and send it to me as a finder's fee!

Among other clues to fish, there is the slick. This may also account for scent, but I have seen it where there was no aroma downwind. Some species, notably the striped bass and the bluefish, often are revealed by sudden slicks that blossom and arise like dots of tranquilizing oil on an otherwise choppy surface. If you are a regular, you will look for these and you will very assiduously cast to them. Again, whether this is the result of excretion, or the oils released by chomped bait, is arguable. They are there, and they are important. Cast to them, and be prepared for an immediate strike.

Less subtle evidence of fish is the sudden spraying of bait. Small stuff may twinkle on the surface or come out in sudden rushes, like an inverse charge of bird shot. Squid jet out like miniature rockets. Shrimp kick and dart. If there are swirls of heroic proportions, or if you can see the flash of game fish creaming in the wake of bait, then this is a dead giveaway. A surf caster must take advantage of any favorable circumstance.

There is a traditional picture—a man in hip boots and foul weather gear, belly deep in a furious clash of combers, armed with a very long rod and casting a block-tin squid halfway to Spain. That's good fish, and quite accurate as a symbol, but the passing years have added certain refinements. For one thing, you will find few honest block-tin squids on today's market and, moreover, the purist has now become a plugger. Most of today's regulars favor chest-high waders over hip boots, and the long cast to Spain now may be a shot at Hawaii, since anglers of all big-surf coasts now enjoy the roughest of all sport-fishing operations.

Each species dictates a specialized approach, yet there are rules of thumb that remain important. Those who can plan no more than a week or two of vacation time should always ascertain peak seasons for the fish they seek. It is a bleak thing to travel hundreds or even thousands of miles to find that the coveted quarry is not there. Peak periods are well documented by local guides and charter skippers. *Salt Water Sportsman* magazine features a monthly fish-finder department that details prospects on all American seaboards. Chambers of commerce are poor contacts. Invariably, they declare that angling is superb at all times, and that is nonsense.

In America, bluefish are resident only on the Atlantic Coast and through the Gulf of Mexico to Texas. Although the great chopper is a favorite in South America and the Mediterranean (where it is called shad or elft) and in Australia (where it becomes a tailor), there are none on our Pacific seaboard. Within its range, the blue is a very important surf fish, even though it dislikes sandy water and is best taken from a beach that shelves off very rapidly.

While there is little surf casting around the Mediterranean, North Africans might well astound the world with record choppers. Hal Lyman has seen fish that would weigh better than 30 pounds toted on the backs of Arabs. There are reports, never authenticated, of Mediterranean blues scaling 45 pounds. Such a fish would be a tough customer on a tight line.

On the Atlantic Coast, heaviest blues are taken from Cape Cod southward to North Carolina. Sometimes jumbo specimens rush bait off Sebastian Inlet in Florida, but the chopper of the Deep South and the Gulf of Mexico usually is small. Moreover, this species is plagued by periods of scarcity and abundance. You can hardly call it a cycle, for there is no observable periodicity.

Normally, the northernmost limit of bluefish range is Massachusetts Bay, south of a line drawn diagonally from the city of Boston to the tip of Cape Cod at Provincetown. In 1971 (as in 1850), choppers ranged far northward of this arbitrary line. In 1850, the glut extended to Gloucester; in 1971, late August and early September witnessed vast schools slaughtering bait as far north as Old Orchard, Maine. If history repeats, and it usually does, there will be a sudden and dramatic decline, followed by a slow buildup over a period of a decade or more.

Where bluefish please surf casters, metal squids still top plugs, if not in thrills, then in fish brought to beach. The chopper can be selective, but when actively rushing small bait he is a very easy mark compared to either the striped bass or the red drum. For this reason some beachcombers scorn bluefish, while others note that, pound for pound, a blue has twice the muscle of a striper, a redfish, or, for that matter, any other finned hunk of dynamite in the immediate vicinity.

One day at the tip of Monomoy Island, Massachusetts, Hal Lyman and a cousin, Ted Lyman, brought this home to me. The point rip on Monomoy can be one of the world's greatest bluefishing locations, yet it encompasses a small area. If you can cast a tin squid approximately 100 yards and drop it right into the elbow of a raging rip, you're in business. If, on the other hand, you miss the target by as much as a few yards, the fish will not oblige.

We took turns casting with reasonably light squidding gear, and then I had an idea. Instead of featherweight stuff, I decided to use a really big outfit with 45-pound-test braided line. Loftily proclaiming that I'd snake those things out like sand flounders, I heaved a 4-ounce Johnson Jig into the elbow and, as usual, scored an immediate strike.

Trouble was, even with an outfit that should have moved a hammerhead shark, I couldn't horse that blue! He simply curved his tail around the rip and stayed out there while I dug my heels into the sand, screwed the drag up to alarming tension, and tried to drag him out. The two Lymans crowed with delight and suggested that I'd better go back to striped bass fishing. The blue weighed 9 pounds.

They're tough, and they're destructive. It is always wise to use a short-wire leader ahead of a tinclad or plug, and only an idiot will employ a shiny swivel. Blues will even strike at clots of goglum or weed on a running line and, when they do this, no razor blade cuts a line so neatly. Often, when a blitz is in progress, one chopper will slash at the lure in the mouth of another.

Blues are spectacular on popping plugs, but an angler's success ratio declines with the number of treble hooks offered. IGFA may not agree, but a single barb, well presented, is far more effective than two or three trebles. A plug presents weight that may be tossed around to loosen hooks, and trebles always seem to work, one against another, to ensure a tear-out. The chopper's mouth is reasonably soft, although well armed with razor-sharp teeth. The best lure is a metal squid, such as the stainless-steel Hopkins or Acme Kastmaster armed with a single O'Shaughnessy or Siwash hook. Retrieve rapidly; a blue is fast and you can't take it away from him if he's murder-bent.

Bluefish are creatures of broad daylight, or so some have said. While it is true that they are taken most often while the sun is well up, don't count them out after moonrise. Some of the heaviest choppers annually belt rigged eels and baits prepared for striped bass from sunset to dawn. Very often I have cursed big blues that cut my rigged eels in half or chopped my lines while I was fishing for trophy stripers in the deep night.

Weakfish, fourth and lowest on a coastal totem pole in the surf, are no longer as important as they were some years ago. But, because the weakie is another of those curious critters that wax and wane with some natural wave of scarcity and abundance, they may again trigger a need for specialized light tackle in the surf. Northern weakfish just about disappeared in 1949. By 1970, they were making a determined comeback.

Originally, weakies were taken with light squidding or popping rods. Nowadays a light to medium spinning outfit is far better. A weakfish is so named because its mouth is soft, and there is no better rig on which to take it than the light fixed-spool outfit with a smooth drag.

Bob Hutchinson of Norfolk fishes the surf for
sea trout. *Photo by Bob Hutchinson*

There are four Atlantic and Gulf of Mexico subspecies, including the famous northern weakfish, the southern-spotted weakfish or sea trout, the sand, and the silver. Only the first named is a high-surf prize if we think in terms of big rigs, but the southern-spotted variety certainly intrigues surfmen who, wisely, take it with one-handed spinning rods, bait-casting outfits, and fly rods. The silver and the sand subspecies are small, hardly worth mention as premier surf-running gamesters.

On the Pacific Coast there are corvina, or corbina, depending on your choice of spelling. These are western versions of the weakfish, quite as sporting and usually larger in size. The corvina is a wonderful game fish, eager to take bottom baits or artificial lures of all kinds. It ranges all the way from central California down through the magnificent Baja country to Central and South America.

All the weakfish tribe, including the corvina, are patsies for properly worked tin squids, bucktail jigs, and sinking plugs. All of them can be taken on flies. They are fine battlers, although not in the same league with bluefish and striped bass, and they are a delight on the table if you dress them out quickly, pop them into skillet or broiler, and serve with love.

Perhaps it is nonsense to stress the big four, if only because they are East Coast species, the place where it all began. Nowadays, surfmen work all sea rims, and there are battlers that challenge the traditional nonpareils. In Baja California and Central America, surf casters are sure that roosterfish cannot be topped. A rooster is a tremendous scrapper, a sort of cross between a jack crevalle and a tarpon in fighting ability. Pez Gallo often works the inshore breakers; he hits like a mortar shell and he promptly goes into the air. He has the bulldog stamina of a jack and the acrobatic ability of a tarpon—he is one hell of a great game fish.

There are areas, particularly on the southern Pacific seaboard, where sportsmen enjoy the taking of mammoth sharks and rays. Surf perch are lightweights, yet they provide much entertainment for good folk with long, limber rods. Pompano, in the semitropics, demand the same basic tackle, a heaver that will get a light bait or lure away out there where it really counts. In most cases the big spin-rig will suffice, but note that there is a definite place for revolving spool when lures or bait-sinker combinations are heavy, when hooks are drawn from heavy wire, and when the cast must be dropped at maximum distance from shore.

Granting favorable conditions—and seasons—the list of fish that may be taken in the surf is lengthy. On the North Atlantic seaboard, southward to the Carolinas, but particularly in New England and New York, tautog have always intrigued surfers in spring and fall. This stubborn, buck-toothed member of the wrasse family is best coaxed with fresh bait, such as sea worms, fiddler or green crabs. I count tautog the northern equivalent of grouper in the tropics, because they esteem rock piles and boast bulldog strength instead of flashing action.

Scup (porgies), whiting, pollock, flounders—even true cod during the springtime when they move close to shore—please surf casters. Moreover, there is ample room for all the tackle combinations, from ultralight freshwater gear for sand flounders and common mackerel on up to unlimited big-game rigs for huge sharks.

Lure fishermen are the self-appointed glamour boys on any seacoast, but they are vastly outnumbered by systematic citizens who employ live bait. I prefer lures and I favor the top-water offering, yet I am too old a sparrow to discount the expertise of a good man with a bottom rig. There is much skill here, and little of that nebulous thing called luck. Bottom fishing is an art and it requires specialized end tackle.

Usually, some variation of the fish-finder rig is employed, although there are occasions when a static sinker and leader does as well. Some think that the big channel bass doesn't mind dragging a weight when he munches on a chunked mullet, crab, or Norfolk spot. I disagree, but lots of bull reds are caught with such rigs. Egg sinkers are great in areas where tidal currents are not very strong and a traveling bait is most effective. Edged weights, such as the pyramid sinker, are best used to offer an anchored hors d'oeuvre on sand, mud, or clay, while variations of the dipsey or rounded weight work best on rocky or rubbly bottoms.

Nylon monofilament is the best line for bottom fishing in the surf. It is supreme because it presents less resistance to tidal currents than braid, so drift is partially defeated. The lighter the mono, within reason, the less drift and belly. Therefore, a surfman will use the very finest single-strand mono that will serve his purpose. Color may be vitally important because a bait fisherman has an advantage when he can see his line. The fluorescent blue shades are good, but I think fluorescent yellow is much better. At night, a couple of wraps of fluorescent tape around the tip of a spiked surf rod will help to indicate a strike.

If fishing is fast, as we always hope it will be, then a surf-casting bottom bouncer is wise to handhold his rod. Sometimes the fish nibble and drop a bait. In this case, the manual operation is important: you can drop back, feel the nibbler, and hook him as he makes that lethal mistake. Often a bait caster can cover ground by reeling in a few feet of line, by waiting for a few minutes, and then repeating the maneuver. Each movement of the sinker-anchored bait stirs a puff of sand or mud and places the tempter in a new location. Moreover, successive movement ensures a greater amount of bait-scent drifting down with tidal currents.

Unfortunately, fish are not always spread out enough to make this strategy feasible, so bottom bouncers go to sand spikes. The best are long-pronged, so that they can't be yanked out by a sudden strike. The reel's drag should be set at striking tension, but not snugged up so thoroughly that a determined gamester can take rod and reel into the deep six. Poorly anchored sand spikes lose lots of expensive tackle.

Gasoline or propane lanterns are favored by nighttime bait fishermen. They're good, so long as they are kept burning in one place. Flashing lights will spook certain game fish, and they should be avoided. Surf casters seeking striped bass along dark shores are so certain of this that they will mutter threats against any colleague who so much as flashes a penlight when fish are in the suds. Any constant light, such as that flashed by a coastal beacon, is accepted by fish, and even helps matters by drawing small bait to the surface and by defeating "fire" in the water. (The billions of tiny dino-flagellates that emit light on being disturbed, and can thus outline a lure so that it glows like a red-hot poker.)

The bait itself is arguable, often a matter of local availability and the desires of the fish sought. No one tempter is all purpose, even with a specific battler. Striped bass are omnivorous, yet they will sometimes feed on sea worms to the exclusion of all else. Within the course of a single tide, big linesiders will switch to squid, herring, mackerel, or spearing. Sometimes, after a strong northeaster has churned the water and thrown thousands of skimmer clams on the beach, they'll settle for nothing other than clam flesh. One must make an immediate evalution.

Good bottom fishermen are quite as observant on all coasts. If hulking channel bass want crabs or mullet chunks or slices of Norfolk spot, the regulars will soon find out. In most cases, the fisherman's grapevine provides clues, and the owners of bait shops will stock up on current goodies. There are few secrets, for the news media are sharp.

In tropical seas, the surf-casting uniform is simple: wear tennis shoes to defeat sharp coral outcroppings and the spines of sea urchins. Wear long pants for wading—not for warmth, but to ward off the stinging tentacles of man-o'-war jellies. Depending on your tolerance of hot sunlight, a loose, long-sleeved shirt may be a necessity, as will a wide-brimmed hat. Dark sunglasses—polarized, if you intend to see fish before you cast to them, or to spot holes, channels, and mussel beds—are indispensable.

Wherever northern seas are cold—and they can be downright arctic even in mid-summer—an angler is wise to choose waders and a foul-weather top. The boot-foot wader is great on a sand beach, but ice creepers or hobnails should be added for work on slippery rock jetties. Felts rarely excel on the seacoast; you'll want "bite," and felt soles don't have it. Spiked sandals are available, and these can be strapped to boot-foot waders.

You'll want a priest, or club, suspended from an elastic cord around your neck or clipped to a web belt, and a gaff if much wading is involved. Gaffs are troublesome because there is no adequate way to shield points. I have tried everything from sponge rubber balls to hunks of cork, and nothing really works. In a raging sea the damned

Light surf-caster's kit includes a shoulder bag to
carry lures, pliers, a folding gaff, a sheath knife,
and a billy club.

hook protectors always work loose and, the first thing you know, you're speared.
Several practical folding gaffs have been invented and produced, but demand has
never been sufficient to keep them on the market.

The gaff used on a rock jetty should feature a long handle, say 4 feet at the least,
and in order to locate it immediately in the dark, better paint the handle white. I
usually add a couple of strips of blaze orange fluorescent tape, which will catch and
intensify any smidgen of blue light.

There is really no need for a gaff on a sand beach. There, a fish will be planed
ashore on a ground swell and may be quieted with a single tap of an adequate priest.
Striped bass and channel bass stiffen out after one solid whack, but blues—like
sharks—are extremely tenacious of life. You can belt the bejabbers out of them and
they'll still thrash, champ their jaws, and be dangerous. Never let your fingers get

too close to the mouth of a live bluefish. Of course, it is wise to be very careful with any large and active gamester that has a treble-hooked plug attached to its face. Hooks pierce human flesh too.

I've had a lot of near-misses. One night Jack Townsend of Shrewsbury, Massachusetts, and I were fishing from a small boat in the surf off Provincetown. Unaccountably—because they rarely hit surface plugs—Jack hooked a sand shark and, disdaining the gaff, swung this mean little critter aboard. I happened to be tied into a very respectable striped bass at the time and was alerted to the situation only when the shark (and plug) swung up against my backside. One of the treble hooks went through my pants but, luckily, missed tender flesh. Believe me, it is a traumatic experience to have a flapping shark and a big, treble-hooked plug fastened to your bottom in a pitching small boat on a dark night! Jack finally pried both shark and plug free, while I broke all bump-and-grind records trying to escape the barbs. I lost my striper into the bargain!

There is mortal danger in the high surf when an angler dares too much in wading or in goat-footing out to the end of a slippery rock jetty. The big sneak wave must always be reckoned with, and an angler burdened down with waders, foul-weather gear, and web belt is hardly equipped to swim against a foul tide.

Waders will not automatically pull you down, as often surmised; indeed, some air will be trapped within, while the pressure of water will force the rubber or plastic tight around one's legs and thighs. Those who do not panic may actually tread water and paddle ashore little the worse for wear. There is a delightful story about the late Reverend Kenneth Gesner, a grand surfman who fished Nauset Beach, at Orleans on Cape Cod, and who habitually waded to the offshore bars when stripers beckoned. One misty, savage, and wave-lashed morning he did this and was swept off a sand spit.

Dozens of regulars were casting into the murk on that particular day, so the preacher heard plugs and tin squids plopping into the water around him as he methodically paddled toward shore. Finally, his groping feet touched bottom and he stumbled out of the suds right in front of a startled surf caster.

"Nothing out there," he said calmly, and ambled off into the mist.

Reaching the bar always entails some difficulty. That ridge of sand invariably lies just beyond a surfman's best heave, so there is a tendency to wade until the combers provide neutral buoyancy and you bob up and down with every step. An educated regular learns the art of wave-hopping—a quick lift-off to ride with a towering ground swell. Wearing chest-high waders with a foul-weather top properly snugged down with a drawstring at the waist (never a rubberized cord) it is surprising how much water can be challenged successfully. You'll wish that your legs were longer, yet there's always the burning necessity to get that last foot of distance in a cast.

At ebb tide it may even be possible to wade all the way to an offshore bar where the flood will ensure game fish chasing bait. Those who are canny enough to gauge height and current flow always return before things get sticky, but all who fish the high surf can recall occasions when the fish were striking and time seemed of no account. When this happens, the trip back is a nightmare of sorts, a wet business of treading water and finally emerging with waders chock full and teeth chattering.

On a sand beach, strong tidal currents present another problem: if you try to stand still, that flow will whip the sand out from under your feet and you will descend like a manic elevator. The only solution is constant movement, a step forward or back—

meanwhile braced against the raging current and the ground swells that often seem to converge from different directions. No surfman lives who has not been dumped by those quartering waves, whopped flat on his back in a racing wash of icy, sandy water. It's part of the game, and you accept it as an occupational hazard, or cop out and become a fair-weather yachtsman.

Regardless of the quarry, surf casting becomes an obsession; its champions are true adventurers and latter-day aborigines who delight in single-handed combat with the elements and with fish that are tough enough to slice through towering combers. There is magic in it—the deep-throated roar of the sea attacking a sand beach or a rocky headland under brilliant sunlight or twinkling stars, or the exact opposite when the ocean is somnolent, its midnight ground swells pulsing evenly while billions of dinoflagellates spark in the suds. There is a constant sea change, a sense of creation and mystery, of tremendous power and dreamlike hiatus when the ocean seems to rest and draw its breath.

A surfman, more than any other angler, goes in cold—with no highly sophisticated equipment or electronic aids to ensure success. He is man against the immortal sea, as it was in the beginning and as it always shall be.

Surf fishermen are content when they are alone on a sea beach.

LINE ASTERN ~ 10

The Mechanics of Trolling for Saltwater Game Fish

A large and overworked dictionary on my cluttered desk defines trolling in one sentence: "To angle with a hook and line drawn through the water from a moving boat." That's pretty basic, hardly enough information to satisfy a prospective fisherman because so much depends on where, and how, and why. There is science involved here, indeed a happy marriage of many sciences. Only the uninitiated—and possibly Noah Webster's descendants—think that it is sufficient to draw a hook through the water.

Trolling can be a very specialized operation, even inland where options are few and problems are minimized by the limited depths of lakes and the absence of tidal flow. In the big, bounding ocean, we not only battle the elements and the reasonably predictable tides, we must consider fluctuating currents, bottom conformation, depth, weed lines, the seasonable abundance or scarcity of migratory fishes, and the often perplexing movements of bait. Selectivity on the part of fish is involved, so presentation of any given tempter depends on an angler's skill, his sixth sense, or his inclination to experiment.

A saltwater sportsman can troll with a variety of outfits, ranging from ultralight on up to heavy. The ideal is a job-rated combination that ensures success while it offers a maximum of joy in use. Unfortunately, we will always have with us the zealot who goes too light, and the meat-fisherman who thinks that Herculean gear is the ultimate answer. Actually, the stunt man with featherweight tackle may be a greater offender than his commercially oriented brother because he tries to prove an unprovable point. Such a man—or woman—boasts about infrequent kills, but is understandably coy about the many battlers broken off, perhaps to die with rusty hooks stuck in their gills. Who needs light-tackle trolling?

We all do, if we are to score regularly!

This is no contradiction in terms, because light tackle is admirably suited to fishing in sheltered waters. Nothing succeeds so well in a brackish river or coastal estuary where small fish are sought, and there are times when featherweight gear is necessary outside, both for sport and fish in the box at day's end. Light, medium, and heavy are words that must be subtly defined; it is the precise matching of gear to a specific fish and angling method that really anchors a definition.

Hinterlanders always think of marine angling as "deep-sea fishing," a view that draws chuckles from veterans. Ninety percent of all saltwater trolling is confined to sheltered waters or the inner reaches of a continental shelf. Only a few troll the edge of the abyss, and they seek the great pelagic wanderers. For every blue water buff there are a thousand kindred souls who drag that hook within the shadow of sand dunes, or well up in sheltered bays and brackish rivers. Where the quarry is reason-

A fine billfish is winched aboard a small cruiser
off Baja California. *Photo by Bob Whitaker*

Bob Whitaker of Phoenix with an albacore, one of
the Pacific Coast's premier game fish. *Photo by
Bob Whitaker*

ably small in size, heavy tackle is an abomination; it not only cancels out sport, it just does not catch fish. I have always entertained the thought that catching fish is the name of the game.

There are folk who troll with a fly rod, one of the worst sticks imaginable for this business, but still feasible under certain circumstances. A fly rod is designed to cast a fly, period. Because it is limber and often extremely powerful, it can be used for light trolling. Perhaps the user derives some measure of joy from playing and landing a fish on the classic long wand. If that is the object, it is sufficient. Most of us place sport above fish flesh, and a man has the right to handicap himself.

With a fly rod, you will either bastardize the classic combination or accept its obvious limitations. Fly lines are not designed for trolling, and single-action reels are ill-advised when a bait or feathered lure is skipped in the wake of a boat. So you go to monofilament lines, or even metal, to get down into the strike zone. It's all possible, but not very practical. I've had lots of fun with dolphin on trolled flies, but it proved nothing; I could have taken more, and perhaps had more fun, with a very light revolving-spool combination. Fly rods can always be used on light-tackle fish, such as shad, weakies, school stripers, and tailor blues, together with a whole host of tropical species frequenting the flats and offshore weed lines. You can even drag a line and conquer something big and spectacular. My point is that other gear is much better suited to the business of trolling.

Spinning tackle is an improvement, but it still falls far short of revolving spool in this technique. Spinning, like fly casting, was designed for and is most efficient in the employment of light lures tossed to a short-range target. Fixed-spool is versatile, so you can troll with it and you can catch fish. Unfortunately, in so doing, you will be handicapped. Spinning makes best use of monofilament line. Braid is almost impossible with fixed-spool, and it is wise to forget wire. Rods usually are too resilient for deep dredging, for jigging, or even for dragging a lure well back in the wake. Trolling, more than any other technique, is wedded to the conventional revolving-spool outfit, and you'd best resign yourself to this at the outset. No tragedy is involved.

Actually, revolving-spool reels and rods to match can be frighteningly delicate, or brutish; they can be fitted with lines ranging all the way from spider web on up to unlimited for big game. A few incurable romantics in southern California bait striped marlin with 4-pound-test mono, and occasionally one of them succeeds in boating a billfish that any other angler would be proud to take on 50-pound-test braid. This is stunt fishing, of course, but it indicates the versatility of the outfit.

Nothing less than 6-pound test is really feasible in saltwater trolling, and even this is too light for all but the smallest of fish and the most skillful of rod handlers. For sheltered water trolling, 8 or 10 is a better choice, and this only when goldfish-bowl conditions obtain. It is rather silly to challenge the odds when a game fish is likely to dart into weed growth, kelp, or a handy rock pile immediately after it feels the hook. Note that a 5-pound fish is quite capable of parting a 10-pound-test line if it can wrap said line around something unyielding.

Probably, status seekers aside, the average light-tackle troller uses something in the vicinity of 12- to 20-pound-test monofilament. Twelve is often employed by blue-water specialists, and it is quite sufficient when there are no handicaps. It is quite as logical to go light with single-strand wire where conditions warrant, so long as the tackle is matched and the angler knows what he is doing. Water, bottom conformation, the presence or lack of obstructions, and the size of fish in attendance all enter the equation.

In river and estuary fishing, light tackle will fill 90 percent of needs, so it is ridiculous to beef up unless you clash with huge tarpon in the tropics. Even in this case, qualifying clauses are required: if a jungle river is broad enough, and there is no major threat from sunken palm trees, weed, or other debris, you can play a big silver king—and defeat him—on a very light line. The great trick lies in gear that ensures sport while it also measures up to practical needs. The two requirements are inseparable.

The best boat for sheltered water is a small craft propelled by an outboard motor of scant horses. You will want to progress steadily, but without any great speed, and you will come to bless the quiet approach. In shallow water, game fish are far more likely to be spooked by motor noise and wake than they will be in a deep, offshore arena. No outriggers here, and no elaborate electronic aids, although some inland anglers have found good depth recorders worth their weight in nuggets. Basically, sheltered, shallow waters are the happy hunting grounds of light-tackle buffs who make their own luck by combining the arts of boat handling and trolling. The skipper is angler, mate, and crew.

Trolling rods, almost always, are shorter than casting rods. You'll want something in the vicinity of 5½ to 6 feet overall, with a butt section of 12 to 18 inches from cap to reel seat. Long butts are troublesome in boats, and even big-game fanciers seldom go beyond 22 inches. You will want a matched revolving-spool reel filled with line calibrated to the rod's strength. If fish are small to medium in size, as most of them are in such quarters, there will be no need for a fighting chair or belt socket. Rod holders, often portable units that may be attached to a handy gunwale, may be a blessing. Some of us use a screwdriver thrust into an oarlock's orifice, and this works very well, although we lose a lot of screwdrivers in the heat of action. The tool simply braces the midsection of a rod while the stick's butt is socked up against something unyielding, like the back of an amidships seat. The rod must be easy to reach in the event of a strike.

Usually, in sheltered-water operation, no more than two lines will be streamed, one from either side of the craft, spaced only by the boat's beam and the length of each rod tip. If lines of equal length, strength, material, and density are dragged, there will be no tangling on turns. Horrendous things develop when the starboard strand is snugged up and the port allowed to stream away out; then a gentle turn may bring the two together and they will tangle.

Quite naturally the selectivity of fishes will have much to do with the choice of a trolled bait. The largest rod and line snook I ever heard of was a 69-pounder caught in Costa Rica's Tárcoles River on a little Creek Chub Pikie Minnow plug. The fish was not admited to IGFA's hall of fame because it was taken on a lure fitted with three treble hooks—but you get the idea.

If plug happy, subsurface swimmers are the best bet. They'll work at all hours of the day and night. Surface swimmers pay their freight at dawn, dusk, and during the night hours, but are seldom much sought after in full daylight. Spoons are effective daytime lures, and bait is excellent at any time or tide. Very often flashing spinners ahead of a bait may make the difference. Curiously, with the exception of the slowly revolving spinner used ahead of a fluke rig, outside, and the big flashers employed by salmon fishermen of the Pacific Northwest, such come-ons are rarely

Balao (ballyhoo) rigged for trolling.

Two standard mullet rigs, one weighted with a pierced egg sinker.

Whole squid rigged for trolling.

Spanish mackerel used in big-game fishing.

Squid, mullet, balao, and Spanish mackerel rigged
and ready for trolling.

used outside of rivers, estuaries, and similar sheltered waters. There, of course, the sea worm, shore minnow, or squid strip streamed on a single hook some 18 inches to 6 feet behind a revolving willow leaf or Colorado spinner is big poison on a whole host of respectable game fish. Logically, the flash of the attractor is sufficient to bring a predator up for a closer look, after which it locates and gulps the following morsel.

Multiple rigs can be profitable in sheltered waters. The plug with a pork-rind or bucktail-dressed dropper hook riding ahead, or perhaps a plug with a bucktail jig may save a day. Twin lead-head bucktails, one ahead of another, are likely to be quite as effective, especially if they are jigged during each pass. In some areas, a trolled bucktail is always sweetened with some natural bait, such as a sea worm or a shrimp tail. Strips of pork rind turn the same trick: they're limber and soft, hence contribute to the illusion of something alive. Such a bait may simulate a longer and larger offering than that actually streamed.

Wobbling spoons are premier attractions in all areas and they also may be adorned with pork-rind strips or feather-dressed hooks. Certain of Tony Acetta's grand little flashers are deadly. The Huntington Drone, Pflueger Chum, Hopkins and Mooselook Wobblers are favorites of mine. If I can't take fish with these standby attractors, I'll change to something radically different.

Johnny Greene, who developed the Mooselook Wobbler, liked to talk about "finding the strike zone," and this is tremendously important. In trolling, a lure or bait must be presented at the level frequented by game fish, else all is an exercise in frustration. Getting it down to a proper level is the most difficult thing for a troller to do, because he must not err by any appreciable plus or minus. Sometimes fish feed close to the surface; on a following tide they may be at intermediate levels, or right on bottom. Finding the strike zone is therefore critical.

Trolling close to the pilings of the Chesapeake Bay Bridge, Virginia.

Milt and June Rosko collect a husky fluke.
Photo by Milt Rosko

You do this with a selection of proper lures, and with weight. Keeled sinkers, split shot, or light wraps of lead may be enough to take a monofilament line down a few feet beneath the surface. Deep dredging requires specialized sinkers or the use of wire, and the proper use of wire is a science in itself. Single-strand stainless steel or Monel is best, since it slices down more rapidly and presents less friction than lead core. Lead core, on the other hand, is easier for a beginner to master. Either will work, although I suggest that you take the time to conquer single strand; it is far superior, a bother only in that it is springy and tends to kink.

Outdoor writers are always tempted to provide tables that tell you precisely how long a line should be streamed. I am not going to fall into that trap, because it is cursed with a lot of ifs and buts dictated by the depth of water and the individual fright tolerance of the species sought. There are rules of thumb, and they vary—subtly altered by conditions. As a general rule, I would suggest trolling 60 to 100 feet behind the transom in sheltered waters, a bit more in the shoals where fish are spooked by a passing boat and must be given a few moments to sooth their shattered nerves and resume feeding. It dosen't pay to be dogmatic. Mackerel tribes will take a bait close to the transom, and so will barracuda. Weakfish, hunted on a flat, require a rather long line. One hundred feet is good sense with striped bass, yet a bluefin tuna or many of the billfishes will grab something towed a few yards back of the stern.

So you choose 60 to 100 feet as a sort of norm with any monofilament or braid—the soft lines that are either buoyant or boast neutral buoyancy. This, whether or not some minor weight is attached to get down a few feet, will probably be best employed at about that distance from the transom. Experiment if it doesn't work. Charley Whitney often succeeds with what he calls "a lot of string." Lengthen it out in shoal water and snug it up over the depths. In deep dredging, contrarily, you may need more line simply to get down to the fish. There are no absolutes, because each case must be decided on the needs involved.

Single-strand wire, depending on test and sectional density, will take a lure or bait down more rapidly than any soft line; therefore, you'll reach bottom faster than you would with a braid or mono. In some areas the regulars always stream metal until they snag bottom, then retrieve a few feet to keep a lure just above mud, rocks, or weed. The admonition: "If you don't hang up now and then, you're not deep enough!"

With wire a leader may, or may not, be necessary. Where soft-mouthed game is sought, a length of monofilament ranging from a few feet to 20 or more is in order. Some deep trollers swear by 100 feet of mono, which serves two purposes: it guarantees a straight-back leader after the wire gets it down into payoff territory, then offers more sport and ease in handling after the metal is spooled back.

Whatever the sinking line employed, trolling speed will have much to do with lure depth. Obviously, the slower a line is dragged, the deeper it will sink. Experienced anglers who know bottom conformation, or have depth sounders to advise them of every bar and hole, will speed up to lift baits over subterranean ridges and slow down to let a tempter drop into a profitable depression. Each game fish will prefer a specific speed, but I am not going to attempt tables because the cusses may be typical among their group, or they may get selective and upset tidy little rules. I advise respect for each rule of thumb, and add that it is wise to experiment.

In river and estuary fishing, a few things are reasonably certain. Trolling speed for example, will be greater during the day than during the night. With a few exceptions you will drag a lure deeper when the sun is up, and closer to the surface from dusk to dawn. If waters are clear and shoal, a long line will help, and there is a good possibility that a long and fine leader will improve chances.

Small-boat fishermen can be very successful just off open ocean beaches. Regardless of coast, the mouths of inlets are hot spots for trolling. Rips, offshore bars, ledges, and drop-offs become very important. All have two things in common; they are concentration points for fish, and they are potential man-killers.

A rather high degree of skill is involved in the safe handling of small boats around inlet mouths, in the surf, and through clashing rips. Come to think of it, big boats can be just as thoroughly mauled by a venomous inlet, a breaking bar, or the sledge-hammer blows of a pounding surf. Annually there are reports of plush cruisers swamped or bashed into the rocks because their skippers miscalculated the literally upsetting power of sweeping ground swells and current in a shallow inlet. Loss of power on a lee shore can be quite as hairy, unless an anchor manages to hold before the keel is brushing sand and ledge.

It would be pleasant to say that anglers rarely shove off unless the sea is reasonably calm, but this would be falsehood of the first order. Fishermen go out when they think fish will be biting, and it doesn't matter a damn what the ocean is doing so long as there's a possibility of getting out there and then getting back. The latter often proves more difficult than the former, one of the reasons why coastguardsmen are easily identified; they forever shake their heads and frown. The only miracle, so far as a coastguardsman is concerned, is how so few actually require the dispatch of search and rescue teams.

The low casualty rate lies in a native awareness. Only the innocent are caught off balance, because old-timers read the tides and the weather and gaze at cloud formations before launching. A growing number of moderns employ radio to monitor weather possibilities—wise, yet not always infallible because weather has a habit of confounding the experts. The meterological conditions obtaining in a coastal metropolis may be quite different from the cycle developing 50 miles north or south. It's still a healthy idea to taste the wind and eye the clouds and recall the effects of specific tidal phases. A seaman doesn't need any printed tables, because he lives in the midst of this cycle. High tide? "Flood about two o'clock. Mought be a mite earlier though, with this breeze."

As an aside, no true coaster ever admits to much more than a "breeze." This can approach gale force, with small craft warnings snapping from every headland, but it's still a breeze. I've heard whiskery old salts admit that "it's breezin' up pretty good" during a full-scale hurricane. One time, hiding in an East Coast bar while a screaming killer swept the beach and neighboring roofs were either flapping or taking off in the general direction of Labrador, a skipper's wife occupied the next barstool. She had to be a skipper's wife, in spite of her youth, red hair, and striped T-shirt sans bra, because she remarked casually, "Goddamn breeze'll ruin tuna fishing for a week."

Well, anyhow, the inlet mouths and shoals close to beaches are hot spots for serious trollers in small boats. Tackle and technique again depend on the species in attendance, which can be small or very large and scornful of anglers. It is not very smart to beef up for Spanish mackerel and summer blues that individually scale no more than 2 or 3 pounds, but some do. The ideal is a very light outfit, something in the 10- to 12-pound-test bracket, with small wobbling spoons or jigs the tempters. You can have a lot of joyous sport this way, and load a fish box for good eating in the immediate future. Moreover, since most inlets are reasonably clean of heavy weed and bottom obstructions, the odd heavyweight that latches on can be handled.

Off-beach trolling with small boats is another step forward. Middleweights swarm close to shore, so the tackle combination therefore edges up to what must be called, for lack of a better word, medium. The options are more numerous, ranging all the way from monofilament and braid through wire to plumb the depths. Because the variety of game fishes proliferates, line length must be studied. Lures are legion.

Generally speaking, you will troll a bait or lure approximately 60 to 100 feet behind the transom, again lengthening the strand in shoal water and shortening it in the depths. Line tests will be 12 to 30 pounds, occasionally going to 40 or 50. Monofilament is practical in these weight brackets, falling off in effectiveness after 50. Nylon braid can be used, and Dacron braid is most efficient, although often unnecessary and expensive for this work. My own feeling is that 30-pound-test mono is adequate for a majority of species found close to the beach, and 20 may do as well, providing that the rod is well chosen and the reel is blessed with a smooth drag mechanism.

Without examining each species of game fish sought, it is, of course, impossible to dictate a precise length of line to be trolled for best results, or to name any lure that is most efficient. If you stick to the 60- or 100-foot length, plus or minus a few yards, you'll strike an average. But, school tuna will want baits snugged right up against the transom on the second or third wave aft. Dolphin can be held within yards, if one is hooked. Don't be in any great hurry to land a firstcomer; keep him out there and stream another line. Always expect company, for dolphin tend to swarm in to see what all the commotion is about. There are dozens of species that will take on top, and many more that require a deepgoing lure. Just to confuse matters, the ordinary surface feeder often gets finicky and wants his fodder at mid-depths or right on the deck.

Light, single-strand wire is invaluable for trolling the bottom, and there are many ways to use it. Generally, it is enough to bend a hundred-foot shot of 20- to 40-pound metal to the end of a 200-yard Dacron-braided backing. Do not use monofilament for backing, because it introduces the destructive process of memory.

Stream all the wire and a practical amount of backing. This ensures weight to get down, but prevents crystallization of the metal against rod guides while jigging. Usually, you will want a short leader that may be attached via a small barrel swivel, and the leader will be made of monofilament where soft-mouthed fishes are sought. If the species is saber-toothed, wire may be extended right to the bait or lure. A short braided steel cable or twist leader, perhaps one of the flexible, plastic-coated types, may save the day because it is more flexible and resistant to wear and crystallization. Such a leader should be at least as long as the fish it is to be used on—within reason, of course, and within the rules of IGFA. Pinch-on bronze sleeves are best to make loops in braided or cable-laid steel leaders. Use a minimum of hardware; one well-made barrel swivel or snap swivel between line and leader usually is enough. There are lures that tend to spin, and these cannot be stabilized with any swivel; even the fine ball-bearing Sampo types will fail to prevent line twist. Therefore, you will need a keel arrangement to counteract the action—plus swivels. Unless desired, a bait that spins is an abomination. A very few are meant to do so, and these require keels and the best of swivels.

There is one wire-line technique that seems to contradict all logic. In some areas game fish inhabit very shallow water and, for that reason, they are spooked by a boat's passage. The canny troller simply streams a full 100 yards of light wire, tipped by a simple lure or baited hook. Obviously, in depths of 5 to 15 feet, practically all this wire will be on the bottom at practical slow-trolling speed, but the technique works if the bottom is not too rough or rubbly to defeat the strategy. The best tempters seem to be nylon-dressed Jig-It Eels, or single hooks adorned with a couple of sea worms, or a strip of squid flesh. The trick can be very deadly on striped bass in shoal waters.

In operation, a troller streams his wire at high speed, throttling down to a trolling pace only after a full 100 yards of metal are trailing aft. He then backs the throttle off and putters along, subtly jigging a worm, or imparting more action to an artificial such as a Jig-It Eel. Plugs and other treble-hooked artificials won't work.

The procedure sounds idiotic, but it is based on common-sense observations. In shoal water, game fish are spooked by the passage of any boat. They veer right or left, out of the path of the overhead juggernaut, and you can see them do so if the water is clear. But, fortunately, their fright is short-lived. Within minutes they sag back into feeding grounds. About this time the long-lined bait or lure comes bouncing along over the sea bottom.

One hundred yards is 300 feet—a lot of string! But it can pay off in shoal water. The regulars stream every inch of it, right down into a foot or so of Dacron backing. Fully three-quarters of the single-strand wire is rubbing bottom, yet this seems to be essential. Experiments with sinker-weighted mono and short shots of metal have yet to succeed. Short lines are catastrophic because the fish need time to get back into their feeding positions. Stream a full 100 yards, or forget it.

Dick Wood, an advertising executive and a very fine fisherman from Cape May, New Jersey, had to learn the hard way. He was fishing with me in a tin boat off Provincetown, and Dick couldn't believe 100 yards of wire. We made a pass and he larcenously streamed about 50 yards, figuring that his bait would reach a hungry fish before mine came bumbling along. Dick caught a fluke (with which the bottom seemed paved at that time) and I caught a nice striped bass. He persisted and boated a few more flatties, while I continued to hook stripers. After a while Dick got the message and streamed all 100 yards. Thereafter he collected stripers. I took full advantage of his tribulations, because he had previously made me look like a rank amateur on a trip to Barnegat Bay.

There is another strange thing about this long-line live-bait trolling in shoal water, and Bob Williams of Worcester, Massachusetts, first clued me in. Bob is an old friend, an accomplished outdoorsman, and an innovator. He never accepts the traditional as a final solution and he always seeks new departures. Therefore he's a very deadly angler.

We'd been trolling single and double sea worms on 1/0 claw hooks and wire line. Bob and I paused for a gam on the grounds. "What do you do when the hook is fouled with weeds?" he yelled across the water.

"Reel the thing in and clean it," I said. "What else can you do?"

Peering left and right, as though about to deliver a state secret, he suggested: "Try dragging weeds and all. You waste time reeling in, unless you have 10 pounds of rocks and clamshells on the hook."

I tried it, and it worked! Sea lettuce doesn't mean a thing to a hungry striped bass when a succulent sea worm is concealed somewhere in the mass; they'll burrow right in and take the goody. Certainly this proves that scent is very important, and the lesson indicated that, with worms, at least, weed is no great handicap. Some fishes employ their noses as well as their eyes. It's my guess that most of them do.

Scent and sight are equally important. I lose patience with people who declare that a fish can't distinguish between colors, because I have seen so many occasions where a subtle hue induces strikes and any off-shade ensures failure. This happens in the bright light of daytime, and it happens at night. I don't care whether you cast or troll, you will find that color is vitally important. There are days and nights when they want red, blue, pink—you name it—and they just won't go for anything other than the hue that is currently favored. I haven't the foggiest idea why this is so, but it *is*.

Daylight trolling on most inshore grounds is a subsurface thing. Usually, you get down into intermediate depths or close to bottom when the sun is high. At night one can work the surface and succeed. Daylight trolling is conducted at standard boat speeds (geared to the needs of the species), while the nighttime operation slows things to a somnambulistic pace. There are rules of thumb, occasionally altered by conditions and sometimes flatly contradicted. Every now and then a surface swimmer or a stick bait dragged right on the surface at high noon will intrigue predators. Swimmers, wobbling along on mono at night, can be quite as effective and, for some reason that escapes me, a surface swimming plug taken into the dark mid-depths on wire line sometimes outfishes plugs designed for that purpose alone. Almost certainly the answer lies in a nuance of lure action.

All of the vast ocean looks alike to a wide-eyed hinterlander, but educated anglers zero in on specific locations. A rip, when it is "working," becomes a natural banquet table for game fish. Bait, caught in strong tidal currents, is swept down into the turbulence caused by a meeting of tidal flows, and is there tumbled. Predators line up, usually just ahead of the current clash, just behind it, and sometimes right in the maelstrom, to feast.

A troller can plan his attack in several ways. Simplest, of course, is to work the edges and the uptide face, particularly that spot where a drop-off is indicated. In some cases, where fish are deep, it is profitable to troll straight through the rip. However, where a number of boats are concentrated, a traffic pattern must be adhered to. There is no problem when helmsmen understand the drill; fevers mount only when a beginner or a curmudgeon insists upon disrupting traffic by cutting in and out or by making successive passes across the bows or sterns of neighboring craft. Such a man is, to say the least, rather unpopular, and he often winds up short of line and temper.

Quartering the rip is a time-honored practice. In execution, a boat under power is held a proper distance uptide of the rip, perhaps sliding to port or starboard, but holding position distancewise. Streamed lines then move laterally across the face of the rip, right in the strike zone. Lead-headed jigs and other deepgoing attractions on wire lines are highly efficient in this work, although they usually require a measure of inspired jigging to succeed. Qualified strippers can work almost gunwale to gunwale if each helmsman knows his business and respects the rights of others.

Even the heaviest of single-strand sport-fishing wire will be buoyed up by the force of a strong tidal current, so there's another method that works very well in the face of a deep, clashing rip—a technique recommended only when traffic is light. It is best explained as a marine version of the inland trout fisherman's downstream wet-fly cast, although, in this case, the lure is trolled on wire line.

Instead of moving against the strong current, or holding in place, cruise well uptide and stream with the flow. Troll downcurrent toward the seaward edge of the rip and then, depending upon the amount of line streamed, turn sharply port or starboard so that the deepgoing lure, no longer buoyed up by current, will swing right across the face of the rip. It will swim deep, and it will be potent.

Any drop-off contour is worth fishing, for the simple reason that forage accumulates at this point and game fish take advantage of the handout. Often there is a "color line" to indicate such a spot, but depth finders do the job accurately and with no ifs or buts. If game species are there and in a feeding mood, you can almost count down to a strike as the flickering dial indicates depths. Sounders are invaluable at any time, but they are pure magic at night.

Offshore bars, where ground swells crest and often break, are ideal concentration points for fish. Predators frequent such places for the same reason they take station in a rip; tumbling water keeps bait confused and off balance. On a flooding tide the offshore edges of a bar are most likely to be productive, together with the break-throughs or passes that lead beachward. On an ebb, fish returning to deep water will fin along the inshore edges, heading toward the passes, gobbling bait that, like the predators, will be heading out to sea with the inexorable flow.

Wherever inshore waters are reasonably shoal and clear, the helmsman who wears polarized glasses will be able to locate "black spots" that indicate weed, kelp, or mussel beds on the bottom. Since any marine growth concentrates forage, such spots should be thoroughly worked. Clean sand or clay bottom offers little in the way of food, so the troller in these biological deserts claims only an occasional wanderer making passage from one feeding location to another. Disregard this advice in the event that some vast school of bait swarms into the "desert" and is followed by destroyers. In the ocean it is always wise to be an opportunist.

Inshore or offshore, trollers often enjoy the spectacular business of fishing a surfaced school of game fishes. These melees may be pinpointed by a gaggle of excited sea birds, or perhaps only by the sudden bursts of white water as individual predators smash into concentrated masses of bait. Schools of big channel bass show as a bronze-red smear under green ripples. Common mackerel—wonderful light-tackle battlers—riffle the surface like a cat's-paw of wind. Bluefish or bonito erupt, and the only simile is a charge of bird shot. Get there fast, and then employ both caution and strategy.

The fish boxes of a cleverly conned boat can be filled if the skipper maneuvers so that his craft never actually enters the surfacing school. Baits are dragged on the perimeters of this moving slaughterhouse, or just ahead of it. The fool who churns right on through breaking fish is roundly cursed by colleagues, and usually winds up with a slim catch. Whether alone, or in the company of other boatmen, work the edges to avoid spooking a school of feeders.

Kib Bramhall displays a "sash-weight" trolling rig.

It must be admitted that there are areas in which accomplished skippers purposely drive right through surfacing fish, a sight that chills the bone marrow of visiting anglers who have learned another discipline. On the Chesapeake Bay, for example, surface-feeding striped bass are immediately driven down by charging hulls, after which patrons stream "sash weights" or other weighty sinkers with bucktail jigs or spoons attached to trailing leaders. The operation succeeds—anglers often snaffling doubleheaders on each streamed line. While light-tackle trollers raise their eyebrows at this sort of thing, heavy-gear enthusiasts chuckle as they winch fish aboard.

The sash-weight operation, peculiarly Chesapeake, has its uses. In essence, the sinker—at one time an actual sash weight—essays the task of an underwater outrigger in that it takes a light line right down to bottom. Weights of 12 to 16 ounces are commonplace, and they are rigged via a three-way swivel on a 10- to 15-foot dropper ahead of 20 to 30 feet of leader. In theory, and in practice when the angler is a veteran, the sinker bounces bottom while a following lure works a few feet above mud, sand, rocks, or weed. The combination can be effective on many species of deep-feeding game fish. Its major handicap is sinker weight, which hampers any ensuing battle.

One sash-weight technique used rarely outside of the Chesapeake Bay is both productive and highly frustrating to a beginner It is the artful working of a rock pile that slopes up or down from a sea bottom. When trolling "up the slope," it is necessary to feel the weight bumping lightly and to retrieve line continuously so that the sinker and following lure will not foul. On a reverse pass, where the bottom descends at a corresponding rate, line must be released a foot or so at a time in order to remain in the strike zone, again without fouling. This is high art.

I am not ordinarily baffled by new techniques, but Captain John Pierce and Russell ("Whistle") Henderson, both of Virginia Beach, recently gave me an object lesson in humility on certain rock piles that protect the subsurface tunnels of the Chesapeake Bay Bridge. Whistle was able to hook up on each pass while I, Al Reinfelder, and Kib Bramhall remained fishless. My own skill is a matter to be argued, but Al and Kib are qualified anglers and they were talking to themselves! After much trial and error we learned to "feel" the rocks and to spool or retrieve line at a proper rate and rhythm, but Whistle made us look like amateurs.

Going "up" the rock pile, he'd stream line until an initial bump indicated bottom. Thereafter, as John Pierce's famed *Shady Lady* trolled slowly up the face of the sub-terranean riprap, he continuously retrieved a foot or so of line at a time, thus keeping his lead-head jigs just above the rubble. Henderson caught a lot of striped bass, and we duffers lost a lot of jigs and sinkers.

The same thing happened on a pass down the slope, a technique we found much harder to master. On a declining bottom it is necessary to stream line constantly, again according to contact established by a big sinker. The method, properly executed, is deadly and it will work anywhere in the world where game fish frequent a rock pile and will not come up to take a bait or lure. You present an offering in a precise strike zone, or you go hungry.

Blue water, that wonderful offshore jungle that lies well beyond harbor bounds, introduces a whole new set of disciplines. Hulls are necessarily larger and power plants complement the stiffer requirements posted by distance and a rolling sea. Very suddenly one finds comfort in adequate electronic aids to navigation—the radar, loran, sophisticated depth sounders, CB, and ship-to-shore communications that have come to be so essential. Whether or not a seagoing sportfisherman is privately owned or chartered, the skipper will be a true captain and boat operator. He'll usually employ a mate, or mates, and those who tend the rods will essay that task alone.

This is outrigger country, a wide, sparkling sea where hinterlanders are completely lost, bemused by endless reaches of heaving water where the twinkling pinpoints of reflected light and the drowsy rocking of a boat can induce nausea or a somnolence that leads to nodding in the fighting chair. I am always lulled and mesmerized by a quiet tray of diamonds under hard, brilliant blue light, but the ocean never seems so challenging as when it is rough and screaming. Those of you who are subject to mal de mer will forgive me, but I enjoy a wild exaltation when the cruiser bucks and plunges, its motors alternately purring and then roaring in cavitation as tumultuous waves rear themselves against the sky and send smoky streams of spume to leeward. If a flying fish launches from a distant wave top and comes arrowing right through the rigging, one suddenly enjoys a moment of awed delight.

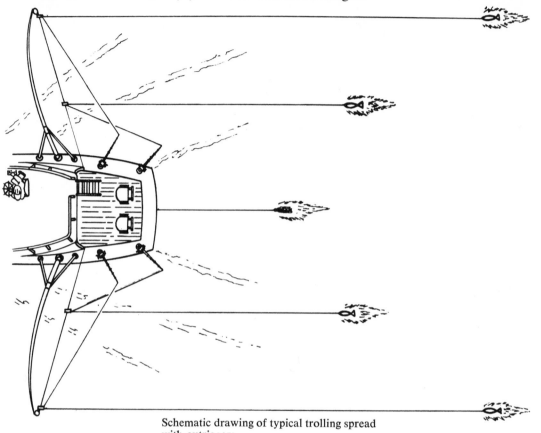

Schematic drawing of typical trolling spread
with outriggers.

Almost always, although there are variations, the offshore cruiser will stream four lines, one from each outrigger and two from rod holders on the deck, the latter called "flat lines." The duty of an outrigger is threefold: it presents a bait at the edge of the wake, far enough to port or starboard so that flat lines will not be tangled; it skips a bait adroitly, accurately simulating a harried forage species such as a squid, mullet, or flying fish frantically fleeing predators in the depths; on strike, the line loops down from a clothespin holder to provide adequate drop-back. Some grand game fish require this blink of time to strike, turn, and to mouth a bait before a hook can be driven home. The delay is important to beginners who might otherwise set immediately and thus score a complete zero. Many of us, who should know better, are reduced to beginner status in the heat of action.

Experienced and well-blooded anglers often prefer to hold a rod. They don't necessarily catch more fish, but they feel the strike—a major triumph in itself—and then win or lose a battle by belting the quarry immediately, or dropping back when that is necessary. There is a very special delight in doing it all by yourself, without mechanical aids. In fact, there are occasions when an educated angler in the chair can "knock down" a line clipped to an outrigger as a fish charges, and then do a far better job of hooking quickly, or dropping back, as the situation requires.

Usually, outrigger baits are streamed farther aft than those on flat lines; the latter snubbed up rather close, right behind the teasers, but again depending on the species sought. Use of fluorescent monofilament lines, where small to medium game is expected, can be an advantage because each line is immediately visible. Yellow or orange tints are best, since they are most vivid against the green or cobalt blue of a following sea. If there is any conflict with the theories of camouflage, a stainless-steel, bronzed cable, or monofilament leader of adequate length evens the score. Recent field tests, under controlled conditions, seem to prove that the glowing line is highly effective and suffers no camouflage handicap.

In tropical waters, but seldom in the cold North, kites are increasingly used to skip trolled baits. These are superb when a live baitfish is used as a tempter, for the properly controlled kite can keep it thrashing and struggling right on the surface behind a slowly moving craft. Kites are really as old as the recorded history of fishing, having been used by Polynesians before modern man ever thought of angling as a sport.

Each game species naturally requires some specialized trolling technique. Billfishes are seldom unduly spooked by motor sound, although some of them will have second thoughts if the engine tempo changes. They usually arrive close astern, glowing with feeding colors and apparently angry at the skipping baits. A white marlin may switch from one bait to another, while the angler on each rod swallows his heart and prays that his tempter will be the one ultimately selected. Wahoo often arrive like a bolt of vivid lightning, zooming high into the air at strike, and then arrowing off in a tremendous run toward the horizon. King mackerel may do the same thing, although the big mackerel is never so tough a customer as its cousin, the wahoo.

Dolphin, common in all warm seas, are school fish. If you hook one, others are almost sure to be in the vicinity. Often an angler will see a hooked fish closely followed by others of its kind, all glowing with that indescribable fluorescent blue-green feeding color. If other baits can be streamed immediately, there is a good possibility that the school can be held and exploited. On the other hand big bulls, identified by size and their sharply sloping foreheads, may be lonesome wanderers of the high seas.

Many members of the tuna tribe seem to be attracted by a boat's turbulence, hence they will strike a bait trolled within yards of the transom. School bluefins, yellowfins, blackfins, and oceanic bonito favor close-range attack. Moreover, these torpedoes of the deep blue prefer a swiftly moving target; if they want it, speedy trolling is an advantage, not a handicap. All members of the mackerel family, the tunas and similar fishes, are delighted by a bait that skips along like a guided missile. Striped bass and channel bass require a more sedate pace. There is an additional rule of thumb: the more line out, the slower the speed.

Most sailfish are taken on trolled mullet, balao (ballyhoo), flying fish, or other natural offerings, plus strip baits. Blue runners and similar forage species are valuable when offered from the clothespin snap attached to a kite. It is worth noting, however, that sails can be hooked and landed on a number of artificials; they have been taken on everything from plugs worked alongside a teaser to big streamer flies and popping bugs worked from a cruiser lying dead in the water after spindlebeaks have been teased to the surface or are engaged in balling bait.

White marlin are suckers for strung eels, squid, mullet, balao, and similar baits trolled 30 to 50 feet astern, but they can also be taken on strip baits, soft plastic eels, and pseudosquid. The man-made offerings pose one handicap: they rarely do well when dropped back after a strike. With an artificial, you hit the skilagalee immediately or, if you're nerveless, you watch him attack and drop the bait right back into a yawning V-mouth one split second before striking. This takes iron nerves; it also requires consummate skill.

Wahoo, tuna, barracuda, and a host of other offshore game fish can be lured with strips, sewed baits, or artificials. These gladiators launch an all-out attack, engulfing bait or lure. You can belt them at strike and be reasonably assured that they have it. Indeed, a strike on the part of an angler often is an anticlimax; if they've taken hold, they either have it or they have missed. Many will come again.

When to strike, or when *not* to strike, is geared to a species sought. There is no norm. Quite often "setting the hook" is unnecessary, because the quarry has already done this in its first precipitous rush. Techniques vary with species, and even change with individuals within a given genus. A sailfish usually requires drop-back when it bashes a trolled bait, but not always. Wahoo, king mackerel, and many others are eager; when they've latched on there is no need to "set," because they have it solidly and will be racing away against the drag before a fisherman is quite ready to do anything other than gasp and grab his rod. If there's any rule of thumb, a delayed strike is good thinking with live, drifted, or trolled natural baits, while artificial lures require immediate action.

In trolling, the forward speed of the boat, usually coupled with a fish's dash toward far horizons, ensures a solid hookup. After a drop-back, however, where line is free-spooled, the angler must take up slack and then hit his quarry a couple of times, hard. Some fine practitioners like to "set" thrice, perhaps entranced by the magic number. There is no standard operating procedure; an experienced fisherman tailors his strike to the fish and the conditions encountered.

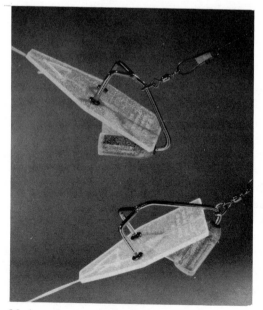

Modern planers, which trip after a strike, were developed on the Pacific Coast.

Jap feather lures may well be the most important artificials on blue water. They intrigue a wide variety of game fish and they are delightfully easy to use. Feathers can be sweetened with strips of bait or pork rind, and they are offered in a variety of color schemes. Blue, white, red and white, green and white, or solid black should be in every tackle box. A single feather may be sufficient, yet many double them up, employing two, or even three snugged up on a single leader.

Far offshore, where the continent is either a dream line on the horizon or is altogether lost to view, the beginner always wonders whether a skipper is simply guessing, or whether he employs some sixth sense in choosing a profitable ground. Almost always the captain knows his precise location and is employing both human sight and electronic aids to pinpoint a hot spot. Bottom contours are important, and water temperature tells a tale. He may seek the edge of the Gulf Stream, where green inshore waters abruptly shade off into cobalt. He works ranges that have produced in the past. He looks for a flurry of bait, the visible fin of a cruising billfish, the investigative circling of a frigate bird or a tern. A skipper scans the surrounding sea, and his mate does likewise. Both are attuned to any unusual activity on the sea or above it, and they communicate in a vernacular strange to the ears of landlubbers.

Colleagues often help, for the radios incessantly squawk and bleat. The shattered, almost indecipherable chatter from other captains, each with his own coastal accent, vectors boats into promising grounds. I challenge any New England skipper to accurately translate the message of an excited Virginia Tidewater guide, and I would equally doubt the ability of a hidebound rebel to exploit the instructions of a Yankee Portuguese or Down Easter who is into fish and quite willing to tell the whole world via radio. We are one people, thee and me, but we speak in a babel of tongues!

Local skippers know, and they waste no time in repairing to a hot spot. Moreover, they know the seas of their ancestors and this means a close acquaintance with off-shore reefs, wrecks, and shoals that always produce. A weed line, where the strange golden sargassum and kelp have been piled by tidal currents, may be a hot corner for finny creatures that hunt miniature crabs, other scurrying weed-borne creatures and timorous minnows. There are lots of checkpoints and signposts out on the glittering ocean, but each has to be evaluated by a man who looks—and sees precisely what he looks for.

Offshore, as well as in the shallows, game fish will take advantage of currents that scour a bar or a shoal and thus tumble hapless bait. The skipper, having checked his ranges and those little, ticking, flickering black boxes on his bridge, will know that he is passing over a subterranean reef likely to pay the freight. Most of the better practitioners have personal charts of such areas, each keyed to certain tidal phases. They are thus able to dictate a certain length of line, with a particular bait or lure, for a gamester they know is waiting.

A subsurface trolling pass on any offshore ground is most likely to succeed if it is keyed to exact depth. Since success may be measured in yards, especially where wire line is streamed, canny operators may toss a buoy immediately after an initial strike. This works well when bluefish are the quarry, for the chopper is a social type. If you snag one, others are likely to be there.

A capped Clorox bottle or something similar, anchored by a length of cod line and a suitable sinker will do. Having made a productive pass, it is then relatively easy to return and cover the same ground. If fish are there in numbers, you're in business. If not, retrieve the buoy and prospect other grounds.

Practically all offshore cruisers are fitted with fighting chairs. These may be portable arrangements, akin to the landlubber's lawn chair, but with a gimbal mount to take the slotted butt of a rod. Unless big game is sought, all are concessions to comfort, not need. There is no real necessity for a chair in working such welterweights as sailfish, white marlin, or other gladiators in this weight bracket. You can play them "like a man," standing upright in the stern sheets. Leave the portable chair for a beginner; tuck the rod's butt into a belt socket, and fight it out. In borderline cases, a light shoulder harness is both comfortable and highly efficient.

The belt-rod socket is excellent. It is nothing more than a cup, into which you tuck the butt end of the rod while playing a stubborn game fish. Some are fitted with gimbals, and these are probably best of all.

Medium-sized tuna, either bluefin or yellowfin, are tough customers; both are given to much sounding, together with strong runs. If the battle progresses much beyond 30 minutes, you begin to feel a certain fatigue in the biceps, and your fingers cramp around the reel's handle. It is nice to strap on a featherweight shoulder harness so that the reel lugs absorb strain and one can wiggle fingers back into a semblance of workability. This rig is a gentle transition between stand-up battle uniform and the fighting chair—kidney harness prescribed for all-out war with big game.

A shoulder harness provides comfort when playing medium-sized game fishes.

Charter skippers provide tackle for patrons and, count on it, this gear will be heavier than the captain would choose for his own use on a sabbatical. Therefore, the average boat rod will be beefed up to handle 40- or 50-pound-test line on species that might easily be conquered on 20 or 30. Guides protect themselves—and their customers—because the citizen who has never fished will need every aid, including a lucky rabbit's foot, to succeed. This is margin for inevitable error and I agree that a beginner is wise to err on the heavy side, to go progressively lighter as he learns to play a fish on fine tackle.

Thirty-pound test, providing an angler knows his business, is sufficient for a wide range of offshore battlers, including most of the middleweights and a few that will ultimately bend the scales to better than 100 pounds. Tarpon and the smaller bill-fishes usually expend their energy in jumping, so they lessen the travail of the angler. Blue marlin up to 480 pounds have been brought to boat on 30-pound test, although this sort of target shooting is not recommended. Almost always, when a big blue is whipped on such fine gear, it develops that he muscled in on a party arranged for smaller game. Sails, either Atlantic or Pacific, white marlin, dolphin, wahoo, and members of the smaller tuna tribe provide lots of fun on 30, yet no one who uses this test will be accused of overwhelming—or dallying—with a worthy gladiator.

Logically, where any number of large or small pelagic game fish may jump a trolled bait, 50-pound test is reasonably practical. Although unsuited to such royalty as the full-blooded blue or black marlin, swordfish, or giant bluefin, it has taken all of these. Fifty is more than enough for any sailfish in the world ocean, for white marlin, striped marlin, wahoo, and yellowfin tuna. The last named is a particularly muscular type, pound for pound a more determined battler than the bluefin, but never approaching the size of its gargantuan cousin. Barracuda, in spite of their reputation as tigers of the sea, are not very convincing fighters, and no striped bass in our watery world will part 30-pound test unless the angler substitutes brute force for finesse, or unless the lineside can find a handy rock pile on which to fray the strand.

Four line materials are commonly used in modern offshore trolling, and monofilament is first. Probably 90 percent of all lures and baits are now dragged on mono, a statistic that ought to demonstrate its worth, but must be qualified. Mono is superior in the lighter tests, say anything up to 40 or 50 for the average game fish. Beyond 50-pound test, and even at that level on some powerhouses, Dacron braid takes command. Dacron is superior because it is inelastic and will survive greater punishment at maximum stress. A lot of chartermen and individuals favor mono for all uses because it will do—and because it is cheap.

Single-strand wire is coming on very strong and will probably dominate deep trolling in the near future. The stuff is handicapped by a tendency to kink—and then to part at the kink—and it is unmanageable in the hands of a duffer. On the credit side, single-strand slices down very rapidly and never conveys the impression of heavy gear. Since such wire is springy and difficult to handle, it is championed by advanced anglers and avoided by amateurs who lack educated thumbs. Metal lines are still barred by IGFA in record applications, but I think that august body will someday relent. Fine wire is sporting and, because it lacks any easily detected stretch, a fish on metal appears to fight much harder than a comparable one attached to mono or braid.

Lead-core line is far simpler to stream and to use, but it doesn't sink as quickly as single-strand, thanks to its greater bulk and a water-resistant sheath of nylon braid. Many use it for reasons of expediency, comfortably noting that it is offered in successive "colors" that immediately announce the amount streamed. Lead-core is good, but never so universally efficient as single-strand. Where charter boats must go deep, skippers prefer this type for obvious reasons. During their busman's holidays, the same skippers will go to single-strand. Learn to use Monel or stainless-steel wire; it takes time, but nobody achieves Nirvana without concentrated effort.

There are other ways to go deep, or at least to work a lure at intermediate levels. Trolling sinkers, which are torpedo-shaped hunks of lead with swivels at either end, can be attached between line and leader. Weights vary, so there's ample opportunity to experiment. Planers are excellent with soft lines or wire, and the best of them can be adjusted to take a bait well into the depths. Pacific Coast salmon anglers have developed the finest models, and these are now appearing everywhere in the world. A good planer is adjustable, to guarantee a specific depth, and it is rigged to trip on a strike, so that you don't have to fight the action of the thing in addition to a powerful game fish.

Underwater outriggers have been with us for years, but the latest models are most efficient. Briefly, a keeled weight that is fitted with a clothespin snap is lowered right off the transom to desired trolling depth. A soft line is clipped to the snap and thus carried down into payoff territory. At strike, the line slips free of the confining clothespin and the angler then plays his quarry on light tackle. Meanwhile, the keeled weight is swiftly reeled aboard and made ready for further use.

Probably the most basic of underwater outriggers is the Pacific Coast's cannonball sinker and quick-release swivel; it is very effective and I often wonder why it has not achieved popularity on other seaboards. Perhaps the answer is the 3-pound cast-iron "cannonball," made to supply a demand on the salmon coast, but available nowhere else. As a matter of fact, quick-release swivels are rarely marketed on the Atlantic or Gulf.

A cannonball is a true underwater outrigger because it takes a soft line down to whatever depth the angler feels is correct under prevailing conditions. Almost straight down, that is. In operation, the spherical iron ball is clipped into the quick-release swivel which, in turn, connects line and leader. When a fish strikes, the 3-pound weight is jettisoned and you are into a grand gamester on a soft line with no fight-handcapping poundage.

There is just one minor irritation: each strike costs one cannonball, and the last time I fished for king salmon off San Francisco's Golden Gate, these were going for thirty-five cents apiece. Without any doubt, in this age of galloping inflation, the magical spheres are now more expensive. Lead would be priced out of the field.

Nonetheless, these things work. Fishing close to the Farallones, far off San Francisco, skipper Hank Schramm suggested that trollers work the 30-foot level. Nothing happened, so—being an insufferable experimenter—I decided to double the depth. Minutes later there was a sudden jolt and, almost simultaneously, a small king salmon soared out of the water in our wake. Schramm courageously guessed its weight at 18 pounds, after he'd swung the net, but I think he was being kind. A nice, silvery, and streamlined fish—yet 18 pounds? Californians are flatterers, and flattery will get them everywhere with me! Offshore guesses make heroes, and dockside scales deflate egos.

There is another West Coast technique that should, and ultimately will, become more popular elsewhere. It's called mooching, and it is nothing more than slow, stop-and-go trolling with a bait that twists and turns in the depths. Moochers come up with very large salmon, plus halibut and a wide variety of rockfish. In practice, an anchovy, a plug-cut herring, or another bait is dropped to whatever level seems appropriate, after which the boat proceeds at low speed or is even allowed to drift now and then or stop dead in the water. Two-hooked rigs are preferred in Oregon and Washington. One barb, which may be either single or treble, is thrust into the tail of a bait. The other goes through the head. The object is a slow, easy squirming, twisting action that is irresistible to game fish like the salmon.

Any troller who is worth cultivating will carry certain equipment aboard his boat. Gaffs, sized to the species sought, are obvious, and every gaff point should be sharp. Landing nets are indispensable when very light tackle is employed, or when the game is soft-mouthed. Weakfish and fluke, for example, often gain freedom at that moment when a triumphant angler attempts to hoist them aboard, sans net. Pacific salmon rarely are gaffed; wide-mouthed nets do the job neatly and cleanly. Nets should *not* be used on bluefish, for their forever chomping jaws will shred the strands.

The gaffs bite into an 800-pound Prince Edward
Island tuna. *Photo by Gene Mueller*

A club or priest is quite necessary. Granting that many fish will be released, those that are destined to grace a dinner table should be dispatched quickly. In many cases it is dangerous to toy with a green battler that is intent on thrashing around the deck with a face full of treble hooks. A loaded hammer or adz handle, a Little League baseball bat, or a well-proportioned dowel of hardwood will be appreciated under such circumstances. Never use a blackjack; they're illegal in many states. Besides, I tried one once, and almost broke my wrist!

Think about some kind of an enclosed fish box to prevent dehydration and spoiling of a fine catch. The motor well, common on many of our larger outboard hulls, may do in a pinch and will keep blood or slime out of the cockpit, but the well has no cover and it often contains a seep of oil or gasoline. Some small-boat jockeys settle for a galvanized washtub; others for a live-bait tank which, when not in primary use, can be employed as a fish box. Well-designed boxes are installed on spacious fishing craft, and the best are fiber glassed to ensure ease in cleaning. Be sure there's a pet cock to drain off excess water during the cleaning process. Styrofoam food coolers are quite all right when the game is small.

Live-bait tanks are quite another thing. The best are aerated by battery-operated pumps, and these are most efficient. An aboriginal, yet reasonably efficient container can be made from a plastic garbage can or a galvanized tub fitted with a jury-rigged cover. If there is no aerating device, it will be necessary to change the water from time to time via a handy bucket. Degrees of sophistication (or labor) will be dictated by the bait carried. Mackerel and herring require well-oxygenated water. Shrimp aren't so delicate. Mummichogs and eels are hard to kill.

Floating tanks, dumped overside when a boat is anchored or drifting, work after a fashion. They fail when a current is very strong or when the boat travels from one location to another. In this case, the inevitable pressure of the flow will pin forage fishes to the downcurrent side of the cage and they will suffocate. Many bait fishes find it necessary to swim constantly, or they will die.

In billfishing, gloves are an absolute necessity because the rough proboscises of sails and marlin can shred skin off the toughest of hands. Cotton gloves are quite as indispensable for handling leader wires and in the playing of big game. Keep them dry, at least until the joining of battle. Wet gloves are both uncomfortable and inefficient; they will soften an angler's hands and cause chafing. Things can be tough enough without inviting trouble.

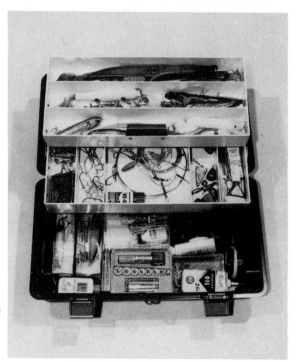

A well-stocked tackle box contains a variety of tools and lures. The box must be engineered for marine use, big, tough, and featuring trays large enough to accommodate man-sized lures and essential gear.

Certain simple tools are as vital to a troller as good teeth in attacking a leathery steak. Always tote a suitable sheath knife. Clasp knives are worthless because they rust, and they are stubborn when a man's fingernails are softened by brine. The knife is a premier tool, used to trim strip baits and to cut hooks out of tough gristle. Veterans usually tote more than one blade—a sturdy sheath type for all-around work, and a limber-bladed filleting tool for dressing the catch or performing imaginative surgery on strips.

Never go to sea without a selection of efficient pliers. You'll want the long-nosed type for subtle work with leaders, wire lines, and lures, plus sturdy cutters. Note that a majority of professional skippers carry both in a belt sheath, ready for instant use. Extras, squirreled away in tackle boxes, make good sense. On too many occasions, wrapped in the excitement of boating a green fish and extracting the hooks from its jaws, I have inadvertently flipped pliers over the side and watched, sorrowfully, as they glimmered into the deep six. Maybe you're an exception, but I lose pipes, flashlights, and knives the same way. My polarized glasses are always slung on a line around my neck, because they also have a habit of sailing away to leeward in the heat of action.

Night rovers must have lights. There is no great problem in a large power boat that produces lots of juice, but even there a powerful spotlight can induce temporary night blindness after it is switched off, and may irritate colleagues on the grounds. The solution is a well-insulated hand flash that can easily be directed on a reel that needs attention, or on a thrashing fish's jaws. In retrospect, I can always chuckle at an Apache war dance in dim starlight, while a big and well-hooked fish is raising merry hell in the cockpit. At the same time, it is no joke, because sharp teeth, fin-ray spines, and even sharper hooks can inflict grievous injury upon the unwary.

Any craft of small to moderate size, particularly those that will operate in shoal water, should be equipped with a paddle long enough to reach the water. This seems a rather ridiculous suggestion, but you'd be surprised to see how many otherwise intelligent outboarders work with paddles so short-handled that it's necessary to do a headstand over the gunwale in order to achieve any bite. A properly shod pole is a godsend in levering a bulky hull back to outboard-operating depth after it has drifted onto a shoal or shell bar in some remote area. When this happens, the Law of General Cussedness will guarantee a foul wind.

One final note: Shipshape and Bristol fashion applies to fishing boats as well as square-riggers. Decks should be cleared for action, with all tools securely fastened in place. A cluttered deck leads to trouble and it may be downright dangerous.

Now check to see that you've stowed adequate buoyant vests and seat cushions for every member of the party, plus foul-weather gear, a signaling packet of orange smoke and flares, a proper assortment of tackle for the job at hand, and an ice chest or galley stocked with sufficient food and drink. Go easy on the hard stuff. There'll be plenty of time to splice the main brace after a long trick is done.

Launch all boats! Trolling is grand sport and it guarantees seven league boots for the angler who knows his gear and his grounds.

BIG GAME ∼11

Techniques of the Giant Killers

Philip Wylie, the genius who wrote those wonderful "Crunch and Des" stories back in the years when *The Saturday Evening Post* was a power in America, precisely stated my feeling when he said that the capture of a giant bluefin tuna was akin to emptying a freight car full of coal with a hand shovel. I still want to catch the biggest horse mackerel in the world!

All big-game fishing entails excruciating labor, and yet the challenge is such that most of us, soon or late, feel an irresistible urge to go out and do battle with the monsters. Specialists think of nothing else and they scorn surf casters, light-tackle buffs, and bottom fishermen. There are plush clubs where a gauntlet is regularly thrown: "How many 'chuna' did you get this year?" (or marlin?) is usually muttered during a cocktail hour over a glass filled with something tinkly and potent.

Depending on area and inclination, some solid citizens are convinced that blue marlin, black marlin, or swordfish—no order intended—should be exalted as the greatest of the great. Some men—and a few women—spend most of their adult lives chasing the royal tunas, the broadbills, or the marlins. Some of them, approaching middle age, have literally been ruined by big fish—old soldiers, broken by the wars they love. Nobody has totted up the score, but big-game fish have killed a lot of people.

Well, matadors die too—and there will always be men in suits of lights. So long as there is a challenge that borders on the impossible, human beings will grasp a lance and mount the white horse. I know a charter mate who is immune to mal de mer, but whose stomach rebels every time a quarter-ton fish engulfs a bait and goes rocketing off into the deep blue while an angler sweats and prays and strains in the chair. There is nothing quite like big game; it is the ultimate, and it can be the most boring business in the world of blue water!

Contradictory? Man, it's a big ocean and mammoth fish are rarely plentiful. Granted, there are areas where you can see tremendous schools of bluefin tuna cruising on or near the surface, but when you seek broadbill, black marlin, or big blues the drill usually consists of endless cruising and scanning, with occasional sightings of fish on the surface or explosive blind strikes. To a neophyte this can be a very dull quest. The endless sea sparkles like a tray full of diamonds. The motors throb, the hull rises and falls; there is wind and spray and a sort of violent somnolence. For those who are afflicted by motion sickness, this can be a junior grade hell. For others it is a lovely calm before a storm, a prelude to life's most glorious adventure.

Certainly all travail and expense are justified when a tremendous game fish is sighted, baited, and induced to take a hook. Who, other than a saltwater angler, can appreciate the excitement generated when a great blue marlin comes up behind the baits or a giant tuna arrives like a gleaming green and gold Polaris missile? Many of the billfishes assume "feeding colors" when they are excited, and then their skins glow with fluorescent, living color. They are magnificent to see, powerful beyond description, and so vibrant with cold life that one always experiences the sinking sensation that *this one can't be beaten!*

Nit-pickers may disagree, but I hold that there are only six big-game fishes, and one of these comprises a group. If, arbitrarily,we assume that nothing under 500 pounds is truly "big," then the list includes giant bluefin tuna, broadbill swordfish, blue marlin, black marlin, striped marlin, and the shark group. Among this latter clan one must salaam to the famed man-eater or white shark, the porbeagle and the mako, the last named a supreme acrobat and a strong fighter.

Sailfish, white marlin, wahoo, and yellowfin tuna are wonderful game fish, but they are far from big game. The yellowfin comes close and, in all fairness he is a better fighter, pound for pound, than the bluefin, but he is small potatoes in size. We still come down to horse mackerel, swords, black marlin, blue marlin, striped marlin, and the most corpulent of sharks.

To catch these heavyweights on rod and line one must go to heavy tackle, the unlimited stuff, or at least equipment testing 80 pounds or more. Stunt men occasionally turn the trick with 50-pound-test gear, but they readily admit (in executive session) that it's a hairy game. You just don't plane a 500-pound-plus fish out of the depths on 50; in fact, you can't lift such a behemoth on this test if he happens to break his heart in battle and dies well down in the sheltering sea. There is no sport or glory in a kill that is lost and wasted.

Respectable blue marlin have been boated on 30-pound-test tackle, and a select group of anglers have subdued better than 500-pound tuna on 50-pound test. The billfishes often defeat themselves by expending energy in leaping, but the 10-to-1 rule pretty well applies. A 300-pound marlin may be taken on 30-pound test, yet the larger ones will almost always break off unless better than twice that clout is employed. It is logical that a man who girds for combat with the monsters must be properly armed. This means the best of rods, reels, lines, leaders, and hooks. Good connections are essential.

IGFA allows the use of a 30-foot leader and 30 feet of double line with anything over 50-pound test. It is smart to take full advantage of this ruling, for the double line and lengthy leader offer an advantage during the final, furious moments of battle. Obviously, you can tighten up and slug it out after a few turns of double line have been winched onto the spool. Where giants are concerned, I prefer cable or heavy monofilament over single-strand piano wire, but this is a matter much argued by big-game fishermen. Mono has yet to work out with giant tuna, but it seems very efficient where other game is sought. Single-strand wire boasts certain advantages, yet it is prone to kinking and tail-wrapping, and parting thereby. Whatever the leader, knots, twists, and splices must be flawless in order to ensure the utmost in strength. There is no margin for error.

Some say that the true giant tuna is the only fish that demands 130-pound-test unlimited tackle. Specialists often go to 80 for the great billfishes, as do some well-educated tuna fishermen who like to live dangerously. Those who seek mammoth broadbill, huge blue or black marlin make no excuses for the use of 130. They need it, and so do the shark hunters who take dead aim at such powerhouses as the man-eater or white. A beginner would have to be addled to employ anything else, for he'll need every ounce of strength to counter his own inexperience in playing the monsters. It is worth noting that we often hear of light-tackle catches because those who are most articulate on the subject are record hunters. There is a tendency to "go light," even when this is illogical and chancy.

First off, the citizen who wants a really big fish must understand that the game is both expensive and tough. There is no way out of this. You can spend a great deal of money on a twin-screw cruiser, in which case you'll also have to hire a skipper and a mate, or mates. Prospective blue-water anglers often mislead themselves by assuming that it is only necessary to buy a boat. Without a crew, they then become boat drivers, while friends occupy the fighting chair. Until a man is really hooked and ready to go for broke, the best way is to charter. It'll be expensive, but never so bankroll-draining as if you invest in a boat, a skipper, mates, and maintenance.

Charter skippers are incurable romantics; they engage in a business that never makes much money. The best of them are there because they love the sea and game fishing. Whatever the latitude and longitude, they have a short season to make hay, and they always shoulder a lot of overhead—bank loans on the boat, dock fees, maintenance, fuel, payment for a mate or mates, and tackle in general. During the season, skippers work from dawn to sunset and often have to spend evenings dining and wining new customers. Their faces are sunburned and sore. Their eyes sting from the constant assault of brilliant sunlight and salt spray. Some patrons are a joy to work with, while others are unmitigated bastards whom it would be a joy to slay and feed to the sharks.

Mates are similarly enraptured by the world ocean. They fall into two general categories: the high-school boy or collegian who spends his vacation months laboring on the sea, and the ancient mariner who may well be a retired captain, a professor of English Lit, or an ex-physicist reveling in the clean medicine of the deep blue. Mates swab decks, scrounge baits from local commercial fishermen, and prepare such baits. They spend long hours repairing tackle and generally getting the boat shipshape and Bristol-fashion before they (the college types) race off to the "meat rack" and a night with the port's glamour girls. They'll be on hand, efficient, if youthfully jaded, at dawn.

Some customers feel that charter rates are excessive; really they're cheap. Price varies with the port and the country, but there is little gouging. From time immemorial seafaring skippers have charged no more than starvation wages for their services. A man has to be an enthusiast to embrace this calling. There's no real wealth in it, only the satisfaction of putting anglers into great fish, of challenging the ocean and making a mark. Seamen are whole men, all over the world.

Everybody has to make a beginning, and the angler who wants big game enters a field that is unlimited—a wide ocean, full of great waves and surging ground swells. This is no place for the citizen with a nervous stomach, but we do have medicines that ease the pain. There are pills which, taken the night before a trip and again at breakfast before sailing, conquer seasickness. Most of these induce a certain drowsiness, but that's better than "chumming" over the rail and wishing to die.

I am not subject to this curse, thank the Lord, having never upchucked on a small craft or a charter boat in the roughest of waters. Yet I have been deathly ill on troop transports during a war, and once on a landing craft wallowing across the English Channel to a beachhead in Normandy. These memories pursue me and there are mornings when I wonder, as the bar is cleared, whether this old hex may still endure.

They say that seasickness is psychological, but try to tell *that* to some unfortunate draped over the rail. A very few people never seem to adjust, regardless of drugs, and these folk should stick to surf casting or angling in sheltered bays where the waves and the ground swells never get very rambunctious. A big-game fisherman must be attuned to the deep-breathing sea because, in the pursuit of his craft, he will have to climb a lot of hills and descend into a lot of valleys—all with lots of flops and wallowings between.

Because of its gargantuan size, speed, and stamina, the giant bluefin tuna usually is considered the most powerful fish in the world, and therefore the horse mackerel intrigues a lot of muscular anglers. Be certain about this: a bluefin can kill you if you're knuckleheaded enough to let him do so. A slim, slight woman can slay a very big horse mackerel, while a virile male may be killed very seriously dead by trying to outslug a giant. Heart attacks are not uncommon on the tuna grounds, and busted muscles are commonplace. Both can be avoided.

A big tuna is a powerhouse of energy; he will come up right in the wash of a charter cruiser, grab a bait, and then uncork a sizzling run that takes much of the 130-pound-test line off a 12/0 or 14/0 reel. In spite of the cruiser's maneuvering, there will be anywhere from 1 to 3 hours, and there are instances of 12 to 18 hours of battle before the behemoth is brought to gaff.

Meanwhile, the angler, seated in a well-anchored chair that is steered by the mate, fitted with a footrest and beautifully designed to fight a monster, may wear skin off his shoulders, his back, and his butt. He will be a very tired man when the mate grabs a leader, the flying gaff is punched home, and the game is ended. Any big fish is well deserved.

Mate David Townsend, biting his tongue, handles the chair for his father, Jack Townsend, as they battle a giant bluefin tuna off Provincetown.
Photo by Kay Townsend

Angling techniques vary with the section of coast. Off Montauk, and northward through Block Island Sound to the shores of Rhode Island, a lot of giants are taken on live or dead baits after liberal chumming. Chum is a soup of ground menhaden, mackerel, butterfish, or other oily, local species. It is ladled out, along with bite-sized chunks, to lure the great gamesters close to an anchored or drifting boat. American sportsmen have even utilized the "chum" represented by trash fish dumped in the van of Russian factory ships well off New York and New Jersey to make fabulous hookups on live bait.

Usually, in this operation, the bait is buoyed up with a balloon or cork of some kind—in recent years with hunks of Styrofoam—which is tied with light line so that it will break off after a strike carries it several stratospheres below the surface. Bottles make poor floats. Most of them sink like deadweights and, if they manage to remain attached, can be dangerous when a fish comes to boat. Baits may be mackerel, whiting, pollock, or any of several other small to medium-sized finfish much in demand by tuna.

Live bait enjoyed a period of popularity in the Gulf of Maine, but is now rarely used there. From Cape Cod northward, the favored rig is a "daisy chain" of mackerel, herring, or squid, depending on the abundance of the specific bait and the whims of bluefin. In this case, anywhere from five to thirteen baitfish or squid may be used, each tied into the 30-foot leader at 18- to 24-inch intervals. Only tail-end-charley is armed with a stout Sobey or Martu hook in the 10/0 to 14/0 bracket.

There are endless variations. Captain Bobby Wood, skipper of the *Dixie* out of Provincetown, had the angling world running a fever in 1971. He'd devised a spreader contraption (actually his mate, Les Shwam, dreamed it up) that simulated a whole school of squid or mackerel. There was the usual daisy chain, plus a crossbar of stainless-steel wire ahead, rigged with four more squid or mackerel. Only the terminal bait was armed, so there was no fracturing of the rules.

Bobby kept his secret from the late fall of 1970 through practically the entire summer of 1971, and he drove competitors to the verge of madness by hooking and landing fish after fish. Luckily, for he worked no miracles, Wood's boat landed twenty-four of the first twenty-five giant tuna hooked during the 1971 season. He was accused of using some sort of tranquilizer, of anointing his hooks with strychnine, of inventing an illegal rig. Competing boatmen crowded his transom and private airplanes circled overhead. Bobby chuckled and let his rig sink into the depths whenever visiting firemen developed nose trouble.

I knew about this very early in the game, but, recalling my unwritten oath as a newsman, kept a zipped lip. Edward ("Spider") Andresen, my associate editor at *Salt Water Sportsman*, a charter skipper himself, cussed me out when I refused to divulge the secret. "I wish you hadn't told me you knew," he growled. "Now I'll have to eat my heart out until somebody spills his guts."

Actually, Spider came very close, and probably knew that he had scored. One morning he said: "Wood must be using an umbrella—everybody else is!" Later, he declared that my swarthy old face paled visibly. A spreader is far from an "umbrella," where all teasers are armed, but it is the same general concept—a rig that offers a whole school of lures or teasers.

Tuna seem attracted by noise, commotion, and glitter, although this is still imperfectly understood. There are boats that seem to be "lucky" because of engine sound, and there is a wide diversity of opinion about the effectiveness of chrome-plating propellers and using such teasers as towed garbage-can lids, strings of shiny automobile hubcaps, crab traps, and such exotic attractors as bunches of varicolored

Saran rope, plastic bags filled with water, and green plastic sink liners fitted with lead weights up front to keep them twisting and wobbling a few yards behind the transom. Some highly successful skippers want no teasers at all; others insist upon them.

In trolling, the daisy chain of mackerel, squid, or herring is dropped back a relatively short distance. Typically, two on flat lines may ride no more than 30 or 40 feet behind, while two more, skipped from outriggers, will be echeloned back a few yards so that the effect of all four represents a school of tempting morsels. In Nova Scotia, mates often arm themselves with long cane poles, to which are attached daisy chains of mackerel or herring, sans hooks, used as teasers. In this operation the tail-end teaser is attached to the armed bait with a light line that will break at strike. Some of the Novies can "play" such a rig in a fantastic and highly productive manner.

Away down in Bimini, where the water is clear as air, the accepted practice is a single-mullet bait on a relatively fine leader. Perhaps multiple rigs would do the trick there, but each coast has its own convictions. At Bimini, of course, one often fishes giant tuna right on the edge of the abyss and this adds to the difficulty.

Tuna may crash a bait, arriving unannounced, but often they are first spotted finning out or pushing water. Often one will vector in from the side and strip most of the teasers off a leader without touching the hook. When this happens, or in the event of a clean miss, an angler may manipulate the baits to goad a second attack. Simply yank the line, so that the baits will appear to rush ahead. Then drop back and repeat the strategy.

Daisy chains of mackerel, herring, or squid are
echeloned back of a trolling boat.

Daisy chain of large mackerel, carefully sewed,
are prepared off Prince Edward Island.
Photo by Gene Mueller

A horse mackerel coaxed into taking a live or dead bait is far more cautious. Usually he comes up rather slowly and often pauses for a fraction of a second before
gulping the goody or turning away. If the water is clear enough for an angler to see
this, suspense builds to coronary-inducing proportions.

Once hooked up, an angler immediately prepares to fight for his life. There is an
immediate necessity to wrestle the rod out of a holder—where it will be bound by a
striking drag of approximately 20 pounds—to fit the butt's nock into a fighting chair's
gimbal, to attach harness straps to the reel's lugs, and to put one's back into a fight
that may be lengthy. Crewmen may help in adjusting the harness, but they can't touch
the tackle. It's your job to manipulate proper drag settings, to don cotton gloves,
and to work like a slave under the whip. A good mate will steer the chair, and a fine
skipper will maneuver his boat so skillfully that you will be spared much pain. If
I keep referring to the skipper's part in this contest, forgive me. He is the difference,
fully 75 percent of clout. When I land a big fish from a boat I congratulate the
skipper. Never forget it—he will make or break you on the offshore grounds.

Possibly the world's record in fighting a true giant tuna, one weighing better than
500 pounds, is 12 minutes. To do this a fish has to come in green, possibly not even

aware that it has been hooked, and must literally be run down by the boat. A monster hooked in the gills or gullet may bleed profusely and prove an easy score. Don't count on it, for there are ample reports of slugging matches that went for 6, 12, and even 18 hours. I'd guess the average, with a man who knows how to pump and apply maximum pressure, would be in the vicinity of 1½ to 2 or 3 hours, although there are many occasions when a wild one, often a tuna in the 500-pound class, will prove more than ordinarily difficult.

Arthur Sullivan of Boston bends a heavy rod as he fights an 804-pound tuna off Prince Edward Island. *Photo by Gene Mueller*

The trick lies in compelling a tuna to kill himself with energy-sapping runs and in exerting all possible pressure during interim periods. A bluefin like most of the mackerel tribe, has no air bladder, hence he must swim constantly from birth to death. Held in tight leash, a tuna can't breathe. Similarly, when he uncorks a sizzling run, his mouth and gills are closed, pectoral and dorsal fins are tucked into handy slots; he becomes more projectile than fish, and he is very vulnerable to the angler who allows no slack line and no quarter.

As a combatant, you pump and reel—a business too often misunderstood—and you never give the quarry a moment of rest. In pumping, the rod is brought back in one smooth, muscular motion in which the back and legs assist. Then the arched tip is dropped as the angler bends forward to spin the reel handle and retrieve as much slack as possible. Weakness or indecision on the part of the fisherman ensures a prolonged struggle.

Lee Wulff and his wife, Joan, with a 651-pound
bluefin tuna she caught on 80-pound-test line at
Conception Bay, Newfoundland.
Photo by Lee Wulff

Often a giant, wearying after a sharp series of tremendous runs, will circle the boat at relatively close range. Then it's time for the angler to lean into his harness and pump like fury. Once a fish is coming, it's well to keep the critter's head up, else an apparently beaten gladiator may dive and unleash a scorching new run. Some plummet into the depths as a last resort, even to burying their heads in the bottom. Depending upon circumstances, this may or may not stymie a fisherman. The angler who is experienced may still lift his quarry by employing very short pumping strokes, retrieving no more than, say, 6 inches of line on each pump. Sometimes there is no way out, and then the crew may employ a grappling hook on a stout line, a ploy that automatically nullifies any record claim.

While fine boats and canny skippers are more than half the battle, there are exceptions. Surprisingly large game fish have been taken from small boats. Indeed, Commander Duncan McL. Hodgson's 977-pound bluefin tuna, which held an all-tackle record for a healty twenty years, was hooked, played, and landed from a banks dory under an ash breeze with one man at the oars. There is a very good possibility that this fish would have scaled a lot of additional pounds had not human exuberance sold it short.

They battled this monster in the way that knights errant are supposed to have attacked smoke-spitting dragons. They allowed it—hell, they couldn't have done otherwise!—to pull the dory as a commercial keg is skipped in the wake of a harpooned sword. For roughly 15 sea miles, and after 1 hour, 20 minutes, of gut-busting labor, Hodgson and his oarsman worked the tuna into relatively shoal water and made their kill. At that time, it was the largest horse mackerel ever landed on rod and reel in the history of our sporting world.

They were young, tough, and spirited men—so they celebrated. After commandeering a flatbed truck, the angler and "crew" toasted victory with a bottle of rum. By the time that great bluefin was loaded and ready for transport to a weighing station, both were comfortably smashed. It's a wonder that they ever got back alive, and the tuna must have lost poundage as it bounced around on the flatbed during a jolting journey over rutted roads. (Unofficially, it went over 1,000 pounds on Hodgson's scales.)

It's easier with a big boat, a well-educated skipper, and a competent crew. Even then, a giant tuna can be a very contrary hunk of finned dynamite when brought alongside. It's the angler's mission to "keep him coming" with all possible pressure after the 30-foot double line is on the spool. The mate, or mates, legally are allowed to do nothing until they can grasp the leader, also 30 feet long where heavy tackle is employed.

On all the sophisticated tuna grounds—which doesn't always mean the best—flying gaffs are used. However, there are many areas of the world where straight hooks are still employed to hold a thrashing monster alongside, while tail ropes or gill ropes are laboriously arranged. I have seen crewmen actually wrap a single-strand wire leader around their hands, prior to gaffing, a good way to get nicknamed "Stumpy" in the event of a sudden, last-minute run.

In most cases, the gaff, whether straight or detachable head (flying gaff), goes home, and the angler may then relax, breathing a prayer for his deliverance while the crewmen bend their backs and get thoroughly worked over, soused with cold spray and sometimes blood. The tuna is a great bleeder. Finally, all gaffs and ropes are socked home; the fish is winched aboard with block and tackle rigged to a gin pole, or manhandled over the transom. How many "chuna" have *you* caught this year?

There are very serious anglers who dispute the notion that a giant bluefin is the most powerful finfish in our world ocean. One faction plumps for the broadbill sword-fish which, pound for pound—as the eternal argument goes—is a far tougher adversary, more spectacular on a tight line, and immeasurably harder to bait, hook, play, and land. I would deny only the "tougher" claim. Nothing is tougher than a full-blooded giant tuna.

The sword is indeed a greater acrobat, sometimes (but not often) soaring out in spectacular leaps. He is absolutely frustrating and often scornful of baits while finning out at the surface; he is difficult to bring to hook, a trial to play successfully, and he may even decide to ram your craft and skewer you if the planks are thin. Incurable romantics hold these things reason enough to consider a broadbill the world's greatest angling prize, and maybe they're right.

In the first place, big swordfish are never very plentiful. You don't find vast concen-trations of them, so each is a glorious adventure, regardless of outcome. Broadbill, at least in daylight hours, are not partial to feeding on the surface, so when you find one finning out he is probably loafing along, thinking his own fishy thoughts, and let-ting the sun warm a well-fed body. He really isn't hungry, so you try to whet his appetite by goading him with a bait so skillfully presented that he just can't resist taking a whack at it.

Most of the time he won't be tempted. Occasionally he will strike, and then the angler finds him difficult to hook very solidly. Once hooked, the sword must be played with ultimate finesse because he has a fairly soft mouth. He's big, but you can't sock it to him after the manner of a bluefin tuna, because that would defeat your own purpose.

Until somebody devises a better method, the broadbill is individually hunted. You cruise the grounds and search for telltale dorsal and caudal fins cutting the surface. Blind trolling has raised occasional swords, and theorists have toyed with the idea of going deep like the commercial long-liners, but the accepted method is a far differ-ent bag of worms. A sighted fish is stalked and the bait is presented with infinite care.

Having spotted a finning swordfish, the skipper carefully maneuvers his boat so that he will pass ahead of the quarry at a respectable distance. The bait, until now carefully refrigerated in an icebox, is streamed by hand, a mate performing the holy office. At this point all aboard become slightly apoplectic.

Ideally, a bait is dragged some 20 feet ahead of a basking broadbill—more or less—depending upon circumstances. Usually the fish will ignore it, but once in a blue moon he exhibits interest by a quick forward movement called "the wiggle." That's a signal for the mate to drop back and let the bait sink, and for an angler to free-spool line and pray. Very often—too often—the trick doesn't work. The sword returns to lazing on the surface, and the whole dramatic procedure is repeated.

It's always a good sign if the broadbill accelerates, wiggles, and sounds after the bait is presented and dropped back. Hold your breath! Offer sufficient slack line and wait to see whether this regal warrior will take the handout and move off with it. If he does, you're in business. If not, join the club of frustrated swordfishermen.

Everything about a broadbill is vexing. They can be huge and extremely powerful, but you can't horse them without chancing loss. Some come out in gravity-defying jumps, yet more drive into the depths or simply churn the surface between powerful runs. The critters are given to much spinning, a thing that can kink stainless-steel leaders. Because of this, 200-pound-test mono is favored for end tackle today.

Broadbill have maimed and killed men, not alone by inducing heart attack, but by premediated assault. The old Yankee harpooners who ironed a sword and then keglined it from a dory quickly learned to stand on the thwarts while hauling line. Object: to avoid being speared by a fighting-mad broadbill arrowing out of the depths. No season ever passes in which some charter skipper does not exhibit, to an avid press, the bill of a swordfish embedded in the hull of his boat. In one classic example, the *Alvin,* a research submarine, suffered an unprovoked attack. The broadbill pinioned itself against the hull of the sub, remained there, and subsequently provided steaks for a crew that had not been frightened by government reports of mercury in the flesh of the species.

Great swords are taken throughout our ocean, and new grounds will be opened up as we move into the tag end of this century. The species is found in practically all seas and seems to tolerate a considerable range of water temperatures. The heaviest of the clan appear to be located off South America's Pacific Coast, and it was there—at Iquique, Chile—that the late Lou Marron caught his all-tackle world record 1,182-pounder in 1953.

Another magnificent world wanderer is the blue marlin, a regal billfish that inhabits all warm seas and "hooks" a vast number of offshore adventurers. Again, as with swordfish, the largest of these huge acrobats seem confined to the Pacific Ocean. An Atlantic blue can grow to 1,000 pounds or better, although the record at this writing is 885. In the Pacific, a 1,153-pounder is on the books and considerably larger fish have been reported. There is the saga of "Choy's Monster," a blue that scaled 1,805 pounds at dockside and was caught in the amazing time of 45 minutes off Honolulu in 1970. Unfortunately, three men took turns in the chair, thus canceling out any chance of a record. The fish was found to have an estimated 100- to 150-pound yellowfin tuna lodged in its gullet, hence the short battle.

The big blue is an oceanic wanderer, observing a seasonal route that brings it into certain angling hot spots annually. On the North Atlantic Coast of America, big marlin are specialty fish off Cape Hatteras, from late June through September, and are caught along the enitre seaboard northward to Cape Cod, although they are never very plentiful in such chilly climes. The Bahamas boast good marlin fishing, and the Virgin Islands regularly yield heavyweights. The largest are caught in the Pacific, usually around the Hawaiian Islands (perhaps because more angling pressure is exerted there) and in other reaches of the tropical Pacific and Indian oceans. As this is written, the world's all-tackle mark is a 1,153-pounder from Guam.

While taxonomists continue to argue whether there is a physiological difference between the Atlantic and the Pacific blue marlins, anglers know that the latter is prone to weigh considerably more than the former, and that the Pacific races seem to favor artificial lures over trolled, fresh bait. This, of course, may be chalked up to local confidence in a given method. Some very big Atlantic blues have been taken on manmade tempters, and a similar herd of Pacific billfish have fallen for the ageless strip baits and whole rigged bonito, bonefish, or whatever is locally available.

A big blue may crash a bait or may come up to investigate—all fluorescent-feeding color and fluid action while he switches from teaser to rigger bait and back to the goody on a flat line. He's reasonably hard-mouthed, so you can fight him hard, and he usually spends a good deal of his energy in spectacular jumps. Some simply bore down, and these are the world's toughest to boat. Every now and then one will defeat the angler—or at least make his lot miserable—by diving straight down to plunge head and beak into the bottom.

"Choy's Monster." Captain Cornelius Choy and his
daughter, Gail, with the 1,805-pound blue marlin
caught off Kona, Hawaii, by three anglers who
took turns in the chair and thus canceled out a
world record. *Photo by Hal Wood*

You'll want big baits or lures, and you'll want to troll pretty fast—up to 10 knots or more with the Pacific "Hawaiian Lure," or Knucklehead, and as fast as possible with sewed baits. You'll find, in practice, that it is difficult to drag a whole bonito or other natural tempter at anything better than about 8 knots without tearing the damned thing apart. We get into the realm of maximum efficiency limited by physical possibility.

Squid, eels, and ballyhoo are regularly employed, as are mullet. On grounds where monsters are anticipated, the baits are correspondingly huge; a 5-pound bonito or bonefish is no more than an hors d'oeuvre for a big, bad marlin. Think about "Choy's Monster," still eager to feed with a 100-pound tuna stuck in its craw!

In Pacific waters the Hawaiian lure, a plastic and nylon-feathered artificial that resembles an East Coast teaser, is favored by a majority of blue-water trollers. Fortunately, the big blue rarely demands a classic drop-back; he's all fury and business, no nibbler or taster. Although the drop-back is still rightly employed with natural fresh baits, it is not only unnecessary, but is a mistake with artificials.

In tropical waters, the black marlin is a true heavyweight and a tremendous adversary. There is no doubt that the black grows to greater weights than the blue and exhibits a somewhat different temperament. As of this moment, the IGFA all-tackle record stands at 1,560 pounds, and this will be exceeded.

Again, as with blue marlin, blacks are world-ranging, yet they seem less tolerant of cool waters. The heaviest specimens have been taken along the Pacific Coast of Central and South America. Alfred C. Glassell, Jr., boated his all-tackle-record black off Cabo Blanco, Peru, a wonderful ground pioneered and publicized by S. Kip Farrington. Huge blacks are regularly taken off Piñas Bay, Panama, and there is good reason to believe that the Pacific Coast of Costa Rica may be a bonanza area. Blacks are hooked well up along the Mexican Coast, as far north as Cabo San Lucas at the tip of the Baja Peninsula and occasionally above that point.

Usually the black requires more drop-back than a big blue marlin. There are the usual crashed baits, so this is a generality. Since a black is big and wide of mouth, hefty baits are preferred. A bonito weighing 4 to 6 pounds is quite acceptable. As with other billfish, tempters are streamed close in and echeloned rather close in the wake, with one or more teasers adding to the come-on. Both flat lines and outriggers are employed.

Drop-back is universally applied in billfishing, and there is much argument about it. This, indeed, is one of the benefits of an outrigger-positioned bait—it ensures an automatic drop-back that keeps the angler from striking too soon. Is this necessary?

In most cases, I think it is. Billfish usually tend to stun a bait, then seize it crossways. There is an indeterminate period during which the predator swims off, then pauses to turn the morsel and swallow it. Some undoubtedly whack the scurrying bait to kill it, and then return to swallow the tidbit as it sinks. Therefore, the drop-back is not only good sense—it is essential. Again, we find that situations alter well-prepared cases.

Some billfish crash baits and hook themselves. Some orbit around the trolled baits and can be teased into accepting one by adroit rod handling. If an angler can steer a bait right into the open mouth of a charging gamester, and sees that lure engulfed and knows that it is well down in strike territory, then he would be a dolt to do anything but strike immediately. Otherwise, the suddenly alarmed billfish might spit the bait. Much depends on circumstances and dead reckoning.

Striped marlin, the smallest of big game because they rarely exceed 600 pounds, may also be easiest to tempt with lure or bait. A striper comes up all color and fury to whack a trolled tempter. If he really wants it, you just can't take it away from him, and he will make pass after pass until the hook goes home. All billfishes exhibit feeding colors, but that of the striped marlin is most fantastic: he lights up like a neon sign when the urge is upon him. Of course, no one has ever really *seen* any game fish unless he has seen it alive. The dead carcasses strung on racks at day's end are sorry facsimiles of the real thing.

We progress to mammoth sharks, and many of them are truly awe-inspiring. Lots of anglers are drawn to these dangerous fishes and make a business of hooking, playing, and landing them. The heavyweights dictate unlimited tackle because they are ponderous and possessed of dogged stamina. Rarely is a shark capable of waging a fast, acrobatic fight, but there are exceptions. The mako does so, and sharkers challenge colleagues to name anything in the wide sea that can jump so well or resist capture. Whites, tigers, hammerheads, and porbeagles are more likely to bore into the depths like submarines. At boatside, practically all of them can be short-fused bombs, fully capable of maiming careless mates and anglers, hard to kill and dangerous until the last gasp.

Hammerhead shark caught by Florida specialist Herb Goodman was loaded with twenty unborn sharks. A spiny lobster was in its gullet. *Photo by Herb Goodman*

Contrary to popular opinion, most of the big sharks are best taken on live or fresh-dead baits such as mackerel, whiting, pollock, or squid; a few are more readily decoyed with huge chunks of animal flesh lowered in a chum slick. Captain Frank Mundus of Montauk, a specialist in the art of "monster fishing," believes that the flesh of a pilot whale is the best lure for gargantuan whites, or man-eaters. Mundus harpoons the little whales, and then uses their flesh for both bait and chum.

If you really desire a toothy trophy, and many people do, the usual drill consists of chumming with something very gunky and smelly, followed by a 10/0 to 14/0 hook adorned with either a locally available bait fish of respectable size, or a hunk of something bloody. Chumming with animal blood, of course, and the use of animal baits—such as Mundus's whale flesh—is frowned upon by the IGFA.

Euthusiasts usually anchor or drift on chosen grounds, making use of much chum. The wonderful thing about big sharks is the fact that they are so plentiful, so potentially dangerous, and so unbelievably powerful. A man can even catch a monster from the beach, although this is about five times as difficult as the offshore boat operation.

A great many sharks are fine on the table if properly dressed and prepared. Lots of people have eaten gourmet "swordfish" that actually was steaked out of a streamlined critter with a bank of sharp teeth. Graying veterans of World War II in Europe consumed vast quantities of fish and chips. Good eating, but the fish were sand sharks.

Our average angler thinks of big boats and outriggers when he visualizes offshore sport. That's right enough, but the traditional equipment is not all purpose. Actually, the outrigger is a fringe benefit, and sometimes a liability. The major function of a 'rigger is to skip a bait properly, to permit a greater spread of tempters in the wake, and to provide an automatic drop-back. Surely this helps beginners and eases the labor of mates.

Kites, used properly—and many are not—do the same thing. The ideal is a natural presentation of baits in an optimum patch of sea behind a cruising boat. Kites are anything but new. They were used by the ancient Polynesians, who fashioned aerial outriggers from broad jungle leaves. This technique came to the American Pacific Coast in the late 1800s and then gravitated to the East, where Tommy Gifford, a great Atlantic fisherman, improved and enlarged upon the operation. Tommy didn't invent it, as some claim, no more than he invented the outrigger, but he sure as hell made both important.

Kites are highly specialized and tough to use properly. Ideally, when weather and wind oblige, a kite can troll a live bait, a strip, or a sewed offering better than a flat line or an outrigger. There is considerable expertise involved, so only the true aficionados do it right. As with an outrigger, you use a clothespin release device that snaps the line free when a fish strikes.

All the great billfishes and the tunas seem strangely attracted to commotion, so they'll come up right in the wake of a crusier. Often the most potent bait is that which is skipped right behind the first wave, and there are annual tales of huge fish that chased teasers a few feet off the transom. To cinch all bets, a majority of blue-water anglers stream lures from a few yards to the 60- or 100-foot mark. A good skipper presents baits in such a way that they simulate a school of tempters. Together with a teaser, or teasers, he has a lot of things going for him, and the fish has a choice. You can't properly visualize a "Chinese Fire Drill" until you've been aboard when a marlin, all fluorescent-feeding color, switches from one bait to another, charges the teasers, and finally comes in to grab one of the hooked baits.

Each species poses special problems. Blue marlin require less drop-back than blacks, and stripers sometimes seem so eager that you can't keep them off the bait. Swordfish are finicky, so the drop-back is not only necessary but in many cases it has to be a matter of finesse and "feel." Giant tuna take with a rush, and you can hook them immediately. No sweat at strike—but lots of sweat thereafter! The big sharks are relatively lethargic, and they fight like absentminded submarines. Some, like the mako and the blacktip spinner, will jump like Atlantic salmon.

Big-game fishes will never be unduly exploited by rod-and-reel anglers, because they require a considerable investment in tackle and time. No matter how you slice this melon, it is expensive and time consuming; there is little likelihood that the game will become very economical. It won't, but men arise to a challenge, so there will always be people who yearn to tangle with the giants. They'll charter boats and buy boats and go in hock. And they'll catch great marine fish.

I am always pleasantly intrigued by the recorded fact that many all-tackle records are posted by beginners on the deep, blue sea.

SEVEN-LEAGUE BOOTS ↗ 12

Boats for Advanced Anglers

Saltwater anglers who travel to the far ends of our watery world are well acquainted with the smooth acceleration of a great jet as it bores down a seemingly endless runway to lift into space. Flight is taken for granted, and the tremendously complicated modern machine is so stable that one seldom feels any transition between ground and air. Recently, pursuing the trade of a writer who scribbles about many things, I flew in an antique biplane, a craft designed and built in the heroic twenties when open cockpits and goggles were still in vogue. That was a new experience and it evoked comparisons.

We rumbled at the start, tail-skid jolting, and then there was raw power and rapid acceleration followed by a very definite change as she took the air and battled for mastery. The sensation was not unlike that of riding in a powerful small boat skimming over ground swells, buffeted by a cross chop, yet steady and well trimmed under the hand of an experienced helmsman. There was ecstasy in it, coupled with a feeling of conquering an element that might be benign, but might also be treacherous.

Boats and airplanes have much in common. Both are well-designed, magnificently tuned machines supported by elements softer than terra firma and more capricious. Both are docile under the hand of an experienced operator, yet either will kill the idiot who takes chances. Planes—and boats—are made for specific tasks; neither is very forgiving of pilot error.

There are lots of corollaries, such as size and type for a given task; power and load capacity, capabilities depending upon weather and sea (or air) conditions; the necessity to use sophisticated instruments and other special equipment; and the need for a helmsman to be both well informed and vigilant. Failure, in either the airplane or the boat, may be fatal.

Fishing boats are safe. So are airplanes. Tragedy, in either case, occurs only when some winsome lad or lass decides that it is sporting to disregard the rules and take a long chance. An ancient saying in aviation goes: "There are old pilots and bold pilots, but there are no old, bold pilots!" Any boat operator who ventures upon the sea ought to think about this, for he also toys with an unforgiving skill.

All sorts of boats serve marine anglers, each in its proper sphere of operations. There is nothing questionable about our modern equivalent of the Indian canoe in a brackish estuary or tropical river. Indeed, that slim and beautifully proportioned craft may be ideally suited to exploration under the rattling palms of our Deep South, or in the broad gray reaches of a northern creek. A canoe, in the hands of educated paddlers, is one of the safest small craft on earth; manned by incompetents it is bad news.

Small boats are best in sheltered waters, for there one seldom needs an ultimate in beam, freeboard, high speed, or seagoing design. There are exceptions, of course, as there are to every rule, but the cartop skiff and the johnboat can be very practical where tides and currents are not strong enough to create dangerous rips or the necessity for brute power to conquer a foul tide. The angler needs only an easily handled small boat that provides a decent fishing platform for the work at hand and is equipped with paddles, oars, or an outboard motor with just enough thrust to satisfy demand.

Seaworthy boats, once lobstermen, serve big-game anglers at Wedgeport, Nova Scotia.

Hull materials are varied, although most of today's small craft are either metal (an aluminum alloy that is not very susceptible to salt corrosion) or fiber glass. There is nothing wrong with old-fashioned wood planking, and the wood-canvas construction ensures both light weight and beauty. The major problem with wood, or wood-canvas, is the necessity for maintenance. You'll have to maintain metal and fiber glass too, but the task is vastly simplified. Usually, although there are many fitted with accessories that add considerable poundage, the aluminum alloy boat is lightest. A well-made wood and canvas craft would be second, weightwise. Wood and fiber glass weigh more. You can buy featherweight glass boats, but most of them are too fragile for heavy-duty employment. Choice is an individual thing. I prefer stressed aluminum skin in any craft that must be manhandled, and fiber glass in models too heavy to portage.

Such small craft range from 12 to 16 feet in length and may be anything from a canoe (possibly an 18-footer) to a planing hull or a flat-bottomed, square-ended johnboat. Motors of 5 to 10 horsepower are sufficient; indeed, they are better for trolling than the big kickers which, in spite of all protestations to the contrary, tend to foul plugs when they are idled down to minimum speeds over a period of hours.

There is now a tendency to trail all small boats, and this is healthy, providing that ramps are available for launching. In many inland brackish waters, there will be nothing more than a slippery, rocky bank to provide access, and there the cartopper that is light enough to manhandle will prove a blessing. You will find that it is possible to muscle any hull weighing less than about 150 pounds into the water. Beyond that, hernias pop. Even a 150-pound hull requires individual transport of boat and motor, plus all the accessories. Since bay or stream banks usually slope to the water, it will be even more muscle-busting to recover a manhandled craft.

There are laborsaving devices in cartopping, such as patent rollers and levers to remove or to replace a boat on a rack. One of the simplest and easiest is a platform with longitudinal stringers. You load or unload from the side, rather than the rear. Basic leverage is employed, and it is possible for a man or woman of limited strength to "walk" a 150-pound hull into position. Thereafter, the inverted boat will slide into blocks and be tied down and secured.

Lightweight outboard motors are just about mandatory for the manhandler. I can wrestle my 25-horsepower Johnson, but that's maximum and, where banks are steep or slippery, I would prefer a 5 or 10. Note that you will also have to tote 6-gallon fuel tanks, plus tackle and accessories. A very light boat can become a very heavy hunk of equipment when you add the power package, plus tackle and gear. Think about this.

In sheltered water fishing, where there is no scouring current that requires power, and where the water is shoal, a light hull and a small motor prevent cusswords. This is inland fishing, no matter if the water is brackish, and there may be no need for sophisticated instruments. You should certainly have a buoyant jacket for every man, woman, or child aboard, plus coast guard-approved seat cushions. You should also ship oars or paddles, plus a suitable anchor with an abundance of anchor rode. I insist that any nonswimmer *wear* a buoyant vest in my boat, but that's up to you. I have never lost a pilgrim, and I do not intend to lose one.

Flat bottoms, or the soft chine that works best in shoal water, are favored. Deep-V configuration is less practical, yet it may be wise to choose a boat that is unsinkable because of flotation built into its sides and bottom. Again, weight is a factor; the truly unsinkable craft usually weighs more than its thin-skinned look alike. If you can launch from a hardpan ramp, the difference is minimal.

Our average aluminum-planing skiff is a highly efficient little craft; in the hands of an educated helmsman it can negotiate some very choppy and turbulent waters. Most of these skiffs now offer Styrofoam flotation, so they won't plunge to the bottom in the event of capsizing. Unfortunately, because Styrofoam seldom is applied high on the gunwales, small metal boats have a tendency to roll like happy porpoises when half full of water. Few of the new glass sandwich hulls do this; they sacrifice something of weight for safety and will remain on an even keel even when completely awash. I once incurred the wrath of a prominent boat manufacturer by stating that the craft he made "couldn't make up its mind—it won't float, and it won't sink!" He carried the day because his craft, if wet, was at least very safe.

In small boats we calculate the benefits of light weight in manhandling, the seaworthy qualities of the hull under specific operating conditions, and the power required. There is no all-purpose boat, so it is impossible to dictate absolute limits or requirements. Much depends on piloting and sea conditions. A skiff can be used on the offshore grounds when all nature smiles, and a mechantman may be destroyed on a lee shore when the sea is angry and some disciple of Queeg errs.

Bowing to the usual exceptions, there are inland waters that snake back and forth for miles, and there a small-boat angler may want the most powerful outboard motor he can safely employ. There are benefits and handicaps. One can move fairly rapidly from one location to another, a credit. But weight will be a factor, always important in manhandling, and, finally, there is an obvous decline in slow-trolling efficiency as horsepower is hiked. One obvious answer is a big motor to get there, plus a smaller kicker, or perhaps an electric motor, for use on the fishing grounds. Total weight of the rig and ease of handling must be worked into any equation.

There are always new departures, some of them ancient ideas resurrected, and some the result of modern technology. A variety of folding boats, assembled via interlocking struts and canvas skin, can be employed for sheltered-water angling. I hold them better for packing into a mountain lake than for marine sport. Rubber life rafts, often military surplus, are intriguing, yet they seldom measure up. The old-timers are subject to decay and puncturing, in which case the craft is rendered lopsided as one of its compartments collapses, or even sinks if there is no compartmentation of flotation chambers.

Soft-skinned inflatable powerboats are now readily available, but are little used for marine angling in the Americas. These craft have achieved some popularity among skin and scuba divers in Italy and the Mediterranean area. While they are far superior to the military life raft, such boats are rarely fitted for the hard labor and punishment of everyday angling.

Then, of course, there are such relatively new developments as jet propulsion. Boats of this type are said to skim over a fine dew, and they will just about fulfill this boast under ideal conditions. The system may become very important a few years hence, but it continues to have teething troubles—such as a workable reverse and debris jamming the impellers. In some cases, a mere hunk of stray nylon rope can mean overhaul because the nylon melts and gunks up hot, whirling turbine blades. Perfected, it is logical to expect that jet propulsion will be the ultimate for thin-water angling.

Airboats are fully developed and very practical in such grassy, shallow, and wide-open water wildernesses as Florida's Everglades. They are hardly comfortable in a seaway; they are relatively small in size and very noisy, yet the things can skim over saw-grass flats that would defeat any conventional boat. Considering that the helmsman and passengers sit well forward in chairs elevated above the hull, it would seem that safety might demand strapping in. On the contrary—since any solid contact with a cypress knee at high speed might lead to flowers in remembrance were the human cargo not catapulted to a wet but soft landing area—you plan to part company with the boat in the event of a too-sudden stop. Obviously, fishing rods carried on airboats had best not be accidentally thrust through the grillwork that protects bodies from a whirling propeller blade. An airscrew is far more efficient than an automobile's slamming door when it comes to masticating rod tips.

So-called surfboats, much used on the North Atlantic Coast and in the Pacific Northwest, resemble inland skiffs, but they feature greater beam, deeper freeboard, and more power. This means additional weight in manhandling, although the problem has been partially solved by the introduction of prime movers, winches, and clever utilization of the sea itself. So-called?

Well, the true surfboat is a double-ender of dory construction, the end result of much experience in boatbuilding and rescue operations, but it is not very practical for the sportsman. Double-enders are supremely safe and stable, yet rarely are they capable of high speeds and they make poor angling platforms. As an aside, landlubbers always feel that a banks dory must be safest because it has enjoyed years of success on commercial fishing grounds. Actually, unless heavily burdened—as it will be in the offshore fishery—the dory is a skittish and tippy hull. Like the great Indian canoe, it is superb in the hands of experienced seamen, but no great joy for a beginner.

Add to this the fact that no sport fisherman ever launches when breakers are smashing ashore during a storm, for his craft is never designed to conquer an angry succession of combers. Beach launching is essayed with planing hulls, units much lighter and more buoyant than the coastguardsman's specialized vessel. Indeed, the art of surf launching, for fun, has evolved only since World War II and has made spectacular advances.

On the North Atlantic Coast we got into this business during the early fifties, usually with antediluvian flat-bottomed wooden boats that were oar propelled. In Washington, Oregon, and northern California, at that time, salmon-fishing enthusiasts were sculling through the surf in similar, if somewhat larger and heavier, craft. They favored a sort of modified Amesbury skiff design with a high bow.

In those days two men usually comprised a team; the craft was manhandled into position, its bow in the suds. At a moment deemed proper, between waves, both pushed off. One leaped to the oars while the other scrambled over the transom and offered moral encouragement. There ensued a few frantic moments of rowing to attain some depth before riding up and over the next advancing wave. Any initial error, such as misjudging a wave or "catching a crab" with an oar's blade, might well mean an undignified return to the beach, possible capsizing, and loss of gear. Since the boats were light and the anglers agile, such an experience might be humiliating, but seldom dangerous.

Recovery was quite as tricky; it involved backing in, because the boat's sharp-bow entry provided less bearing surface than a broad stern. Oars were very important tools for a few short years, and then anglers solved part of the problem with power. Launching remained a matter of manhandling and scrambling aboard to man an ash breeze, but he who swarmed over the stern immediately fired up an outboard motor to thread advancing swells and move safely offshore.

Small outboard motors lacked the push to land bow first, so oars were still used in recovery until larger kickers were mounted. Then, of course, the helmsman found it very possible to circle, to pick up a wave, and come ashore at full throttle. The trick then, and now, is to ride right on the reverse slope of a looming ground swell and to apply full power an instant after the wave bursts to send its wash racing up on the shingle. Properly executed, powered recovery is both safe and spectacular, with hulls sliding high and dry on that swift wash. Botched, humiliation is always bitter. It is quite easy to overshoot a wave and come down with a tremendous crash, after which a following wave is sure to smash into the cockpit. Undershooting is quite as perilous, for the craft is then stranded well down, at a point where another wave will tumble it, fill its length with sandy water, and generally sear the hearts of all concerned.

A small outboard powered boat may be quite sufficient for sheltered water angling.

North Atlantic anglers very quickly turned to the "tin" boat, or aluminum planing skiff, with outboard motors ranging from 18 to 25 horsepower. These could be man-handled down a smooth sand beach and swiftly dragged up to the high dunes after recovery. Practically everyone invested in extension-operating handles for outboard motors, and these are still favored by all small-boat surfers. The extension handle allows a helmsman to stand erect in the stern sheets, to see where he's going and to trim his craft properly. In addition, the handle serves as a brace or clumsy cleat. Most of us would be lost without it, and I am always scornful of chairborne writers who declare that no one should stand in a small boat. They have a point only in that beginners should learn a trade. Seasoned backwoodsmen propel Indian canoes with the setting pole, and all laborers on the sea find it necessary to stand. Quite naturally one masters a trainer before he flies a fighter.

Small boat surf launch—one man at the oars and another pushing off.

Nicely trimmed, a 14-foot aluminum surfboat is stable and easy to manhandle.

Without any doubt, the small, light surfboat still outnumbers larger craft, but there is a definite trend toward much heavier hulls and more powerful motors. These are the 16- to 20-foot fishing machines that require prime movers, such as four-wheel-drive carryalls and jeeps. They are too heavy for manhandling, yet they are superb performers in the suds, much safer than lighter skiffs. Fiber-glass boats are better than those constructed of wood or metal, because glass offers less friction in landing. Under sufficient power you will zip up through the breakers to land high and dry.

For several reasons, the cathedral-hull conformation is better suited to surf launching than a traditional round chine or flat-bottomed planing type. I am particularly impressed by the 17-foot Boston Whaler for this task, although I am not fond of the craft for any high-speed work in a rough sea. The Whaler's three-point entry lifts, rather than digs, into advancing waves during launching. There is little of the veering common to single-entry hulls. A Whaler type rides up and over, comfortably. In recovery, the configuration is no handicap; this craft hits the beach, leans to port or starboard, and slides smoothly on two points.

The only real problems are those dictated by weight and an inability to manhandle. Any heavy surfboat requires a prime mover, usually a powerful four-wheel-drive vehicle fitted with flotation tires, a power winch, and a buffer device securely bolted to a front bumper, portside. The winch is useful on many occasions, but is primarily effective in loading the craft on its trailer. Half-inch hemp or nylon lines perform other offices.

Use of big surfboats puzzles citizens who feel that such trailered rigs should be launched from hardpan ramps in the fishing area. Unfortunately, many of the better angling grounds are far from ramps, yet easily reached via four-wheel-drive beach buggy and trailered boat. Note that the trailer, in this case, must also be equipped with oversized flotation tires. Sand launching may be easier than takeoff from hardpan.

On the crest of a sand dune, some 30 or 40 feet from the water, a big boat is unceremoniously dumped off its trailer bunkers to lie stern toward the surf. A line is then secured to a stern cleat and bent to the prime mover's trailer hitch. Within moments the craft is whirled on its axis, so that it faces the suds. There is nothing further to do than to push it forward, and this is accomplished with the help of that aforementioned padded front bumper. Portside, because there's better visibility for a driver.

After recovery, such a boat can be snaked up beyond the high-tide mark with a simple line, or winched beyond the ocean's reach. Power and well-chosen machinery take all the labor out of launching and recovery. It's an expensive business, but we always pay for the ultimate in performance. An increasing number of sportsmen seem to think that costs remain in proportion.

An extension operating handle permits the small boat helmsman to stand in the stern sheets where a high angle of vision aids the spotting of fish.

Nowadays, 16- to 20-footers are not uncommon in the surf, and they pay off in better-casting platforms, more comfort for trollers in a rough sea, and the vital necessity to be there when any action develops. Like corsairs, these on-the-spot enthusiasts shove off when a target is apparent. Thanks to the internal combustion engine, they are immediately mobile, and larger hulls permit space for a few basic aids to navigation and fish-finding.

Small tin boats remain important for adventurers who work with a minimum of equipment, perhaps a gimbal-mounted compass to assure rough direction, together with a basic chart tucked into a tackle box. Larger craft may be graced by remote controls, an ideally located amidships console, and an electrical system that complements a CB radio and a depth sounder. There will be more stowage space for everything from tackle to foul-weather gear, plus flares and smoke bombs in the unlikely event of trouble. In addition to a primary power plant, usually something in the 50- to 75-horsepower range, it is wise to bracket an auxiliary 5 or 10. You'll never need it, of course, but it will be there in the event of accident.

Surfboats, generally, are operated by men who know their particular reach of ocean front. Night or day, they read the ranges and know their location. No night is so dark that shoreside contours and silhouettes are lost; indeed, there is always a surprising amount of light out on the water, unless fog obscures all reference points and reflects illumination so that the fisherman's craft seems tucked into a sphere of baffling cotton batting. No seaman is fond of fog, so compasses, charts, and depth finders are lifesavers. Even in a 12-foot skiff, the man who launches without a compass of any kind (even a cheap woodsman's pocket model), plus either a chart or a good mental picture of the coast he works, is an idiot. When cloud descends to surface level, it is all too easy to motor out to sea, supremely confident that land lies in that direction. Human nature errs, but the compass rarely lies.

Practically all prime fishing grounds on American coasts feature good hardpan launching ramps. The small outboard motor is used as a spare in the event of trouble with a primary power plant.
Photo by Milt Rosko

Usually, outboarding off a sand beach in the night hours, it is possible to recover under the shadow of a waiting beach buggy by noting the contours of the dunes above. The buggy will be indistinguishable, unless you have placed a flashing light on its roof or hood to guide return. Spotlights seldom help, for the white beam directed over more than a hundred feet seems to probe a limbo. You want to make an accurate landfall, guided by some terrain feature or a fixed light.

Harbors and ramps are more easily located. Usually there are range markers on a chart or indelibly impressed upon the subconscious of the helmsman. There will be a necessity to thread a proper channel, else you may spend perspiring hours poling off a shell flat. Straying from a channel is common enough during daylight hours, so it is a major threat at night. If you're confused, proceed slowly and look for markers. They may be coast-guard buoys and beacons, inland waterway range markers, or maybe no more than saplings thrust into the mud by local commercial fishermen.

Surf launch and recovery are, almost always, a soft-beach operation. If the waves are breaking, thus necessitating a full throttle run-in, any rocky beach threatens destruction of expensive equipment and these should be chosen only in emergency. Any hull will be worn by successive sand-beach landings, but damage will be minimal. The rivets on a "tin" boat may loosen after a few seasons of hard use, and it may be necessary to renew the glass matting or gel coat of a glass hull at touchdown points each fall. In a well-executed recovery, the throttle is chopped before the hull really touches down, so there is no appreciable damage to the wheel. Be sure that the outboard motor is not locked in the down position; it should be able to kick up on contact. I have ruined a couple of transoms by carelessness.

A small metal boat is brought ashore at full throttle.

A botched recovery means trouble. This boat has bogged down in the suds, and weed-laden waves are roaring aboard.

Larger boats, such as this 16-foot whaler, are now used very successfully in surf launch and recovery.

All fishing boats are compromises; the best are highly specialized, built to perform one task and often poorly suited for other work. Floridians have created a whole fleet of very fast shoal-water hulls that are ideally suited to cruising the flats and the mangrove back country, an alluvial wonderland where considerable distances must be covered and the water is shallow enough to frighten any offshore enthusiast. Since the weather usually is pleasant in tropical or subtropical fishing areas, and because warm-water angling demands much casting, hulls are wide open and uncluttered. Most of the better boats feature a control-console amidships, with casting platform fore and aft. One or two outboards will be bracketed, and they'll be big jobs, capable of high speed.

Such flats boats are planing hulls; they have to be in order to get up on top and skim over ground so close to the wheel that a rooster tail often throws mud and sand. Fiber-glass construction is favored, for these craft usually measure 16 to 18 feet and are trailered or moored in coastal slips. Equipment becomes specialized, but the depth sounder is of less importance than a compass, a CB radio, and a footed pole for labor on the flats. Your skipper may thread channels and zoom over air-clear flats at high speed, but he will cut the gun and pole—from bow or stern—when it is time to present baits to cruising tarpon, permit, or bonefish.

Visiting northerners are impressed, and some of them feel that this shallow draft, high-speed creation with its beautifully designed hideaway duffel compartments and uncluttered decks would be ideal anywhere. They forget the flat, planing bottom that would mean a very bumpy ride in a real seaway, and lack of a sheltering windshield or cabin to turn wind or spray on a northern ground. The tropical outboard fishing machine is highly specialized, and many of its better features are now appearing in craft designed for work elsewhere. Uncluttered casting platforms, smoothly faired duffel compartments, and built-in bait wells are admired by fisherman on all coasts. The shoal-water hull configuration is not so universally admired.

There are compromises. Back in 1965 Jim Martenhoff of Miami, a fisherman, an ocean racer, and a very competent boatman, designed and had built a craft he called *Miss Print*. She was very possibly the predecessor of all modern outboard fishing machines, a boat big enough to horse around offshore, yet with shoal draft to navigate the flats—everything from blue marlin to bonefish in one hull. Is this possible? Not ideally, but a good compromise. Jim has dabbled in ocean racing and he is a highly respected marine writer, so his thoughts are worth study.

Prototype of today's magnificent, wide open fishing machines, Jim Martenhoff's *Miss Print*, here numbered for an early race, was built in 1964.
Photo by Jim Martenhoff

When outboarders actually go to sea, or operate in regions where winds are cold and waters are rough, the deep-V or modified-V hull is a much better choice. Length escalates a bit, where poling is unnecessary, and there will be a need for some shelter. This may be a small cabin up front, or simply a windshield or canvas Bimini top folded forward. The windshield becomes just that, something to stop spray and wind, but not to peer through. It'll usually be so doused and beaded with salt water that a skipper would need radar to see through it. The thing will keep him half dry and half warm while he stands at a center-mounted console and conns a true course.

The best medium-sized (18 to 24 foot) outboard hulls for sea work are the deep-V types pioneered by master designer Ray Hunt. They feature sharp entry and longitudinal lifting strakes, together with the V bottom. Such boats are reasonably comfortable in a healthy sea, their only handicap a lack of grace in very shoal water, except at high speed when planing. Actually, this hull form is not fully utilized in any very small boat, but it is a far better choice for rough going than the hard chine or round-bottomed planing skiff that skips from wave to wave with all the subtlety of a thrown brick.

Another choice is the modified sea sled or cathedral hull that features a three-point bottom. This may be the most stable fishing platform in the world, and it is a delight when seas are reasonably calm. Roughly shaped like a huge pumpkinseed, the wide-beamed and squat sled, regardless of its size and triple entry, is a bucking bronco in an open ocean. It's wet and it is hard riding. An ocean racer it is not.

This wide and rather squat power platform undoubtedly is an offshoot of the great Gold Cup racers, a testimonial to the influence that competition has on the design of all sporting craft. The point forgotten by enthusiasts of an era now passing was that Gold Cup racers were best employed on quiet waters. Today, Ray Hunt's magnificent deep-V Bertram types, with a host of minor variations to defeat patent rights, are triumphant in ocean racing. The pendulum is swinging back toward a relatively lean hull form that combines the best features of displacement and planing design. Each advance adds something to the science of fine boatbuilding. Perhaps of major importance is the fact that citizens now embrace a greater knowledge of the physics involved, and know that an all-purpose hull has yet to be designed.

Binoculars are a must for any serious marine angler. Claude Rogers's boat is equipped with three outboard motors, each designed for a specific task.

Outboarders who travel more than a few miles offshore are wise to carry all possible aids to navigation. While the kicker-equipped small craft is not really suited to any beyond-the-horizon work, veterans make it do. They succeed because they never venture too far out and they scurry shoreward whenever the weather deteriorates. A properly compensated compass is a necessity, as are suitable charts. A practical depth sounder is worth its weight in fine-minted gold, and a CB radio is essential. Twin outboard installation offers a form of insurance, or one big power plant may be augmented by an auxiliary small motor either bracketed or stowed away against a moment of need.

Limited range is one handicap of the small- to medium-sized fishing machine, and fuel-tank placement is arguable. Built-in tanks are excellent if they are well designed and properly located to ensure balance and trim. Some of the finest new models, holding 40 to 60 gallons of gasoline, are secured under the amidships consoles of boats in the 19- to 24-foot bracket. Even larger tanks are optional, together with auxiliaries fore or aft. If tanks are built in, filler pipes should be easy to reach, preferably gunwale level high, portside.

Where portables are favored, and this usually is a necessity with smaller outboard hulls, an angler can choose between 6- and 12-gallon types. Many prefer the 6, because it is easily shifted from place to place in order to ensure precise trim. Such small tanks are joys to handle, easily topped off at dockside. You will carry 2, 3, or possibly 6, depending upon the fuel-guzzling potential of a given power plant and distances to be traveled. It is wise to insist upon a more than adequate supply, for the small-boat skipper who cruises far offshore turns his back upon marine bush leagues. The sea is a big place, and it is seldom kind to erring innocents.

From the 18- or 20-foot hull, on up to about 26, there is a sort of middle ground where the outboard may give way to the stern drive, or so-called inboard-outboard. Stern drives may bridge a gap, for they can be used in shoal water or deep, and they are highly efficient four-cycle engines with the added advantage of lower unit tilt. The type has one Achilles' heel: it usurps valuable space in the after cockpit because of a boxlike engine housing that does not permit an angler to belly up to the transom in playing a fish. Inboard engines are positioned under the deck, or above deck level amidships, in which case the engine cover affords a handy working space to cut baits and rig lures.

A well-appointed stern drive certainly extends the safe operating range of small to medium fishing boats; the type is economical and relatively foolproof, highly maneuverable, and better suited to shoal-water operation than an inboard, although still inferior to an outboard in the shallows. Craft so equipped are readily trailered and launched, since the motor's lower unit can be tilted at will and there are no fixed rudders or delicate drive shafts to worry about.

As hull length increases, so do the possibilities for storage, bunks of a sort, and a head. The latter, actually its lack, is one argument against the magnificent wide-open small to medium fishing machines so popular today. Optional heads are offered for most of the largest outboards and stern-drive designs, but seldom appear on smaller craft. This is no great problem with an all-male party, but the ladies are challenging our mastery of angling and most of them like a bit of privacy from time to time. Few of the fully liberated are content to ask that gentlemen study the sea ahead while they . . .

In America, the highly sophisticated offshore sportfisherman was born shortly after

Sportfisherman *Mitchell II*, skippered by Captain
George Seemann, is typical of today's highly efficient
offshore fishing machines. *Photo by Milt Rosko*

World War II. Prior to that time ocean anglers made do with converted lobster boats, banks dories, an assortment of small draggers, and practically anything capable of floating and ranging close-in grounds. True to the Jekyll and Hyde nature of mankind, today's magnificent sporting craft were direct results of an illicit traffic in booze and war. Necessity is a fertile culture for invention.

It started with Prohibition, that ill-fated American Eighteenth Amendment which, in the late twenties and early thirties, spawned a lucrative trade in forbidden liquids. Rumrunners found it necessary to outrun coast-guard vessels, and they did. The solution was a series of very fast planing hulls, many of them powered by resurrected World War I Liberty aircraft engines. These will-o'-the-wisps could outperform anything the government then had in service, and they were recalled in later years when hulls were built for a gentler pastime and the tommy gun had been replaced by a fishing rod. It is a matter of record that the first sand-beach surf landings were made by latter-day pirates in overpowered Jersey sea skiffs. Hotly pursued, they'd slam ashore at full throttle to unload a valuable cargo and disappear into the mist before federal shore parties could be directed to the scene.

Offshore anglers were already thinking about hull design and power for comfortable offshore fishing when World War II called a four-year halt to peaceful development of this new breed. Naval personnel, as well as fishermen, had witnessed the evolution of the fast boat and so all powers built patrol and torpedo boats that, like heavyweight boxer Muhammad Ali's boast, floated like a butterfly and stung like a bee.

Naval small boats were of necessity heavily armed and, although extremely fast, they were fuel guzzlers. Nonetheless, a proper combination of hull form and power gave them speed and maneuverability previously undreamed of. Marine architects, who waited only for peace to resume boatbuilding for sportsmen, sucked their pipes reflectively and prepared blueprints. War had provided new materials for hull forms, new designs, and engines that turned up greater horsepower per pound of weight than anything ever seen on blue water.

Progress was rapid. Rybovich and Pacemaker hulls were among the first truly revolutionary offshore fishing machines. Later, Bertram became a deep-water angler's household word and Hatteras Yacht pioneered fiber glass in the construction of sleek cruisers. Bill Hatch and Tommy Gifford, both great and imaginative charter skippers, had already resurrected the outrigger and the kite. Topside helms, then pretty aboriginal, soon gave way to elaborately equipped flying bridges and tuna towers, initially called "Texas towers."

A fine offshore sportfisherman must be fast, because time elapsed in cruising from slip to fishing ground is time lost in angling. It must be both seaworthy and comfortable in a seaway, for there is no joy in wallowing like a jug in a millrace. Such a craft should boast range sufficient to its needs, plus creature comforts. Dead reckoning is no longer enough in the wheelhouse; one requires a host of electronic black boxes that hum, flicker, and compute ranges, depths, temperatures, and the presence of other craft or floating debris. There is a fully synchronized flying bridge, radio telephone, radio direction finder, a depth sounder, radar, loran, and intercom systems. The modern, sophisticated sportfisherman is a microcosm of a pocket battleship, although its only intended victim is the great game fish of the sea, and its primary task is comfortable, functional operation well beyond harbor soundings.

An offshore cruiser has been defined as "a hole in the water into which man pours his money." The big ones are indeed expensive and they require professional crews, plus much maintenance. Unless a sportsman is prepared to pay the freight, he had best charter. There are degrees of sophistication, each logically tied into a specific sphere of operation.

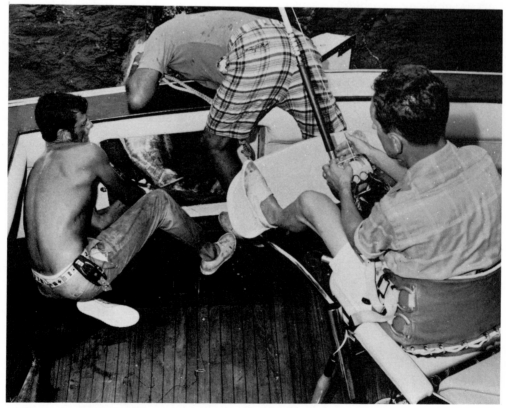

Modern skippers feel that the transom door is more efficient than the time-honored gin pole to bring a big fish aboard. *Photo by Milt Rosko*

Increasingly, small- to medium-sized boats make use of outriggers.

A small ocean sportfisherman ranges from 25 to approximately 36 feet; it can be beautifully equipped, and usually appeals to folk whose budgets squirm at mention of a larger boat. Such craft are surprisingly able and well chosen for angling within, say, 30 miles of shore when the weather is obliging. They can be fitted with suitable flying bridges, outriggers, and all the goodies encompassed in little black boxes. The better models are designed for fishing alone, although they provide creature comforts, including bunks, galleys, and heads. Such a boat is quite capable of challenging any of the big-game fishes, providing that such monsters cavort within safe operating range and in waters that are not too rough.

Most of the vest-pocket fishing machines are single-screw, a little too delicate for heavy work in a crashing sea, and usually limited in the matter of range. No doubt a capable skipper can take them almost anywhere, fuel supply permitting, but there is the matter of comfort and efficiency in playing or landing a huge fish when the ocean is roaring. Single-screw is a disadvantage in a loppy sea because it hampers maneuverability just when that benefit is most needed.

Off Bermuda's Challenger Banks, one fine and screaming afternoon, I watched a capable angler play an estimated 250-pound blue marlin on 30-pound-test line. Following 2 hours of give-and-take combat, superbly waged, he had the billfish beaten and ready for a gaff. Unfortunately, the sea was wild and it proved just about impossible to back down. Time and again, with single-screw propulsion, a wave caught the stern of his charter boat and caused it to veer off just as the mate was about to plant a gaff. Finally, desperate, the skipper attempted to range alongside this tired blue, rather than to back down—and it didn't work. The marlin summoned up one last burst of energy, turned under the transom, and cut a tortured line on the wheel.

If you want the very best for offshore fishing, then it will have to be a well-designed sportfisherman in the 42- to 60-foot bracket, twin screw, and equipped with every

Another of the great modern fishing boats is the
Boston whaler *Outrage. Photo by Kib Bramhall*

Wide open fishing machines, consoles amidships,
are increasingly favored by anglers who cast to fish.

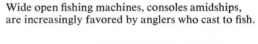

Aquasport's 22-footer is typically arranged for
modern saltwater sport fishing.

MacKenzie-Gray Cuttyhunk bass boat is one of the
first of the classic fishing machines. This one is
owned by Captain Bob Smith, a famed
Cuttyhunk guide.

aid to navigation and angling. These are highly sophisticated machines and are understandably expensive. In this range the traditional $1,000 per foot may well escalate to twice or even three times that figure. There will be certain niceties; in addition to a fast, soft riding hull and an abundance of power and fuel to span distances that may add up to a 150-mile round trip, modern electronic aids are essential. The entire ship must be designed for fishing, yet it should also provide faultless living accommodations. Today's sportfishermen boast such fine sophisticated aids to creature comfort as fully equipped galleys, washers, dryers, freezers, water makers, air-conditioners, ice makers, and even—if you are so inclined—water beds.

While living accommodations will be built in, the cockpit should be spacious and uncluttered, with a modern fighting chair anchored smack center. Supplementary chairs may be ranged to port or starboard aft, for lounging or for playing small game. Rod holders are necessary, usually one built in or attached to either arm of the primary fighting chair, plus additional holders faired into after gunwales. Spare rods and other gear will be stowed in customized compartments or racked under the cabin's roof during a day at sea. Gaffs must be ready to break out, although never underfoot. Shipshape and Bristol fashion on a sportfisherman mean an absolute elimination of clutter. Clear the decks for action applies here as it does on a man-o'-war, and for the same reason.

Every inch of such a craft is designed to complement angling and gracious living, from the intercom system to radio communications and a bank of instruments that determine course, depth, exact position, water temperature, and the presence of other craft in the immediate area. Aerated live-bait tanks will be built in, as will a separate refrigerator to preserve fresh bait, and a fiber-glassed box to receive the smaller gamesters brought aboard. There will be a stout gin pole, although recent years have seen a definite preference for the transom door on highly sophisticated craft.

A practical offshore sportfisherman will be equipped with whip or trussed outriggers. There's much argument over which is most efficient, but all are now made of fiber glass or tempered, lightweight metals, and are easily raised or lowered and secured, depending on necessity. Properly employed, an outrigger's tip will extend to a point just opposite or perhaps slightly aft of the fishing chair so that a knockdown will not send line billowing around angler or crew. Line release pins are easily positioned where they troll baits well outside, or close to the wake, as the skipper or angler desires. Variations are common, but usual practice is to stream two lines from the 'riggers and two "flat" over the transom.

There is an overriding need for the skipper to see what is happening, so his flying bridge should present an unobstructed view of the cockpit and the surrounding sea. Any overhang of cabin roof that prevents unlimited vision is a handicap because the skipper must be able to note every development as a fish rises to the baits, switches from one to another, finally decides to take one, and turns away—hook hopefully in mouth. In addition to the flying bridge, of course, most modern machines include a complete set of synchronized controls in a forward corner of the cockpit, so that the helmsman can be a few feet from his angler and right in the action when that is necessary.

A good skipper is coach and crew chief on the offshore grounds; he is positioned high enough to see what happens and his advice is worth heeding. Usually the captain is first to spot a game fish vectoring in on the baits, and he will communicate his knowledge to the mate and angler below. From that aerie, aloft, a skipper often knows whether a great gladiator has engulfed the bait, or has only stunned it and may come back to take the offering when it is free-spooled. Similarly, once hooks are set and the fisherman's harness is adjusted to wage battle, a skipper initiates offensive maneuvering with rudder and throttle. A quick and easy boat is master of almost any situation, but such a craft must first master the deep-breathing sea on offshore grounds. It can be rough out there, but that's part of the magic. You can always play croquet on a country lawn.

Most of us ship on sophisticated offshore sportfishermen as charter patrons; a very few tournament buffs enjoy the wealth necessary to purchase, crew, and maintain big boats. Of course, it's far cheaper to charter, although fees may seem high. Take a good look at the equipment and the manpower involved. Note that the skipper is sunburned and that his eyes are bloodshot from too much squinting into the pitiless sun and from a work load that often begins before dawn and ends after the last customer has been sent on his happy way—and the next patron insists upon another highball long after dinner.

There are other sport boats and they are important. One is the West Coast party packet that may be 80 feet in length and designed to host a number of passengers on an extended voyage. All creature comforts are assured, plus fishing fit for the green gods of the sea. These queens of the briny sail out of southern California ports, often bound for border or Mexican waters, and they offer royal sport at an astonishingly low price.

Similarly, there are multitudes of party boats, in all tourist areas, which carry greater or lesser numbers of patrons and offer full value. On the Pacific seaboard, these may be called open party boats, or, if you are acid-tongued, "cattle boats," because they carry so many enthusiasts. In the Atlantic, they are "party" or "head" boats. All offer excursions at budget rates, whether the quarry is a long-finned albacore some 40 miles off San Diego, or a tub full of cod and haddock winched out of the depths in the cold Atlantic due east of Gloucester or Nantucket. In chill climes, there will be enclosed cabins, well heated, often featuring efficient galleys. Away down South design changes. You get into broad beam and canopied decks to ward off hot sunlight.

All are sport-fishing operations, whether the quarry is king salmon in Oregon, or a tilefish dredged out of the depths off Long Island. The boats are big, relatively speaking, and well equipped for the task at hand. Bait will be available, and there'll be crewmen to advise and help. Many rent tackle and offer bunks for overnight adventurers, and the big ones all feature well-stocked galleys. Practically all are equipped with electronic equipment that ensures sport while it guarantees safety.

Party boats—and charter craft—have been involved in disaster, but this is rare. Maritime authorities now check passenger-carrying boats and skippers' credentials more rigidly than they did in the past. Overloading is seldom charged today, and few boats venture beyond harbor bounds without electronic aids to navigation that help ensure safety. A patron probably faces less danger afloat than he would at a church social. Unless he's stupid enough to stick a 3/0 forged hook in his thumb!

Finally, perhaps, there is the houseboat—a mobile campsite that is designed for leisurely cruising in sheltered waters. Never designed to challenge a heavy sea, this descendant of the old Mississippi River stern-wheeler is flat-bottomed and variously propelled, often with outboard motors. It can be a superb choice in shallow, inland bays or estuaries where weather is unlikely to threaten disaster, and it really excels as a floating base camp in a sun-washed back country. Smaller fishing skiffs are either towed or carried on deck.

Citizens who charter may be perplexed about the matter of tipping after a day at sea. Often the mate's salary is small and much of his income will depend on gratuities, but the key word is there. This *is* a gratuity, offered for good service rendered. If a mate is helpful and handy, he deserves a stipend at least equaling 10 percent of the agreed-upon charter fee. If he is lackadaisical and surly, he deserves nothing. Good mates usually collect tips well above the standard 10 percent figure, and poor ones cry about cheap-skate patrons.

A skipper, on the other hand, has stated a specific fee for a day on the grounds and he is entitled to no more, unless you feel that he has performed so well that some reward is due.

Prior to shipping aboard, it is well to have an understanding about the disposition of any catch. In some areas skippers offer no objection when a patron takes all the fish he has caught. Elsewhere, the captain thinks it fair to give his customers a fish or two, while he retains the greater portion of a catch to sell or exhibit. Local custom often governs usage, and discussion prior to boarding will prevent hard feelings later.

Any boat serves as a fisherman's seven-league boots. Whether it is a "tin" skiff used on a coastal estuary or a full-blooded cruiser droning out beyond harbor bounds, the angler's transportation and fighting platform is always specialized and equipped to do a prescribed job well. Each hull and power package should be chosen with care and tailored to use. There is just no such thing as an all-purpose fishing boat, but there are lots of boats that scale Olympian heights for specific tasks.

Rods neatly racked, a Florida party boat heads for the fishing grounds. *Photo by Milt Rosko*

GENTLEMEN, START YOUR ENGINES ～13

Beach Buggies, Airplanes— Mechanization on the Sea Rim

Away back in the autumn of 1949, sixty-two surf-casting enthusiasts met on a grassy upland adjacent to Nauset Beach, at Orleans, Massachusetts, to organize a club. Since sportsmen are forever fond of banding together, this was no world-shaking event, yet the association these men formed was dedicated to a new concept. Each of the sixty-two owned a motor vehicle specially rigged to run sand beaches, and each recognized a need to cooperate with coastal town fathers, to operate within the law and, most of all, to prevent littering, pollution, and the destruction of natural resources through mechanization.

Today, the Massachusetts Beach Buggy Association counts its members in the thousands; its code of ethics has been adopted by similar organizations on all American coasts, and has guided the federal government in controlling vehicular traffic on every national seashore.

The code was written by Francis W. Sargent, then a recently mustered-out line officer of the 10th Mountain Division and director of the Bay State's Division of Marine Fisheries, and by me. Sargent later became governor of Massachusetts, and he still boasts MBBA Number 1, awarded by popular acclaim. Mine, MBBA-13, was pure chicanery. Since I was chief cook, I simply appropriated it, while other charter members observed a more democratic process and drew numbers out of a long-beaked swordfisherman's cap.

Since the code is important, I think it wise to quote all fourteen points. Whether or not a mechanized angler boasts membership in any of the beach buggy associations, common sense dictates certain rules of conduct. The following is MBBA's version, almost universally used as a prototpye.

1. To enter and leave beaches in prescribed ways.
2. To eliminate speeding and reckless driving.
3. To respect local ordinances and the rights of property owners, particularly in regard to parking.
4. To offer aid to any fisherman or buggy owner in trouble on the beach.
5. To respect picnicking and bathing groups by (a) avoiding them whenever possible and, (b) by slowing to minimum speed when passing picnicking or bathing groups.
6. Do not litter the beach with any type of trash. Carry all trash and garbage off the beach and dispose of it in the proper receptacles or dump areas.
7. To leave no dead fish or bait of any kind above the high water mark. Throw dead fish and bait back into the surf where they will be found by gulls and other scavengers.
8. Use public toilets when available. When not, respect the beach and carry a portable toilet in the buggy with you, and use it in the buggy. Refuse then to be carried off the beach and disposed of in the proper manner.

9. To avoid overcrowding any one area and elbowing other fishermen out of their chosen spots. This is particularly important where surfmen without buggies are concentrated.

10. To leave the track when a halt is made, so that other buggies will not be forced to detour.

11. To fill in holes after getting stuck, and to avoid indiscriminately crisscrossing tracks.

12. To observe the rules of common courtesy on the beach.

13. To simplify passing of vehicles meeting head on on a single track, the driver who has the dunes on the right will be required to turn out of the track to the right. This rule to be tempered by common sense in difficult circumstances.

14. It is requested that all members carry extraterritorial insurance on their vehicles.

Beach buggies weren't spawned in war, but the internal combustion engine certainly impressed a few million soldiers who trudged across Europe and Asia during World War II. When the fishermen among these reluctant warriors came home, their thoughts quite naturally turned to mechanization. Why walk when you can ride? In many areas, but particularly in the American Northeast, surf casters began to feel underprivileged unless they owned wheezing Model-A Fords.

Model-A Fords, now collectors' items, were the first of the practical beach buggies. This one was used by Frank and Dick Woolner during the late forties.

Early Model-A Ford was intricately rigged for
beach fishing.

Of more recent vintage, a four-wheel-drive carryall
—owned by Frank Woolner—is rigged for
beach work.

In those days—and I still hate myself for giving my last Model-A to a friend—one of Henry's masterpieces (now collectors' items) could be purchased for less than $50. Equipped with oversized flotation tires, and lovingly maintained, such a machine could chug over the dunes and carry three or four anglers, plus basic gear, to hot spots previously inaccessible. If the radiator boiled over, as it often did, we simply bailed salt water out of the surf and poured it in.

There were teething troubles. We all thought that a light motor vehicle was essential, and we had no real appreciation of adequate running gear. The first Model-A Fords to hit the beaches were fitted with prewar "balloon tires," or war-surplus airplane tires, which worked, although they tended to wear rapidly. We fooled around with military sand shoes, again war surplus and well made, but they were six-ply and therefore much too stiff for the light Ford. Someone discovered the then 820 x 15 four-ply, and that was it. Deflated to 8 or 10 pounds of pressure, that tire served more than a decade of anglers and is still wistfully recalled by old-timers.

With the exception of the military jeep, war-surplus vehicles never really paid their way in that slice of time. Four-wheel-drive army ambulances and staff cars, amphibious Jeeps and Dukws arrived and departed. Most of them churned mightily and burned a tremendous amount of fuel. It should be added that we were poor in those days. Anyone who suggested the purchase of a brand-new vehicle for beach fishing would have been ticked off as a playboy or a dreamer. New motor vehicles were reserved for the highway; beach buggies were patched together with the proverbial baling wire and chewing gum.

Tubular metal or plastic rod holders, bolted to front bumper, tote rods on the beach. The angler is Stan Gibbs, a famed North Atlantic surfman.

Sometime in the early fifties a few pioneers introduced the big, elaborate camp on wheels, usually a walk-in truck or coach-camper, the latter mounted on a pickup chassis. These early birds were all two-wheel-drive models, and some of them still grind over the dunes. For some twenty years Jack Townsend of Shrewsbury, Massachusetts, has employed a 1941 Ford walk-in, beautifully appointed with creature comforts and scrupulously maintained. Jack has a modern four-wheel-drive Jeep Wagoneer as a chase car and prime mover for his boat, but the old walk-in seems indestructible. Equipped with positraction and 890 x 15 flotation tires, it humps along like a medium tank and it is a comfortable camp on wheels. Jack's truck sleeps four people on foam-rubber mattresses, and it boasts a chemical toilet, shower bath, propane-fueled refrigerator, galley, and lights. There is a CB radio, a winch to drag a boat, and duffel compartments that hold all sorts of fishing equipment.

Once we made wry jokes about ancillary equipment, noting that "first thing you know they'll have a television set and a helicopter on a rooftop rack." The chopper never materialized, but lots of big home-on-wheels buggies boast TV, the antennae strangely incongruous on a wild beach where the terns swoop overhead and the surf mutters or roars. Increasingly, we utilize the printed circuit, the marvels of electronics, and the advances of technology to tame a wilderness. And then we have the unmitigated gall to declare that we look for solitude and life in the raw.

The walk-in truck, possibly a former conveyor of milk or bread, is superbly designed for use as a fisherman's camp on wheels. It is spacious, maneuverable, and ideally suited to specialized rigging. Strangely, in an age of motorized camping, few vehicles of this type are equipped with four-wheel drive. In fact, those offered by recreational camper outlets usually are fitted with dual rear wheels that are an abomination on the beach and suitable only for highway and hardpan travel. For a back-country angler, the present production walk-in camper is an expensive white elephant, no great joy on the road, and impossible in the boondocks. It is a fine choice for the "nature lover" who is satisfied with commercial campgrounds where water and electricity are piped in, bugs are regularly sprayed with insecticides, and a roofed-over area features square dancing nightly.

Practical walk-ins are custom-made. You can buy a factory model properly rigged for off-highway work, but it will be very expensive, and it will be necessary to insist upon options that the makers seem to view as impossible. The best bet is to acquire a used bread truck and convert it in a home workshop. There are no very difficult conversions; the basics lie in a proper selection of flotation tires and distribution of weight. You will want most of the load aft. Remember this, and 90 percent of the battle is won. Positraction is an aid, almost approximating four-wheel drive. A four-speed transmission is helpful, indeed almost essential.

With one of these big jobs, you will require tires in the 950 x 15 or 890 x 15 class, usually six-ply to take the weight. Don't think in terms of speed; the big buggies must move slowly, because they are always loaded with creature comforts and equipment. The best of them grind along in first or second gear on soft sand, capable of moving faster, but never urged, because this would put an operator in the glass business. Broken glass, that is.

Beach buggies have evolved. By the mid-sixties, enthusiasts began to think in terms of brand-new vehicles, either customized or easily converted to sand-dune travel. The big rig remains a camp on wheels, but now there is a trend toward the four-wheel-drive coach-camper, never so practical or spacious as a walk-in on the beach, but easier to acquire at reasonable cost and possibly superior because it is suited to other uses. Sans camper, the pickup becomes a general-purpose carrier and a workhorse.

Mechanization triumphant! A North Atlantic regular employs a coach-camper (equipped with all comforts, including television), plus a modern four-wheel-drive chase car that is also used as a prime mover to launch and recover a heavy surfboat.

Live-in beach buggies lined up on a North Atlantic sand beach.

Whatever the big rig, bearing surface will be important. We need tires that will suffice on the highway and still prove adequate on a soft sand beach. There is no need for "bald" shoes, but there is good argument for the high-walled flotation types. Low profile has its uses, but not on a beach. There, you will want something that will mush out and *track*—not grip. For the same reason, snow treads or knobs are the worst possible choices for sand driving. Ordinary road treads are best and, where considerable weight is a factor, install tubes. Tubeless tires are fine with light, modern chase cars, because weight is minimal and tires need not be deflated to the perilous levels where there is danger of rolling at the rim.

There is an unfortunate belief that any four-wheel-drive vehicle can go anywhere. It can't! Unless flotation tires are fitted and properly deflated, the four-by-four can hang up quite as miserably as the two-wheel-drive machine and, even if it progresses after a fashion, there will be much wear on motor and clutch, plus overheating and subsequent damage. Proper tires and deflation are necessary, and this is true whether you essay the task with a Universal Jeep or a huge camp on wheels.

Periodically, I am stymied by folk who request advice on the right tires and pressures to run a beach. I can't tell them, because the answer depends on so many factors, such as the weight of the loaded buggy and the consistency of sand to be negotiated. At Daytona Beach, Florida, you can forget deflation and whip along at road speeds on tires inflated to road pressures. Don't try it at Provincetown, where the sand is deep sugar. Weight will make a difference; my Chevy four-wheel-drive carryall, lightly loaded, will zoom over any dune with tires balanced at 14 pounds of air. If I add two or three passengers, plus their duffel, I must inflate to at least 15 or 16 pounds. The sand driver will find it necessary to experiment in order to choose the pressure best suited to his vehicle and load on a given beach.

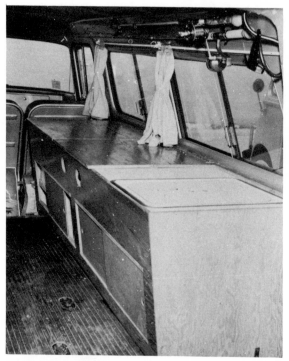

Compartmented refrigerator, propane stove, and sink are covered to provide bunk space at night.

Fresh water is gravity-fed from a tank in a roof rack. Light rods are rigged above. Stove cover hinges back in use.

I don't think there is any need for custom-built wide-rimmed wheels. You need adequate clearance, to avoid plowing sand, and you need flotation. The tires should be high-walled, not low profile. Nylon construction is better than rayon, because it does not disintegrate with heat. Bald tires may be most efficient on the beach, but most of us find it necessary to travel over highways, and a bald tire is slippery, dangerous, and often illegal. Even the so-called sand tire, with its squiggly tread, can be very bad news on a wet hardtop.

There's always lots of help when tires must be changed on the beach.

So what do you choose for a given vehicle? In recent years tire designations have undergone much change, and dealers seem to be as perplexed as consumers. The old 820 x 15 four-ply is just about forgotten, although it was ideally suited to any light machine used on the beach. Today, the 900 x 15 is probably closest, but be sure that it is high-walled and nylon reinforced. Low profile may be fine for dragging on a hardpan highway, but it won't do in sugar.

Light vehicles, such as the Universal Jeep, Land Rover, and Toyota, require tires in the modern 850 x 15 class, four-ply rated. They must be limber and prone to mush out at low pressure. Width is important, but width is just one requirement. The sand tire *must be soft*. You track; you don't dig out. Beginners who feel that they can gun out of any bog-down are mistaken; they'll simply go down. Rapidly.

Larger tires are required on heavier machines. A carryall or suburban will need something like the present L-78 950 x 15 nylon high flotation type, again four-ply. The same basic shoe, 890 x 15, 950 x 15, or larger, will be used with big walk-ins and coach-campers, although these will be six-ply or even eight-ply where weight is excessive. It is wise to use tubes on the big rigs, although tubeless tires are adequate on smaller vehicles. Practical operating pressures always depend upon buggy weight and the consistency of sand on a given beach.

Now I am sure to be accused of dodging a question: how much pressure? There is no pat answer, because ideal tire pressure will depend on such variables as the weight of the vehicle, its load, and the terrain. Some beaches are hard, and others are very soft. A mechanized angler must personally determine that pressure which is ideal, under existing conditions, for the machine he drives. There is no norm.

Carry a good tire gauge, and be very sure that pressures are balanced. In sand driving, there should be no ounce of difference between the inflation of opposing tires. If the right front shoe is blown up to 15 pounds, then the left front shoe should be precisely equal—else it will drag and dig. The same equalization is important on rear tires, for they generally provide driving force. There is a general reluctance to deflate, because citizens worry about ruining good tires. They may do so, but without deflating they ensure greater stress on clutch and engine and cooling system. Penny-wise strategy can be costly.

There is always an optimum pressure for best results on a given sand beach. If the tires are well chosen, this will be far from dangerous, with no chance of creasing or rolling of rim. You can generally deflate, safely, to a point just above creasing. When this happens, look for trouble, but don't worry about low pressures above the creasing point. At low speeds, and all beach speeds are low, the shoe will take it. Even on a hard highway, traveling from sand dune to the nearest gasoline station, there'll be no difficulty if you maintain a low speed. Heat is the destroyer, and heat cannot build up unless friction is introduced.

Once, manual transmissions were necessary in vehicles used off the highway. This is no longer so, and the automatic transmission is now far better suited to beach work than is standard stick shift. The automatics are no longer delicate, accident-prone mechanisms; they are both tough and efficient. Indeed, there is now less difficulty with the automatic than with the stick shift. For a beach driver, the automatic offers one very important benefit.

With stick shift you start in low or low-low, and then progressively bump up. A very experienced driver can do this without difficulty, but most of us lose some momentum while shifting. Since sand is both soft and damnably retarding, the tendency is to shift too slowly and therefore belabor the clutch. An automatic transmission cancels out human error; it is smooth and efficient, mechanically ironing out the faults of human time lag.

Salt is a destroyer, hence vehicles used by marine anglers tend to rust out and corrode more rapidly than those driven over inland highways. The very best defense is a thorough washing with fresh water after each excursion, but this is sometimes impossible. Undercoating has its champions and detractors; certainly salt moisture works its evils under any film. In some coastal areas, beach drivers prefer a periodic spraying of underparts with fuel or linseed oil. Sand should always be whisk-broomed out because it contains salt and will hasten rusting.

On the beach you will need certain accessories. A suitable jack is important, because flat tires are always possible. Sand is soft, so a hardwood plank—to support the jack—must be carried. Maybe you can find a hunk of suitable driftwood, or maybe you can't. A hardwood plank is insurance. You will want a suitable towrope or chain—hopefully to help other unfortunates, but perhaps to help you. A shovel is indispensable; it can be one of the folding war-surplus infantry types, or a standard spade, but it must be there. And you will need a good tire gauge. These are basic requirements. Carry them or stay away from ocean beaches.

Regardless of equipment, you're going to get stuck! Accept this and learn how to get out. A beginner always feels that power is the answer, and he tries to gun out of a bog-down. This never works in sugar; indeed, it is the worst possible solution because it compounds difficulties. Spinning wheels dig like frightened sand bugs. Pretty soon you'll be suspended, with a new flood making. That sort of thing is coronary-inducing.

Usually, overinflated tires are the primary reason for digging in. A lot of penny-wise souls hate to deflate, because they feel that this will ruin expensive shoes. They forget that hard tires ensure ruinous stresses on engine, clutch, and cooling system. At the standard low beach speeds, tires are safe until they begin to crease. In this sugary arena you must have flotation and you must track, rather than dig.

Having driven into an abnormally soft spot (assuming that tires are properly deflated), the first step is fore and aft tracking. Go forward a foot or two, then halt without application of brakes, and back slowly. With any kind of luck each pass will pack sand and "make a track." Raw power won't work, and spinning wheels are bad news. Often it will be necessary to deflate all around. The difference may be as little as 2 or 3 pounds of pressure. A veteran, finding that his machine is laboring, always halts and lets the air out. Sometimes no simple procedure works, and there's a necessity for mule work. Break out planks and a jack. Sweat a little; you surely will—if there's a coming tide and you're stuck well down on the shingle!

Jack each wheel separately, first paying attention to that which is most abysmally mired. Get the thing well up, and then shovel sand into the depression. Stick a plank under the tire; on most ocean beaches driftwood will be available. Almost anything solid will do, so long as it provides a foundation. Having built a track, it is usually best to back out, because there's no certainty that the soft spot does not extend beyond a bog-down location. You came in blithely, so you should be able to retreat. If that isn't possible, due to a steep slope, examine the terrain ahead and plan operations. Often a mushy spot is no more than a depression where the ebb has pocketed water. Very suddenly you'll be very fond of shovels, jacks, and hardwood planks.

Old-stagers are seldom caught napping, but hinterlanders on a sea rim for the first time court another disaster; they park sleep-in buggies too close to a supposed high-tide mark. Tides vary in height, a thing adequately calculated and predicted. If today's height is, say, 9 feet, and tomorrow's is 10, you know that the water level will rise a foot under normal conditions. Unfortunately, that doesn't tell the tale. If an unannounced onshore gale whips the sea, that tide will arrive early and may well peak far over the estimated height. A full-scale hurricane can double the flood.

Years ago, parked on a northern ocean beach during a northeaster, I awoke in some impossible midwatch to find the buggy shuddering under blasts of wind and swirling waves. With each successive ground swell I felt the machine sinking, settling in a morass of sand and hissing salt water. The racing brine had already swept across the floorboards, so we were parked in about 2 feet of angry suds. A panicky look at a wristwatch proved that the time of flood was well past, so there was nothing to do but doze and worry and wait. The worst should have been over, and it was.

The cloud-curdled dawn found a line of beach buggies mired, right down on their chassis. We all slaved with shovels and jacks and planks, meanwhile nursing drowned engines with WD-40 moisture repellent. Those vehicles that started were pressed into service to yank others out of position and up on the high dunes, for another tide was coming, pushed by a manic wind. That was an expensive mistake, for most of the buggies had brake drums packed with sand, and the water had damaged provisions and equipment.

Love the sea, but never trust it. Read the tide tables and listen to weather reports. Scan the sky and be wary about flat calms that often precede abrupt changes in wind direction. Remember that a gale force onshore wind will add X number of feet to the estimated height of tide. It isn't very joyous to awake at 3 A.M. to find an expensive beach buggy buffeted by waves and sinking into the sand. I still have nightmares about dropping a hand out of my bunk to find 6 inches of cold salt water coursing over the floorboards!

Every beach buggy is rigged for action, and rigging depends upon necessity. Usually, there is a need for duffel compartments and rod holders, the latter positioned on front bumpers or rooftop racks. Big rigs feature creature comforts, while smaller chase cars are geared to use as prime movers for boats, and light reconnaissance or angler transportation. Where surf fishermen are concerned, vehicles are used for fishing, and not for joyriding. The beach buggy is a means to an end. Big rigs are camps on wheels, and chase vehicles are employed to follow the fish and provide basic transportation for active anglers. Any carryall or suburban can be a sort of transition, rigged to sleep two and equipped with some creature comforts. Obviously, such a vehicle will lack the necessary space for comfortable living room, but it is nimble and immediately mobile. The type is ideally suited to use by a couple of hard-rock anglers who can thrive on basic amenities; it is not the answer for a family.

Houseboats are grand living quarters in sheltered
waters. The small outboard powered craft ensures
mobility in fishing a back country.
Photo by Max Hunn

ATVs (all-terrain vehicles) now crowd the sports pages, yet most of them are unsuitable for beach use by serious anglers. The great mass range from tracked machines to those that employ huge flotation tires—the rolligon concept—plus motorcycles and so-called "dune buggies."

Most ATVs are fine for an afternoon of cruising in the back country, but they lack the load-carrying capability so necessary to a mechanized angler. There simply is no room for tackle boxes, rods, and ancillary gear, let alone more than a couple of passengers.

Similarly, there is a subtle difference between a true beach buggy and a dune buggy. The former is designed for off-highway transportation and duffel carrying, while the latter is a small, joyriding machine. Properly rigged, some of the dune-buggy types can be used as chase cars, but it is unfortunately true that most of them are manned by youthful adventurers who care little about fishing and desire only to crisscross the coastal dunes at high speed.

Improper use of ATVs and dune buggies has worked a hardship on dedicated sportsmen, because authorities in coastal townships tend to ban all off-highway vehicles when a few drivers persist in destroying anchoring dune grass and endangering bathers on public beaches. The mechanized angler can only hope that law-enforcement personnel will differentiate between the destructive joyrider and the fisherman who travels slowly on established tracks. There is, of course, no excuse for the occasional angler who insists upon using a chase car as a dune buggy. Those who litter, tear up anchoring uplands, and endanger bathers or other fishermen by traveling at high speed should be ruled off the beaches.

Of course, the internal-combustion engine is not confined to terra firma. If you must be a nit-picker, mechanization on ocean beaches began with Wilbur and Orville Wright, a couple of bicycle mechanics who flew a rickety, motor-driven kite off the sand dunes at Kill Devil Hills, North Carolina, in 1903. There is nothing to suggest that Wilbur and Orville ever took a sabbatical to catch channel bass, but they *might have*—and I hereby invent a rumor.

American fish-spotter aircraft vectors over a
Russian commercial vessel off the North
Atlantic Coast.

Super-Cub fish-spotter aircraft is fitted with a
long-range cruising tank under the fuselage.

In those days the Wright brothers couldn't care less about airplanes, per se; they just wanted a machine capable of spotting fish! Any angler will agree that this is logical.

Airplanes are great fish spotters; indeed, they are employed by a host of commercials who seek, among others, menhaden, mackerel, tuna, and swordfish. Some sport fishermen consider this aerial reconnaissance less than cricket, while others regularly employ flying machines. A gull's-eye view is revealing, and I see nothing reprehensible about locating schools of game fish from the air. A rod-and-line angler will still find it necessary to land, to wade into the surf, or to launch a boat in order to close with the quarry. Whether we like it or not, light planes have become very important tools. The flying machine offers rapid transportation and a bird's-eye view. Both are valuable.

There are marine fishing grounds, usually back in the world's boondocks, where you go in by bush plane or you do not go in at all. That's an oversimplification, because it is always possible to journey tortuously by land or boat, as the pioneers did. We, in our hurry-hurry civilization, can't take the time, so we fly. We span the continents in huge, supersonic jets, and then we charter lighter kites to shuttle over the rain forests of the tropics or the forbidding granite ridges of the North to reach paradisiacal coasts or brackish rivers where game fish are still very plentiful and, hopefully, naïve.

Statistics indicate that a citizen incurs less risk on a commercial jetliner than on a back-country light plane ferrying passengers over rough country at low altitude. In either case, the danger is slight. Pilots are seldom bent on suicide, and they never take chances. Like man, the modern airplane is capable of enduring stresses and strains well beyond the limits of belief. Most of them come in safely and the casualty rate is low—even on bush planes where maintenance is questionable and well-being seems to depend on that old air-force bromide—"a wing and a prayer."

One springtime Hal Lyman and I repaired to San José, Costa Rica, by jet out of Miami, and then boarded a single-engined craft to fly to the Colorado River, which serves as a border between that country and Nicaragua. It developed that the motor of our chartered bush plane was being torn down and reassembled immediately prior to departure. Parts were scattered over a dusty hangar floor, and wildly gesticulating Latin types rushed hither and yon while a hot and steady wind blew sand particles over the assembled, oily parts.

Commendably, they got it together and brewed up a hell of a storm with the propeller in a wheel-chocked hangar test. Then we piled duffel aboard and got strapped in. As usual, the aircraft was tremendously overloaded, by American standards, but our pilot seemed unconcerned. He smoked a final cigarette and cast it aside. We taxied well out on a grass strip and turned into the wind. Then our hero checked his instruments and, before pushing the throttle forward, crossed himself.

I am no enemy of religion and I respect all faiths, but I do not believe in asking the Supreme Being to bless an undertaking that is questionable from the outset. Later, our host, Carlos Barrantes, said that all Spanish pilots cross themselves before taking off. I wondered, but I did not ask him, whether all Spanish pilots also circle for an interminable time while an overloaded aircraft gains height, and then shake their heads before boring into a cloud mass that conceals a rugged mountain slope?

Our pilot was accurate and we drilled through the mist into bright sunlight over a seemingly endless tropical forest. There were few emergency landing strips, only an occasional cleared patch on a jungle finca. We were jolly and full of savoir faire, but if that aircraft's single engine had ever sputtered, I guarantee that black despair would have replaced levity. It is no joke to go down in the bush.

In Central America, in Africa, in remote Canada—in fact, anywhere in the outback regions, including those of our country—a basic air strip is likely to be a rather rough hunk of topography. You come down over palm or pine and sometimes have to buzz the strip to chase the cows off. Then, on final approach, trees loom up and the rough sod leaps toward extended wheels. The plane touches down, bounces, rattles alarmingly, and seems to slam into the hostile earth. Bush planes must be the toughest mechanical contraptions ever invented, because they take this punishment regularly without disintegrating. Accidents are rare.

Take off can be quite as exhilarating. Once, again in Central America, we gunned off a runway bordered by tall palms. There were four of us crammed into the cockpit, plus the usual overload of freight, and the Chinaman strapped in to my right must have weighed 300 pounds. He was a delightful guy with a patent smile and none of my apprehensions. I add, as a sidebar, that there are lots of Chinamen in Central America, plus lots of ex-Nazi officers, and other expatriates who are here for one reason or another. Perhaps the climate is healthy.

It was a long run and we took the air sluggishly. Mesmerized, I watched palm trees swimming up ahead of the windscreen. They are feathery trees on postcards, but each frond is leathery, tough, and as unresisting as a scalloped chunk of plywood. In this case, the wheels must have cleared by a matter of inches, and then we were in clear air with nothing but jungle below and the usual worries about stuffed clouds over the mountains.

The pilot was a slim, aesthetic type, hardly a prototype of the accepted soldier of fortune. He seemed a gentle man, but first impressions can be deceptive. It turned out that he'd flown fighters and was a very resolute killer, but only in a cause he deemed right. Recently sprung from a Nicaraguan jail, our birdman was, in the words of a Spanish friend, "a bad boy, but he's learned his lesson."

He didn't cross himself and he flew a straight course to our base, landing so smoothly that there was no rumble of undercarriage.

One of the irritating things about commercial airline travel is a general reluctance to carry long fishing rods. Unless they are transported in crush-proof containers, such sticks will be mangled by baggage smashers. A nomadic angler must keep this in mind and choose weapons that are jointed and easily taken down. With the single exception of the fly rod, I prefer one-piece sticks—but not for long journeys. Fortunately, an increasing number of tackle manufacturers now offer a wide range of take-down rods. Only the true high-surf rod is lacking—because of excessive cost in manufacture. If the future witnesses sufficient demand, these can be produced. In fact I have one, handcrafted by Fenwick, but not currently in production.

Bush pilots are far more accommodating than the antiseptic commercial airline jockeys; these worthies will shrug their shoulders, grin, and tote just about anything. I have flown into wilderness ponds with a canoe strapped to the top of a pontoon and, on many occasions, stuck 11-foot surf rods back into the fuselages of single-engined aircraft. A few pilot-anglers have devised strut or underwing racks for rods so that they'll be handy immediately after landing on a remote beach.

Ocean beach landing and takeoff are prohibited in most of our metropolitan areas, undoubtedly for good reason, but there are vast reaches of seafront—even along heavily populated American coasts—where the light plane is an angler's flying carpet. Quite naturally, aviators study the terrain and prefer touchdown points that are firm and reasonably level. Runout and takeoff—with a light airplane—are surprisingly quick, for sand acts as a natural brake in landing, and there is usually a good deal of wind on an open beach to buoy an aircraft's wings.

As a result, vast areas of wonderful fishing grounds—which would otherwise be inaccessible to the fisherman whose time is limited—have been opened up. In addition to remote beaches, there are countless uninhabited islands where angling is superb, and there is no competition aside from the odd boat or another small party of flying fishermen. With a light plane it is often profitable to reconnoiter the waters, find schools of fish, and then land to work them over with sporting tackle.

Air spotting, for rod and line anglers, is particularly valuable with such surf-running species as striped bass and channel bass; it can be quite as profitable with the monsters offshore. While it takes a bit of practice to identify species, fish are easily seen from an altitude of 200 or 300 feet, or higher, where marlin or broadbill are sought. If billfish are the quarry, the plane will be in CB radio communication with a boat on the surface, vectoring it in. Modern surf casters also use CB, although they can be apprised of schooling gamesters by the plane's circling or dipping a wing—even by throttling down overhead while the pilot shouts basic advice.

Spider Andresen is an angler and a sport flyer. His brother, John ("Winkie") Andresen, is a professional spotter pilot for the commercial fleet, so the two often get together on a busman's holiday. Spider clips a CB walkie-talkie to his hip, while Winkie orbits overhead, offering advice.

"A school of bluefish at one o'clock, 50 yards! That's a good cast, a little beyond them, but they're turning out. Okay, start reeling. They're coming! Reel faster and make that thing pop!"

Wham! Spider drives the hooks home in a big chopper, and his brother, circling overhead, makes ribald remarks. Spotting, aided by a CB radio, is a tremendous help, yet it never automatically ensures success.

For some years, those of us who roamed Cape Cod's surf for striped bass started each long weekend by chartering a light plane to locate fish. Almost always we found them, a school here or there, loafing around the offshore bars or concentrated in a slough. Strategy then indicated beach-buggy travel to the hot spot and much inspired labor with big surf sticks. Sometimes it worked. On other occasions, when we knew that the bass would feed at night, daylight air spotting failed to pay off because the fish would move with tidal currents and turn up at some remote location that was a biological desert at high noon.

Where fish are actively feeding, air-ground cooperation really pays off. Lots of Virginia and North Carolina surfmen use aircraft to find big red drum rooting in sloughs, after which precisely placed baits result in trophy battlers on tight lines. Tarpon and cobia are easily detected as they range over fairly shallow waters in feeding or migrating, and any surface-feeding school of fish, such as blues, can be pinpointed. On one Costa Rica trip, prior to landing on a rough strip, we flew the length of Rio Parismina and found two tremendous schools of sabalo rushing small bait on top. No sight could be more welcome to the eyes of a traveling angler. After we'd landed, distributed suitable payment to a host of eager children who—in Central and South America—are always on hand to tote luggage, there was no delay in boarding an outboard and pushing off.

Offshore spotting may be quite as efficient a sport-fishing method as it is in commercial operations. Airplane and boat communicate by CB radio, and the boat is fitted with a loudspeaker mounted high, so that all hands can hear the spotter detailing pertinent information. Clock hours and boat lengths are used as units of direction and distance. Ideally, the aviator and the skipper should be sympatico, used to each other's patter and needs. The pilot's monologue goes something like this:

"Okay, Captain Turtle, I got a swordfish over here at four o'clock. He's pretty deep and swimming from port to starboard. Come around to five o'clock. Keep coming— he's at one o'clock, about fifteen boat lengths. Dammit, you've gone too far! Come back to eleven o'clock. Hold it there. You're looking good. He's eight boat lengths at twelve o'clock, swimming from port to starboard. Better come a touch to starboard to cut him off.

"Now you're looking good at five boats. The bait is right. Beautiful! He's coming up a little. You should see him in a few seconds. Watch out! He turned around and is swimming starboard to port. Come port! Hard port! More, more! Keep coming to port—three boats at ten o'clock.

"Steady up! Only three boats and the bait is perfect. He sees it! There's the wiggle! He's got it!"

Fast aircraft are unsuitable for spotting, and impossible if beach landing and takeoff are contemplated. The swifties are great if you simply want to reconnoiter a ground and see where the charter boats are concentrated, but they are far too sophisticated for close-range examination and, peradventure, to land immediately and take advantage of a promising situation. For this you need a machine that is capable of flying low and slow, versatile enough to land and take off on soft sand. Light, single-engined tail-draggers appear most efficient, so long as they can carry enough fuel for a long day's fishing.

Curiously, float planes and light amphibians are not very suitable for a saltwater sportsman. With either, a water landing must be made in some sheltered bay or estuary that may be far from the open ocean. Most amphibians require a considerable hardpan strip to get off, or to land on terra firma, and they need just as much space to operate on a reasonably quiet bay. They are comparatively heavy and most of them have the glide angle of a brick when bereft of power. Featherweight float planes are better, yet they are limited because they can't touch down on a beach or land on rough water.

Helicopters seem an obvious solution for the marine angler, and they are used to a limited extent. Problems are associated with excessive cost and maintenance. A small chopper sells for something like four times the price of a well-equipped tail-dragger, and it ensures no major benefits other than vertical takeoff and descent. There is little luggage space in a small helicopter, speed is minimal, and the ability to hover is questionable, since you can see a great deal of ocean from the cockpit of a light plane flying just above stalling speed.

Until there is another major breakthrough, the back-country angler's airplane will be a very light, single-engined tail-dragger—a Super Piper Cub, a Cessna, or a Helio-Courier. The last named is America's improvement over Hitler's famed Fieseler Storch, an aircraft that could land on the proverbial dime and take off on a pfennig.

Some sportsmen, usually those graying at the temples and the brain, war against the internal combustion engine; they protest the use of beach buggies, ATVs, and airplanes. Admittedly, all must be utilized with reason and under intelligent controls, but nobody has yet succeeded in turning the clock back. We are an automated people and we progress, for better or for worse, with the sound of engines in our ears.

If we use them wisely, the engines will be no more than an extension of the basic oar and sail.

FISH FOR CASH ⌁14

Rod and Line Commercial Fishing

Coastal residents, since the first crack of recorded time, have always considered it their right to "make a buck on the bay." The moonlighter who spears eels through a winter coating of ice on a brackish coastal estuary, the clammer who sells his allotted harvest of soft-shells or cherrystones, the rod and line angler who peddles each catch to a nearby fish house or restaurant, all subscribe to the same reasoning: Why can't a man enjoy a sport and, at the same time, realize some monetary return?

Why not? If any given species is plentiful enough to sustain a commercial fishery, if the laws of the land permit this harvest, if marine biologists conclude that a renewable resource permits such exploitation, then the rod and line angler who sells his catch is no pariah. He *is* a commercial fisherman.

Make no mistake about this: anyone who sells fish is, by inescapable definition, a commercial. The wicket gets sticky only when one or both of these forever argumentative groups, sport or commercial, favors hypocrisy. Then we have the holier-than-thou gentleman who wants to sell rod and line catches but who raucously seeks a legislative ban on netting, long-lining, dragging, or other basically commercial activities.

Or, conversely, the businessman of the sea who feels that it is his sole right to harvest the available resource for cash, and that anglers should be prevented from selling any portion of a meager catch. In either case, class legislation is favored, with whatever lobby capable of making the most noise (and delivering the best bundle of votes) triumphing over biological honesty and moral right.

Unfortunately, a lot of sportsmen defeat their own ends. In some states, where the rod and reel commercial is scorned by fellow fishermen as a mercenary and a traitor, self-appointed sportsmen have backed legislation that denies the right of a citizen to sell any rod and line catch, or limits the daily bag, while true commercial operators, working the same grounds, are licensed to fill their holds with the same fish. The reasoning is curious.

American insistence upon a sharp division between sport and commercial fish-kill is the end result of a guilty conscience. We are almost psychotic about the near extinction of buffalo on the Great Plains and the complete wipe-out of passenger pigeons, and we forget that the bison was destroyed by federal edict in order to starve hostile Indians, while the pigeon succumbed to land use, not hunting. Closer to home, anglers and assorted ecologists (many of whom remain a bit hazy about the word's definition) charge commercial fishermen with the destruction of Atlantic salmon, conveniently forgetting that these grand silver hordes were the victims of industrial dams and pollution.

Marine fishes require intelligent management so that they will remain a renewable natural resource, and the great seafaring nations are fully aware of this. Very recently, the North Atlantic haddock suffered a precipitous decline because there were no major year classes of hatch over a period of seven seasons. All the commercial fishing nations agreed to curtail dragging on the spawning grounds until such time as the haddock could recoup its losses. No emotion was involved—just sound management.

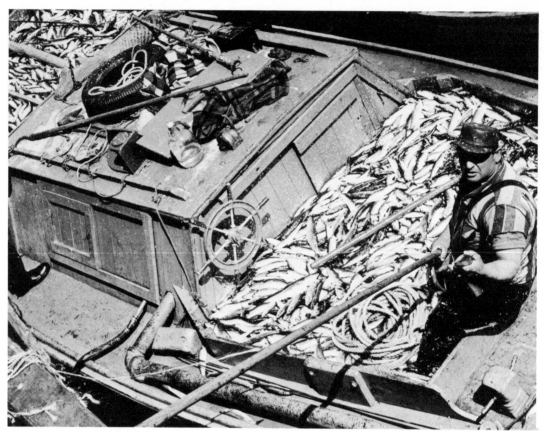

Herring, plus a variety of other species, are harvested by trap fishermen.

Great Britain, the land that originated most of our legal processes and sporting ethics, takes a far more liberal view of this sport-versus-commercial situation. There, management of natural resources supersedes emotion. The salmon caught on a Jock Scott by a sportsman in Scotland is swiftly iced and offered for sale on a fishmonger's tray in London. Red grouse, harvested on well-managed moors, are sold a day later. By manipulating the harvest so that a resource remains in balance, fish and game prosper, while citizens realize a fair return. We will come to this, in our new land, but it will take time and an honest meeting of minds between the rod and line and the commercial fishing groups. Sale is no sin; guilt lies only on those who rape a resource.

Meanwhile, the double standard is particularly disgusting. Few coastal marinas lack the wealthy sportsman who owns a plush, twin-screw cruiser and who pays for the services of a skipper and mate to guide him during posh coastal tournaments where all codes are scrupulously observed and IGFA rules supersede the Ten Commandments, but who orders his skipper and crew to "get out there and fish commercially" on off days, in order to pay expenses when he, the Big Man, returns to a city desk.

It is a different ball game when the owner sanctions charter operations in his absence, in order to pick up some of the tab in fees and income-tax write-off, unless such chartering involves the too common practice of killing fish for advertising purposes alone. And how about the tycoon who professes sportsmanship but employs his considerable rig (on weekends when there are no status angling tournaments) to iron giant tuna and swordfish for the pure joy of sticking them? Or to pick up a few dollars for fish flesh—money that he doesn't need? Perhaps I am a maverick, but my sympathies are all with the honest coaster who loves fishing with rod and line but who makes no excuses for selling every legal fish he drags aboard. At least he is no hypocrite.

One surprisingly durable myth should be destroyed at the outset: nobody ever made a good living at rod and line commercial fishing. The very idea is preposterous because the possible harvest is limited. You simply cannot catch enough fish in this way! Sporting tackle is just about the worst sort of gear to collect fish flesh in marketable volume.

Lots of industrious romantics have tried to make it work. Arnold Laine of Templeton, Massachusetts, probably the greatest rod and line commercial striped bass fisherman who ever lived, gave it a whirl during the forties and fifties. He was good enough to boat approximately twelve tons of bass during each season, working day and night from mid-May through October, but he finally quit in disgust and went back to his old trade as a machinist.

The bad news about commercial rod and line fishing is twofold: a season is short, and fish, when they are plentiful, sell at starvation rates. While a consumer may pay— grabbing a figure out of the air—89¢ per pound for any given hunk of fish flesh, an angler may, if he is lucky, get about one-third of that sum. A local glut of fish will lower the market price within 24 hours, and there are fluctuations caused by ethnic holidays. Stormy weather and the usual inclination of fish to move in and out of an area in pursuit of bait guarantee occasional good hauls—and more barren days.

Overhead is always there. At the very least, a rod and line commercial will require a boat and an outboard motor. He will have to invest in tackle, bait, fuel, and necessary food. If he operates off a sand beach, a four-wheel-drive vehicle will be necessary, and they don't sell any of these things for peanuts.

Great days fever the imagination of a prospective commercial. The boast "I caught 800 pounds on one tide and made $200" may be factual, yet the happy angler neglects to mention a preceding week of high winds and no fish at all. Usually, if we are honest, hard scrapes outnumber the lush. You burn the same amount of gas—often more— on a poor day. Sometimes sharp-toothed fishes spitefully cut lures off tight lines, and these lures sell for anywhere from $1 to $5 apiece.

These are things that should be emphasized, because there has been too much nonsense about the money to be made fishing with rod and line. There simply isn't any, and you'd better believe it. The game provides a few dollars to defray the cost of tackle, fuel, and other expenses, yet it never adds up to any substantial income. While a coastal resident can profit by fishing in leisure hours, he'll never make sport pay off in real folding money. If you want to be a true commercial, better invest in a big boat, a lot of nets or long-line gear, and then prepare to fight the weather and the sea. It isn't the easiest of callings.

Having punctured the bright balloon of easy money earned in the most delightful way, I still champion the right of any man to make an occasional dollar by selling fish that are rated commercial. It is quite ethical to fish for sport—and then sell the catch on an open market—providing that laws of the land are scrupulously observed. Your tackle is nobody's business but your own. Usually, as a fish-for-cash angler, you will employ reasonably heavy gear, although in some cases the light stuff will prove most lethal. Great rod and liners use everything from spinning and flycasting outfits on up to heavy-surf and wire-line trolling rigs. The business *must* be fun, even though it adds up to a lucrative poundage at day's end.

After all, "sport" is just another word, variously defined. The citizen who irons swordfish or bluefin tuna from the pulpit of a private cruiser may get a big bang out of hitting them and following a skipping keg. I do not count this true sport, and that is a personal opinion, but I will fight for the right of any seafarer to harvest legal quarry as he pleases. The broadbill and the tuna are commercial fishes, therefore fair game until such time as marine biologists and administrators declare that they must be taken in lesser numbers.

Sport commercials fall into pretty well-defined categories. There is, first, the coastal resident whose very tradition includes that right to make a buck on the bay. He counts this right inviolate, and he fishes after daily working hours, on holidays, and whenever there is leisure time to spend. Usually he is just about the worst angler imaginable. His tackle is atrocious and his methods were good enough for grandfather, so they remain good enough for him. He never reads the literature and he never experiments with new developments in angling. He doesn't slaughter many fish.

Next, there is the retired citizen who may live on social security or a pension and can use the pennies he makes by selling fish flesh. He has unlimited time, but usually is slightly incapacitated by his age and unable to maintain a killing pace. He's a fair-weather angler, often a habitué of beach or pier. His tackle may be sophisticated, yet he seldom knows how to use it. In fact, business is seldom so important as yarning with old cronies. Fish brought to gaff, net, or beach are ceremoniously sold, and the money received is as welcome as the gentle rain from heaven; it is a gift from the gods, but never a calculated income.

Every coast boasts charter skippers who sell every prize left behind by patrons. There is no wrong in this; indeed, it is right and proper to dispose of fishes that would otherwise wind up in the town dump or be consigned to the sea. A lot of skippers engage in commercial fishing when bookings are slim, and most of them are very skillful. They'd do better with a gill net, but guides are anglers first and foremost; they delight in sport and try to make it pay.

Among sport commercials, there are the deluded, money-hungry sharpies. Great fishermen, usually well read and schooled in the arts of rod and line, they conspire to buck the odds and succeed where others have failed. A great majority fish on weekends, holidays, and long summer vacations. They labor like galley slaves but, because it is "sport," forget the long hours and the grinding attrition. Their eyes are bloodshot; their skin is burned by the sun and stung by salt spray; their hands are lacerated and sore.

I know men who have invested in big, live-in beach buggies, plus chase cars (usually modern four-wheel-drive station wagons), plus big, fiber-glass surfboats powered by gas-eating motors, plus the best in tackle, who still think that they make a buck on the bay. A few even boast airplanes, written off as company expenses, to ferry them from inland cities to the salt chuck. Their investment is astronomical, and their return is miniscule, yet they scrabble for each penny per pound of fish sold.

Finally, among regulars, you have the man who can only be described as a fishing bum. He ceases gainful labor at the birth of each new season and repairs to the seacoast, where he remains until the last catch is recorded and it is time to quit collecting unemployment checks and return to a plebeian trade. Very often these are master anglers who make enough, through the sale of fish flesh, to pay for basic equipment, to buy provisions, and to live like hermits during a long summer on the grounds. This may be a lovely way to live, but it is not very lucrative. There is no future in it. I would guess that every seacoast in our weary world hosts a limited number of fishing bums who are expert anglers, grand companions, incurable romantics, and parasites on the body politic. A few seek no welfare handout, are fiercely independent, and try to make it on their own.

Arnold Laine, until his awakening, was typical. A well-read man, he always kept abreast of world news and great literature. Arnold spent his few leisure hours listening to the best music on a phonograph that he carried in his cluttered beach buggy. Modern rock infuriated him, yet he could discourse even on this subject. Self-educated, Laine was no unfortunate driven to the beach.

Tough and self-reliant, for years he launched a frail surfboat in pale dawn or darkness. He waded the sand beaches and challenged great waves on rock jetties. His beach buggy was first on the dunes, and last off. Sometimes, when the fish were not there, Arnold was "bushed," shaggy-haired, and wild of eye, no fit companion for old friends and certainly a sworn enemy of tourists. He caught a lot of fish and he became a living legend, but Laine could never make it pay. I recall a sportsman from New York, fishing the Cape Cod grounds, who said: "This has been the greatest week of my life; I caught a striped bass and I met Arnold Laine!"

Any saltwater food fish is a marketable commodity and can be sold. There is, as I have said, no sin in sale, but there is corruption in trading foodstuffs that are suspect because of improper processing or plain, old-fashioned neglect. Professionals respect the fish they catch; each is properly dressed and iced, still red of gills and firm of flesh when tossed into a buyer's scales. Some amateurs forget that fresh fish means just that; they are prone to peddle carcasses that have been dried by the sun or allowed to soften over a long weekend. Buyers are not stupid; they expect a certain amount of spoilage and compensate for this by paying less where a rod and line angler is the seller. Who needs the trash that will be relegated to cat food or discarded? The amateur commercial is suspect, if only because he is an amateur.

Some states currently require licenses to sell food fish, while others are lenient in this respect. Some permit residents to sell without a ticket, while nonresidents have to pay a healthy fee. There are instances of black marketing, where a species is considered to be endangered, but is much in demand by gourmets. Fortunately, this is rare in the salt chuck.

I think it is too early to demand saltwater sport-fishing licenses (although some states levy them now), primarily because no really suitable apparatus has been set up to funnel license funds into wise and productive research-management programs that are divorced from pork-barrel politics and will benefit the angler who casts a line for fun. On the other hand, I am firmly convinced that the rod and line commercial should support state and federal research that seeks a fine balance between conservation of the available resource and a healthy, renewable harvest.

Every man who sells a fish should contribute a small amount of cash to the funding of established research and management programs. This need not be much, in the case of the coastal resident or retiree who is making his simple buck on the bay—certainly never so generous a bite as that put on a full-time commercial—but it should be there. The largess of the sea is not inexhaustible; therefore, if you sell for coin of the realm, you must be willing to channel some small part of the profit into programs designed to maintain a viable fishery and to ensure a practical harvest in future years.

Of course, the universal saltwater sport-fishing license will come; it is inevitable, because we now witness a marine-angling boom that shows no sign of reaching an apogee and is unlikely to do so. Even now, some coastal species are more thoroughly harvested by rod and line anglers than by true commercials. There is a great need to study the fishes of the sea and to manage each fishery for the benefit of all users. Unfortunately, marine biology is still an infant art, and the wisest of the scientists are still struggling in the spider web of political bureaucracy. Sport fishermen will see the logic of a license when state or federal planners convince them that this is in their best interests. They will resist, like a tiger defending her cubs, so long as licensing appears to be taxation without representation and a simple, fund-raising device, bereft of intelligent programming. Logical research and management of marine sport fisheries is in the offing. So is the sport license.

Meanwhile, a sport fisherman who sells his catch must observe certain rules of the game; if he is to create a reputation for honesty, the fish he peddles must be both fresh and properly dressed. Depending on species, this catch may be sold in the round without any dressing-out, or gutted and gilled. The hard-fleshed types often go as is, while more perishable game must be gutted. Usually, the former command highest prices, but they are less plentiful than the soft-fleshed hordes. In any area, buyers dictate conditions of sale, and the angler must comply.

Fish houses and co-ops buy most of the catch, but coastal anglers who operate in prime tourist areas often develop lucrative markets in restaurants that cater to the great American pilgrim. A restaurant buyer seldom scans the daily "green sheet" to gauge fluctuations in price, but, although he usually pays considerably more than the commercial fish house, he is always ahead of the game when he buys from a local angler.

Often, in this case, fish must be filleted so that they will be ready for instant freezing and equally instant preparation for the table. All the better restaurants pride themselves on impeccable cuisine, so foodstuffs must be wiggle-fresh. The seller who palms off tired merchandise soon runs out of customers.

This restaurant market is, of course, limited. A buyer will stock X number of pounds of a specific fish for the season, and will then cry quits. He will always buy from locals who have demonstrated an ability to provide good fillets or steaks, and he will be wary of newcomers unless his need is great. Whether restaurateur or bulk purchaser, those who trade in fish will insist upon the highest of standards. Those species that spoil quickly, such as the common mackerel, sea trout, and bluefish, are critically examined. A buyer is always happiest when the catch is cold, damp, and still in rigor mortis with bright eyes and red gills.

Regardless of species harvested, an angler who wishes to compete with true professionals succeeds only when he offers a superior product. Hustle them to market as quickly as possible. Use ice whenever it is available and, lacking ice, cover the catch with a salt-wet blanket of burlap to ensure radiational cooling and to avert the damage caused by hot, drying sunlight. Gut or gill those that must be so treated, and don't wait until day's end to do so. If you sell, each catch should be treated precisely as it would be prior to gracing your own table. Remember that, unlike beefsteak, a fish is most delectable when fresh—not aged or even cooled in a freezer.

There is no stigma attached to the honest sale of marine fishes that are esteemed as food and sold in the open market. If the rod and line commercial is slandered by his blood brothers who fish for sport alone, we must regard this as a sociological phenomenon and a narrow definition of the word "sport." Moreover, if we truly desire to utilize a renewable natural resource in the best possible manner, we'd better work with, and understand, the commercial operator. Any conflict between sport and commercial defeats the very goal we all seek—an abundance of fishes for the tables of the world and the taut lines of joyous anglers.

Award full credit to the citizen who releases every game fish he cannot use, but reserve a measure of compassion for the man who honestly, and within the letter of the law, feels that he must make a buck on the bay.

DANGER AT SEA ⌁ 15

The Real Perils—and the Fancied Ones!

Let psychologists tell you why all men derive a certain pleasure from pulling the whiskers of the reaper. I only know that a spice of peril in any sport is a benevolent narcotic. There is always a delicious element of danger in the sea, perhaps one of the reasons why saltwater angling is such an intriguing game. There *are* dangers, usually those ignored as unworthy of attention. Human miscalculation, which results in accident, is the foremost trigger of tragedy. Man-eating fishes are not very abundant, nor are they prone to launch unprovoked attack.

Still, the world ocean remains a largely unknown frontier; reputable scientists admit that strange animals *may* inhabit its depths. It is well to remember that the coelacanth was thought to be extinct until one was discovered, vibrantly alive, off South Africa in 1938. No mammoth sea serpent has been proved to live, yet accounts of sightings are chilling because so many of them are offered by highly educated and observant seafarers.

Fear springs from ignorance and is fed by folktales of monsters in the deep. Few men are entirely divorced from superstition, and it is very easy to exchange logic for panic when sea and sky merge in one opaque wash of darkness, when the tidal currents gurgle and the recurrent boom of surf sounds like a dirge from another world. At such a time, alone and under the infinite stars, any sea monster is possible. I have been thoroughly frightened by things that, under a blue and sunny sky, would have been easily explained and accepted as normal.

Once, when anchored in a small aluminum surfboat off Cape Cod, casting for striped bass in the dark hour before dawn, a whale broached within 50 feet of my craft. This behemoth came out like an animated island—huge in the pewter light of the stars. He arrived with a rush of waters and a deep, groaning sound, and I saw the black, glittering bulk of the creature with the seas sliding off. There was a sudden stench, for all whales seem to have halitosis. Probably a finback, some 60 or 70 feet in length, and he meant no harm.

Yet, suddenly, I was seized with unreasoning terror. The pulsing sea was alien and I was a very small atom in a vast nothingness of chuckling brine and pale horizons and unforgiving stars in a blue-black zenith. The striped bass could wait; I hauled anchor and planed ashore at full throttle.

One other night, when the only illumination was that strange and hardly perceptible difference between sky and water, with little flecks of phosphorescence in a running tide, I waded belly deep in a scouring current at Cape Canaveral—now Cape Kennedy —plugging for the big southern spotted sea trout that have made this region famous. That night the warm and flooding tide seemed to be alive with huge shapes that thrust occasional fins above the bubbling surface; they were sharks and rays, and I conquered fear only because local colleagues ignored the visitors.

228

There *are* monsters in the ocean. At Big Pine Key one opalescent evening, I was lounging on a bridge abutment, gazing down into Florida's air-clear water as one tide changed and the sun began to sink in those curious green-edged cloud formations that you sometimes see in the tropics. A sawfish appeared, and that leviathan must have weighed 800 pounds. Right behind him a ray braced the tide, and that ray could have blanketed a Volkswagen!

Bill Walton, a Massachusetts friend of mine, was frightened in broad daylight. Bill was live-lining a mackerel bait off Cape Cod, anchored in some 20 feet of water, seeking big striped bass. He saw a swirl, a thing that fishermen usually love to see, but this was a rather unusual swirl. It was 30 feet in diameter and it stirred sand and eelgrass off the bottom some 20 feet below! Walton hauled anchor and went ashore very rapidly, after which he beckoned me to share a jolt of something we never mix with gunpowder.

No danger, but fear was there. The whale chased me to bed, and something big and unknown gave Bill Walton a case of the fidgets. Nobody had been bitten or swamped, yet we were frightened. Imagination is a force to be reckoned with in the big, brawling sea. Logic is better suited to a well-lighted dining room. Almost always the big marine animals go their way in peace, ignoring mankind and usually fleeing from human beings or motor sound.

Usually.

Wading or boating, you are more likely to be struck by lightning than hit by a shark, and there is almost no chance of a whale either upsetting a boat or actually launching an attack. Even the orca, or killer whale, seems loath to harry human beings. While sportsmen on Atlantic and Pacific coasts give the big black and white killers a wide berth, authenticated reports of attack are almost nonexistent. Big whales, the Moby Dick type, like to keep well away from men; indeed, they generally accelerate when a powerboat skipper attempts to range alongside so that passengers can take pictures.

Once, in my experience, there was an exception. Larry Helin of Detroit, scion of the Helin Tackle Company, was with me in a small outboard powerboat when we spotted a huge pod of whales spouting. Larry wanted motion pictures, so we chased them and—that day—the great finbacks seemed almost contemptuous. Larry, manning a camera, asked to take the helm so that he could shoot pictures of me bouncing tiny spinning lures off the broad backs of whales. (If anyone ever inquires, I can state that it is very difficult to hook an adult whale on a ⅝-ounce plug and one-handed 10-pound-test spinning tackle. The hooks simply refused to penetrate the leathery hides of the animals.)

Cinematography went well until Larry became so absorbed that he forgot to steer our boat. Quite suddenly, and with startling clarity, I saw that we had veered right over the tail of a cruising monster. There seemed to be 20 feet of flukes on one side of the boat and 20 feet on the other! If that whale had been so disposed, we'd have emulated Melville's famous sea hunters and been "drawn upward as by invisible wires!" I cursed Larry in several languages, but he only grinned, and the whales continued to ignore us.

Sharks are unpredictable, and this is a first thing to consider in dealing with them. There are records of attacks on small boats, usually launched by the white (*Carcharodon carcharias*) or man-eater, a species that grows to considerable size and is, without doubt, bad news. Makos and other large sharks have been known to assault small boats and, of course, human beings caught swimming or wading. While unprovoked attack is a relatively rare thing, it certainly occurs in all seas, most often in the tropics or subtropics. Australia and South Africa annually record tragedies.

There are an estimated 350 species of sharks in the world ocean, and perhaps twenty of these actually threaten mankind. Beware of any heavyweight equipped with rending teeth. In addition to the infamous white, makos, porbeagles, tigers, lemons, white tips, hammerheads, and sand sharks have been found most dangerous. In Costa Rica and Nicaragua, a subspecies of the bull shark ranges well up into fresh water and is particularly abundant in the Colorado-San Juan river systems up to and including Lake Nicaragua. Until very recently, this was considered a unique freshwater species, but studies now indicate that the Central American bull thrives in salt or fresh, and is a dangerous customer in either environment. Certainly Costa Ricans and Nicaraguans fear the critter, apparently with good reason. The first time I fished the Colorado, back in 1964, my host, Carlos Barrantes, warned: "Don't fall overboard here!" People do not swim in these waters.

Living dangerously, an angler gets his legs too close
to a shark being hauled aboard.
Photo by Hal Lyman

Unreasonable panic always ensues when a shark's caudal fin is seen cutting the water close to a bathing beach, yet waders of tropical flats exhibit no more than clinical interest in a huge predator weaving through the brine at close quarters. Scuba divers have visited with sharks in the depths and have found most of them inquisitive, rarely threatening. There is always the possibility of a rogue, however, and there is the matter of conditioned reflex triggered by some outside influence. Never be terrified of sharks, per se, but respect them and try to understand the things that motivate their dull brains.

It is quite possible that an individual killer, having dined on humankind, will enjoy every opportunity to satisfy a new hunger. While the evidence indicates that this may be so—a cessation of attacks after the hunting down and slaughter of sharks in an area that has witnessed unprovoked assaults—there is no empirical proof. At any rate, anglers seldom figure in these ghastly affairs because they either work from boats or wade reasonably shallow waters. By comparison, a swimmer is an easy mark for a murder-bent shark.

Sharks, like many other sea creatures, are excited by commotion and scent that is generated by a slaughter of bait. Any trace of blood in the water will turn them on, and then the slowly finning, undulating monster suddenly moves very rapidly and with vicious accuracy. A cruising shark is a symphony of slow, graceful movement; one that has been charged up by the scent of blood is a switching, darting menace. Always beware of those that seem to be employing afterburners, for they often seem to grow bolder by the moment. Never create this situation by dragging dead fish on a stringer while wading the flats, or even by dragging captured gamesters behind a boat.

It is a most disquieting experience to have a large shark, on the flats, arrive from dead astern to nip fish off a trailing stringer. You always wonder whether he'll shear off after the last tidbit has been devoured, or whether he'll decide that your legs and buttocks might provide dessert! If he gets too close, whack him with the rod tip—hard! And don't worry about fractured glass or bamboo. In this case, things will have progressed too far for comfort and gentle persuasion.

Bill Burton of Baltimore exhibits the awesome bite
of a shark. *Photo by Bill Burton*

Thousands of great game fish, having been fought to gaff and then tail-roped to tow beside a boat, have been devoured or disfigured by sharks. Lacking a gin pole to hoist the catch aboard and out of harm's way, there is no foolproof way to prevent a determined assault. Lances, shotguns, pistols of heavy caliber—even submachine guns in the days when these were legal and readily available to well-heeled offshore anglers—seldom save the catch. An excited shark is single-minded and very difficult to kill.

Guns are not the answer. In many states they are illegally carried, unless the person concerned is able to wangle a permit. Moreover, they are dangerous in the heat of action; bullets will ricochet if fired from an angle against water. Charges of bird shot can be deadly at close range, yet equally deadly if the shooter is thrown off balance by wave action and his shot goes into a boat's gunwale or, more ghastly to contemplate, into other human beings.

Paul Kukonen of Worcester, Massachusetts—a fine fisherman and a motion-picture photographer—once recorded a shark attack on school tuna he towed behind an 18-foot outboard skiff. There were three bluefins, each weighing 50 to 75 pounds, bobbing along in the wake, and two more in the cockpit, when a large and determined shark arrived. This suddenly frenzied animal systematically devoured all three of the towed tuna, and then came back to seize the outboard's lower unit in its jaws! While the boat was shaking and vibrating under this attack, Paul threw the remaining fish overboard as a peace offering. It apparently worked. He has the whole sequence on film.

"Dead" sharks may be quite as dangerous as live ones! The creatures are very tenacious of life, and those brought to boat or beach as trophies are potential mantraps so long as they retain any spark. There are ample tales of monsters gaffed, clubbed, lanced, and pierced with high velocity rifle bullets winched aboard on a gin pole, only to chew expensive splinters out of a mahogany gunwale. Hours later, at the dock, an apparently dead and sun-dried shark may snap its jaws with all the authority of a bear trap—and with more knife-edged peril.

Since a great many offshore anglers count "monster fishing" a supreme thrill—and it is—the drill consists of cautious playing, landing, and boating of any toothy warrior. It is well to remember that a shark is a cartilaginous fish that has the ability to double back fully two-thirds of its length and bite anything in the immediate vicinity. There is no margin for error in dealing with these killing machines. By all means, be cautious.

Any large sea creature is dangerous—potentially—yet few threaten the angler who observes basic rules of intelligence. It is quite possible to be skewered by a green sailfish or a marlin if you are idiot enough to grasp the bill of the animal and point it toward your windpipe or chest while hauling it over the transom. One final surge of body and tail might be enough to drive that rapier into human flesh. It has happened on too many occasions.

A loose and flailing leader wire can be quite as dangerous during the last, hectic moments of battle with a brute of the depths. If such a strand should be looped around the arm or neck of angler or crewman, something has to give, and it could be somebody's neck. Once the mate has a leader in hand, it is a fisherman's duty to slack off drag. Needless to say, a good mate will wear gloves, and he will so handle the leader that any breakaway will not find him firmly attached.

Lines must be awarded equal respect, for they can burn and cut. A few ill-instructed folk insist on standing aft of a line leading to an outrigger, or will even hold the line to one side of the transom when trolling. There is a mistaken tendency to haul braid or mono in, off an outrigger, while standing aft. If a fish happens to strike during this maneuver, the line will come ballooning down so rapidly that it will be difficult to get out of the way. And, when a large, determined game fish is on the other end of that potentially dangerous connection, a mistake can lead to serious trouble.

It should be obvious that men or women with known heart conditions should consider the wisdom of challenging tremendous game fish on offshore grounds. Most true heavyweights will wage grueling battles, often over a period of hours. The slugfest will leave an athlete bruised and weary; it may kill a sedentary human whose physical condition is poor, but whose pride prevents him from admitting that the struggle is unequal. Death in action may be glorious in fiction, but it is unnecessary on the offshore grounds.

Usually, we bring trouble down on our own shoulders. On the Saint Lucie River in Florida, Charley Whitney and I chased a manatee and cub with a 12-foot aluminum skiff. We shouldn't have done this in the first place, but neither tarpon nor snook were hitting, and this seemed an adventure. Finally the big female turned and arrowed straight for our light craft. I had visions of colliding with something big, bulky, and angry, so I turned hard starboard and gunned the outboard. Charley performed a neat half somersault out of the bow and landed in the stern sheets, right on top of a very expensive German camera. Served us right for harrying a sea cow. She dove under the boat. The camera wasn't insured, so I learned about sea cows from that!

Conceivably, a manta ray could demolish a boat if the critter jumped out of the water and came down on the deck. Mantas aren't likely to do that, but tarpon are very apt to come aboard after they have been hooked. On that same Saint Lucie, I had one arch out of the water a full 15 feet and then bounce off the gunwale. If that powerhouse of energy had actually come aboard, I'm sure that Captain Bill Todt, Whitney, and I would have jumped overboard. Think of this possibility when hunting the silver king. Note that it is not very good strategy, in confined waters—such as a "hole" in the mangroves or a narrow pass—to place one's boat between a tarpon and the open ocean. The hooked fish will have nowhere to go but up, over, or into a boat. There is no future in a small craft, or even in a large one, when a green tarpon visits; he'll break everything in sight, including the bones of anglers who insist upon close-quarter combat. Lots of fishermen have been injured by tarpon.

Among biting fishes, the great barracuda is much maligned and often unfairly blamed. A 'cuda seldom attacks man deliberately, doing so only when some coil of circumstances suggests another target. It is not very wise to trail a hand over the side of a boat in water frequented by barracuda, or to cool one's feet in the wash. The flickering of fingers or toes may suggest small bait, and the 'cuda attacks. Divers seldom worry about this so-called "tiger of the sea," and the wading angler can operate without fear.

On tropical flats, a barracuda often lies quietly with nose into the tidal flow. If he spots an approaching wade fisherman, the creature will turn like the needle of a compass—to point right at the encroacher. There will be no attack, just a sort of Mexican standoff until the angler approaches a point where contact seems imminent. Then the 'cuda will whirl off for 50 or 100 yards to halt, turn, and maintain the original position. He won't hit a lure, and he won't attack. He's not dangerous.

Beginners always fear sea snakes. On North American coasts—and generally in all cold waters—these are akin to "ice snakes," because they do not exist. There are several varieties in the tropical Pacific and many more in the Indian Ocean, but all are fairly docile and rarely given to unprovoked attack. Some will even bite and, somehow (marine biologists don't understand the process), will refrain from injecting venom. While highly venomous, sea snakes are distinct hazards only to men who are handling nets or weirs in areas where the reptiles are plentiful. One species, the yellow-bellied sea snake, ranges from East Africa to Australia and thence eastward to the Gulf of Panama, but is never plentiful and is hardly a menace to the sport fisherman.

There are, of course, certain cone shells with stinging spines that contain venoms comparable to a cobra's poison, and a few fishes that secrete equally lethal venom in their spines. The European weevers are dangerous, but an angler is unlikely to meet them. A man who fishes with rod and line seldom comes into contact with the potent poisoners, but he meets certain nasty critters that are unlikely to rattle him into a grave, yet may well make his life very difficult. Some of these menaces are common, hence we tend to disregard them.

In all tropical waters there is the stingaree or stingray. Some of the species grow to horrifying sizes, but most of them are small; all feature a whiplike tail that is armed with a serrated spine or spines containing mild venom. They won't kill you, but they can sure as hell inflict a painful and long-lasting wound.

Stingrays aren't aggressive; they don't come looking for a soft ankle in which to bury that daggerlike spine, but they protect themselves. Therefore, in stingray country —which means any warm-water area—look for this member of the ray family wherever the bottom is soft and oozy. If you step on one, the critter will whip its tail around and drive a saw-edged stinger into your leg or foot, after which you will spend much time swearing and sighing with pain until the wound heals.

There is a very effective defense against stingrays and it is practiced in all tropical waters. Simply shuffle your feet. That's all there is to it. The stingray dosen't want any part of you and he will flush ahead if he knows that something is coming. Don't step high and mighty. Properly warned, stingarees will depart in a smoke puff of mud.

A man or woman whose feet are tough enough to defeat northern clamshells and sharp-edged rocks can wade barefoot in a cold surf. Some do this in the tropics, but it is not very wise. There you have sharp coral outcrops that can produce painful lacerations, and there are always sea urchins. The latter boast sharp spines that tend to break off after they penetrate flesh. The spines are difficult to remove and they often create festering wounds. Wear tennis shoes, at the very least, in warm waters.

Long pants, rather than Bermuda shorts, also make good sense in tropical shallows, not alone to ward off hot sunlight—a very real danger in itself—but as armor against the stinging tentacles of a jellylike hydroid called the Portuguese man-o'-war. This false jelly is very common in the warm Atlantic, the Hebrides, and the Mediterranean Sea. A close relative annoys seafarers in the Indo-Pacific.

A man-o'-war is most easily identified by its sky-blue float, a thin-walled balloon sail that harnesses wind and wave action. Suspended from this innocuous bladder are masses of purple stinging tentacles that may stream 20 to 50 feet in a tidal flow and which are capable of inflicting painful stings. Swimmers who absorb a full charge from a number of tentacles may be in serious trouble, and no season ever passes without a few deaths attributed to the man-o'-war. Fatalities usually occur when a person suffers respiratory paralysis and heart failure after massive stinging. Immediate medical treatment is imperative.

Anglers are unlikely to court death, but few tropical fishermen entirely escape the attention of these jellies. Bits of stinging tentacle often are picked up by a trolled line and, of course, there is contact in the surf or on the flats while wading—the reason why it is prudent to wear long pants.

You'll never forget contact, because these things hurt like blue hell. One bit of tentacle draped across shinbone or wrist will feel precisely like a red-hot branding iron, and the pain lingers. Old sailors advocate urinating on the affected member. More fastidious and possibly better informed souls first remove the tentacles, scrub with sand in an effort to scour out the miniscule poison barbs buried on contact, and then wash with ammonia, alcohol, or gasoline. Calamine lotion helps to relieve pain. The man-o'-war is no joke, even though tropical kids derive great joy in stamping upon the sun-dried air sacks, piled upon a beach, just to hear them pop.

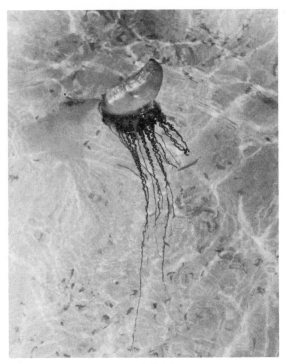

Portuguese man-o'-war jellyfish is a menace to tropical anglers. The trailing tentacles boast a dangerous sting.

There are other stinging jellies in the sea, few of them so annoying and plentiful as the sky-blue and purple man-o'-war. One, the sea wasp of northern Australia, the Philippines, and the Indian Ocean, can shuttle a man into a hospital bed or even into one of Melville's graveyard trays. Fortunately, sport fishermen of the New World are unlikely to make their acquaintance.

Similarly, tropical seas are sparsely populated with corals that sicken human beings unlucky enough to touch them, with certain cone shells that secrete a venom of great potency, a few rogue sea worms, spiny fishes—such as scorpions and weevers—and even octopuses, which can inflict a venomous substance when biting with their parrotlike beaks. Again, Australia seems to have more than her share of the little nasties; that continent's tiny blue-ringed octopus isn't aggressive, but when it bites a human being a death may be recorded within 5 minutes. Octopuses of the American Atlantic and Pacific coasts can bite, and they can cause much pain thereof, but fatalities are almost unheard of.

While the European weevers and some other fish can kill man with one thrust of a sharp-edged spine, those in American seas are more likely to inflict painful, but not serious, wounds. Most of the catfishes boast sharp fin-ray spines that are mildly toxic.

The common spiny dogfish has a sharp, venom-lined spine ahead of each dorsal fin, and these are said to be capable of inflicting injury. I have handled thousands of them, albeit carefully, without ill effect. Most of the troublemakers are small and of little interest to a sportsman, so injury usually is the result of carelessness or handling an unknown creature captured by accident.

Lots of snappers and other game species boast nonvenomous spines in dorsal, pectoral, or anal fins. Northern surf casters, for example, have found that it is lunacy to kick a beached striped bass. Spines in the fins of that great gamester are not venomous, but they are sharp, prone to break off in human flesh, and to cause festering and pain over a considerable period of time.

Having written a flood of words about the dangerous business of kicking a striper out of the suds, I periodically do so in the heat of action. The last time it happened, I felt a very sharp pain and realized that a spine had broken off in my foot, just above the toes. Cursing my own stupidity, I proceeded to shed waders, and found that the boot foot was thoroughly nailed to my flesh! There followed a rather blasphemous dialogue under the dim beam of a flashlight, during which the broken spine was finally extracted with a pair of rusty pliers. My foot hurt for a month.

Quite as accidental, although also due to carelessness, is gashing and slicing by sharp-toothed fishes that have been brought to boat or beach. A bluefish is called a "chopper" for good reason; that wonderful battler snaps its jaws until it is completely dead, and it is rather hard to kill a bluefish. A big one is capable of taking a rather large hunk of flesh out of the human frame, so it is a first order of business to avoid those chomping jaws. A blue, like a shark, seems to consciously turn its head and bite, even after capture. Smart fishermen respect those jaws, for they are mighty efficient.

Other toothy fishes must be handled with care. The barracuda has teeth like a timber wolf and will use them in like manner if given a chance after capture. All the sharks should be respected, even the little ones. King and cero mackerel have ripped human flesh on many occasions, and even the lowly fluke or summer flounder boasts needle-sharp teeth. Flatties don't bite like crocodiles, but a tyro who sticks his hand into a fluke's mouth makes the immediate discovery that the species is well armed.

There are, in addition, fishes with razor-edged gill covers. A snook can slice a man's hand from fingertips to wrist if he is careless enough to grasp any lantern-jawed catch by the gills. You can manhandle a snook by grabbing his pugnaciously outthrust lower jaw, but keep well away from the sides of his head.

Of course, saltwater game fish rarely are the mild, soft-finned creatures of inland lakes and streams. Precisely because they are big, muscular, and rambunctious, the collector of marine trophies faces another peril—loose hooks. Any green gladiator with a big, treble-hooked plug stuck in its face must be subdued quickly. No horror quite matches that of being foul-hooked by a loose barb, the other end of which is firmly attached to a very angry, flopping monster. It happens all the time, and I've been spooked right up on a boat's console by huge bluefish that managed to squirm off a gaff at night, and were thrashing around in the cockpit with treble-hooked plugs jangling and teeth chomping. A loose fish, so adorned, is bad news.

Annually, anglers impale themselves, or friends, on stout hooks. One night, fishing with Charley Whitney, I got careless and felt a sudden jolt as I cast a 5-ounce rigged eel from our small boat. Charley yelled and swore that I'd knocked his hat off, and I retrieved my eel to find his hat firmly pinned to one of its three 8/0 single hooks!

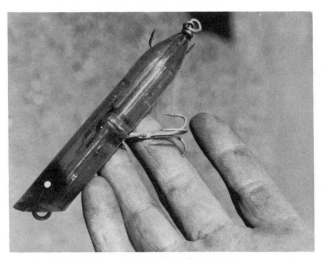

Anglers regularly spear themselves with barbed
hooks. Removal is painful.

One inch lower and I might have seriously injured a good friend. For me, the night's fishing was ruined. I was humiliated by my own inept performance and shaken by a near tragedy. Fish get hooked—and people get hooked. Sometimes there is comic relief.

There is the tale of a very tough Massachusetts steelworker who, with his teen-aged son, was throwing eel-skin rigs into the Cape Cod Canal on a dark night. The boy was unfortunate enough to be plagued by a drunk who staggered down from the high road to observe proceedings. One of the lad's casts hooked him right through the cartilaginous tissue of the nose, and the drunk howled with pain as he went reeling down the riprap.

The youngster was understandably rattled, so he finally whipped out a sheath knife and cut the line. His father was hardly complimentary. "You dumb bastard," he roared, "whyn't you play him in and land him? That line cost money!"

Fishhooks buried in human flesh are occupational hazards. It is a traumatic experience to find a point driven in well beyond the barb, especially if that hook is constructed of heavy wire. The thing has to come out and—if you're away out in the blue—the operation will be essayed by a layman. There are several techniques.

Time honored and well tested, the barb's shank is cut with stout pliers and the point is pushed on through tissue until it emerges and can be removed. In recent years, some surgeons have recommended the quick-snatch theory—quite similar to that timeless operation in which a child's wobbly baby tooth is yanked out with the help of a string attached to a doorknob. It's quick and can be relatively painless. Here, a length of stout fishline is looped around the bend of the embedded hook. The shank is then depressed to ensure a straight pull and—whap! It's all over. Dr. Theo Cooke of Guramulka, South Australia, first detailed this method of extraction.

Dr. Warren T. Longmire, Jr., of Hitchcock, Texas, offers another route. *Emergency Medicine Magazine* has described Dr. Longmire's method, in which he inserts an 18-gauge disposable hypodermic needle along the curvature of the hook, with the bevel toward the inside of the curve "so that the needle opening can engage the barb." When the needle finds that barb, Dr. Longmire states, "it has a very positive locking action and both needle and hook can then be withdrawn by rotating the hook and holding the

Gaffs strike home only after a mate or skipper has
the leader in hand. *Photo by Gene Mueller*

needle tightly down over the barb." In some areas, it should be noted, possession of a
hypodermic needle is illegal. Courts would probably be understanding if such a needle
were mounted on a wooden handle, with no syringe present.

Almost always, the danger involved in saltwater fishing is a by-product of accidents
like this, or to miniscule pests we shrug off as unimportant. Sea monsters rarely
threaten, yet some of the tiniest of insects can ruin a trip. Mosquitoes, sand flies, no-
see-ums, chiggers, and such may be greater perils than the much touted and advertised
killers.

Contrary to popular opinion, insects are a greater menace in far northern regions
than in the tropics. During our brief northern summertime, mosquitoes arise in clouds,
no-see-ums are everywhere, and black flies—which must have teeth like hyenas—emerge
in uncounted billions. There are deer flies and other biting horrors that make life a
constant battle, especially during periods of still, hot weather. Head nets, "bug dope,"

and insecticide bombs offer some protection. Tobacco smoke helps, but to be truly effective it must be issued in such quantity that the sportsman risks nicotine poisoning. Bugs can drive a human being to the brink of a funny tank but, unfortunately, when bugs bite, fish also bite. Bug time is fishing time.

Sand flies are the southern equivalent of the northern no-see-um; they sift through the finest of protective netting and they descend like tiny, red-hot embers. Mosquitoes are seldom lacking in the tropics, and one usually suffers the attention of chiggers or red bugs. These mites cling to the brush and attach themselves to passing humans. They diabolically creep up one's pants legs, drilling into shins, thighs, and groin. A tight belt curbs the invasion, but red bugs often cluster shortly south of the belt, and that is a very tender area. Having drilled in, they secrete a venom that results in a quarter-sized area of all-out itch. In polite company, scratching such areas is frowned upon, so torment is heightened for all but the modern uninhibited.

There is one good defense against red bugs, plus another that helps. Wherever possible—and it is not always possible in the back country—bathe immediately after any trip into the bush. This usually will wash the mites off before they have a chance to drill in. Lacking the prospect of a bath, the attention of red bugs may be discouraged by anointing one's ankles and shanks with kerosene, a practice that may—depending upon the angler's hide—introduce other problems. There are various salves and lotions guaranteed to defeat red-bug infestation, and I have found none of them very effective. Fortunately, chiggers and other biting bugs never plague me to a point of distraction, but I have seen men hounded out of the back country by hordes of little destroyers. There are people so allergic to such treatment that they require hospitalization after massive exposure.

Wood ticks are problems in many areas, and some of them transmit disease. They are slow-moving little creatures, prone to fasten in groin or armpit. The defense is a daily inspection of the entire body, with particular attention to prime target areas during shower or bath, or similar inspection where a bath is impossible. Ticks may be felt while they are crawling upon one's person, but you will never feel them drilling in. They don't hurt; they are simply repulsive, sometimes disease-carrying, obscene little parasites.

In tropical areas, one must think about spiders and scorpions. Only a few spiders threaten mankind, and most scorpions deliver a sting not much worse than that of a healthy wasp. A small minority are dangerous, capable of delivering enough venom to dump a human being into a hospital, or even to kill. Scorpions often are plentiful in warm climates. They are members of the spider tribe and must be taken into account.

Of the spiders, most Americans consider the black widow and the brown recluse most dangerous. Either can induce lingering illness or even death, but the casualty rate is low. Huge and vicious-appearing spiders, such as tarantulas, want no part of mankind, although they will bite if provoked. Black widows and brown recluses live in dark, dank places, and they are physically incapable of biting through the thickest of human skin, so stings usually are suffered in some tender area. Much-used, old-fashioned privies are grand spider habitat, and many a nip in the butt has sent a contemplative angler into low orbit.

Preventive measures are stereotyped in any tropical area. Never, for example, place a hand under any timber or other ground cover where scorpions or spiders may be hiding; use a staff or cut stick to move such an object. Always, upon disrobing, hang clothing well above floor, deck, or ground. Before donning shoes in the morning, shake them out. Unless your feet have become as tough as those of the local natives, refrain from going barefoot in the tropics.

First-timers always worry about venomous snakes, and usually they waste their time. Deadly reptiles often are there, but they always seek to avoid humankind. Few live close to salt water, and those in brackish reaches are furtive. In a lifetime of rambling the salt seacoasts and the jungle rivers of the tropics, I have seen few venomous snakes, and all of those actually observed were either basking on banks, dry brush piles, and other sunny loafing spots, or heading away at a fair rate of knots. However, in snake country, it is wise to carry an antivenin kit. These are available at low cost, and they offer first aid to counteract the rare accident in which an angler blunders upon a dangerous reptile and is struck. Possession of such a kit ensures confidence, too, so it's well worth toting.

Fear of wild animals sometimes borders on the psychotic. Occasional anglers live in mortal terror, worrying about everything from crocodiles and alligators to jaguars and bears. None is very threatening, unless you insist upon invading their domestic lives. The alligator in a wild place is shy and retiring. Crocs, found in the American tropics, are quite as anxious to avoid human beings, although those in certain East Indian rivers have been conditioned to feasting upon Homo sapiens through funeral practices that seem curious to Western man.

Now and then the news media headlines a man grabbed by a shark, ripped by some other toothy creature of the sea, or painfully mauled by a stinging jellyfish. These tales are newsworthy, precisely because they are rare. Multitudinous drownings caused by the inept handling of boats, or by venturing too far out on wave-lashed jetties, are taken for granted and listed on obituary pages. They're frequent, hence, like automobile accidents, such tragedies boast little "news value." No one raises an eyebrow when a dog bites a man. Yet these *are* the major killers, *not* things that go bump in the night—or animals, predatory fishes, snakes, spiders, scorpions, jellyfishes, and other stingers.

High surf is seldom dangerous, but anglers often get wet and pummeled.

Sportsmen who buck for last rites usually underestimate the lethal power of waves and tidal currents, line squalls, and vicious electrical storms. They dare too much and so they die—sometimes dragged down by a piece of equipment that fails in an emergency, but more often swept away by the elements that have been miscalculated. The shambling sea is no country mill pond; its moods change with startling rapidity, and a prudent marine angler had better learn to read the sky and to anticipate those moods. Pogo's "We have met the enemy, and he is us!" should be pondered by every sportsman who insists upon pulling the weedy beard of Neptune.

A marine version of Russian roulette can be simply described. You clamber out to the end of a slippery jetty at night when ground swells are vicious. Perhaps the fish are obliging, and this seems worth scrambling to another rock pile, just a bit farther out. Gung-ho anglers are always immortal, until that terrible moment when a big wave slams home and the world tilts in a cold, black maelstrom of thundering water. Many have survived this treatment, and many died—caught in swirling tidal currents, pulled down by the weight of their waders and foul-weather gear, swept seaward and utterly lost in a hostile void.

On all coasts there are rocky shorelines and precipitate cliffs where the great combers smash ashore, each charged with tons of energy. There is a magnificent feeling of omnipotence and excitement in fishing from such a coast, in tempting the fates and snatching wonderful game fish out of a boiling caldron. Annually, a predictable number of unfortunates are swept off their perches and either drowned or beaten to jelly by the hammer of the waves against the anvil of the rocks. Tidal waves or tsunamis are unnecessary, for there's always the sneak ground swell that, for some reason or another, looms like Judgment Day and sends the alert operator scurrying, while the laggard is caught.

Even on a sand beach, scouring waves and swift currents can be treacherous. In spite of rough water, there is an almost overpowering desire to "reach the bar," that ridge of sand or rock that always seems to lie just beyond a long cast. Often, on sand, a wader must step lively, for otherwise the swift flow will wash bottom out from under his questing feet and he'll go down abruptly. There is the added danger of waves that often converge from two or three directions and can knock you flat in a swift race of suspended sand and cold water, plus the current that can very rapidly take you out to sea after such a mishap. The ocean's a big place.

Up to a point, any freshwater angler can afford to ignore weather; while cold fronts and rain may be uncomfortable, they are not likely to send him to his ancestors. On the sea a fine understanding of wind direction and velocity, tidal rise and fall, the development of violent rips, and probable effect of any weather change may be the difference between life and death. In some coastal areas the tides are tremendous and heightened by storms. An unwary sportsman may camp far above normal tidal bounds, only to have his tent and equipment inundated by a high-course tide pushed by a booming wind. It is quite possible to enjoy a flat, calm sea at sunset and awaken to a roaring terror before dawn. Line storms stir the briny so rapidly that the transformation seems impossible.

Long ago, conning a tin surfboat along a quiet shoreline at night, I saw a leaden cloud build in the northwest, but the stripers were hitting and I was loath to leave. The weather came with a rush that converted July into November, a chill, screaming wind and a deluge of rain. My beach buggy was parked 2 miles up the coast, and I decided to navigate beyond the outer bars. That was a mistake, because I temporarily forgot that I'd have to turn shoreward at some point in time and then thread a wicked series of breaking bars to make landfall. Visibility was almost nil.

Finally, reading the dune formation in silhouette, I knew it was time and swung hard starboard for the run-in, a demoniac wind behind me. Following seas were terrifying, and it was necessary to jockey the throttle to climb crests and to prevent plowing right into the depths of successive troughs. At the beach, colleagues tried to help with flashlights, which thoroughly blinded me so that I could not choose a proper wave to aid recovery. There was nothing to do but brace myself and go in wide open, which I did and—luckily—rode a smashing comber right up on the high dunes.

A friend was not so fortunate; together with a colleague, he launched a small tin boat at two A.M. in rough water and was cruising the edge of a turbulent offshore bar when he struck a floating log. The craft immediately capsized, and two men were struggling in a wild boil of hissing brine and punishing ground swells. They had no flares and it proved impossible to jettison the outboard motor because it had been fitted with a lock to prevent theft. Flotation was therefore just enough to keep the upended craft awash and there were no handholds. While the wind was blowing inshore, it took a considerable time to drift back to the beach, and my friend's companion was unequal to the task; he was dead on arrival.

Such tales are legion, and they usually contain some evidence of pilot error. Nor does the size of a boat have much to do with it. "Seaworthy" is a relative word. A battleship of the line may be sorely tried by typhoon winds and great waves, so there is no pat answer other than a comparison of size, hull configuration, power, and a helmsman's skill against the combined fury generated by storm, wind, and waves. Panic is an able contributor to disaster; a cool hand will ride out some very difficult situations.

Weather, on the sea, is a major killer. Experienced fisherman forever check the meteorological reports, scan the sky for revealing hints of coming attractions, and waste no time in seeking sheltered waters when a blow is imminent. Electrical storms may be accompanied by line squalls, but lightning is no great threat. In a metal boat passengers are relatively safe because they enjoy the Faraday cage principle, which routes charges around the skin of the craft and into the water. Most of today's wooden and fiber-glass crafts are fitted with lightning arrestors, which prevent damage. It isn't very wise for a surf caster to operate during a violent electrical storm, yet there are few records of tragedy laid to the forked lightnings. Sudden, violent winds are greater reivers.

Often, line storms build after a dead calm. One moment the sea is slick as wet silk, breathing deeply, and then a leaden pall builds on the horizon. There is a sudden rush of cool air, followed by a tremendous wind and lashing, almost horizontal rain. The white horses build and spume blows off the top of towering combers. In shoal water, peril is intensified by bursting ground swells. Offshore in a small boat, or a boat of any size, haul that bow into the wind and hold it there. Your life may be at stake.

The angler in a small, outboard powerboat working inshore waters had best go ashore as quickly as possible when a squall develops. If the craft is light enough to manhandle, there is no difficulty; you simply pick a ground swell and plane ashore on its crest. The landing, depending on your skill in judging the wave and jockeying the throttle, may be very smooth—or a sudden, crashing stop. In either event, you'll be home free, even if soaking wet, bruised, humiliated, and a mite sandy. There is a talent involved in beach landing, and we will discuss this in another chapter. It's really very easy—unless you don't know how to turn the trick!

Jack and Frank Woolner use Citizen's Band radio
to contact colleagues on the inshore grounds.

Inadequate equipment often leads to tragedy. It is very easy for a fisherman to gamble when the ocean is somnolent. Beginners may be excused by colleagues, although the sea is unforgiving. There is no word of praise for the ancient mariner who can read cloud formations and wind changes, yet who tarries on a ground that has become threatening. Only a damned fool tosses the dice when a crap out is death.

It is axiomatic that large and well-designed boats can master rougher water than smaller craft. Still, there is a point at which any hull may be defeated, so it is no more than common logic to understand the capabilities of a given boat and to operate well within that craft's sphere of efficiency. Only idiots and inexperienced landlubbers take small outboards far beyond harbor bounds. That's country for twin-screw cruisers fitted with the best of electronic aids to navigation.

While fishing boats in the 26- to 42-foot range figure in coastguard casualty reports, usually due to fire aboard, navigational errors that run them hard aground and into buoys or wrecks, or by misjudging the tidal fury at dangerous inlets, major killers are small, outboard-powered skiffs. Most of these boats are well designed and capable of absorbing much punishment, but they are regularly pushed beyond all safety limits by well-meaning folk who are, to be blunt, very ignorant.

A whistle buoy marking dangerous ground.

Overloading is a common sin—four or five people in a skiff made to carry two. A lack of basic equipment, such as a buoyant vest for every person aboard, or at least a coastguard-approved buoyant cushion, often accompanies overloading. Thousands of tyros annually challenge the ocean without a suitable anchor and 50 feet or more of line. Many fail to carry a paddle, let alone a pair of oars to use in an emergency. They launch in thick fog, without so much as a pocket compass, and they scorn any study of weather conditions. It is inevitable that a certain percentage of these gamblers must pay, and it is a sorry commentary that most of the victims never know that they gamble!

There is a hard and fast rule that one stays with the boat in the event of capsizing. This goes against the grain in a vast sea that seems utterly bereft of human life, especially when the shore seems fairly near. It is tempting to swim to safety, yet this decision commits every blue chip. The shore always seems nearer than it is, and an average man will quickly be exhausted by wind, wave action, and strong tidal currents. Those who swim for it usually die, while those who cling to disabled boats will survive for many hours unless the sea is very cold. In metropolitan waters, help is seldom very far away; a missing craft immediately becomes the object of a coastguard search-and-rescue operation.

A few happy warriors seem to think that any fishing trip is a heaven-sent opportunity to consume great quantities of firewater. An occasional cold beer is no menace, but the gentleman who imbibes copiously is booking passage with Davey Jones. Whether high surf or jetty, small boat or sportfisherman way out beyond harbor bounds, any immoderate use of alcohol is a form of Russian roulette. On this exacting ground you want keen reflexes and a sharp mind. Fish now, drink later—back in the lodge after a great day with rod and reel.

Inland anglers who gravitate to the sea often find it difficult to grasp the enormity of this big pond. The more intelligent of beginners study seamanship and piloting in a Coast Guard auxiliary or United States Power Squadron course. Both are magnificent primers and the instruction is available in every major American city.

There is little danger from the creatures that live in the sea. Some of them are huge and quite capable of inflicting injury or death upon man, but usually they go their strange, subterranean ways in peace. There are smaller hazards, such as stinging jellies and biting fishes and cone shells that protect themselves with sharp spines and venom. There is the stupid, inevitable accident, assured by carelessness.

But the sea itself is the real reiver. Respect it, because—with wind and weather—the world ocean is quite capable of overwhelming and drowning and destroying men who are silly enough to gamble against long odds.

THE GLORY ROAD ~ 16

Tournaments, Contests, and Trophies

Some years ago, thirsting to serve mankind—and to make an honest dollar—I spawned the brilliant idea of publishing a monthly list of marine fishing tournaments under way along American coasts. It seemed reasonably possible to do this in a boxed column, tastefully decorated with a bit of artwork, and I made some initial inquiries prior to scuttling the entire project and gulping a generous beaker of Old Sea Dog.

During the summer months there are roughly 900 fishing contests under way from the northeastern Canadian Maritime Provinces down through metropolitan New York and New Jersey. There are just as many for each comparable length of seaboard southward, through Virginia, the Carolinas, and Florida, into the Gulf of Mexico, around the Horn, and up the Pacific Coast to Alaska. Ten to one, if you outboard across the Bering Sea, there'll be a Soviet tournament official waiting with a wide smile and an entry blank.

Man is a natural competitor, so any complete list of contests, even in fine print, would pack a considerable volume. In addition to the famous tournaments, usually touted as international, there are thousands of state, city, town, and club derbies, plus awards offered by magazines and industry. All these runs for the roses emphasize sportsmanship, and there is no doubt that attendant publicity contributes to the current boom in marine angling.

Unfortunately, any clinical analysis of a fishing contest turns up certain crawling things under the tinsel and glitter. Tournaments, generally, are promotional devices, calculated to vector well-heeled customers into a coastal tourist area and plunk them aboard boats; to sell food, beer, booze, lodging, golden girls, and other human necessities. The pitch is forever glowing, and the denouement may hurt a sport that can ill afford to be plagued by dead-meat trophies and the chicanery that always surfaces when prizes are worth the efforts of a larcenous minority.

Credits, sorrowfully, are always snowed under by debits. A very few contests plow all proceeds back into marine research or management. The Shinnecock Swordfish Tournament on Long Island annually raises funds to construct artificial fishing reefs or to fund other benefits for marine anglers. Some of the brewers and dispensers of hard liquor leaven propaganda with the financial patronage of good causes. This, incidentally, is increasingly characteristic of the big-business approach; promotion of a product remains paramount, but there is a tendency to recognize responsibilities and contribute funds for research and management of a fishery.

No such compliment can be paid to a majority of coastal entrepreneurs who sponsor derbies, tournaments, fishing rodeos, or whatever these advertising gimmicks are called. The object is promotion and exploitation, the placement of feature stories, photographs, and news items that will decoy tourists into a specific area. Too often the marine resource is considered expendable, and no thought is given to intelligent management of an important fishery.

Every other coastal town has its local or "international" fishing derby. A lot of states get into the act, awarding trophies and certificates for the capture of big fish, and fish above an arbitrarily selected weight. In some inexcusable cases, local contests are scheduled during a slack tourist season when motels and hotels are empty and the economy of the region is at poverty level. Sponsors are not overly concerned about the fact that fishing is similarly in the doldrums, and it is worth noting that most of these promoters are chamber of commerce types who wouldn't know a game fish from a bullfrog, and couldn't care less. Their job is the exploitation of tourists, and they are quite capable.

The worst of all contests is that which stresses poundage above all else. It may be newsworthy to report that X number of white marlin or sails have been brought into a vacation city's docks, yet conservation of a magnificent natural resource is not served when dozens of carcasses are daily carted off to the town dump or towed out to sea and cast off for the attention of waiting sharks. Fortunately, public opinion is currently damning this practice, and it will be phased out. Even in Central and South America where, a few years ago, anything boated was killed—edible or not—there is a healthy trend toward release of any game fish that is not desired for food or important enough to become a mounted trophy.

Lusting for publicity, too many tournaments offer rich purses—automobiles, television sets, savings bonds, or choice lots of land. These treasures automatically appeal to a minority of rascals who acquire great game fish outside the contest area and rush them to weighing stations. The only logical defense is a retreat from the rich purse, and an increasing number of contest administrators have seen the light. Ringers are still possible, but never so likely as when a valuable prize is offered. The larcenous brothers aren't interested in a silver cup. Usually, that is.

Attempting to solve the problem, while ensuring promotion, many tournament officials have stressed release. That is good fish all the way, but it has led to some very strange shenanigans. No fish is considered caught until the mate, or skipper, or angler has the leader in hand, yet we have the spectacle of the "long-line release," in which a gamester actually gets off the hook before any leader is at hand, yet is chalked up as a true release. Sometimes the business of turning a fish loose—for honors—can be rather ludicrous.

Hunting cruiser snook on Florida's Tamiami Trail Canal one morning, three of us found a section of the ditch alive with small black bass that had been driven out of the everglades by a drought. Each cast, with spinning tackle, drew an immediate strike; none of those bass would weigh more than a pound, and most of them were in the 8- to 10-inch class. Tenderly, we released each fish. Our tackle, geared to snook, was hardly ultralight for this task, and I don't know how many we landed and slipped back into the water. Our Florida companion was counting.

Later, on the way back to Miami, he insisted on stopping at a tackle shop to fill out release applications. Solemnly, he announced that he had caught and released something like sixty-seven black bass—probably true. Amused by the procedure, I wouldn't admit to catching a one—although it seemed to me that I had matched my host—and I thereby forfeited a beautifully engraved plaque. Proof of skill? That day you couldn't keep the damned things off a hook!

Release is tremendously important, so any contest that awards trophies for fish returned to the water contributes to the future of a grand sport. It doesn't matter whether the charlatans count swarming black bass in a goldfish-bowl canal or miniature snook winched out of the mangrove pockets. If long-line releases are worth an engraved certificate for sportsmanship and valor, those actually brought to boat and turned loose will live to fight again. The phonies will be with us until the last sunset, but their prevarications cannot alter good conservation practices.

In order to further the knowledge of game-fish movement and well-being, tagging is now popular prior to release. The return is small, because the sea is vast, but marine biologists punch their computers every time the cycle is completed, and thus add new data to fuel the engines of truth. It would probably be wise for all release tournaments to specify that each catch be tagged, a thing that, in all cases other than those of the outright liar, would cancel long-line releases.

Tagging has faced and surmounted a lot of hurdles. Initially, sport-fishing skippers opposed the practice because they wanted fish on the rack at day's end. Marking meant release, so they fought it by declaring that a tired gamester was no more than shark bait. Some of them, according to Ernie Lyons, editor of the *Stuart News* in Stuart, Florida, were "real sons of bitches. One, I remember in particular, would lift a sail in by the bill, grab it by the tail, bend it quickly to break its back, turn to the angler who wanted to release it, and say, 'the poor thing died.' "

Ernie, who fishes, raises tropical ferns, and is a prize-winning editorial writer, caught, tagged, and released the first sailfish ever to be recovered, proving that they can live to fight again. It happened back in 1948, and Lyons never got his fair share of credit because Captain Curtis Whiticar's handwriting was a mite hard to decipher. Whiticar tagged this spindlebeak in the water, bill-holding it overside, and resting it for a few moments before release. When he scribbled "Ernie Lyons" on the card sent to Miami, the university misread it as "Eric Lang," and a mythical "Eric Lang" still enjoys the honor of being the first angler to release a sailfish that was later recaptured.

Sport-fishing clubs are legion, and practically every association of anglers sponsors an annual derby or tournament. Such contests help to generate interest in marine angling, and they often decoy a rash of new, dues-paying members. They also create the usual by-products of larceny and hard feeling. Every club boasts a few sterling characters who regard truth as a delusion of the establishment. These amoral citizens enter ringers, or fish that were never actually boated. Occasionally, they submit sales slips that note, laconically, "60 pounds, large," when the catch was not one 60-pound fish, but two mediocre 30-pounders.

Since most contest rules require sealed scales, witnesses, and affidavits from weigh-masters, questionable entries get the old heave-ho, and tempers rise to apoplectic levels. Administration of a club derby is a difficult and thankless task, often made virtually impossible by ill-advised rules and a lack of adequate controls. Differences of opinion poison lifelong friendships and may lead to back-alley punching parties.

Even where the scales are sealed and the witnesses impeccable, professional jealousy creates a deal of trouble. The old story about loading a fish with sinkers to improve its weight is not without justification; some unscrupulous anglers have done this, and some will continue to do so. Where rod and line commercials sell fish in the round, lots of things are done to increase weight—like a Coke bottle filled with sand, thrust into the gullet of a sizable catch. More imaginative pirates simply stuff baitfish into the gut of a trophy. Since this is possible, cynics assume that it is standard operational procedure. I say that it is not.

Back in 1958, Ralph Gray of Southville, Massachusetts, caught a 68½-pound striped bass off North Truro on Cape Cod. The wiseacres said that he'd stuffed his fish with menhaden to make the weight, but they were careful about mentioning the possibility while Ralph was listening, because he is a big guy with the normal complement of ham-sized fists. Today Gray is a successful charter skipper out of Provincetown on the tip of Cape Cod.

The rumormongers were and are wrong, because I was there. At the time, no striped bass approaching that size had been caught since Charles B. Church boated his famous 73-pounder in 1913. Ralph and I pushed off in a 14-foot tin boat in a heavy surf whipped by a half gale. We had no fresh bait aboard, only a selection of big, treble-hooked plugs, That fish was the first of the day, and it wasn't a very formidable battler. After we had wrestled it aboard, Gray opined that he might have a 50-pounder, and we thought no more about it— because bass were all over the place. We caught four more, all big fish, before the wind increased to gale force and we planed ashore.

Ralph weighed his catch on a beach scales that registered a maximum 60 pounds, and the needle clunked. That's when he jumped into his beach buggy and headed for town. He had no menhaden or other bait aboard, and none was immediately available. He was so damned excited that he couldn't have warped the rules, even if so inclined. I have fished with Ralph Gray for a number of years and he is an honorable gentleman. The cynics were wrong.

Many of the state tournaments are social events and perennials; there are ladies and gentlemen who attend them with almost religious fervor and who associate all marine angling with competition. It is not unusual to hear of a citizen who has purchased six sophisticated offshore sportfishermen in as many years, just to keep ahead of the maritime Joneses.

There is a uniform for combat, and proper dress ashore, the former rather unimaginative because it often features an African bush jacket. How this garment muscled into the act I will never know, for it is not a very effective saltwater angler's coat. The bush jacket is made of light poplin, belted at the waist, and blessed by a plethora of pockets. It may be very dashing, but it doesn't turn rain, wind, or spume, and it has no parka or built-in warmth. It does provide lots of bearing surface for patches, and patches appeal to a majority of ardent contest anglers.

Some veterans of the circuit are ambulating advertisements for watering places on all coasts. The beautifully embroidered insignia proclaim everything from participation in assorted tournaments to boasts that the wearer "field tests" tackle, outboard motors, assorted beers, Scotch, and mechanical (as opposed to human) lubricants. There are additional badges, lapel buttons, pins, and brooches, all attesting to consummate skill in the high art of yanking fishes out of the ocean, or membership in some high cult of the swinging sea.

Patch-ism is healthy, a lighthearted and friendly flaunting of honors and campaign ribbons, but it is not very wise to judge an angler's merit on the amount of heroic fruit salad he has accumulated. Some of the frightening authorities are grim-visaged old characters who forever dress in comfortable chinos or weather-turning oilskins, and avoid social gatherings as they would a convention of white sharks. They are sunburned, often whiskery, seldom very articulate, substituting a grunt or a muttered observation for a wordy exposition, but they know the sea and the fishes in it.

If any of the foregoing seems a backhanded slap at tournament angling, let me mend my ways. Competitors always further the technology of marine sport fishing. These pioneers may go to extremes in donning correct dress for breakfast, lunch, and dinner, in flaunting a uniform spattered with patches, and in religiously following the circuit, but mark the fact that they are keen students of tackle and technique. All forsake healthful rest in selecting, maintaining, and improving gear. They experiment with knots and splices, seeking an ultimate in performance. Like the Indianapolis automobile racer, a tournament angler tests new equipment and improves that which has become standard. He needs the edge, and he finds it, thereby benefiting colleagues who fish for fun instead of trophies and campaign patches.

Every tournament angler is gung-ho about opening up new grounds, thus adding much to a grand sport. Solitary pioneers too often are inarticulate; they seek out great fisheries, and they succeed, but infrequently pass the word along. Contest-oriented folk sound the tocsin, thereby adding to general intelligence. Without the effort of S. Kip Farrington, Wedgeport, Nova Scotia, might still be just another sleepy little Canadian fishing village, and Cabo Blanco, Peru, a nonentity. In Kipling's words, tournament fishermen have "skirmished ahead of the army," and they are due full credit.

Quite similarly, the release tournaments have promoted conservation and sportsmanship. In spite of the few who will always take advantage for personal gain, progress is inevitable. Contest anglers have their little idiosyncracies, as we all do, but they publicize new grounds, make a lot of friends, enjoy sport supreme, contribute to the knowledge of mankind, and have a lot of extracurricular fun in the bargain.

There is one important record-keeping organization, the International Game Fish Association. It has its faults and it endures continuous sniping from those of us who treasure a lover's quarrel. Now and then IGFA relents and changes one of its rules. Always, such changes are preceded by much study. Like western democracy, the association can be accused of error, but no better system has been devised. IGFA is honest, nonpartisan, and accurate. Other saltwater record-keepers cater to specialized angling methods, but IGFA is the final authority on a worldwide basis. Indeed, the association's recognition of a 6-pound-test line category in 1972 was an instance of moving with the times.

Fly-rod marks are another bag of worms, because they are calculated on leader test rather than line (although there are other important stipulations). Feather merchants cannot comply with IGFA requirements, so they must set their own standards. These are nicely set forth and there is no conflict. With the exception of fly-rodding, where SWFRA rules should be observed, a citizen who covets prizes or world records had best be governed by IGFA rules affecting tackle and technique.

There is a certain Alice in Wonderland aspect about record-hunting. No one sneers at an all-tackle mark, but line-test triumphs sometimes engender impolite smiles. It is still quite possible for a hungry exhibitionist to take dead aim at a specific line-test record and bust it with the greatest of ease. Some records are impossibly low, and some thrones aren't even occupied. The astute and trimly bearded Nelson Bryant of *The New York Times* recently told me—tongue in cheek—that he planned to shatter the all-time world's fly-rod record on common Boston mackerel. Nels won't find that very difficult because—to date—nobody has applied for the honor.

A quick check of IGFA record lists will disclose a number of line-test marks that are insults to the intelligence of anglers, and the Salt Water Fly Rodders of America has dozens of open ends. All you have to do is catch a fish and enter it. You'll be a hero.

Record-keepers and contest administrators are bound by the rules of their specific organizations, and said rules may be remarkably dissimilar. All serious record-keepers require absolute proof of a catch, together with a line sample for testing. There must be witnesses, a photograph of the fish, and a notarized affidavit from a weighmaster. Local tournaments and club contests may accept the word of a contestant, but most of them want proof, signed and sealed.

Any sharpshooter can draw a bead on specific contests that are run—for the milk and honey of promotion—by magazines, brewers, importers of hard booze, and various townships, states, or territories. All of these tournaments require some proof that a catch is kosher, although they often suffer the attention of charlatans who enter fish never caught within the boundaries of the derby or strictly according to its rules. The larger the monetary return for a first-place award, the greater the chance of finagling.

There are highly competent people who have roamed the sea for half a lifetime without beaching or boating one record fish, and there is the beginner who, on his first trip to the briny, comes up with a monster that goes into the record books. This sort of thing irks veterans, but it happens. Very often the beginner—precisely because he is a babe in the woods—wrecks his own chances for immortality. Charter-boat mates regularly help to demolish record claims.

I have, previously, discussed the necessity for a mate to help an abject beginner in setting a hook or adjusting a drag. In so doing, the crewman aids his angler, but he cancels all hope of a record certificate if the hooked fish happens to be a trophy. All rules specify that the fisherman must do it all. He must hook his quarry, play it, and land it without any aid from an associate. No one can touch the tackle, adjust a drag, or otherwise physically interfere until it is time to grasp a leader, apply the sharp point of a gaff, or dip a net. A mate can adjust a fighting harness and can swing a chair. He can offer advice, but if he touches that tackle until a leader is at hand, your record is gone with the wind.

Legions of charter-boat mates, conditioned by duffers, seem to think it their duty to set all hooks and to adjust drags during an offshore battle. Most of them are intelligent lads who like a tip at day's end, so it is wise to acquaint them with standard operational procedure prior to any strike. Mates are good fisherman, so they won't sob if you make it plain that all rules must be observed. Indeed, a majority of these deckhands will applaud an angler who really knows how to strike, fight, and boat a trophy. Remember—they've been exposed to a lot of nincompoops.

If it gets down to hot argument, note that *you* have chartered the boat. Good skippers may like, or dislike, the people they ship aboard, but the patron is boss because he's paying the freight. For an infinitesimal moment in time and space, within reason, the charter customer owns that craft and he has a right to declare his desires in angling practices and techniques. Moreover, his desires should be honored by skipper and mate, again within reason. Usually there is no conflict when a fisherman exhibits some natural skill and outlines the ground rules he considers pertinent.

Tackle geared to IGFA standards is necessary where records are coveted. Practically all the rods and reels offered by reputable makers fall within the association's butt and tip limitations, so lines, leaders, and lures are major offenders. One poor rule is that which allows no more than 15 feet of double line and the same length of leader where big game fishes are sought on 50-pound-test gear. This works a particular hardship on the monster-seeker who elects to use light tackle.

The problem, from IGFA's point of view, is a blanket rule to cover all applications. No one needs 30 feet of double line and the same amount of leader for the typical offshore catch. This is necessary only where very large gamesters are baited and hooked. Perhaps some future decision may be keyed to the size of the fish boated, rather than to the test of tackle. While no such edge is needed with, say, 30-pound test (indeed, it would be a handicap), the man who uses 50-pound mono or braid on a monster weighing 500 pounds or more is entitled to some consideration.

Unlimited means 130-pound test or heavier. Anglers get into trouble when they range down, because a lot of strands simply do not part at a point advertised. The cheaper the line, the more likely it is to be stronger than the label attests, and more prone to stretching, instability, and fraying. If a fine fish is offered as a 20-pound-test record and the line sample parts at 21 or 22 pounds on IGFA's machines—no record.

All the better line manufacturers now offer strands that are engineered to break a few ounces *short* of any given test. Such lines are stable and well braided or extruded, for they are built to the specifications of perfectionists who desire the best and sneer at astonishing claims that a given line is, say, "the strongest 20-pound test in the world." Blood pressures rise when a probable record is cast into limbo because a sample of line tests a pound or so over its rated strength, proof that the maker had provided a built-in margin for error.

Wire lines are still scorned by IGFA, although accepted as sporting by many contest officials. Until 1971, no treble-hooked plug could be used for record, and this rule has been relaxed only to a point where a lure fitted with two trebles qualifies *if it is cast*. The plug fitted with three treble hooks, or one that is trolled, rather than heaved, remains an outlaw in the official view of IGFA. American saltwater sportsmen generally protest this thinking, and practically all club or area tournaments accept any lure designed to catch one fish at a time. The so-called "umbrellas" and other spreader rigs, where a number of armed lures makes it possible to catch two or three gamesters simultaneously, are regularly attacked as meat-fishing instruments and rightly banned in contest angling.

Most of us regard all-tackle world records as lucky strikes, but there are reputable folk who gird for combat and very actively stalk honors. They are perfectionists, and I salaam to them, for they advance angling techniques and improve tackle. Zealots will replace a line after one hard battle with a large game fish. They study knots and splices, choosing only those that approach the utopian 100 percent strength factor, and they select every swivel, leader, and hook with the painstaking care of a brain surgeon at work. Nothing, or at least nothing that can be detected, is left to chance, and that is commendable because there is no such thing as fisherman's luck. We make our own luck, and a competitor forever seeks the edge.

Poundage pays off. Therefore, ignoring the minority of shallow souls who will actually load a fish with handy bait (or sinkers if he lacks imagination), certain facts become apparent. A fish that bleeds copiously loses weight, so gaffing should be immaculate. Place the hook well forward where possible, or back in some fleshy side of the body where it will not rip the belly or pierce an artery. Netting, of course, is a better procedure with fish of a size to enter the mesh.

Winched out of the water, any fish immediately begins to dehydrate and will lose a certain amount of weight before it is suspended from an accurate, sealed scales. Figures vary, but there is no doubt that loss is there, escalated when the catch is submitted to drying sunlight over a period of hours. Rush any possible record-breaker to a scales. If this is impossible, keep the prize both cool and wet. Drenched burlap will serve as an impromptu covering. Icing is dandy, if you have a suitable fish box—and ice. Even under the most favorable of conditions, a catch that is kept away from the weighing station for a number of hours will lose poundage through seepage and natural dehydration. The seepage loss is sometimes partially prevented by plugging the quarry's vent immediately after capture. Ounces count, so it's wise to move rapidly and plan a campaign!

There is an awful tendency to rattle a possible record-breaker into the first available scales that may, or may not, be accurate, and then to weigh the trophy again on a second scale. If the two conflict, you're in trouble; nit-pickers will immediately point to the discrepancy, and you may have to accept the lesser of the two figures. It is logical to select a proper weighing station beforehand, to get one accurate reading, plus accurate measurements of length and girth, and a signed affidavit from the weighmaster. It will be necessary to submit a proper sample of line and, in some cases, the lure used. You'll need a photograph, preferably a sharp, clear print that shows the angler and his catch. Judges will be able to make a reasonable comparison. Don't indulge in the common deception of holding a fish out at arm's length, so that depth of focus will make it seem larger than it actually is; the trick is very evident. Finally, prepare an accurate statement of fact and submit the entire package as quickly as possible. Data prepared for IGFA will be accepted elsewhere, if you yearn for trophies and occasional cash awards.

In the business of record-hunting, one must count ounces as well as pounds, so fish-house scales are sometimes questioned. There is a tendency in some areas to pay on the pound, subtracting ounces if they add up to a minimum, or adding them beyond the half. Remember that in the books of IGFA, any catch under 100 pounds must be at least 8 ounces heavier than the existing titleholder, or a tie is declared. Trophies of better than 100 pounds must be a full pound heavier to be recognized as new champs. If you're serious about this, by all means correspond with the International Game Fish Association, 2190 S.E. 17th Street, Fort Lauderdale, Florida 33316. Rule books are available at minimal cost.

Some anglers profess scorn for prize awards and records, and they are gentle prevaricators. We'd all like to shatter a mark or accept a bauble for the best fish of the year. Most of us troll or cast hopefully, not really expecting to bag a monster, nor even striving for a line-test triumph. The small minority of men and women who gun for records comprises a tiny group, and most of these are scrupulously honest.

Cheating is possible and the law of averages ensures attempts to beat the system. I have thought about this, out on a dark ocean with nobody to bear witness. I could, conceivably and were I so inclined, boat a tremendous battler on an illegal outfit or lure, then rush it ashore for beachside witnessing and later commitment to the scales. I could lie about the tackle, collect prizes in various derbies and, perhaps, a certificate from IGFA. I could be a hero, but I'd know that I had cheated, and so the triumph would turn sour. One has to live with oneself, and truth is a very strange thing; you can trample it, spit upon it, and declare it a decadent tool of the Establishment, but truth forever bounces back to confound mankind.

In the category of man bites dog, all-tackle records sometimes are eaten before the angler knows he has scaled Olympus, but failed to stake a claim. This is folklore, occurring just often enough to add credence to each tale. It happens, yet more often the weight of a given catch is estimated and exaggerated. Any sizable fish is a monster to the beginner, and there is no scales to prove or disprove a good story. You can't weigh a memory, no more than you can feast on filleted strikes and broiled long-line releases. Anyone can be deceived.

One night, fishing with Jack Townsend, I caught a herd of very big bluefish. The two largest seemed, to me, monsters of their kind and I kept them segregated, tails slit with a sheath knife to establish identity. Come morning, the unsympathetic scales indicated that each weighed 17 pounds, right on the button. They were big choppers, but a mite short of the glory road. I'd have sworn those fish went better than 20.

Tournament casting is another popular diversion among competitive anglers and, like the fishing contest, it continually aids the improvement of tackle and technique. There is a measure of old-fashioned hokum involved, because the spectacular "unlimited" events usually feature gear that would be utterly inadequate on any fishing ground. Four-ounce weights, in surf-casting contests, can be heaved to better than 500 feet when a shock leader is backed with 10-pound-test monofilament. Try to do it with 36-pound braid! In fly casting, special shooting heads are employed and reels discarded.

From an angler's viewpoint, the most valuable casting tournament is that which is limited to actual fishing tackle—the standard rods, reels, and lines calibrated to everyday use rather than one performance gauged by a tape measure. Winners in either category deserve praise, for they become champions through much practice, training, hair-trigger reflexes, and the precise timing of an athlete. The great competitors may be poor anglers, or even scornful of angling as a sport, but their zealous development of tackle to attain an ultimate performance always benefits colleagues on the beach or in the back country.

In casting, the lighter the line, the farther a given weight may be heaved. This is one secret of the beach bum who astonishes onlookers with tremendous casts. Within reason, light lines are feasible when tipped with shock leaders. Since a distance rod must feature a good deal of backbone, it follows that a hooked fish must be played rather carefully when a line is light. Most of us go too heavy, but a few grandstand artists woo the other extreme. They pop a lot of lines and they lose a lot of fish—and lures—but they sure throw it out there when muscle and gear are properly synchronized.

Accuracy contests may be more important than distance, if only because this art is very necessary to a working angler. The citizen who can toss a fly or plug into a hat-sized hole in the mangroves, or plunk a lure right in the swirl of a surface-feeding fish at any distance from 50 feet to 100 yards enjoys a definite edge. An ability to make a long cast will help, although its greatest importance lies in flawless performance at the standard short to medium killing ranges.

Chairborne, while writing about far-away places, I often procrastinate by gazing at a bonefish on the wall. My first, it weighed 8½ pounds and was caught a long time ago on a live shrimp. (I always admit the truth when cornered.) The trophy went to Al Pflueger in Miami and was a handsome thing when delivered.

Now that lovely creature displays cracks around the gills and ventral fins, no fault of Pflueger, as we shall see. Invariably, the spoiling of a fine trophy must be laid at an angler's doorstep, and deterioration can begin very early in the game. If a mount is coveted above all things in heaven and on earth, there are ground rules to observe. First, as the old bromide goes, catch a fish.

From the outset, any prospective mount must be handled with care. Gaffing should be flawless, through the lower jaw if possible. If not, then one side of the trophy will be marred while the other, hopefully, remains handsome. Be very picky about any loss of scales or ripping of fins. Strive to take a sharp color photograph of the specimen immediately after it is caught, while still alive and flaunting those almost impossibly vivid colors that landsmen never see. (A taxidermist who is familiar with the fish in question won't need this aid, but "stuffers" tackling new and unfamiliar varieties are confused. That's why a tropical or semitropical trophy is best delivered to a sun-country craftsman, and a northern battler placed in the capable hands of an artist who knows frostbite fishes.)

Having reduced to possession, as biologists say, wrap the catch in salt-wet cloth or sacking and get it into a capacious icebox. Keep *that* fish on top of others, so that it can't be damaged by pressure. In the event that ice is nonexistent, employ the wet sack and keep your trophy in deep shade. Dehydration is a major enemy.

Often it will be found necessary to quick freeze a fine specimen prior to shipment. Keep it wrapped in wet cloth, but add a layer of paper to prevent the fabric from sticking to a freezer's shelves. If there's a "best" side, see that it's uppermost, and refrain from placing any other object on the fish until it is rock hard.

Finally, hand carry or air freight to the taxidermist of your choice. Instruct him about the position you desire, whether a complete mount, or simply head and shoulders—incidentally a very effective choice with a billfish that would otherwise occupy too much space on a rumpus room's wall.

Mounts are expensive, so they deserve care. Sometimes, a year or so after delivery, a proud sportsman finds that his stuffed beauty is developing fine cracks around the gills or elsewhere. This logically triggers a yearning to caress the taxidermist with a blunt instrument.

Occasionally, a craftsman will be at fault, due to some unstable filler that expands or contracts on drying. Usually, if this happens, he will pay freight charges and make repairs at no cost, *so long as the mount has been out of the shop for less than one year.* Beyond that period there are too many owner-induced deterioration factors involved.

A fisherman wants the fish he caught, not a facsimile. This means an actual skin mount, instead of a plastic copy. Any fine taxidermist can oblige, but he has problems. Skin mounts are subject to cracking after a period of years, and the process is accelerated by heat without humidification. Excessive humidity is quite as damaging, and then there is rough handling that leads to broken fins and more hairline cracks.

Fish mounted with gills closed are especially subject to cracking, since the gill covers keep pressing outward to assume their natural, flared position. One solution is to open the gills on all species, and many taxidermists do this in self-defense. All offer advice about maintenance in the home, and few citizens are able to meet the standards cited.

A mount should be positioned well away from heaters or air-conditioners and shielded from direct sunlight. Temperatures must be even, because a quick change is damaging. If humidity is not controlled, forget it! Never lower than 50 percent, and not too high either. Trophies are best cleaned with a soft, slightly moistened cloth.

So my bonefish is cracked and a bit discolored, but I'm rather fond of it. Still, photographs are pretty good and I cotton to the idea of "shooting" your quarry and releasing it too!

Fishing, according to some philosophers, is not a competitive sport. I disagree. It is one of the most competitive games ever invented by mankind. One always seeks a fair share of the fishes available, whether or not they are released, and it is pleasant to wipe the eye of one's partner, so long as he does not go hungry while you collect all the goodies. If I have a pilgrim aboard on beach or open ocean, I want him to catch fish, and I like to see his best conquest top mine by a pound or so.

But, if he manages to hook and land a world's all-tackle record while I am guiding, then I have dark thoughts about breaking a couple of his arms or legs and tossing him to the sharks!

Competition is always there, even when it is a solitary desire to outwit a spooky fish when no other angler is in sight. Trudging a lonely beach, or conning my small boat through the offshore rips by night or day, I talk to myself and curse my ineptitude when a cast is backlashed or too much pressure pulls the hooks out of a possible trophy. I am supremely alone with the elements and the quarry, and I fight *me,* as well as the deep-breathing ground swells, the fish, and the burgeoning tides.

If there is ho competition, why do my friends—all over this watery world—drive themselves to slave labor on the flats, in the high surf, and on the big, blue-water grounds? Why are they willing to suffer sunburn and cracked lips and eyes forever tinted with the red of exhaustion? Come on, ladies and gentlemen, we compete against our own skills and wage a gentle war with colleagues. Otherwise, there would be no point to the operation.

A fish is just a fish, available on any supermarket's slab. It becomes something more important when the seabirds are wailing and the surf is booming and the bait is showering. I think I'll rest my case.

THE TRAVELING ANGLER ~17

Logistics for Jet-Age Nomads

I am tempted to say that all nomads find it necessary to travel light, to select duffel with great care, and to eliminate all things weighty and frivolous. This was so when the American Indians and the Bedouin of North Africa trekked, and it is also true to a certain extent when modern man boards a jet plane. We seem to have arrived full circle, and yet motor vehicles serve those of us who can't be happy without a long ton of gear and goods within reach. Fitting out remains an important prelude to any adventure, for there is a need to include basics and to cull out items that may be used, but probably will not.

Perhaps airline travel has reached a point of excellence, yet I always feel like an overburdened refugee lugging a large, well-packed suitcase, two tackle boxes, a crush-proof container loaded with rods, and an assortment of cameras into a terminal—and out at the end of a long trip. There are helpful gentlemen to shoulder the load for a reasonable fee, but I'm always late, perspiring and wondering whether the tickets are truly confirmed and the planes flying on schedule. Most of the time one is directed to Gate 8, which turns out to be 7 miles east and turn right. There is the matter of customs, on any trip out of the country.

Invariably, I forget something very important, so the great trick lies in organization well prior to packing and boarding. A checklist sounds pretty dull and academic, but it's a worthwhile gimmick. One should plan logistics a week ahead of flight time, rather than wait until the last call and then realize, on the way to the air terminal (all terminals are located approximately 50 to 100 miles away from point of departure), that polarized glasses are still tucked in a leather case, at home, or that the baggage contains no foul-weather gear. One may shrug this off if the destination is reasonably civilized, but there are innumerable fishing grounds back in the world's hinterlands. In these paradisaical spots, the local markets sell plantains and yams and tourist gimcracks, but little in the way of modern sunglasses, rubberized garments, or decent fishing tackle.

Much, therefore, depends on destination. I am not overly irked when the target area is close to a large city. Obviously I can, while muttering about my own idiocy, purchase just about anything available at home. Indeed, it is sometimes wise to take advantage of local industry. I can't see toting a batch of chino pants or short-sleeved cotton shirts to Florida, because every corner haberdasher will have them piled to the ceilings. Similarly, a traveling tropical type can buy all sorts of woolens in the cold North, *if* he visits a population center. I couldn't pass through Seattle without repairing to Eddie Bauer's emporium and purchasing a delightful goose-down vest or jacket.

It's still best to outfit with care and to tote everything necessary to ensure both sport and health. The angler who travels southward, and especially a pale northerner who is not acclimated to broiling sunlight, will want clothing that covers his body, but is light enough to be comfortable. Figure on chinos or poplin pants, not Bermuda shorts, unless these will be worn at an evening cocktail party. Swear by long-sleeved cotton shirts, with a few short-sleeved models for pleasant hours after the sun, no longer an implacable enemy. Pack a wide-brimmed straw hat or, in the event that you prefer baseball caps or long-billed swordfishing types, include a selection of bandanna handkerchiefs that can be worn, Beau-Geste style, to keep your neck and earlobes from crisping like well-done bacon. Tropical sunlight is nothing to trifle with; even the local guides go to shady hats and surgical masks to protect their lips.

Never pack waders into the tropics. The best footwear for wading in palm-tree country will be ordinary tennis shoes. You'll want them because coral outcrops are sharp, and there is always the possibility of stepping on a sharp-spined sea urchin. Light foul-weather pants and tops are advisable because, even in the lands of eternal sunshine, you get torrential rains and occasional chill winds. For the same reason, always include a shell jacket as a windbreaker, and a light woolen shirt or two. On any fishing ground it is possible to remove excess clothing, but it's hell when temperatures plummet and you don't have anything to turn the weather. Sometimes nights can be distressingly nippy in the semitropics; I have seen thermometers plunge to near freezing in Miami in March. When that happens, residents fire up electric space heaters and shiver like Old Joe Pelican on a piling.

Warm clothing is a necessity in the North, and the air traveler saves both bulk and weight by toting well-made quilted jackets and pants. Foul-weather gear is an absolute necessity, both to ward off the wet and to turn chill winds. A surf caster will need waders, for even in midsummer these northern seas are cold. Any jacket or foul-weather top should be equipped with a parka hood. Sure, there'll be days and even nights when a North Atlantic or North Pacific sportsman will be able to dress like a tropical beach bum, but don't count on it. Remember the old rule—you can take it off, but you're up the creek if it's cold and no warm clothing is available.

Almost always, a saltwater angler needs sunglasses to defeat glare and reflection. The best are polarized, because they permit a measure of visibility *through* the water, and tan is the best choice for anyone who boasts normal color vision. Color deficients are more numerous than you'd think—almost 9 percent of the American male population and 1 percent of the female. These folk are not color blind, a term loosely used; they can distinguish colors, but often have difficulty with reds and greens. For them, tan may be a poor choice, and either neutral gray or an olive-green shade is best. Lenses should be dense wherever light intensity is high. As a rule of thumb, on beach or open ocean, if you can see a person's eyes through his sunglasses, the lenses are insufficient to offer adequate protection.

Fine wraparound glasses are available at low cost, say $2.50 to $5. More sophisticated glass sandwiches, with a polarized layer of gelatin positioned between two optically ground-glass lenses, are more expensive; they resist scratching, but are never true wraparound. Where peripheral light is a problem, as it often is on tropical flats, blinders are necessary. On the credit side, such glasses are cooler than the close fitting wraparound. There are prescription shades, but they are rather expensive. If an angler must wear spectacles, clip-on polarized lenses are available.

All glasses are a sort of necessary evil. One may need them for no other reason than to see, or to divert the damaging white glare, ultraviolet and infrared rays of strong sunlight. Glasses are an abomination in the rain, and they are forever falling overboard during some hectic wrestling match with a big fish. To prevent this, I favor a length of ordinary braided fishline attached to the end of each earpiece and looped around my neck, but some colleagues can't abide the practice because the line feels like a crawling thing. Better carry an extra pair of sunglasses if you don't use an anchoring device. They're very important to defeat glare and thus conquer eyestrain, and to see through the water when fish are hunted on a brilliant tropical flat.

In packing for a trip, primary items will be carefully selected, but you are likely to forget some little gimmick that adds a measure of comfort. I smoke a pipe—and apologize for the habit—so it is necessary to tote one extra briar together with a packet of cleaners. Since the tobacco of my choice may not be available in some foreign port, it is also good sense to transport a supply of the weed. Initially, I employed a plastic bag that would take a full pound or more, but I have found it more efficient to pack several ordinary oilskin pouches, each secured with a rubber band. If you dote on cigarettes, a nasty habit at best (I once smoked four packs a day), it may be good sense to transport a supply of your favorite brand. Ditto cigars. I have tried to puff native twists in faraway places, and I am simply not man enough to master them.

Since we seem launched on a discussion of questionable creature comforts, there is the matter of booze. Good stuff is available just about anywhere on this globe, and local beer usually proves delightfully cool, tasty, and divorced from Montezuma's curse. There are areas where spirits are expensive and then it may be wise—if you care to indulge—to stock up en route. Almost always liquor is more expensive in the United States than it is in other nations, but there are exceptions. Noting these, one can transport a quota of duty-free spirits when leaving this country.

Even in the land of love beads and Establishment, there are places where John Barleycorn is officially discouraged, if unofficially popular. Cape Hatteras is a lovely place to visit and to go fishing, but I wouldn't want to live there because you have to travel weary miles northward to buy a bottle of good Scotch or any other alcoholic beverage. Therefore, if you like a before-dinner cocktail, better inquire whether it will be necessary to arrange for the ingredients before packing in.

Bathing and shaving may be the hallmarks of civilized man, but there are occasions in rough jungle camps, and even on remote beaches close to a metropolis, where ablutions must be planned. Away out in the blue I can endure my own aboriginal muskiness for a period of several days, between trips to freshwater swimming holes or occasional showers under the omnipresent oil drum, but whiskers itch and I want them off. It is always possible to boil a basin of water and lather up with a cake of Ivory prior to wielding a safety razor. Aerosol cans of lather are fine, although they usurp more space in the duffel. An increasing number of traveling anglers favor the self-contained electric razor, although it adds bulk. Be sure it's self-contained; there are few electrical outlets on wild beaches and jungle rivers.

Scheduled airline travel is a far different thing from flying bush planes, where you can safely tote anything, including a pet python. The commercial scheds evidently employ professional baggage smashers, and woe to any item of equipment that is not thoroughly boxed and armored. It is not enough to close a tackle box with the patented snaps they feature; if you're smart, you'll also encircle the thing with a well-tightened web belt or a securely knotted hank of rope. A few sophisticated models, like the Vlchek Adventurer Model 2022, a fine saltwater choice because it is capacious, rugged, and boasts a brace of adequately compartmented trays, can be padlocked. That's a simple thing, and yet it is very important—not to discourage thieves, but to prevent accidental opening and spillage in transit.

Rod cases, like tackle boxes, must be resistant to shock or crushing. The best are made of high-impact aluminum. Ordinary cloth cases, with stiffeners, practically guarantee mashed guides or fractured sections at journey's end. Short, jointed rods can be hand-carried, but this is difficult when an angler needs a selection of sticks. Therefore, the true airplane rod is a jointed item that can be packed in a crush-proof container with a number of its fellows and consigned to the wicked luggage compartment where it may well be dropped off at Rome when you are flying to Nairobi, but at least will not be thoroughly masticated.

Cameras and other delicate instruments are best hand-carried. I always board an airplane with a leather case stocked with two or three still cameras, a motion-picture machine, and a lot of film. The package rarely quite fits under a seat, but at least I preserve it from the destroyers.

Customs officials, in traveling in or out of any country, rarely pose a problem. These worthies, regardless of nationality, seem to enjoy *fingerspitzengefühl* (a feeling in the tips of the fingers) for wrongdoers. If you're clean, they usually make a swift, cursory examination of baggage and then wave you through. I always feel, just as I feel when a state policeman stops me for some nonsense like a malfunctioning taillight, that I *must* have inadvertently robbed a bank or committed some heinous crime, else why would this uniformed janissary flag me down? Always the grim visage parts in a smile, and the customs official asks about fisherman's luck while he probes dirty laundry and motions me on. Nobody hates an angler!

I have been told that it is a rather good idea to carry bills of sale or an insurance policy on expensive cameras toted out of the country, and I do this. Curiously, no customs inspector has ever so much as opened or looked at the reinforced leather bag in which I carry some $2,000 worth of photographic equipment. They've asked about contents, and I have told them, and they have yet to evidence further interest. Nonetheless, it is good policy to document anything of worth. Carry all papers in one folder: tourist card or passport, bills of sale, health certificates, or whatever. Don't try to beat the system. Only professional smugglers get through, occasionally, and they're often tripped by stool pigeons. Amateurs are sitting ducks.

On a long trip to some exotic ground, selection of tackle is a soul-searching thing. There is the problem of weight and the need for specific lures. You can't take everything, yet you are fully aware that lures and ancillary tackle may not be readily available after touchdown. Prior correspondence with a contact on the scene is in order; a skipper or guide will detail needs. Take his advice, because he is there and he knows, or should know. If you desire to tote a few extracurricular goodies, that is your right, and maybe you can surprise him. At the very least, carry the gear that he feels is necessary.

There is a very human desire to confound the experts and to prove that a lure or rig that produces on one seaboard will revolutionize angling on another. Maybe it will, but human beings are pretty equal in intelligence, regardless of their home ground. Often the fishes sought, and the methods of luring them to a hook, change with the area. When in Rome . . . There is nothing reprehensible about experimentation, but only a stupid man scorns the tactics and strategy employed by his guide on a new ground. Some items of equipment are cosmopolitan.

There is an art to the proper stuffing of a tackle box, and note that the box itself should be designed for marine fishing. Too many of the inland models feature miniature compartments and trays too small to hold a healthy saltwater plug or spoon. All equipment used in the briny is beefed up, by comparison with sweetwater gear, and the box is no exception. Several tough, roomy models with man-sized trays and compartments are now marketed.

The basics? Leader materials, a wide selection of hooks in different bends and sizes; snaps, swivels, assorted trolling, egg, pyramid, and dipsey sinkers. Bronze sleeves and a proper crimping tool go into every well-appointed tackle box. Pliers often are carried on an angler's belt, but an extra set should be packed. Think about one needle-nosed type, and another all-purpose job with a sturdy wire cutter. There is a lightweight Diamond combination pliers that features a small, adjustable wrench, a screwdriver, and wire cutter, a fine tool for tackle tinkering. You'll want a separate screwdriver as well, with interchangeable blades.

To guarantee a measure of maintenance in some wild watering place where the guide doesn't speak English and the nearest tackle shop is a few hundred miles that-away, over a rain forest and mountain range, stock at least one rod guide and tiptop calibrated to each of your traveling sticks, spare parts for reels, particularly bail springs for fixed-spool winches and Teflon drag disks for both spinning and revolving-spool models. A small roll of plastic electrician's tape serves many purposes. Dental floss, a spool of nylon wrapping thread, and another spool of good old-fashioned linen Cuttyhunk will be handy. Every tackle box should carry a small, screw-capped can of machine oil and a stick of ferrule cement, a tube of Ambroid, and/or a bottle of lady's fingernail polish. There is need for a couple of sharp bastard files to touch up dull hooks, proper needles for stringing and sewing bait, a penlight, matches in a waterproof packet, and Band-Aids (either the Johnson & Johnson trademarked variety, or something similar). I always tote a few in my wallet, for a slight cut can bleed copiously and make life very unpleasant in the field. My fishing boxes also contain a tube of suntan lotion, a stick of lip ice, and a can of lighter fluid to fuel the ever-present Zippo. Nonsmokers can save a few ounces here.

Some countries will confiscate a knife at customs and, if you're lucky, return it when you leave. Where no such restrictions are posted, it is a good idea to carry either a stainless clasp knife or a sheathed blade. The latter will be most effective, although it may usurp a bit more space. There are, in addition to the folding variety (which may be hard to open when fingernails are softened by salt moisture), two excellent types. One is an all-purpose sheath knife with a rigid blade, ideal for general work, adequate for cutting strip baits, and great for carving the hooks out of tough gristle. Browning, Buck, and many other makers offer magnificent tools.

Then there is the filleting knife with a blade that is long, slender, and resilient. The very best, for fish-house work, are made of high-carbon steel with a plain, rough wooden handle, but an angler may be better served by a stainless type, regularly touched up with a stone. Normark produces excellent blades with man-sized birch or plastic handles. Nothing is better designed for dressing food fish or for the artful trimming of a strip bait.

A saltwater sportman's knife requires no great blade length or fancy blood drains. Too many are offered with saw-edged fish scalers, bottle openers, hand guards, and other useless gadgets. Scalers never work and they impede clean cutting action. The ideal is a very basic sheath knife, trim, sharp, and built of metal that will retain an edge. Wherever possible, carry one on your belt, and another in a tackle box.

Lures must be chosen with care, tailored to the requirements of the ground you will fish and the techniques employed. Sometimes the plug that is so successful in one region will be a total loss elsewhere, so prior research is indicated. Spoons are effective everywhere in the world, as are Jap feathers and bucktail jigs. Standard streamer flies and popping bugs serve marine flycasters on all waters. Choice of lures often narrows down to size and, in the case of jigs, weight. Again, contact your guide, charter skipper, or lodge owner to ask for details on specific needs.

Lures considered hot in any tourist mecca will be available in local tackle shops and it's often best to purchase them on the scene, unless you know the precise models prior to departure and can buy them at city rates. Tackle, in any vacationland, will bring top prices—no sin on the part of merchants, for they make hay during a short tourist season and then starve for X number of months. The difference in price is infinitesimal anyway. Again, make a mental note of the fact that efficient gear may be very scarce and hard to come by in an exotic location. Take everything you'll need, plus extras, such as bulk line or additional reel spools well packed with the strand of your choice.

There is a good possibility that you won't need the extras, but they become tokens of goodwill in many remote locations. At the end of a trip, your guide or host may be delighted to receive bulk line, plugs, spoons, or other lures that are hard to obtain in his bailiwick. In Central and South America, American tackle is both scarce and expensive. I have tipped guides with coin of the realm, often generously, but their eyes really light up when I offer, in addition, a gift of line, lures, or polarized glasses. A very serviceable pair of sunglasses will cost you less than $5 in the United States, but they are priceless treasures to a foreign jungle guide. One, smiling like a youngster with a new toy, made me happy by declaring, after I had whipped glasses off my face and handed them to him: "Meester Frank, with *these* I can see to Miami!"

Since most fisherman dote on cameras to record their triumphs, protection of an expensive instrument is vital. This boils down to a completely waterproof container, and there are two basic choices. First, there is the customized tropical case that is built for a specific camera and fitted with rubber gaskets so that no moisture can seep in when the case is locked. A war-surplus steel ammunition box, the .30 caliber for miniature cameras, and the .50 caliber for larger models, will prove satisfactory, and both are inexpensive. One warning: even where packets of silica gel are strategically placed to defeat condensation, never keep these cases closed over any considerable period of time in traveling to or from a fishing ground. Air circulation, so long as the air is dry, is kind to delicate shutter mechanisms. Moisture, whether spray, spume, a tropical downpour, or condensation in a tight metal case, leads to stabbing pains in the wallet.

Incidentally, and perhaps more important than you might think, a war-surplus steel ammunition box lined with foam rubber is a fine camera case for one reason other than its low price and rugged efficiency. I think Lefty Kreh, a superb fisherman and a master of timesaving kinks and gadgets, first noted that an olive drab, slightly rusty tin box in an automobile is unlikely to vector in thieves. A leather camera case, on the other hand, often leads to jimmied doors and a tearful visit to the insurance adjuster.

All cameras are fairly delicate instruments, as are binoculars. Careless beginners often place them on a console, a fighting chair, or an icebox while trolling offshore grounds. If the boat then wallows or pitches in rough water, camera or binoculars may hit the deck with a resounding crash and become so much junk. Unless a foolproof bracket is built into the console, keep cameras and glasses boxed and on the deck from the very outset. If they're not insured, that old Law of General Cussedness will prevail.

Long years ago, at Marathon, Florida, a lovely lady named Billie Anderson and I dumped a tin boat in launching, because we were too eager to chase tarpon. Very shortly she whipped a baby sabalo and I caught a bonefish, but the swamping was expensive. One of my Rolleiflexes got wet and repairs added up to a whopping $147. No insurance. Since that time, all my cameras have been fully covered, and I am rather petulant about the fact that I have never dunked another.

Every marine angler covets binoculars, a boon to nodding noodniks who prefer to glass the exertions of other fishermen until action develops—and then hasten to the scene—and quite as valuable in checking bird action to see whether gulls, terns, and pelicans are over game fish or a garbage slick. There are miniature models that serve air travelers, but the most efficient are standard-sized 8 x 35 or 8 x 50 types. Beyond 8 x 50, power is of questionable value because you get into jiggle caused by motion, or even heartbeat. The better glasses, American, German, or Japanese—not necessarily in that order—feature coated, light-gathering lenses. There is no such thing as a "night glass," unless you tinker with infrared, electronics, and little black boxes that hum with evil precision, but a fine pair of binoculars will aid human vision in inclement light or during the hours of darkness. Unless fog cloaks the sea, it is surprising how much light is generated by the stars and the moon. Looking out, from an ocean beach, the void seems impenetrable. A boatman, on the same ground, enjoys fairly good vision.

On any well-touted fishing ground, a visitor can be reasonably certain that guides and charter skippers will offer adequate tackle for the task at hand. Of course, gear will be tailored to the average patron, which means it will be too heavy for specialists, and there is always the possibility that lines will be veterans of combat, perhaps slightly frayed and weary. Top hands maintain tackle, but there's no lack of grooved guides and erratic reels where the equipment is hard used. If there are luggage problems, a traveler may find it wise, at the very least, to carry reels well loaded with proper lines. The skipper will be pleased, because no insult is intended, and the captain's expenses are lessened if a patron chooses to bust his own lines.

There is an additional benefit. A personal reel always feels comfortable on any reasonably matched rod. You know that winch's capability, and all the little aids are instinctively operated—the star or lever, free spool, click, and antireverse. There is nothing so nicely calculated to make an experienced angler look like a duffer as the unfamiliar outfit, particularly one with some irksome feature such as a sticky bail, improperly spooled line, grooved guides or—very often—a rig fitted with line too heavy for the flawless casting of light lures. Reels, comparatively speaking, take up little space, unless they're the big 12/0 to 16/0 models used on big game.

Where light tackle is specified, there may be no need for harnesses or cups on waist belts. Today's surf caster simply tucks that long rod between his legs, and the flycaster, bait caster, or spinning enthusiast requires no edge. If "light" means, say, 30-pound test on offshore grounds where reasonably tough customers are expected, a belt socket fitted with a gimbal nock pin will be much appreciated, and a featherweight leather or canvas shoulder harness often eases the strain of combat. All the better big-game boats tote kidney harnesses, but some of them are hardly worthy of the name. It's always wise to pack your own, nicely adjusted to proper fit, for there is no joy in slugging it out with a monster when an ill-fitting harness is alternately rasping skin off your shoulders and your butt. The skippers will have gloves, too, but you'll be happier with your own—tailored to fit, and dry until the last wet line is pumped back on a tortured reel spool.

Blessed is he who has the time and the specialized motor vehicle to carry a great deal of tackle, plus a trailered or cartop boat. In this case, there is no sorrow about the necessity to use multiple-jointed rods or to divine the precise lures to pack in a couple of always inadequate tackle boxes. With the exception of big game, light spinning, bait-casting, and flycasting rods, the one-piece stick is infinitely superior to that which is jointed. It is lighter, tougher, and carries its action fluidly from tiptop to butt. Theoretically, all rods are more efficient when they are of one-piece construction, with the possible exception of the big-game instrument that features a very heavy locking reel seat. However, even where beach-buggy racks solve transportation problems, the fly rod is too long and limber to excel in anything other than two pieces; bait-casting sticks still feature a variety of drop-center butts, and one-handed spinning rods can be had either way—with little to choose from in the matter of efficiency.

The special delight in ground transportation is an ability to carry whatever *might* be useful. If two tackle boxes are insufficient, add a third or fourth. Throw in a veritable raft of rods, plus an icebox filled with cold drinks on the way out and, hopefully, fish on the way back. There's room for every conceivable item of clothing: short boots for boating and waders for the surf; adequate foul-weather gear, gaffs, nets, camp stoves, and provisions, even a scales to weigh the odd record breaker.

Any motor vehicle can be fitted with external rod racks, usually tool-clip or sponge-rubber clamp-ons ranged horizontally, or tubes fastened to a front bumper for beach work. The only real problem is thievery on a long trip, or where an automobile is parked while anglers go fishing. Provision must be made to lock all valuables inside, preferably concealed in proper containers. In too many metropolitan areas, light-fingered types will strip a vehicle of goodies while you turn your head to sneeze. Treasures, such as cameras, rods, reels, and other expensive items, should always be stored in a motel room during an overnight stop. It is a sorry commentary on our times that city folk are forever hostile, while the farther you get out into the boondocks the more honest and hospitable the people. This is true the world over, and perhaps it has been true since time began.

Saltwater anglers forever play a game of musical chairs. They may have great fishing in their own backyards, but there is an urgent desire to go elsewhere—to tangle with new battlers on exotic grounds. Often that mania is triggered by a book or a magazine article, or perhaps a television show, and too often the enthusiast absorbs nothing but spectaculars while neglecting a certain amount of fine print. Chamber-of-commerce types don't help, for they often clarion the fact that "in our area fishing is always good!"

That's unmitigated nonsense. Every ground has its peak seasons—and months when angling is at low ebb. During the "season," charter boats will be well booked and guides will work long hours. Motels and hotels will display no-vacancy signs, and coastal townships are sure to discourage those who would camp out on the dunes. It may be impossible to book a boat or to obtain suitable lodging without reservations.

That, of course, is the key. Anyone who plans to catch a specific game fish in an unfamiliar arena had best do his homework long before repairing to the rod and reel bonanza. Contact guides, skippers, and lodge owners who will provide accurate data if you ask intelligent questions. Zero in!

You will want information on peak seasons, lures or baits that score, proper tackle, and accommodations. Having acquired this vital G-2, make a reservation with the skipper of your choice, plus a reservation at a motel or hotel in the immediate vicinity. Always a charter captain will recommend places and procedure; he wants you to enjoy your fishing vacation and become a regular, annual patron.

Going in cold is frustrating. Granting that you arrive in a specific area at the height of a game-fish run, the better boats and guides will be solidly booked, so you may wind up with some half-crocked beachcomber with a ratty craft and tackle that wouldn't sell in a flea market. The good lodgings will be loaded with customers who have made reservations, and the poor ones will be swarming with hairy hippies. No season ever passes in which I fail to receive weepy complaints from good people who spent too much time and money traveling to famous fishing grounds, only to find no decent accommodation and no adequate guides or skippers with open dates. Early inquiry and reservation would have solved all problems.

Very possibly the best approach is to work through a reputable travel agent who will set up an entire itinerary. This costs nothing extra, for the agent skims his cream from airlines, ground transportation, motels and hotels. An unscrupulous hotelier may care less about an individual's request, but he will honor the reservations contracted by an agent who may send him much business in the future. Travel services, including those that set up safaris to foreign lands, guarantee accommodations as advertised, and they smooth the way of the pilgrim.

On any long journey, it is a timesaving device to call a local agency. I simply dial Four-Seasons Travel in Worcester, Massachusetts. Mary Winchester, who currently handles these things, gives me a lot of jovial flak about being lucky enough to fish around the world, and then asks a few pertinent questions. She'll call back, in an hour or so, with data on precise departure and arrival of airplanes on which I will be booked. There is no charge for the service and it saves much time and travail. Good travel agencies are located in all big cities.

There are, unfortunately, handicaps to sport and a mutual admiration society on any seacoast. An adventurous type may choose to prospect a true marine back country where residents aren't geared to a tourist economy. There it may be necessary to trail or cartop a boat, although rental skiffs usually are available. Lodgings may be far from plush. Perhaps the mosquitoes and sand flies will exult in the absence of toxic sprays. Mornings may be frosty in the North, and remote southern camps alive with cockroaches big enough to scare a Yankee mud turtle.

Fortunately, boondocks people—North or South—are both friendly and hospitable, unless you are stupid enough to insult them with some inanity based on race, creed, or supposed sophistication. Most back country folk are sensitive, immediately aware of any slur or patronizing attitude. Many of them are graduates of accredited universities and they live out there because life in a clean countryside triumphs over the smog and hypocrisy of a big city. Spanish Caribbean types and Mexicans worry about arrogant gringos, and the gringos, in turn, expect communism in every hamlet south of the border.

And it's all nonsense! Wherever you go, this wide world over, back country folk embrace the golden rule. If fishermen held the reins of government, there'd be no animosity or hatred. Anglers comprise a true brotherhood of gentle men.

FISH ON! ~ 18

Today's Potential in Marine Fishing

"Expert" and "authority" are words that forever create a squeamishness in my soul. The cynic's definition—a man with a briefcase who is 50 miles from home—seems peculiarly apt. Unfortunately, I have a briefcase and I often migrate out of natal territory. When this happens, good people forever ask me to list the greatest of all game fishes in order of importance. This is a thing I will not do, because it is impossible.

The greatest is always the one that happens to be on your fast line at any given moment in time and space.

If that's heresy, make the most of it, but go back over the years and winnow out experiences before voting for any current favorite. Was that tomcod winched over a bridge railing in youth any less exciting than the latest broadbill swordfish baited, hooked, fought, and boated on offshore grounds? Who says that a big-game enthusiast, with his bluefin tuna, marlin, and broadbill, enjoys greater sport than the light-tackle buff who wades a crystalline flat for bonefish and permit? If a striped bass seldom exceeds the magic 73-pound mark, what experienced surf caster is willing to bad-mouth the delightful, unpredictable nature of the beast?

For that matter, what's wrong with Norfolk spot and common mackerel, grunts, sheepshead, sea trout, snappers, surf perch, and lingcod? All offer grand sport and gourmet table fare. Each, if taken on tackle calibrated to its size and strength, provides a full measure of anticipation, plus the thrills of hooking and playing that make salt-water angling an absolutely fascinating sport. I have seen some of the world's foremost outdoorsmen as intent on catching a 10-inch bait as they would be in luring a monster of the deep blue.

There is a stereotyped thing about fishing books; practically all of them feature a chapter on X number of favorite fish, or fish identification. But there is really no such thing as a complete identification manual of marine fishes. It would be possible to fill a book of this size with nothing but brief biographies of species that inhabit the sea, and still—in view of present knowledge—ignore a surprising number of battlers. There are strange fighters in remote sections of the world that may well be cataloged by ichthyologists, but are rarely identified in popular literature. Even the natives of a given coast offer a variety of colloquial names, so it would take a highly skilled, world-traveled scholar to zero in on all.

Nobody has done so. There are brilliant books, such as *Fishes of the Gulf of Maine*, by Bigelow and Schroeder, now published by the Harvard University Press. This classic fills almost 600 pages of fine print, and yet it only discusses that which it promises—fishes of the Gulf of Maine. Some of the coastal states offer grand identification manuals keyed to their regions. *Common Ocean Fishes of the California Coast*, offered by that state's Department of Fish and Game, is a fine example. Francesca La Monte's *Marine Game Fishes of the World* is very good, yet it only scratches the sur-

face. There are hosts of local guides and otherwise decent books full of strange draw-
ings, psychedelic colors, and much misinformation. There is, simply, no complete
book of marine sport and game fishes, nor will there be in the immediate future. We
still dabble on the edges of a vast puddle.

The scope of the thing is immense, and this is a first hurdle. Next, you have the
well-meaning experts who list, say, "fifty favorite fishes." They do so, safely, so long
as these are *their* favorites. I can list three times that number and still fall short. Who
can declare that one rod-and-line prize is more important than another, or prepare a
roster that ignores certain small and often delightful finfish because they are not
coveted by self-appointed purists? If any species provides sport, it is important.

There are specialists who delight in taking a myriad of tiny, colorful coral dwellers
on spider-web strands and miniature hooks. More power to them. A few academic
types are entranced by "life lists" of species taken on sporting tackle, and such a list
can be very long. Critters regarded as "trash" by one angler are held important to
another, and who is to judge?

Not I, although I am rather amused by area promotion that states that sportsmen
can take some 600 species in a given locality. There's no doubt that this is possible,
but most of the "trophies" will be small, slimy, spiny, inedible, and incapable of
waging a satisfactory battle. A few may even be toxic, nasty little brutes with no
saving grace other than additions to a list of conquests. The roster of true sport and
game fish is extensive only because it includes a multitude of subspecies. There are,
for example, some twenty-one known Pacific surf perch.

There are fringe types. Should we dwell on eels, which are often sought and are a
gourmet's delight? Or sea robins that pester anglers and still yield delicious fillets? Or
elusive, fluorescent deep-bottom feeders and coral fishes and remoras? One wonderful
day in the Gulf of Mexico, fishing with Del Chaplin of Marathon, Florida, and Charley
Whitney, three of us caught forty-eight different species of fish. Some of them fought
well and some were deadweights; a few were edible, while others were kept for bait
or released with a sigh of relief. The world ocean is alive with fishes.

Latin is touted as the solution to all identification problems, but scientists who
complain so vociferously about a rash of popular monikers are quite as likely to
change Latin designations so that the lay citizen is confused. There are continuous
variations in the supposedly worldwide keys to specific fishes. Sometimes the busy
taxonomists even manage to establish, in the minds of laymen, a Latin word for a
great gamester, and then capriciously change it!

Striped bass, for example, have progressed from *Roccus lineatus* to *Roccus saxatilis*
and, finally, to *Morone saxatilis*. Usually, changing the name of a fish works hardship
only on students and compilers of identification manuals. Occasionally, though, such
a change illogically scuttles a Latin designation that has become popular. To a majority
of enthusiasts who catch them, *Roccus* means striped bass, and *Roccus* will not be
very easy to discard. Therefore, the taxonomists—who are so critical of colloquial
names—often defeat their own purpose.

Regional nicknames are quite as difficult to erase. Some years ago the American
Outdoor Writers Association wasted valuable time and pelf in compiling a booklet
listing the proper names of all popular game fish, salt and fresh, together with collo-
quialisms to be banished. This was an exercise in futility because a majority of citizens
prefer the language they and their ancestors have used for years beyond reckoning.
Examples are legion.

Take the common northern weakfish, *Cynoscion regalis*. In the New England states it is called squeteague, or squet, an American Indian word that has endured. From central Connecticut southward through New York, New Jersey, Delaware, and Maryland it is a weakfish, a weakie, or a weak, but it becomes a gray trout in Virginia, North Carolina, and points south. In some areas, a big weakfish is a "tiderunner" or a "yellowfin." Take your choice.

A southern spotted weakfish, *Cynoscion nebulosus,* is rarely called a weakfish! It is a sea trout, a trout, a speckled trout, or a speck. Channel bass, depending on location, are red drum, redfish, or even spottail bass. The cobia is a ling, a sergeant fish, or a crabeater. In American North Atlantic waters a giant bluefin tuna is a horse mackerel—pronounced "hoss mack-ril"—and it is a tunny off the British Isles. There is a snail's pace trend toward standardization, often strenuously opposed by local usage. Better learn the language—even if you won't drink the water!

It would be very easy to prepare a selected list of great game fishes, the remainder, by inference, relegated to second-class status. Fortunately, we humans are very complex machines, no two of us alike. In selecting, say, fifty of the greatest, I would only impose my preferences on you. Maybe I like a blue marlin vaulting into the sky with 300 yards of line trailing, while you are quite content to catch Norfolk spot or surf perch off a pier. And maybe it's just the other way around! In any event, we are blood brothers, yet our requirements differ. It is not a matter of wealth. Lots of folk who could buy and sell charter fleets take their ease on the bonefish flats, finagle cagey dock snook, or go out on the party boats to winch up cod, snappers, or kelp bass. We fish as we like and the harvest is multitudinous. We fish for sport, and that makes all the difference.

Each technique has its disciplines, and he who thinks otherwise is a loser from the outset. To be successful you will take dead aim at a specific species; you will study that fish, its habits, and habitat. You will arm for combat—light stuff for the lightweights in shallow water, and increasingly heavy artillery for those in the depths or for the monsters. You will embrace the credos of sport, but scorn luck. Luck is for dreamy people who never control any situation; they win only when some fluke of nature offers them a break.

And so I break with tradition, holding it no office of a book such as this to delve into the life histories and identification of each sport and game fish. Each, and there are literally hundreds of them, is entitled to a separate volume. The good identification manuals cannot do the subject justice, but at least they provide reasonably accurate information on life cycles, range, habits, idiosyncrasies, and size of the more popular marine battlers.

Great anglers are catholic in their tastes; they fish for everything from big game down to tiddlers, and find each species intriguing. Normally, the well-versed saltwater sportsman has experimented with a number of disciplines and gamesters, but specializes in one or two. There are men and women who pursue big game only, scorning anything other than a full-blooded giant tuna, a huge marlin, or a swordfish. Occasional single-purpose individuals hunt great sharks as Ahab scoured the seas for Moby Dick. The monster hunters are magnificent folk, and yet they are a minority. Theirs is the arena of the big offshore sportfisherman, the winking blue sea far beyond harbor bounds, the affluence and the leisure and the patience that must be part of any calculated offensive against true heavyweights.

Unlimited tackle men seek a very few gladiators deemed worthy of attention. The roster is short and the quarry, unlike smaller and more prolific game, boasts no extensive family of subspecies. The greatest remain a matter of personal opinion, and arguments always founder in a backlash of qualifications. A giant bluefin tuna has to be, pound for pound, one of the most powerful monsters in our ocean, yet it is a minnow compared to the regal and evil white shark. No bluefin is an acrobat, so in the minds of other specialists black marlin and blue marlin are far superior because they are wont to come clear in spectacular leaps and greyhounding surface dashes. Where the three are concerned, there is not much difference in maximum weight, although the Pacific black marlin and blue marlin seem to have a decided edge. Actually, taxonomists are still scratching their heads, not quite certain whether the Pacific blue is a separate species, or is identical to the Atlantic variety.

One self-appointed elite group holds a broadbill swordfish the greatest marine game species that ever lived because this magnificent world wanderer is toughest of all to locate, to hook, and to play successfully. Broadbill grow to well over 1,000 pounds, yet they have soft mouths that prevent undue horsing. The heavyweights are solitary, and it takes a great deal of cruising, skillful maneuvering, and flawless rod work to boat a trophy. Contrary to popular opinion, the broadbill is not a great acrobat; while it sometimes comes clear in a stunning leap, the usual fight is subsurface, with much spinning and determined diving. There are men who have racked up three, four, or even five giant tuna in a single day, but only a few who have managed to collect more than one sword during a comparable time span. It is possible to count on the fingers of one's hand those who have accomplished the hat trick by whipping three broadbill in any twenty-four-hour period.

Great sharks comprise a separate category, certainly big game, yet often studiously avoided. The man-eater, or white shark, attains horrifying weight and is a worthy adversary on unlimited tackle. Makos grow to well over 1,000 pounds and are spectacular performers, often leaping time and again when hooked. The tiger and the relatively phlegmatic hammerhead may go 2,000 pounds. Some men seek these killers over all other game, and it is quite possible that—if sharks were not so abundant—they would be treasured over many of the universally recognized gladiators.

Sawfish grow to heroic sizes in tropical waters.
Photo courtesy Marineland of Florida

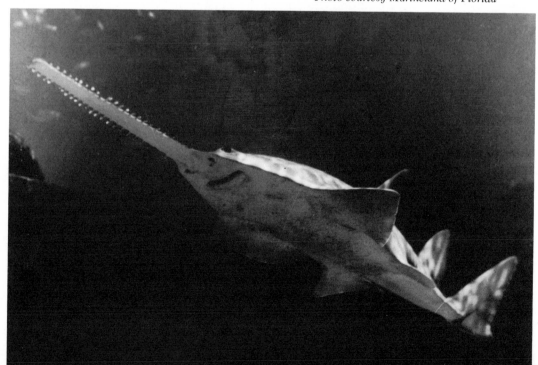

There are second-class monsters—like the sawfish, an offshoot of the skates and the sharks that may tip the scales to better than 1,000 pounds, plus skates and rays themselves, popular on many seacoasts. One must make mention of jewfish and black sea bass that approach the magic half-ton bulk. Surprised anglers have landed giant squid in the tropics, huge creatures measuring 20 feet from siphon to tail. There are giants in *these* days, but only a few of them qualify as game. The second-class heavyweights are unspectacular, ponderous sluggers.

With certain exceptions, all the billfishes are magnificent aerial battlers, yet only a few of them grow to heroic sizes. Progressing down the list, after blue and black marlin, there is the striped marlin, which sometimes squeezes into the big-game category by ranging up to, or beyond, 500 pounds. Silver marlin also enter the circle, but some taxonomists now feel that this is not a separate species, but only a misnamed blue.

White marlin and sailfish are much smaller, a white rarely attaining more than 180 pounds, and a sailfish (Pacific), possibly to 250. Atlantic sails, for some unknown reason, are smaller than those taken in the West; they average 50 to 60 pounds and are unlikely to attain weights of more than 150 at best. There is a unique and rarely caught spearfish that looks like a junior-grade edition of the sail with a much less impressive dorsal fin. It doesn't grow very big and is never anything other than a curious catch.

A white marlin comes clear in an arrowlike leap.

True big-game fishes never swarm in the sea, but middleweights are abundant. Tremendous battlers, ranging from 50 to 150 pounds, are reasonably plentiful, and there are a few that push monster figures by growing to more than half the accepted 500 pounds that designates big game. Tarpon exceed 300 pounds, as do yellowfin tuna. The blackfin tuna may actually approach 500, and there are any number of lesser sharks in this size range, many of them—like the blacktip or spinner—highly spectacular fighting machines.

The great trouble with categories of game fish is a very human tendency to specialize. Poundage is deceiving, because some of the bulkier middleweights are far inferior as fighters to their smaller, lunate-tailed neighbors. An Atlantic cod may grow to better than 100 pounds, and a black drum to some similar figure, yet neither is considered a very spectacular battler. Both have their champions and it is useless to make comparisons because, as I have said, the greatest game fish is always the one hooked and running against a tight drag.

Among the middleweights there are some very capable performers, fish that merit the superlatives. Anyone who has hooked a wahoo is unlikly to forget the experience, for this streamlined member of the mackerel-tuna tribe is piscatorial TNT with a short fuse. He strikes, often rockets into the air, and then unleashes a torpedolike run. The roosterfish of Central and South America's Pacific Coast resists like a jack and jumps like a tarpon. Cobia are deceptive; some of them come tamely to gaff, and others are holy terrors, often most dangerous right at boatside. A big, green cobia yanked aboard a small boat is likely to demolish that craft and its contents. An amberjack is mean and tough, probably one of the most difficult game fish to exhaust and to land. Having taken a respectable amber, you'll know that you've been in a back-alley brawl.

North Atlantic anglers often catch huge cod. This one-time record holder, caught by John Michna of Dudley, Massachusetts, weighed better than 74 pounds.

They're all great! I have been cleaned by a king mackerel, abused by a looping yellowfin tuna, and humbled by a great dolphin. Hawaii's ulua, another of the incredibly tough, pugnacious jacks, grows to considerable poundage and, like all of that wide-ranging family, is murder on a tight line. The Pacific yellowtail, another cousin of the jacks, will wring you out, and the albacore, a world-ranging member of the tuna tribe, uses its long pectoral fins, streamlined body, and lunate tail to make many of us look like rank amateurs. What a wonderful way to be humbled!

Barracuda, and particularly the world-ranging great barracuda, enter the lists as upper-echelon middleweights, famous if only because they are reputed to be "tigers of the sea." The appellation is erroneous, because a 'cuda is unlikely to be dangerous—unless you are stupid enough to stick your hand into its mouth—and it is nowhere near the fighter, pound for pound, of other great middleweights. A barracuda may make one or two halfhearted jumps, one run, or possibly two, and then it will be led to gaff. A wahoo, or even a king mackerel of comparable size, would make the "tiger" look like a mewling kitten.

There are, as always, qualifications. Small 'cuda, hooked on light tackle in shoal water, are great performers; they'll leap time and again. The subspecies caught on American Pacific coasts rarely grows to frightening sizes, but provides much sport and good table fare. Elsewhere, barracudas are suspect as food, because some appear to be toxic.

Among noteworthy middleweights, although not yet recognized by IGFA, there are groupers of considerable size that will not only grab a bottom bait, but will rise to strike a spoon or plug. Having done so, they immediately repair to a coral cave where it is impossible to move them with any tackle yet devised for sport fishing. The only strategy is deception; you slack off, count the minutes, and wait until it seems reasonable to believe that the quarry has discounted danger and emerged. Then you sock the drag up tight and make every effort to horse that mule to the surface. Sometimes it works. I have defeated groupers with this strategy—and they have defeated me.

If there is any rule of thumb in our world ocean, it is this: the smaller the quarry, the more numerous the representative species. Overlapping is inevitable, yet there are hosts of fish that range from tiny on up to something just below the 100-pound mark. Some of these gladiators are very important because they dominate a regional sport fishery or are the major prizes of specialists. There is the case of the striped bass, a dominant medium-sized game fish from the Chesapeake Bay to New England, and almost as deified in the Pacific adjacent to San Francisco.

From the Virginia Capes down through North Carolina's Outer Banks, channel bass become the trophy supreme. Bluefishing is a seasonal madness from New Jersey through southern New England in the summertime, and it prospers elsewhere in spring and fall. While the blue doesn't grow to mammoth size, a run of 10- to 20-pounders—not uncommon in the late sixties and early seventies—engenders something approaching hysteria in angling circles. Blues are quite as popular in Australia and New Zealand, although they then become "tailors." In South Africa and in the Mediterranean, they are called "elft" or "shad." In America, the species is limited to the Atlantic Coast and the Gulf of Mexico.

On America's great Pacific seaboard, three species really dominate the sport fishery. One, in the Pacific Northwest and ranging down through central California, is the salmon, with chinooks or kings most important and silvers or cohos close competitors for favor. All the West Coast salmon die after spawning, and all are eager strikers in the salt chuck or in the lower reaches of natal rivers. The Atlantic salmon of the East is anadromous too, but is rarely caught on rod and line in salt water; it is the target of inland anglers who intercept it in the northern rivers of Canada and Europe where it engages in round-trip spawning runs. Although many other important game fishes are available in the Pacific Northwest, salmon reign supreme and dominate the sport fishery.

Down coast, in the Pacific United States, yellowtail and albacore become the great prizes. When either are running, all other varieties take a back seat in the minds of sportsmen; they are the most sought-after trophies, and nobody challenges their superiority. It is useless to point out that more rodsmen may seek flounders, corvina, surf perch, rockfish, kelp bass, and a host of other gladiators, such as bonito and barracuda.

So-called specialty fishes are not limited to western seas. There are many that, for one reason or another, have captured the imagination of anglers. Among these must be listed the tarpon, a spectacular acrobat that grows to considerable size, yet is often taken on light tackle because of its habit of feeding in shallow water and expending its energy in tremendous leaps when hooked. I love tarpon, and I am afraid of them! They are among the most spectacular of game fishes and they are fully capable of jumping into your boat, tossing tackle hell, west, and crooked, breaking your bones, and jumping out again.

Lefty Kreh, a Florida light-tackle specialist, strains
to lift a big tarpon he caught on a fly.
Photo by Lefty Kreh

Frank Woolner releases a spent bonefish. Often the
fish needs "artificial respiration" before it regains
strength enough to swim free.

Bonefish have been quite as well publicized, and they rate every rave review. Any bone stalked on a thin flat is a spooky, hair-triggered bundle of nerves and explosive energy. He must be hunted with care, and a bait or lure will be presented with utmost finesse, or it will fail. Once hooked, the thin-water bonefish will streak away like a torpedo, often essaying an initial run of more than 100 yards. That's a full 300 feet, and no exaggeration is involved.

Bones are not always caught in the shallows, but that is where they are most impressive. Hawaii boasts some monsters of the species, and they are usually taken by blind baiting in relatively deep water. In this case the famous white fox is just another very strong gamester, seldom capable of raising a fisherman's blood pressure to apoplectic levels.

In recent years the permit, king of the pompano tribes, has been placed on a pedestal as the greatest trophy of a flats fisherman. Very few anglers have hooked and landed a permit on a fly. Many have turned the trick with natural bait or bucktail jigs. Like the bonefish, a permit is fury incorporated in thin water—spooky to an extreme, fast and powerful. Offshore, where it congregates over reefs and wrecks, the same great gamester is relatively easy to tempt and no very difficult prize to boat.

Initially, intending to list the important game fishes available to a marine angler, I prepared a rough roster. It went to better than one hundred species before I quit counting. Even at that, I had not worked around to subspecies and the exotics, all of which fever the supposedly placid brows of "contemplative anglers." There are so many!

Inshore and offshore, we are blessed by abundance. The offshore operator welcomes yellowfin tuna, a fish that—pound for pound—I believe humbles the mighty bluefin. There are hosts of pelagic wanderers: the wonderful chameleonlike dolphin, blackfin tuna, a half-dozen pugnacious bonitos, another great family of ferocious jacks, a tribe of mackerels and runners, a host of snappers, a legion of surf runners and bottom feeders. The list is not endless, but it seems to be. Those who dote on life lists of conquests are unlikely to run out of targets.

Much of our current sport-fishing literature dwells on the glamour species, those that are very large and acrobatic, or the flashy performers of shoal water. Actually, more people seek the plebeian bottom feeders than the spectacular surface gladiators. Depending on coast and water temperature, legions of anglers prefer such species as true cod, haddock, pollock, halibut, hake, whiting, wolffish, cusk, and a veritable grab bag of tautog, flounders, sea bass, porgies, tilefish, cunners, and eels.

All the aforementioned are North Atlantic, yet many of them are represented elsewhere. There are halibut on both coasts of the United States, although the eastern species is larger. With poetic justice, the western is both more abundant and more readily available. Flounders are cosmopolitan, and practically all the flatties are grand table fare. Filet of sole, in America, is almost always the flesh of native flounder, not the true European sole.

Claude Rogers of Virginia Beach gaffs a trophy
black drum for George Heinold of Connecticut.
Photo by Hal Lyman

Bottom fishermen enjoy new conquests as they travel from place to place. Southward, on the Atlantic Coast, one finds sheepshead—not the sheep-head of the Pacific—in good supply. There are black drum, croakers, groupers that often grow to considerable sizes, and a host of snappers that range from the wary little mangrove on up through the toothsome red, mutton, and dog. All boast subspecies, most of which fight like hellions and are fine table fare.

On the Pacific Coast another grab bag of great deep feeders fever the imagination of sportsmen. In the Deep South there are the groupers again, called cabrilla in Latin America, plus a few unusual croakers such as the totuava, which grows to better than 225 pounds and is an overgrown cousin of the Atlantic weakfish. Corvina, another of the croaker-weakfish tribe, are taken on bottom, but also at midlevels. White sea bass, still western representatives of the croaker, are much sought after. They get pretty big, possibly growing to 80 pounds, but seldom exceeding 30 or 40.

Western anglers enjoy a multitude of kelp bass and rockfish, sheep-head, cod, again a subspecies of the eastern variety; lingcod that grow to 70 pounds or more and are not true cod at all. This character wins no beauty prizes, boasts a large mouth full of wicked teeth, and has an insatiable appetite. Lingcod are determined battlers and fine table fish, so they are much sought after.

Sablefish, another one-of-a-kind type, is a fine food variety taken by sport and commercial alike. The sable is reported to attain weights of better than 50 pounds, but specimens over 25 are noteworthy because they are uncommon.

A number of flatfish, led by the regal Pacific halibut, intrigue millions of saltwater sportsmen along the West Coast, and there are at least twenty-one species or subspecies of surf perch available, some of them habitués of deep water, while others frolic in the suds or stooge around dock pilings.

Certainly, south, east, west, or far north, there is no dearth of marine bottom feeders to thrill anglers, and there is a wide range of sizes. There are specialists on all coasts who hunt sharks alone, or get fevered over huge rays. Britons set great store by the tope (a soupfin shark) and big skates. They also catch lots of true cod, pollack—which are similar to, but are not the American pollock—conger eels, a number of flatfish, bass, mackerel, and many lesser warriors of the sea. The British bass is comparable to the American striper in that it frequents inshore surf and is somewhat similar in appearance, although lacking the longitudinal stripes that give the American species its name. In addition, the European bass never attains the size of the Yankee striper.

Popular game fishes are well known on all coasts, but there are surprises in store for a traveling angler. Down on the west coast of Costa Rica one memorable day in springtime, Dr. Carlos Marine, a member of our party, caught a hard-fighting and brilliantly colored gamester of about 10 pounds. The specimen looked like a subspecies of the jolthead porgy, yet no book in our library ever offered positive identification. That cuss took a bucktail jig and waged a furious battle, so it would have to qualify as game. We snapped photographs and yearned to preserve the critter for examination by Harvard University's savants, but we were away out in the blue with no refrigeration, indeed without so much as a radio-link communication with the world of men. In that breathtakingly beautiful corner of the tropical wilderness, jaguars were more plentiful than human beings.

Without doubt, there are many potential game fish still unknown to anglers, most of them subspecies of recognized genuses, but prospering only in remote bays and estuaries of the world ocean where man has yet to penetrate with fishing tackle. History indicates that some have always been there but, for one reason or another, have escaped the attention of sportsmen. Only in very recent years have North Atlantic party-boat anglers begun to take tilefish on rod and line. This middleweight feeds in depths exceeding 200 feet, far offshore, and is both a commendable fighter and a joy on the table.

Tilefish weren't even discovered until 1879, when commercial operators began to take them off Nantucket. The fishery was short-lived, because some natural cataclysm triggered a massive die-off in 1882. At that time men believed that the species had been utterly destroyed and was extinct, gone—dead as the dodo.

Fortunately, a few survived and, in 1882, eight were boated off Martha's Vineyard. The harvest steadily increased although, until the late years of 1960, no sport fisherman ever took dead aim at tilefish. Then a few enterprising party-boat skippers prospected offshore grounds and began to book long-range trips. Unless there's another catastrophic die-off, the deep-down slugger that looks like a thing from another world, fights valiantly, and then rewards a gourmet with delicate, lobster-flavored flesh, will continue to gain friends.

In addition to the famous light-tackle species found on all seaboards, a modern angler may take delight in hunting a separate world of colorful, unique reef and coral dwellers. Many of them are tiny butterflies of the ocean, rivals of any tropical fish in an aquarium. Since many feed only on coral, or are vegetarians, baiting becomes fine art based on knowledge of the specific fish's feeding habits and habitat. Usually such prizes are preserved for a taxidermist's attention, or photographed and released. A few boast venomous spines, and some—eaten by man—will send man to his eternal rest.

The seas are full of fishes, great and small. It is inevitable that some still escape the taxonomists and will be "discovered" in the years that lie ahead. Known varieties are legion, so any list of game species must be incomplete, often condensed for a lack of space, or limited to those that have excited the imagination of sport-fishing pioneers.

There is something for every desire and every tackle combination. You can gun for the monsters or wrestle with middleweights, stalk wary shoal water speed merchants, plumb the depths for ponderous bottom feeders, or go to gossamer tackle for delectable midgets. The variety is immense, and our playing field is so new that much remains to be discovered. We are entering an era of joy and abundance in saltwater sport fishing, not recording past glories.

Please do not ask me to name the finest of them all! My heart thumps almost equally when an 8-ounce smelt takes a bait or a 1,000-pound tuna crashes the daisy chain, yanks me out of a fighting chair, and promptly breaks off. All lost fish are lunkers.

If you love the sport, every striker or nibbler will become a worthy foe. The challenge, in terms of skill, is always there, and combat can be made delicious by a simple choice of tackle. The potential is awe-inspiring: a plethora of game fishes ranging from monster to minnow, a staggering arsenal of modern gear to turn the trick, and a hunting ground that is still wild and largely unexplored because it covers three-quarters of the earth.

GREAT GROUNDS ⌁ 19

Game Fishing's Great Locations

January—and the cold is intense in my inhospitable, wintry New England. Outside, snow is driven by a manic wind and good fishing lies approximately 3,000 miles south of Cape Cod. At this time of year it always intrigues me to answer the phone and make the acquaintance of some gentleman who itches for the good medicine of offshore sport. Innocently, I cannot bring myself to believe that he means—now!

"Where can I go to catch a blue marlin?"

Hesitantly, with Boston's gray, frigid skyline just outside the window, I say: "Cape Hatteras is pretty hard to beat, but the season begins in June and it won't be hot until July and August."

The voice is brusque, impatient. "I want to catch a marlin right now! Money is no object. Where do I go?"

Frantically, I rack my brain for the idea that should be stored there. Are the Virgin Islands producing at this time of year? Not likely, or at least not in any numbers. The Hawaiian Islands chain will have blues, but they won't be at peak. It's summertime in New Zealand and Bay of Islands skippers will be baiting big billfishes. Half around the world? That's what the man wants, so I provide details, plus a contact to arrange accommodations and bookings. (Later, he'll cuss me out or praise me, depending on results.)

Modern saltwater sport fishing has become an earth-spanning game. While a relative few are able to jet half across the globe on a whim, millions of citizens now travel to known hot spots, planning their vacations to coincide with peak seasons of game fish. Slowly, but very surely, the great grounds are opening up. Each year sees new bonanzas explored and publicized—after which accommodations are developed.

No chauvinism is involved in the statement that America has led and still leads the world in saltwater fishing tackle, techniques, and ancillary equipment such as specialized fishing boats. Australia and New Zealand are second, because both are geared to a new world flexibility and initiative. Great Britain straggles, handicapped by senseless tradition and a hidebound aversion to change. A Briton always has to be thoroughly beaten at his own game before he will grudgingly admit that the tools of the victor are superior. Then, characteristically, he will jump light years ahead in designing an improvement. It was an Englishman, you will recall, who made the spinning reel practical.

Yet it's still America—and America alone—that is responsible for most of the great advances in saltwater sport fishing. The star-drag reel came out of California and was fabricated in Brooklyn, New York. The tubular fiber-glass rod was a product of Yankee ingenuity. Synthetic lines evolved here, and lure development is predominantly American. No other country has advanced the design of sport-fishing boats so rapidly and so cleverly, perhaps because no other had the requisite affluence and the demand for finished products.

Similarly, saltwater sport-fishing grounds of the Americas have been more thoroughly plotted and publicized than those in other watery corners of the earth. There is much to learn, yet hundreds of productive grounds off Canada, the United States, Central and South America are now familiar. Like the ancient whalers of Nantucket, our sport fishermen have pushed out and conquered a watery wilderness.

Every coast boasts fine saltwater angling, with resident species foremost and migrants claiming the spotlight when they arrive in optimum seasons. There are concentration points, thanks to currents and temperatures and an abundance of bait, and such spots often become famous. Ocean game fishes usually observe a cyclic schedule, arriving and departing on cue unless some unforeseen vagary of current or temperature drives them out of traditional channels. In many instances, it is quite feasible to predict the arrival of a given species almost to a calendar day. The wanderers, guided by light intensity and water temperature, are punctual. Residents, on the other hand, are obliging during those months when they are feeding most avidly or, perhaps, accomplishing a minor migration by moving from deep water to coastal shallows.

There are famous jumping-off locations, usually well publicized by tub-thumpers who use the fishery as a lever to extract cash from tourists. This is good business, and I offer no argument—other than to note that boats from many self-appointed hot spots fish areas far removed and seldom mentioned in press releases; they are sally ports, no more and no less. For this reason, and with few exceptions, I intend to discuss areas of importance rather than springboards.

To do so at all amounts to a measure of impertinence. Quite obviously, I can only touch the peaks and I am sure to omit grounds that many anglers consider unique. It would take a quarto volume to cover all the great fishing areas in our watery world, and I guarantee that the author of such a masterpiece would miss some of them. The canvas is gargantuan.

In order to dodge the charge of favoritism, too often valid because we all nurture prejudice, I proceed from north to south on the Atlantic Coast of the United States, into the Gulf of Mexico, and then up the Pacific seaboard from the Mexican border to Alaska; then to Central and South America, both coasts; Bermuda, the Caribbean, and Hawaii. With a bit of luck I may even touch on a few faraway places like Australia, New Zealand, and Fiji.

No mile of this vast ground is bereft of fish, aside from a few sorry locations where raw sewage is pumped into the sea or where toxic chemicals are similarly discharged. As a matter of fact, sewage draws some gamesters. The north Atlantic's famed striped bass is a garbage hound, and so is the tarpon of Florida. Unfortunately, pollution ultimately kills important organisms in the ecological chain, and then there is a general breakdown of the biosystem. Each separate stream of filth is a worm in the heart of a clean sea, and some respectable marine biologists have plotted the time it will take to destroy an entire world ocean if we maintain our current pace of thoughtless violation. They speak in terms of years, a few centuries at most—not millennia—so the warning is hardly academic.

I am going to write about great grounds, and I will sometimes sound like the chairman of a local chamber of commerce. The problem lies in a natural conflict between that which is available, and that which is accommodating. A fisherman can drive his keel over solid phalanxes of fishes and never catch one because the water temperature is too high, too low, or maybe the sea is roiled by a storm. There are all sorts of spoilers, not alone our ineptitude as anglers. Trophy fish, even on great grounds at the peak of a season, are unpredictable. We have to arrive at the right time, fish the proper tides, use the right baits or lures, and pray that weather conditions will oblige. Any abnormality can spoil our sport, even though the bottom is paved with fishes. We play the odds, bolstered by statistics compiled over a span of years.

Away up in the Maritime Provinces of Canada the sea is a rich soup of plankton and other nutrients, so it is capable of supporting a tremendous poundage of fishes. Cold seas are always crammed with life, while the supposedly beneficent tropics offer much less in the way of forage and are therefore more sparsely populated. Sportsmen cannot visualize this, because a majority of the arctic species are bottom feeders and the angling season, dictated by weather conditions, is short. Many of the northern gamesters are lethargic, although a few rate all of the spectaculars.

The finest giant tuna fishing in the world occurs in that stretch of North Atlantic between Montauk and Newfoundland, and it sometimes seems that the farther north you go, the larger the fish. Away back in 1950, Duncan McL. Hodgson set an all-tackle record for the species at Saint Ann Bay, Nova Scotia. Hodgson's catch, a 977-pounder, endured as a record for a full twenty years. Then, in 1970, it was repeatedly shattered.

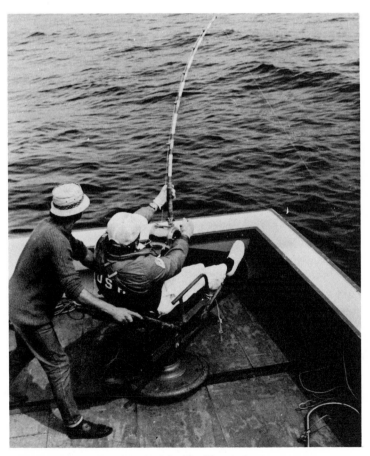

Johnny Wilson, a Fort Lauderdale, Florida, outdoor writer, plays a giant tuna at North Lake, Prince Edward Island, Canada. *Photo by Gene Mueller*

One of the great horse mackerel came from Montauk, but all of the others were Canadian, and the honors now rest with a 1,065-pound monster from Nova Scotia. In recent years. Conception Bay, Newfoundland, and Prince Edward Island, Canada, have come on strong as hot spots for the giants. Nova Scotia, opened up by such stalwarts as Mike Lerner and S. Kip Farrington back in the thirties, remains important, although many believe that the Prince Edward Island grounds will become paramount. In 1969, Hal Lyman predicted that the next world-record tuna would come from P.E.I., and he was wrong. In 1970, a Montauk angler was first to smash Hodgson's twenty-year mark, but in rapid succession three Prince Edward Island monsters topped the list. Then a Nova Scotia fisherman, Glen Gibson, copped all honors on November 19 of that astonishing year with a 1,065-pounder from St. George's Bay. Larger fish are there, and they will be taken, possibly before you read this.

The Maritimes have always been prime hunting grounds for broadbill swordfish, although the largest of the species have been taken off Chile. Louisburg, Nova Scotia, is a sally port for anglers who are tough enough to brave cold and loppy seas in quest of the much-touted greatest prize of big-game fishermen.

Other than giant tuna and swordfish, the Maritimes simmer along with a grab bag of not very spectacular cold-water species. Cod are abundant, and pollock very plentiful. During the summer months mackerel and pollock swarm into the provinces, and anglers find striped bass in the river systems. Sharpshooters, usually codfishermen seeking targets of opportunity, collect occasional huge halibut. There is no genuine sport fishery for this acknowledged king of flatfish because it has been reduced to relative scarcity by centuries of commercial harvesting.

Giant tuna, striped bass, and bluefish all typify New England to a legion of traveling anglers. The wide Gulf of Maine plays host to astonishing numbers of big bluefins during the summer months, and similar schools cavort in Block Island Sound between the rocky coast of Rhode Island and Montauk. Record-breakers are quite possible in any of these waters.

The old Yankee coast is, of course, a mecca for striped-bass fishermen. More trophy bass have been landed in Massachusetts and Rhode Island waters than in all other favored locations combined. Maine and New Hampshire stripers usually run small and are concentrated in the river systems. Monsters tempt the multitudes in Massachusetts Bay, in the surf of Cape Cod, and down the wide sand beaches to those legendary islands of Martha's Vineyard and Cuttyhunk. Nantucket is higher rated for its bluefishing than its bassing, but the rips around that ancient whaler's island are stacked with stripers during each late fall season.

Rhode Island's seaboard is another striper concentration point with hordes of schoolies and medium-sized fish swarming into Narragansett Bay, plus trophy-class battlers on the outside from Beavertail to Watch Hill. Connecticut sportsmen enjoy fine runs of bass, but relatively few big ones. The path of monster migration seems to stream right across Block Island Sound from Rhode Island to Montauk. Anglers of the Nutmeg State harvest few over the magic 50-pound mark.

In normal years bluefish range to a line that, roughly, might be drawn from Boston across Massachusetts Bay to the tip of Cape Cod. In 1971, however, a glut of choppers sent masses of them streaming as far up the seaboard as Old Orchard, Maine. The previous "high tide" was recorded in 1850 when these voracious travelers reached Gloucester, Massachusetts, in numbers. Peak bluefishing is most likely along the southern shores of Cape Cod, down through the Elizabeth Islands, and on into Rhode

Island and Block Island Sound. Connecticut, New York, and New Jersey anglers enjoy a bonanza that often extends over better than five months, from mid-May through late October.

New England's cold waters offer prime habitat for cod, haddock, pollock, and a number of other bottom feeders, plus hordes of mackerel. South of Nantucket and Martha's Vineyard white marlin and swordfish become specialty targets in blue water. Rhode Island's Narragansett Bay offers fine sport with northern weakfish, here called squeteague, and the weakie is increasingly plentiful along the Connecticut and Long Island seaboard.

Striped bass are most sought after along the North Atlantic Coast. These are school fish.

New York and New Jersey are population centers, but wonderful game fish feed and frolic within the shadow of metropolis. Montauk is a famous jumping-off spot, but there are literally hundreds of harbors, boat basins, and launching ramps available to the saltwater angler. Striped bass range the entire seaboard, but the monsters are apt to be concentrated off the tip of Long Island and at Sandy Hook, New Jersey. Farther southward, bass tend to be smaller, albeit plentiful in spring and fall.

Nelson Bryant cuddles a 46½-pound striper he caught off Virginia Beach.

Swordfish, white marlin, huge sharks, and giant tuna—the latter becoming more abundant north of Long Island—please big-game fishermen. School tuna are present during the summer and early fall, and bluefishing is superb. While the Coxes Ledge ground, combed by boats from Long Island, Connecticut, and Block Island, are famous for cod, pollock, and those massive flounders called "snowshoes," all three species are in good supply along the entire coast. There is, quite naturally, a veritable grab bag of other fighters, including some semitropical types, like dolphin, that are sporadic visitors during the midsummer months.

Delaware and Maryland sportsmen enjoy the same general plethora of northern game fish, although giant tuna and swordfish are unlikely. As recompense, this coast is one of the world's great white marlin grounds. The whites congregate here and provide royal sport through summer and early fall. Ocean City, Maryland, is a foremost port, but boats from many others, including those of southern New Jersey, share the offshore fishing.

Bluefish are here in numbers during any peak year, and striped bass are crowd-pleasers in bays and inland waters. Except in spring and fall, the blues are small to medium in size. Stripers also tend to be small, although a fair share of brutes are hooked. School tuna range the seaboard, and summertime finds a minor influx of dolphin northward, and greater concentrations of them in the southern third of the section.

While some channel bass are taken from southern New Jersey, Delaware, and Maryland, the world's most important fishery for giant red drum is limited to that stretch of coast from the Virginia Capes down through the Outer Banks of North Carolina. All major world records on the species have been posted there. Great locations include the barrier island water-wilderness of Virginia's eastern shore and North Carolina's Outer Banks from Nags Head southward through Cape Hatteras and Ocracoke. Spring and fall are the magic seasons.

Giant tuna are rarities here, yet offshore anglers catch lots of white marlin, a lesser number of yellowfin tuna, school bluefins, some sailfish, and a host of dolphin, false albacore, blues, and other gamesters. Blue marlin are well represented off Virginia, and Cape Hatteras has become one of the Atlantic's premier billfishing grounds. Big blues range well to the north, but there is no doubt that North Carolina's offshore waters are most heavily populated.

Hatteras has been called "the graveyard of the Atlantic" because of the treacherous shoals that claimed so many ships during the age of sail. A nicer nickname is "gamefish junction," which is true because these waters mark a fairly well-established boundary between the semitropics and the cold North. Off Hatteras there is a clash of cool water and warm, with fishes from both environments butting heads against an invisible barrier. Some go on through as strays; many pause, mill around, and provide grand sport before departing for more familiar and comfortable grounds.

There is, between the Delmarva Peninsula and mainland Virginia, the great Chesapeake Bay, a major spawning ground for striped bass and a playground for millions of people. While the Chesapeake offers sport throughout much of the year, excepting the midwinter months, best catches of Virginia and North Carolina stripers are racked up during late November and December. At that time migrating fish, both schoolies and heavyweights, congregate around the Chesapeake Bay Bridge Tunnel and the shoals off Virginia Beach. By December, trophy bass have completed a terminal southward migration and have arrived on the Outer Banks of North Carolina, where they are caught sporadically on rod and line, and viciously haul-seined.

Bluefish are seasonal favorites here, although the average size is meager. In spring and fall, for brief periods, trophy choppers arrive, and then records topple. Such was the case in 1971–72, a time of abnormal bluefish migrational patterns. In December 1971, Rita Mizelle caught a 24-pound 8-ounce prize at Nags Head on North Carolina's Outer Banks. This fish edged the then existing world record by 5 ounces. On January 30, 1972—long after the blues should have vacated this seaboard—James M. Hussey landed an astonishing 31-pound 12-ounce monster off Hatteras Inlet to set a new all-tackle mark. The lure? A Burke Jig-A-Doo "rubber" eel.

Virginia and North Carolina boast fine runs of sea trout or southern spotted weakfish, plus good supplies of common weakfish—here called gray trout. There are the usual hosts of bottom-feeding gamesters and assorted warriors such as Spanish and king mackerel, cobia, and ponderous black drum. Nowhere may an Atlantic angler find so unusual an assemblage of northern and semitropical species.

South Carolina and Georgia are more thoroughly oriented to the South; they share an offshore jungle that is practically virgin. Great game fishes are there for the taking, but the ground simply has not been opened up. So far the sport fishery has been coastal, geared to summer blues and Spanish mackerel, sea trout in the surf and the creeks, plus fine cobia and channel bass. There is a healthy striped bass fishery in the Santee-Cooper empoundments but no stripers of note along the coast itself. From here on southward and into the Gulf of Mexico, striped bass become inland fishes, thriving in the rivers, freshwater lakes, and brackish deadwaters, but not in the salt chuck.

These states are blessed with hordes of channel bass, yet few of them attain the awesome weights racked up in Virginia and North Carolina. There are exceptions. In recent years some very big red drum have been reported out of South Carolina, and especially from the Cape Romaine area. Otherwise, the bulk of the catch consists of puppy drum, locally called spottail bass.

Florida's east coast is a tremendous hunk of seaboard, and no mile of it lacks fine saltwater angling. In the northern half of the state, say from Jacksonville down through Cape Kennedy to Vero Beach and Sebastian Inlet, there are fine seasonal runs of channel bass and bluefish, the former running to good size, but again far from the Virginia and North Carolina jumbos. Blues are generally small to medium, although there are occasional flurries of monsters. Tarpon and snook thrill anglers in midsummer and fall. There is a steady supply of white marlin and sailfish, in season, plus cobia, king mackerel, Spanish mackerel, and reef dwellers. Sea trout are abundant, and that area in and adjacent to Cape Kennedy—the Indian River country—always yields trophy trout.

James Hussey's all-tackle world record bluefish,
a 31-pound 12-ounce monster, was caught off
Cape Hatteras early in 1972.
Photo by Aycock Brown

Arbitrarily, since there is no abrupt dividing line, South Florida might be said to exist south of Fort Pierce, Jupiter, or Stuart, and the Saint Lucie River. There it begins to be reasonably warm in wintertime, although you can still shiver like Old Joe Pelican on a raw day in Miami during February or March. Sailfish Alley is that stretch of coast from Fort Pierce through Stuart and the Palm Beaches. No other Atlantic seaboard is so blessed with the spectacular spindlebeaks, although they are taken in considerable numbers down through the entrancing Keys. Sails are available throughout the entire year, but they're at peak in the midwinter months. There's an additional flurry of hectic activity in June.

All the books say that bonefish range as far north as southern Massachusetts, and strays are sometime collected in Yankee country. However, if you want peak sport with the white fox, it will be necessary to visit the Florida Keys, Bermuda, the multitudinous Caribbean islands, or maybe jet out to Hawaii where bones (o'io) are taken by blind casting.

For all practical fishing purposes, the Keys begin just south of Miami and extend down through the Marquesas. There are air-clear flats along this entire seaboard, from Biscayne Bay down to Key West, and westerly to the fabulous Marquesas. If you're thinking "south," think again; the Keys curve westward.

Captain Jimmie Albright bills an Atlantic sailfish for Joe Brooks. This was a 12-pound-test line catch off Islamorada, Florida.
Photo by Joe Brooks

Not so very long ago a traveling angler could see bones tailing close to the famous Overseas Highway. That's still possible, but not probable, for the greedy land barons have dredged once immaculate flats to create housing developments. In order to catch one of saltwater angling's grandest light-tackle prizes, you'll want to book an experienced guide with a small, fast planing boat. He'll take you out of some paradisaical slip in Islamorada, Marathon, Big Pine, or Key West, and you'll scream away into the blue to some far-off flat where civilization is still no more than the contrails of a continent-spanning jet aircraft. The Contents are justly famed, and the Marquesas ground is coming on strong.

All this is bonefish country, from Biscayne south and west, on both the Atlantic and Gulf sides. It is also the domain of the permit, a big brother of the pompano and an elusive battler that has become a supreme challenge to all light-tackle anglers. Tarpon range the entire area, cruising the flats in their endless search for food. There are hosts of barracuda, large and small sharks, mammoth rays, and pugnacious jacks.

Offshore, in this South Florida mix-master, sportsmen find a wide variety of pelagic and resident game fishes, from sails and wahoo through blackfin tuna, amberjack, big cobia, groupers, and snappers. There is ample opportunity to employ every fishing method, from fly casting on up to unlimited, although the latter is minimal. South Florida now boasts the finest light-tackle anglers in the world, people who have advanced every skill in the books.

Proceeding up the Gulf Coast of Florida, there is the mangrove back country centered on Flamingo, a great place to find tarpon and snook, redfish, sea trout, and a galaxy of other small to middleweight scrappers. It's a wild and beautiful wilderness of salt water and jungle islands, still basically remote and teeming with tropical life. Unless you have prospected carefully, a guide is necessary, else it is a good bet that you'll get lost, spend too many uncomfortable hours poling off shell bars and battling mosquitoes before the indefatigable park rangers complete a search and rescue mission.

Springtime witnesses a massive migration of cobia along this seacoast, a stream of hungry fighting fish that travels northward at a measured pace and affords hectic sport for pier-casters and boatmen from the mangrove country up to the Panhandle and beyond into the southern Gulf states. There are king mackerel and Spanish mackerel galore; bluefish, a host of snappers and groupers, and—always—a spring and fall bonanza of redfish and sea trout. Tarpon move northward as water temperatures climb, and Fort Myers' Boca Grande is a famed angling location where the silver king is often taken on deep-water grounds.

With a few notable exceptions, the Gulf Coast of Florida has not been so ruthlessly exploited as the Atlantic seaboard and the Keys. Therefore, accommodations may not be so plush, and boats less sophisticated. On the credit side, residents are more hospitable and there is a sense of delightful wilderness. You'll slap more mosquitoes and sand flies, but you'll also see dawns like the beginning of creation, with all the world a blaze of opal fire and the shell bars or river mouths alive with grand game fishes.

Away up on the northwestern tip of Florida, Destin boasts its "miracle strip" of white beaches, and the ports of adjacent Alabama share the same cornucopia of joys. This is far from Deep South, if we think in terms of the Keys, for angling falls off to ebb tide in the winter months. Sport is always available, yet spring, summer, and fall are the seasons to savor.

Once, and not so very long ago, the sport fishery relied on such stalwarts as cobia, migrating northwestward in the spring and tarrying through the summer months; spring and fall bonanzas of sea trout and redfish, hordes of Spanish and king mackerel, bluefish, snappers, groupers, and a grab bag of other species. All continue to oblige, but the canny skippers of this Panhandle area have opened up new grounds for offshore addicts.

Southward, in the Gulf of Mexico, charter men have discovered a blue-water arena that is stacked with grand game fishes. Nowadays, the beautiful outrigger-equipped sportfishermen land spectacular hauls of blue marlin, white marlin, sailfish, wahoo, and dolphin. This is a relatively new fishery, discovered in the mid-sixties; it is a summertime delight and it will be more important with each passing year.

Westward, into the Gulf of Mexico through Mississippi, Louisiana, and Texas, the spring-summer-fall season assures fine sport. Offshore anglers collect billfishes, but in no great numbers, together with lots of dolphin, king mackerel, Spanish mackerel, cobia, and bluefish. There is much inspired angling around offshore oil rigs for all of these battlers, plus groupers and snappers. Redfish and sea trout are important to the light-tackle buff, and both are most abundant in spring and fall, although taken pretty regularly throughout the year. As usual, there is a grab bag of inshore game: the croakers, black drum, flounders, sheepshead, and pompano that make life interesting. Well offshore, tuna are available, and big sharks forever challenge the muscleman. At proper seasons, tarpon arrive to try the nerves of specialists.

Jumping straight across the continent, southern California offers magnificent sport with a wide variety of game fishes. Following the seasons, yellowtail come first, migrating up out of Mexico and appearing around the Coronado Islands in March and April. Some so-called mossbacks remain there the year around, but they are never very certain and anglers appreciate the spring migration. White sea bass are much sought after and taken on bottom baits. By June, the first true albacore appear, usually far offshore, and then the long-finned warrior reigns supreme.

Modern big-game fishing was born on the Catalina Island grounds, so history's footnote is ironic; aside from the odd shark or broadbill swordfish, there is nothing here to test an unlimited outfit! During late summer and fall, striped marlin migrate up the coast to provide thrills. Bluefin and yellowfin tuna still make their annual rounds, although the former is never a true giant and the yellowfin simply does not grow to big-game proportions. A tuna of 183 pounds may have been "big game" in Dr. Holder's golden age, but the magic of the star-drag reel has transformed it into a light-tackle prize.

This fishery is dominated by yellowtail and albacore, although less spectacular species may command more attention from rank-and-file anglers. Kelp bass and rockfish are crowd-pleasers. Pacific barracuda and bonito oblige multitudes. Corvina, a West Coast cousin of the Atlantic weakfish, has its champions, and a good many enthusiasts hunt for halibut. Some specialists concentrate their attention on the vegetarian opaleye and here, as elsewhere, there are musclemen who are happy only when tied into a big shark or ray.

Southern California is big-boat territory. Nowhere in the world are there better party boats for offshore angling. The craft are huge, spacious, equipped with the best electronic aids to navigation and fish-finding, creature comforts, and modern tackle. You can sleep aboard and awake to drop a line into waters that are alive with game fishes. Chumming with live bait, usually anchovies, is almost taken for granted.

There are one-day trips, overnight jaunts, and extended cruises to hot spots well down into Mexican waters.

Progressing northward, the various Pacific salmonids take over as specialty fish. Albacore still sound a tocsin during the summer months when their long-finned phalanxes sweep up the seaboard, usually well out beyond harbor bounds where none but the most seaworthy of boats may participate. There are lots of wonderful resident species, like halibut, lingcod, the multitudinous rockfishes, sea bass, surf perch, flounders, and sturgeon, but the salmon occupies a psychological ivory tower.

In and around San Francisco there is strong competition from the striped bass, an East Coast species planted in the late nineteenth century. Stripers are caught throughout the year, sporadically in the winter months far back in delta impoundments, and regularly in spring, summer, and fall by trollers in San Francisco Bay and by surf casters operating from adjacent ocean beaches. Here, and here only on the Pacific Coast, the striper is considered a very important game fish. Northward, in Oregon—where bass are quite as plentiful—the lineside is never so eagerly sought and quite definitely plays second fiddle to king and coho salmon. Many residents of San Francisco agree with this point of view.

Oregon and Washington are salmon oriented. The chinook is king, and the coho is crown prince. Both are plentiful, although declining in numbers, thanks to heavy commercial exploitation and the damming of natal rivers. During any peak season, always the warm months, these great salmonids support a major sport fishery. They are taken, primarily, from boats working the offshore grounds, although there are river mouths where a shore caster can fill his limit. Even during the winter season carry-over salmon are available and are hunted. However, if you want a trophy king or silver, it would be wise to plan a trip to Oregon or Washington in late June, July, or August. Boats, baits, and facilities are readily available.

Debbie Waterman of DeLand, Florida, weighs a fine chinook salmon from the Pacific Northwest. *Photo by Charles F. Waterman*

North again, British Columbia is a spectacular seaboard, with great runs of king, silver, and pink salmon (the latter in alternate years) on tap for sportsmen. There are notable exceptions, but accommodations and facilities deteriorate as you move toward the Pole. A fisherman may find it necessary to improvise, but he will enjoy waters that are generally clean and stuffed with fish.

Alaska is America's last Northwest frontier and it is still delightfully sylvan. Gleaming salmon swarm into natal rivers, where they are taken with nets, spears, and sporting tackle. Accommodations are hardly comparable to those in the other states, but they are adequate and—in some cases—sophisticated. If there is any handicap at all it is the brevity of the sport-fishing season. Alaska's summer is both breathtakingly beautiful and short, so an angler's paradise is compressed into a very few months of magnificence. June is springtime, and September sees the first frigid blasts of winter. The salmon is king, and the salmon is abundant—chinooks, silvers, and humpies thrive in these cold, clear waters. If you take dead aim at a trophy, this is the place.

Salmonids dominate the Pacific Coast from, roughly, San Francisco northward, but dozens of other fine game fishes command respect. The Pacific halibut is very important and is more often taken by sport fishermen than is its East Coast look-alike. There are shoals of rockfish, kelp bass, flounders, and surf perch. Huge sturgeon—together with a lot of small suction mouths—populate the rivers and bays. Again, as on the chill North Atlantic, a veritable soup of plankton ensures a tremendous proliferation of life. Our northern seas almost throb with fishes and many of them offer a challenge to the rod and line angler.

Americans may lead the world in saltwater sport-fishing activity, but the United States has no monopoly on great marine grounds. Obviously, Canada enjoys a resource that has been no more than scratched. Australia and New Zealand boast important fisheries. South Pacific anglers are opening up fabulous grounds in the Fiji Islands, and there is much interest in South Africa, the Indian Ocean, particularly those warm seas around the Seychelles. Britons go down to the sea for tunny (bluefin tuna), cod, pollack, tope, skates, and a host of other species. There is much marine angling off the coast of Ireland.

Closer to home, providing that you are American, the vast and lovely Caribbean, with its legion of magical islands, must become a future angler's playground. Fabulous sport awaits the citizens of tomorrow, when new grounds are opened up and facilities provided. In some areas, such as Cuba, political differences must be arbitrated.

Central and South America now witness the first trickle through of sophisticated anglers from other lands, and this probing will become a flood as facilities are provided. A few Latin American countries recognize the tourist potential now and they are wooing the northern angler. There is magnificent marine sport in Nicaragua, Costa Rica, and Panama. Ecuador, British Honduras (Belize), and Venezuela are increasingly important for their sport-fishing grounds.

Well up in the North Atlantic, British-administered Bermuda is an island gem warmed by the Gulf Stream. While a year-around vacation spot and a legendary honeymoon isle, prime fishing is reserved for a seven-month period—May through November. Bermudians have championed the joys of light-tackle angling and have always discouraged so-called meat fishing. The variety is impressive and grounds vary from good bonefish flats to offshore banks where rocky drop-offs march up to cobalt depths. Accommodations are excellent; charter boats are well equipped and skippers are capable.

Yellowfin tuna may lead the hit parade. Almost always called Allison tuna here, they are the same magnificent battlers. *Thunnus albacares,* found around our watery world. Challenger Bank is a hot spot and that wonderful reach of blue ocean where the reef abuts the abyss also pays off with wahoo, white marlin, blue marlin, amberjack, blackfin tuna, and a host of other battlers. While there are flurries of hectic activity, billfishing is not spectacular off Bermuda. Look for some hefty bones, yellowfin tuna, wahoo, amberjack, a host of snappers, barracuda, dolphin, blackfin tuna, and a nice assortment of false albacore, oceanic bonito, and other rovers. It's light-tackle country, never a ground for the unlimited muscleman.

For some hundreds of years the Caribbean Sea has been a synonym for romance; even its place-names evoke the scent of flowers and the clatter of palm fronds in a brisk trade wind. Mention of the West Indies stirs something long forgotten and poignant in the soul of a city dweller, a vision of pirate gold and raw pearls weighing down the bleached bones of buccaneers. The Antilles, Tobago, Martinique, and the Grenadines—one cannot breathe these lovely names without visualizing azure seas and veils of soft rain to leeward.

Bill Burton, a Baltimore outdoor editor, exults over
a wahoo on light trolling gear. The place—
Challenger Banks, Bermuda.

Of course, the Caribbean is a very vast area, lying between the West Indies and the coast of Central America, buttressed on the south by the shoulder of South America and on the north by the Greater Antilles. It is a sea of scattered, gemlike islands that, on a map, often appear to be located cheek by jowl. Sometimes this is true, but one can also fly 1,000 miles across the blue sea, a vault of azure above and a bowl of indigo below—without any landfall.

Cuba was one of the first incubators of modern big-game angling, and that wonderful island, together with its outlying atolls, such as Isle of Pines, remain prime territory for offshore and flats fishermen.

Within scant air and sea miles of Miami, the Bahamas—Nassau, Andros, Walker Cay, and a skein of outlying jewels—are familiar to saltwater anglers, and yet that sun-warmed chain still covets secret places where few men have wet a line. Cat Cay and Bimini are famous for giant tuna in the spring; the great bluefins congregate here before they slant across the Gulf Stream and drive northward toward a cold New England coast and the Maritimes. Blue marlin, wahoo, dolphin, and a cornucopia of other wonderful game fishes tempt a traveling angler. Moreover, the air-clear flats of the Bahamas offer magnificent sport with bonefish.

Grand Cayman, Little Cayman, and Cayman Brac, almost due south of Cuba, used to be happy hunting grounds for bonefishermen, but sport has been far from classic in recent years, and nobody knows why. The surrounding depths certainly play host to billfish, wahoo, dolphin, and additional goodies. Eastward, Jamaica draws anglers from all over the world with some good marlin fishing off Kingston. Haiti and the Dominican Republic are blessed with fruitful grounds, but the political climate remains such that tourism has been retarded. This unfortunate situation will be corrected in the foreseeable future.

Puerto Rico and the Virgin Islands of Saint Thomas, Saint John, and Saint Croix straddle an important fishery. Here, big billfishes are almost taken for granted. The current world's all-tackle record for Atlantic blue marlin came from the waters off Saint Thomas, and a lot of big-game buffs are sure that much larger blues range this coast. Add wahoo, yellowfin tuna, blackfin tuna, dolphin, and the usual reef species. San Juan is Puerto Rico's major sally port; its charter boats are efficient and the skippers well versed.

Although it has only been tasted by keen North American anglers and residents of the country, there is no doubt that the waters off Venezuela boast record numbers of white marlin. This may, indeed, be the world's foremost ground for the little cousin of the big blue. Sails are abundant, and offshore anglers are finding considerable numbers of blue marlin. La Guaira, east of Caracas, is a major jumping-off point, and there is rapid improvement in facilities, accommodations, and boats.

Worth noting is the fact that the largest rod and reel tarpon in the world, a 283-pounder, was taken from Lake Maracaibo, Venezuela. The "lake" is a saltwater bay that curves well inland and is sheltered by land masses, except for a relatively narrow passage to the Caribbean between Maracaibo and Aruba. This coast is an angler's dream of good things and it will become more popular with each passing year.

Every mile of South America's great shoulder on the Caribbean is important. From Trinidad, Port of Spain, on up through the Orinoco Delta, Isla de Margarita, Caracas, Aruba, and into Colombia, a spectacular fishery is hiding in the wings, waiting only for facilities to be improved. There are white marlin, blue marlin, sailfish, tarpon, wahoo, snook, and a marvelous array of other saltwater game fish waiting for the pioneers to arrive.

Carlos Barrantes with a grouper from Costa Rica's
Bay of Parrots.

Lack of facilities—boats, lodging, and transportation—continues to plague Central and South American sport fishing. There is a measure of political turmoil that often deters tourists. All of Latin America fashionably hates the United States, but this seems to be a generic and collective rather than an individual thing. Almost always the visiting gringo is treated courteously. Outright hostility is an exception.

Facilities! Only recently have some local entrepreneurs, usually financed by Americans, provided modern lodging, boats, and tackle on the great locations. Some of the grandest grounds are still absolutely virgin, and you will plumb them only as a pioneer —able to suffer the attention of wind and sun and rough campsites. This will change, for the fish are there, an astonishing variety of magnificent fighters on a sea rim that is both spectacular and fruitful.

The east coasts of Nicaragua, Costa Rica, and Panama swarm with tarpon. They are not the record-breakers of Maracaibo, the Florida Keys, or Mexico, but they are healthy 70- to 100-pounders, so abundant that (when weather and water conditions oblige) one does not speculate on a possible strike, but expects many during the course of each day. In Nicaragua, the San Juan River produces silver kings in a setting reminiscent of northern Atlantic salmon fishing. Costa Rica's Colorado and Parismina rivers are spectacular. All are now graced by modern lodges, good outboard-powered small boats, and guides who will fish all day and into the night.

The guides are marvelous; often they speak little English, but hone their skills with each passing day. They may be Indians, Negroes, Spaniards, or various mixtures of races, but practically all are hard-working gentlemen who want to see their sports catch fish. They appear tireless and forever enthusiastic; they will be itching to shove off at dawn, and loath to return until the tropical sun plunges into cabbage palms and the howling monkeys have awarded the jungle to such night workers as the jaguars and tapirs.

This east coast of Central America is river country, black water, and jungle. There the tarpon is supreme in season, and hulking snook arrive when the time is right. One finds a host of other battlers, many of them unfamiliar. The machaca, which looks and fights like a northern shad—although more of an aerial acrobat—frequents brushy riverbanks and will crash a well-presented plug or fly. There are quapote, a look-alike of the Florida-Gulf tripletail, but a fish well armed with sharp teeth; the majarra, a large, brackish-water facsimile of the bluegill and a far more formidable battler. Snook are always hiding under ground cover, and big jacks often thrash the dark water into foam. Tarpon are winter fish, most numerous from December through March. Look for commendable runs of trophy snook in the late summer and fall.

Honduras offers fine sport with tarpon and snook, plus some almost unexplored grounds for white marlin and blue marlin. Most of the boats are primitive by modern standards, as they are along the short coast of Guatemala. The fish are there, legions of them, but the facilities have yet to be developed. Commercial anglers report lots of sails, white marlin, and blue marlin, but almost nobody seeks them with rod and line. King and Spanish mackerel, dolphin, and wahoo are plentiful, yet rarely hunted. Both Honduras and Guatemala boast fine bonefishing, again a resource that has been little exploited.

British Honduras—better call it Belize if you want to make points with the local citizenry—is another proposition. There, fine accommodations, good boats, and guides are available, both on the mainland and on offshore Turneffe Island. The people speak English, and a sportsman can seek anything from bones and permit to such offshore game as marlin, sails, and wahoo. Snook range the rivers and the brackish bays. Groupers and snappers are abundant on offshore reefs.

Belize is a good port of call and there are no major problems at the moment. Sometimes these Latin American countries seem illogical and engage in suddenly furious passions that threaten the health of a visitor. Over a few potent drinks in a tropical bistro I learned the reason why—a few years back—Honduras and El Salvador went to war. A soccer game triggered the whole unfortunate bloodbath. Somebody won, and somebody lost on a playing field, and so a bemedaled general ordered the troops to march and the bombers to fly!

Latin America boasts great fishing grounds and her people are hospitable, unless inflamed by some new revolution. As elsewhere, pay attention to seasons, winds, tides—and politics.

More than 100 years ago, Melville thought that Mexico was "America's fast-fish" and would ultimately be landed and incorporated into the United States. He was wrong, because the United States and Mexico have become good neighbors and the old boundaries endure. Indeed, Mexico is among the most advanced of all Latin American countries and probably draws more North American tourist anglers than all the others combined. East and west, this nation's seaboards offer grand sport.

Mexico's east coast has been ignored by too many anglers, although sportsmen from Texas and Louisiana often range its river mouths and beaches, where they collect fine hauls of redfish, tarpon, snook, and king-sized jacks. Lack of facilities and rapid transportation hamper exploitation; only those who are willing to rough it have penetrated the wild regions of this coast and savored its delights. Cozumel, away down off the Yucatán Peninsula, offers fine sport, with sailfish on offshore grounds. There is a never-ending supply of reef fishes, groupers, and snappers, many of them huge, plus a leavening of tunas, dolphin, and other wanderers. The variety has been no more than tasted, and the taste is sweet.

This is tarpon ground, and the big silver kings swarm into all major river systems. There is too much pollution, and there is a great overkill in the commercial fishery, but the mouths of the Rio Grande and the Pánuco are famous for trophy battlers. Most of the monsters are caught on live bait or trolled lures, and gear is relatively heavy. There is little interest in light tackle, although this must become important in future years.

South of the United States, in the vast Gulf of Mexico, weather forecasts are erratic and uncertain, so offshore fishermen must operate like the old seafarers—studying the sky and the cloud formations, rather than heeding the meteorological data radioed to ships at sea. From midsummer through early fall, sudden, furious storms are probable, so a boatman must be prepared to seek a sheltered harbor at the first sign of elemental fury.

For many North Americans, South of the Border now means Mexico's astonishing Baja California, a warm and sunny vacationland that extends southward from San Diego, to and beyond Cabo San Lucas, incorporating the vast and protected Sea of Cortés. While surface transportation remains a bit rough on Baja, there are air links to all the great locations and adequate facilities on site. Fishing rates the superlatives. In addition to resident species, which include corvina, Sierra mackerel, cabrilla (grouper), and many others, the wheeling seasons witness grand sport with sailfish, striped marlin, yellowfin tuna, yellowtail, dolphin, and the giant totuava, king of all weakfish-croaker tribes. Trophy snook lurk in the river systems, and milkfish, a West Coast cousin of the tarpon, often thrill anglers.

Cabo San Lucas, like Cape Hatteras on the Atlantic seaboard, is a sort of game-fish junction. There, black marlin become fair game, together with sails and striped marlin. There, also, an angler will find roosterfish, the astonishing jacklike battler with a high and mighty dorsal fin. There is really no way to describe a rooster; one can list its green and silver tiger markings and its fighting tactics—a combination of pugnacious power and soaring acrobatics—but you'll never know all the truth until that magic day when Pez Gallo takes a lure and exhibits his considerable talents.

Southward, Mazatlán and Acapulco are favored jump-off locations for marine anglers. Both are sophisticated, with plush accommodations and boats to suit any taste. Sailfish are bread and butter here, and they are big spindlebeaks—most of them far larger than those of the effete Atlantic. The bill of fare includes striped marlin and black marlin, roosterfish, and a host of other species such as dolphin, yellowfin tuna, and wahoo. There are the usual residents, some of them big enough to yank a man over the transom. A visitor can enjoy great sport in the surf or offshore. Mexico welcomes traveling anglers and offers Old World hospitality. Of all Latin American countries, this land of romance and legend best understands the needs of a tourist and strives to smooth his way.

Central America's Pacific coastline is volcanic, rough, and breathtaking in its aboriginal beauty. Until you get down to Panama it is also a rather wild frontier, practically untouched since the dawn of creation. The blue seas are alive with game fishes—black marlin and sails, striped marlin, roosters, and tuna. Dolphin chase bait in bays that have never seen a sport-fishing line. In many areas, facilities are almost nonexistent and the vast cornucopia of abundance is sampled only by residents and occasional whiskery pilgrims out of the north—people tough enough to enjoy life in the raw, a hard bed on volcanic sand, a dip in the sea for a bath, and tinned rations for food. There is a vast no-man's-land between Mexico and Panama, yet all of it is prime saltwater angling territory, destined to become famous in some not too far-distant future.

The fish are there, and I have seen them off Costa Rica's rugged west coast: sails and dolphin and roosterfish; runners, groupers, and strange battlers that have yet to grace the identification books. Shrimpers find 200-pound black marlin entangled in their nets, or mourn over meshes that have been torn into shreds by larger gamesters. The largest snook I ever heard of was caught in the Tárcoles River on Costa Rica's Pacific Coast; it was a 69-pounder, but it never made IGFA's record lists because the angler, Bernal Fernández P., used a treble-hooked Pikie Minnow plug, then out of favor—and still *verboten* because it was trolled.

Bob Whitaker, a Phoenix, Arizona, outdoor writer,
displays a husky roosterfish taken on spinning
tackle in Baja California waters.
Photo by Bob Whitaker

The prospect is eyebrow-raising and, with notable exceptions, this is par for the course all along Central and South America's Pacific Coast. Lodging, facilities, transportation, sophisticated boats, and modern tackle are required. When they arrive on the scene as they must, a rash of new and important sport-fishing grounds will be opened up. There are ample precedents.

Possibly the heaviest rod and line snook in the
world, this 69-pounder was caught in the Tárcoles
River of Costa Rica by Bernal Fernández P., right.
Carlos Barrantes, San José fishing authority, is at
left. *Photo by Carlos Barrantes*

Piñas Bay, Panama, sets the pace. There, a modern lodge, fine boats, erudite
skippers, and a good deal of know-how put visiting anglers into black marlin, sails,
dolphin, and a grab bag of other game fishes. In the Canal Zone, members of the
fabulous Schmidt family, originally from Baltimore, have been operating sportfishermen for half a lifetime. In this area, whether unlimited or light tackle, the field is
wide open. Practically all of Central and South America's West Coast offers the same
prospect, but too few of the prime grounds are geared to a jet age.

S. Kip Farrington, a Long Island aristocrat and a roarer par excellence, opened
up Cabo Blanco, Peru. Kip is a sea rover, a pioneer, and a big-game fisherman; he was
instrumental in publicizing the grand tuna fishing off Nova Scotia, and he then
switched far southward to promote the broadbill and black marlin of Cabo Blanco.
Farrington was a foreloper in our joyous art.

Cabo Blanco, at one time, was the mecca of all big-game anglers, the place where
record swordfish and black marlin were most likely to be taken. It is still a grand
and imposing seacoast, but for some reason—perhaps the usually accepted shift in
ocean currents, or possibly Farrington's unswerving conviction that Japanese long-
liners murdered a fantastic fishery—the old magic is gone. This entire seaboard plays
host to billfishes beyond compare, and much of the water is still absolutely virgin.

S. Kip Farrington, an American angling pioneer,
with a brace of black marlin he caught at Cabo
Blanco, Peru, in 1952. The larger fish was a new
all-tackle world record at the time.
Photo by S. Kip Farrington

Note that the world's record broadbill swordfish, a 1,182-pounder, was taken off Iquique, Chile. South America's Pacific Coast is a sleeper, still largely unexplored by anglers, yet still prominent in the record books.

Hawaii is a promised land for saltwater sportsmen. Water temperatures vary little from month to month, yet there is a seasonal variation in the number of certain fishes. Spring and summer witness the greatest influx of blue marlin and yellowfin tuna, but both are present throughout the year. Wahoo, dolphin, and skipjack tuna are plentiful. Bonefish (o'io) have their seasons, and ulua—king of the jacks—swarm close to volcanic shores. There is no end of profitable sport fishing, yet the off-islander entertains one very erroneous belief: he thinks that Hawaii is a single atoll in mid-Pacific.

It is, in fact, a vast and far-flung chain of islands, each with its separate marine ecology and environment. The major sport fishery centers around Honolulu because that is a population center and a crossroads for air travelers. Entirely aside from geographical accident, Kona, at Honolulu, is a great jumping-off spot. The outlying Hawaiian Islands are quite as fruitful, and perhaps more so in some cases, but are never so well advertised for the simple reason that they are remote.

Some of the largest blue marlin in the world fin these waters. The yellowfin tuna grows to heroic sizes. Bonefish, although here a deep water rather than a flats feeder, achieves record weights. Until a Zululand, South Africa, bone vaulted into the record books to take all-tackle honors, Hawaii was a front-runner. Offshore fishing is profitable the year around, but, as elsewhere in the Western Hemisphere, is best in spring, summer, and fall. A tremendous number of sport and game fishes present themselves to the rod and line angler.

With few exceptions, big-game fishes of the Pacific seem to grow larger than those of the Atlantic. Excepting the regal bluefin tuna, there are few challengers. Although a larger specimen has been taken (illegally in the eyes of IGFA) off Hawaii, Guam holds the record for blue marlin, a tremendous 1,153-pounder. Australia and New Zealand support burgeoning sport fisheries; in fact, an Australian, Alfred Dean, is credited with taking the world's largest game fish on rod and line. Dean conquered a white shark that scaled 2,664 pounds. Talk about light tackle! On unlimited 130-pound-test line, that monster from Ceduna in southern Australia was better than twenty to one!

A blue marlin is winched to the dock on Hawaii's grand Kona coast.
Photo courtesy Hawaii Visitors Bureau

765. TRUSSELL.

P. GOADBY.

1137.

CAIRNS
GAME FISHING
CLUB

ANGLER	PETER GOADBY.
FISH	BLACK MARLIN
WEIGHT	1137 lbs
TACKLE	130 lb.
LAUNCH	STRIKER I
DATE	8-11-68

Peter Goadby, right, a famed Australian angler-
author, with a 1,137-pound black marlin he caught
off Cairns, Australia. *Photo by Brian and
Ann Vicary*

New Zealand is prime territory and many record catches have been made off Mayor Island and Bay of Islands. Blue marlin and striped marlin grace that fishery, together with huge sharks of many species. To date, the heaviest yellowtail in the world, a 111-pounder, is credited to Bay of Islands. Saltwater fishing is a way of life in this corner of the world and there is much sophistication in tackle, boats, and techniques. Australians and New Zealanders bow only to the United States in equipment, strategy, and know-how, and they'll never admit it, because they are Anzacs, the toughest and most imaginative people in our New World. Next to Americans, of course! Did you expect anything else from a rock-ribbed Yankee born within the shadow of Concord Bridge?

Australians and New Zealanders catch big bluefish, which they call "tailor." In South Africa, the blue is a "shad" or an "elft." Names change, and sometimes species are unique, tied to a seaboard. For example, the Australian salmon is far removed from American and European salmonids; it resembles a shad and is a much sought-after game fish. Things change. Even the seasons can be reversed, for it's summertime Down Under when winter is smiting our Western Hemisphere. All the better for world-ranging anglers who have the ambition and the necessary wealth to travel half across the world at a moment's notice.

American whalemen ranged the South Pacific long years ago, but that entire region remains a "loose fish" so far as rod and line anglers are concerned. Australians and New Zealanders are beginning to penetrate its fragrant fastnesses, but the seas are vast and it will take many years to pinpoint all the hot spots. Fiji is the latest of the prime grounds, a place where wahoo grow to record proportions and great billfishes chase bait. October through February is the optimum season to hook a trophy black or blue marlin. Yellowfin tuna, dolphin, and many other game fishes are readily available. The major sport-fishing ports are Suva and Yanuca, and the international airport is located at Nadi on Viti Levu.

Tahiti also caters to sport fishermen, and the waters off that romantic and legendary island chain host big blue marlin, king-sized wahoo, and yellowfin tuna. There are sharks big enough to scare a bluebearded angler, plus lots of sailfish, bonito, and other gamesters. New Caledonia, the Cook Islands, the Marshalls, and the Marianas offer big billfishes and tunas, together with such shallow-water species as bones. Papua and New Guinea boast wahoo, sailfish, dolphin, and small billfishes. There is a trend toward the use of light tackle along the Gulf of Papua. Australians and New Zealanders lead the way, staking out new fishing grounds off beaches where an Allied soldiery defeated the Japanese Empire in mortal combat long years ago. Today, Japanese sportsmen come to fish—and to marvel at the rusting hulks of war machinery left on these sun-washed shores.

Wherever you travel on this earth, there is saltwater sport fishing. Often it is aboriginal. Invariably the fish will be there and—thanks to the Law of General Cussedness—they'll be larger and more plentiful in areas where you can't scrounge up a decent tackle combination, an adequate boat, or a skipper who knows his trade. It is impossible, in a single book, to blueprint all the wonderful grounds. They are worldwide, glued to each continent and island; they are multitudinous in silk-smooth tropical bays and roaring northern seaboards that have seen little of man other than the native hunter and an occasional mat-bearded adventurer searching for the unknown.

The marine fishing grounds span our globe: South Africa, where cliff-hanging daredevils use side-cast reels to flip metal lures to big bluefish and tuna; Great Britain's cold wash, which yields cod and sea bass and conger eels; the big seas of Cairns, North

Queensland, and the thin flats of Florida and the Caribbean. A man who wades chest deep in the crashing surf of New England, trying to catch a trophy striped bass, is blood brother to he who seeks ulua off a precipitious Hawaiian headland. Whatever the offshore ground, a fisherman is mesmerized by the rise and fall of a rolling sea, burned by the sun, stung by salt scud, fully alive to a sudden fin or bill behind the skipping baits. There are always men who, as Kipling sang, "preach in advance of the army" and "skirmish ahead of the church." Most of us remain innocents on the great, dark, all-encompassing ocean.

And this, of course, is a gauntlet thrown. The great grounds constitute an infinitesimal fraction of those still to be discovered. My account is fractional, drawn from personal experience and the records of pioneers who went out to see for themselves. Much remains to be seen.

As marine sport fishermen, we emulate the first hunters and trappers who penetrated the wilderness to challenge unknown continents and faceless perils. The shambling sea is our jungle and prairie, ours to conquer and—hopefully—never to defile.

FLOOD TIDE ~ 20

The Promise: Tomorrow at Sea

Reading the future is a tricky game at best, yet we require no seances, ESP, or tea leaves to predict a continuing boom in saltwater angling. During the tag end of this hurtling twentieth century, new grounds will be opened up by knowledgeable nomads, and tackle will be improved. Gradually, we will learn the secrets of the sea, as astute marine biologists and oceanographers study each problem and provide answers. There will be a greater sharing of scientific information by all the seafaring nations, and by anglers themselves. The trend is apparent now, with an obvious thirst for basic data on all continents and much to-ing and fro-ing of sportsmen who range the entire world. Quietly, commercial fishing authorities of the maritime nations are pooling their information in businesslike seminars divorced from power politics.

Sport certainly remains in its infancy, still lacking accepted prophets and an extensive literature, but rapid transportation, the deterioration of inland resources, greater affluence, and leisure time guarantee that it will be the premier game of future generations. The sea remains a lush frontier. We have yet to destroy the ecology of the salt chuck, but, of course, we'll do that too—if we continue on our present collision course. There is one bitter consolation: it will take many years. And there is one almost infinitesimal glimmer of hope: we now witness a citizen ground swell of outraged protest against flagrant desecration. Perhaps man will slacken his ferocious assault upon the life-giving biological ecosystem, if only in self-defense. We can only hope that there is still time to do so.

Marine angling flaunts one trump card: every saltwater fish is a better battler than its inland counterpart. A tinker mackerel that weighs less than a pound will outfight a Rocky Mountain rainbow trout of twice that weight. There is no comparison at all if you match recently stocked inland fishes with the wild, sea-nurtured spawn of the ocean. Marine species pull harder, jump higher, run farther, grow to larger sizes, and are more plentiful than their inland counterparts. Some of them will bite your hand off if you take liberties, and a few monsters, carelessly approached, are quite capable of killing and eating a man.

Among advances will be both weather control and more accurate forecasting, the former a long-range goal that may never be entirely successful. Meteorology has scored notable successes, most apparent in the current plotting of hurricanes and typhoons. On the other hand, daily or short-range predictions that concern sunlight, rainfall, wind direction, and velocity often fail. Although founded on good and true information pounded out by computers fed by scanning satellites and weather ships, the world spins and local patterns change rapidly enough to humble a country forecaster. Often a seaman—or a farmer—studying cloud formations and tasting the wind proves a more accurate soothsayer than the scientist with his bank of sophisticated instruments. This, too, will change.

Marine anglers of the future are sure to place greater reliance on electronic aids such as depth sounders and fish-locating devices, yet there will be a cut-off point at which the little black boxes will be considered too efficient for the collective conscience of sportsmen. This has already happened with the so-called "electric reel," a motor-driven device used by some party boatmen who fish great depths and desire to take the work out of hauling a fish to the surface. Such tools may be godsends to physically handicapped people, or to butchers, but they are scorned by a majority of responsible anglers and usually disqualify a tournament entry.

Equipment forever improves, yet no revolutionary departures are likely in our fore-seeable future. Most striking, perhaps, will be further rapid improvement in boats designed for sport fishing and the power plants that complement them. Hull forms will change subtly, but rarely radically. Clever technicians are now researching paints boasting special properties that, when applied to a hull's bottom, might remarkably increase any given boat's maximum speed. Marine biologists, going to nature for some of the answers, note that certain fishes utilize slime coatings that measurably increase their velocity in pursuit of prey or escape from predators. While the chemistry and the mechanics of this process are understood, fishes in a sense burn off a part of their "high-speed slime" during a hard run and are then capable of replenishing it. The busy laboratory workers search for ways and means of duplicating nature's minor miracles.

Tomorrow there will be greater attention to comfort coupled with efficiency in boats designed for use on inshore and offshore grounds, with cleverly fashioned storage compartments built in to defeat the elements and keep clutter to a minimum. Practically all small boats will be equipped with transistorized CB radios, depth sounders, and fish locators—the two latter combined in one instrument—plus workable compasses. We are only beginning to realize that a small craft on the sea must be able to conquer difficulties seldom encountered in an inland mill pond.

Power plants will be better and more efficient with each passing year. Weight, commensurate with horsepower, will continue to plummet as power rises. There will be further advances in jet propulsion and the electric motor, the latter beefed up to defeat marine corrosion and provide silent propulsion on shoal grounds. Wankel rotary engines may well be important to tomorrow's outboarder, because the design is simple, light in weight, and capable of high performance without excessive wear. Like the gas turbine, another promising power source, designers are still battling to defeat a few problems inherent in the Wankel.

Mechanization will be increasingly important to anglers who go down to the sea, yet this development will be rigidly controlled in many metropolitan areas, first through gradual elimination of the big, live-in beach buggy, and emphasis on small four-wheel-drive chase cars or new ATVs with sufficient load-carrying capacity to satisfy the needs of serious anglers. Except in undeveloped and unexploited areas, live-in beach vehicles will be herded into special campground acreages administered by state or federal park authorities, and all smaller vehicles will be restricted insofar as indiscriminate exploration is concerned. Drivers will be required to utilize well-marked access and exit tracks.

Similarly, light plane operations off many beaches will be halted because of the hazard to public safety. Airplanes will be extremely important, though, for they'll bring anglers into remote fishing locations, spot fish, and otherwise serve as the eyes of the angler and his magic carpet to great grounds when the time element prohibits leisurely ground travel. Aircraft will, of course, become far more efficient in all dimensions, in speed calculated to ship a latter-day nomad to the far shores of the world, and in the ability to land or take off on short strips.

Thanks to affluence and the demand of sportsmen, new grounds will be opened up with breathtaking regularity. Unlike inland fishing, the surface of this marine bonanza has not even been scratched—it has been lightly tickled! Vast reaches of sea, teeming with sport and game fishes, are still virgin, while other continent-sized arenas have hosted only a few back-of-beyond adventurers who suffered to attain paradise and—in many cases—are violently opposed to the development of facilities. These idealistic gladiators joust with windmills, for the facilities will go in and the treasure chests will be opened. In this hemisphere, when and if political strife subsides, the perfumed Caribbean, Central and South America (both Atlantic and Pacific) must become North America's ultimate playground. Spectacular sea sport may well become Latin America's most valuable product. We, the English-speaking gringos, had best absorb a few crash courses in Spanish.

Fishing tackle jumped light years ahead in those magnificent two decades following World War II. The great revolutions are well behind us, yet no technology ever remains in suspended animation. While entirely new departures are unlikely, there will be spectacular improvements and variations in basic gear. I see no phase out of any fishing technique; indeed, the challenge posted by each tackle combination will ensure that each survives. Fly casting, bait casting, spinning, surf casting, and trolling will continue to intrigue multitudes of enthusiasts. A healthy contingent of salty zealots will always haunt the charter and party boats, the piers and jetties where bottom baits provide satisfaction. Big game, on a wild and open ocean, will take the place of yesterday's elephant and Bengal tiger. We return to the sea.

Look for a steady phase out of the wooden rod. Split bamboo is delightful in a light wand used on fresh water, but it has become an anachronism on the briny. Modern, tubular fiber glass is far superior because it ensures a maximum of quality control in manufacture, it is lighter than bamboo, and far less susceptible to the ravages of salt moisture and mildew and rough handling. Superb glass rods are inexpensive, yet they are the finest fish-fighting tools ever created by man. The modern marine angler who uses anything other than fiber glass does so because he is a victim of romantic tradition, forgetting that he is engaged in a relatively new sport and that he enjoys the privilege of building his own dream castles.

Grimly resisting, the incurable romantics declare that no glass rod has the quick return action of fine split bamboo, or the "feel" nurtured by traditionalists over a weary span of years. Their arguments become tedious, for today's champions are winning casting tournaments, distance, and accuracy, and they are catching tremendous numbers of great game fish on tubular fiber glass—the rod material of the sea. Naturally, this new synthetic shaft has its faults.

Once upon a time there were weight and action standards, quite possibly erroneous, but nonetheless an industrywide effort to standardize. Tubular fiber glass and synthetic lines scuttled all this careful departmentalization, and the makers of modern rods must sooner or later return to truth. Standardization of weight and action is necessary, if only to provide a guide to line matching, a thing very important in fly casting.

Fortunately, all the better manufacturers of fly rods, having adopted numeral rather than letter designations of line weights, are stressing balance by recommending proper lines to match given rods. Some go so far as to market combinations, each a rod, reel, and line in ideal balance. Others clearly mark rods with proper line weight to ensure maximum performance.

There is a healthy trend in the manufacture of trolling sticks to designate each rod by pound-test rating, an indication that it will be best employed with a line of that particular breaking strength. Unfortunately, standardization again suffers because a rod, say a 20-pound job made by one firm, will be much stiffer, or more resilient, than that offered by a competitor. There is a need for all hands to compare notes and come up with figures they agree upon. Since the logic is inescapable, this will be done.

Quite as logically, tubular fiber glass will see improvement in certain areas. Glass, like every other material, deteriorates. When a much-appreciated stick breaks in the middle of a cast, the angler looks for flaws or accidental injury. The rod may simply have worn out and become brittle through long use, exposure to sunlight and dry air, which leaches bonding resins out of the foundation material. You won't hear or read much about this, but it occurs, and research technicians continue to seek cures. They'll solve the problem.

Future anglers will enjoy more efficient rods because competition between manufacturers is keen. In addition to general excellence of the basic stick, I would expect increasingly better wraps and gel coats that serve as armor against the odd stress exerted by accident. There will be less accent on decorative windings and more on pure efficiency. The intricately wound rod is on the way out; it may be pretty, and the winding pattern may be a trademark of some status custom builder, but fancy wraps invariably fray, part, and cause trouble. You wind up anchoring them with an unsightly hunk of plastic tape, or strip the entire stick and refinish it.

Metal ferrules will phase out, to be superseded by the glass-to-glass joint. This offers greater strength and no interruption in the action of a given blank under stress. The only exception—and this too may be overcome—is that of the big-game stick that requires a heavy, well-machined reel seat to absorb the pounding administered by monsters of the sea, plus a keyed tip locked into this rugged butt and reel seat unit. One-piece unlimited rods are feasible, and any elimination of a joint increases overall strength. Perfectionists will increasingly demand that which cancels out any possible weakness.

Hardware is always important in a decent fishing rod, and is sometimes the only obvious indication of quality, since it is difficult for the average consumer to determine whether glass blanks have been properly manufactured and cured. Roller guides are available in degrees of excellence, but the best now leave little to be desired. There is a need for smoother and tougher rings, and these will be provided. The present Carbaloy type is most efficient, although still far from friction-free. Metallurgy will provide alloys hard enough to resist grooving, yet slick as the old-fashioned agate that was so faultless in its pristine state, but prone to cracking or shattering upon any light contact with an immovable object.

We will see steady experimentation with rod action, a thing that has been going on for many years, but is only currently emerging from the lairs of piscatorial witch doctors and faddists. The trend is toward a tip calibrated to a specific job. Therefore, tomorrow's throwing rod will feature a more or less planky action, whether it be fly, spin, or high surf, and the trolling stick will feature greater parabolic action and the necessary backbone to kill a powerful battler. Always, there will be specialized weapons, like the limber-tipped power rod used on Pacific Coast live-bait boats. This hunk of ordnance needs light-tip action to throw very light live baits, such as anchovies, together with considerable amidships backbone to pummel large game fish hooked on tiny tempters.

In any rod, the angler often seeks an impossible combination of virtues. There is, for example, no reason why a variable action stick could not be developed—one that, by the pressing of a button, might be extended and made limber enough to cast a tiny bait or lure, and then retracted to offer the planky power necessary to play a robust game fish. This is feasible, and yet there is much doubt that anglers would accept so radical an innovation. Fenwick explored the possibilities with its "purple shaft," a stiffener shoved into a tubular glass fly rod after a big fish had been hooked, and the idea drew jeers from perfectionists who insisted that this gimmick involved the use of two separate systems in conquering a trophy.

The future is sure to witness a whole host of combination rods—fly-spin, spin-bait, troll-cast, and multiple breakdown types designed for travel. None will measure up to the specialized article, but each has a place in a society forever on the move and traveling with two suitcases, plus toothbrush. I reserve greater respect for the clever little breakdown outfits than the combinations, which always seem to be either-or and not quite up to either.

Though spinning is probably an older method than revolving spool, fixed spool is technically far behind conventional, and its failures will be corrected by technicians of the near future. Among problems to be ironed out are line twist and the delicate construction that leads to mechanical failure at the most inopportune time. Bails, gearing, and drag systems remain antediluvian. Corrosion, or a few grains of sand in the wrong places, can render these reels inoperative. The very serious defect of line twist, a congenital fault of spinning, must be overcome, and then the fixed-spool reel must be beefed up to a point where it is no longer a gentle left jab in a back-alley brawl.

Whatever the reel, spinning or conventional revolving spool, there is a need for tougher and smoother drag systems, perhaps automatic drags that will slack off just before a line's breaking test is reached. This, admittedly, would be a major benefit to the amateur, because an advanced angler derives an edge by manipulating his drag. Like a host of antibacklash devices, it would handicap the expert, while foolproofing the inept performance of a duffer.

All reel spools must be, and will be, strengthened to prevent sudden disintegration under pressure. Gearing will be improved to resist normal wear and the stresses encountered in playing great game fishes. There will be a steady phasing out of the star drag on big-game grounds and substitution of the micrometer-adjusted lever-action brake with its graduated stops and silk-smooth operation. (Many of the current models are far from "silk smooth," and some are quite as jerky as the old-fashioned star that has been given no maintenance.)

All future fishing lines will be single-strand synthetic extrusions, or metal. We're not ready for this in the seventies, because the tireless technicians have yet to solve all problems with monofilament, or wire, for that matter. The former still is cursed with "memory," which can explode a heavily burdened reel, and the latter tends to be springy and cursed by crystallization after it has been kinked. Mono is grievously elastic, compared to modern braids, and is more subject to fatigue over a period of time and hard use. Up to approximately 50-pound test, monofilament now suffices; beyond that it is currently questionable. There will be improvements.

We are going to see perfection in monofilament, advances that will doom all braid to limbo and will even make today's beautifully designed and fabricated fly lines obsolete. Our technology will control stretch in the single-strand extrusion, remove memory, achieve absolute quality control in diameter and strength, even where tapers are desired. It will become possible to produce monofilaments that will float or sink, that feature weight where weight is needed and buoyancy where that is a benefit. Within another twenty years braid will be forgotten and only single-strand wire will challenge mono as the fishing line supreme.

One very possible breakthrough lies in the realm of spectacularly bright built-in color. All previous attempts to camouflage lines have stressed translucence or the mottled effect of neutral splotching. This is logical to the human mind, yet not necessarily right. There is, currently, some upsetting evidence that a fluorescent yellow monofilament is less visible to a fish than any of the supposedly clear or shadowy strands.

A couple of scientific types long ago concluded that "all fish see as through a yellow lens." Fluorescent yellow monos, introduced by Du Pont in 1970, are now being evaluated on the grounds. I have found them highly efficient, in some cases apparently superior to near-translucent, gray, blue, and green.

We may well progress into an era of "bright string," a trace easily followed by human eyes yet deceptive to the fish. It is worth noting that all trout and salmon guides warred against the first white fly lines—developed to please tournament casters and outdoor photographers. The guides were wrong, because these snowy lines have never spooked fish.

Whether or not the fluorescent colors are a major advance remains to be seen. They have certainly proved themselves in many arenas and they offer a new concept. All of tomorrow's fishing lines will employ color, both to deceive fishes and to ease the task of the angler.

Wire certainly has a stake in the future, because no other material is better suited to the deep dredging of lures. Metal will be recognized by IGFA, and the line will be a far better product than that now offered. Although single strand, the wire line of our future fishing adventures will be both tough and limber, resistant to kinking and malleable enough to be handled with impunity by beginners. The strand will be well marked at regular intervals, say 50-foot sections, with plastic sleeves just large enough to be seen during daylight hours and to rattle through the guides or be felt at night. Diameters, per rated pound test, will diminish, an achievement that will add to the joy of tackling game fish in deep water.

Tomorrow's leaders will be fabricated of kink-resistant wire or special monofilaments that will be harder and tougher than the extrusions that must serve as running line. Knots and splices will always be valuable, yet our technology will provide new methods of fusing soft leaders to soft lines without benefit of knots, bends, or sleeves—perhaps with some special tool designed to utilize the properties of the line-leader material. Shock lines and backing will be connected in the same way, smoothly, and yet boasting the utopian 100 percent strength factor.

Any reasonably well-informed angler can list basic lures used in salt water—or in fresh, for that matter. The roster of types is surprisingly short, yet there are legions of variations on each standard design. This is not only a healthy state of affairs, it is entirely logical. Our future will see a proliferation of variations, together with a very few new departures. Once-popular types (if they ever possessed true merit) will return to favor and will be hailed as discoveries, and then relegated to limbo for another course of years. Great changes are likely only in materials used to manufacture lures and in such barrier-breaking innovations as the imaginative use of color, scent, and sound as attractors.

Wooden plugs will phase out—no very erudite prediction, because their manufacture is expensive when mass production is initiated. Actually, there are areas in which the action of the old wooden lure has yet to be duplicated, but it's a dead duck because hard plastic comes very close and adds the benefits of stability, quality control, and ease of manufacture. Although a mold is rather expensive, once a maker has absorbed initial costs he can turn out plugs like love beads. Moreover, the plugs will be remarkably similar. If design engineers have made the right guesses, the mass-produced plastic lure will not waterlog—as will wood—and it will remain serviceable until such time as some overeager hero snaps a line and consigns it to the shambling sea.

Hard plastics are versatile. They can be used to fabricate floating, neutral buoyancy, or sinking lures. They may be translucent, delicately colored and scaled, or fired with the unnatural blaze of fluorescent pigments. Since color can be molded in, ordinary wear and tear may only dull a surface. If hardware is tough and stainless, such a lure may be the most indestructible of its type.

I have in my possession a plastic Finnish minnow plug that, obviously, was lost by an angler at some point in time and fouled on bottom. It is one of Plastic Research and Development's "Rebel" swimmers, and it is almost entirely covered with barnacles! The high-carbon steel hooks are gone, long rusted away to basic elements, but hangers and split rings, made of stainless steel, are still bright and clean. It would be quite possible to scrape the barnacles off, attach new hooks, and catch fish with this lure. A wooden bait, similarly drowned in the sea, would be waterlogged, worm-riddled, and useless.

Soft plastics will be quite as useful as the hard types in our future sport fishery. Manufacturers have learned, through costly trial and error, that it is not enough to build an exact facsimile of a forage species; such lures must also feature built-in action to be effective. There is much room for development in this area and we are sure to see exciting new developments of synthetic building blocks.

While wood must become no more than a home mechanic's substitute for plastic, metals will continue to come on strong in lure-making. Spoons and jigs, depending on types, are best served by steel, brass, or lead. In this field, the major change will lie in a gradual replacement of natural fiber dressings. Hair and feathers will disappear as new synthetics equal or even surpass the benefits of the original. These man-made "feathers" and "bucktails" will be far more durable than the real McCoy, and less expensive. Look for them to take over immediately after science has solved a few problems, such as the synthetic's current lack of fine taper and supple action, the ability to "breathe" in the water and look alive.

Very possibly the next major advance in lure-making will be radical employment of color, scent, and sound. All have been essayed but, with one exception, have yet to achieve a spectacular breakthrough. During the past couple of decades, anglers have proved that color can dictate success or failure in the hunt for certain fishes, even during the hours of darkness. Aside from grotesque and brilliant hues unlike anything in nature, presumably effective because they awaken anger rather than hunger in fish, more or less exact simulation of bait has paid off in big catches. There is no norm, because the various predators differ in degrees of selectivity.

Fluorescent pigments offer an entirely new concept. Sometimes these highly activated finishes will scare a wary fish right over the horizon, yet often they work well. The lads and lasses in laboratories cannot resist impolite smiles when they hear that "unlike anything in nature" bit, for a measure of fluorescence has always graced creatures of the sea. The brilliance of modern fluorescing pigments is most closely approached by fishes that "light up" with feeding color, a change roughly akin to humankind's emotional flush.

Gradually, lure makers will temper the first extravagant application of fluorescents and will use them subtly, as nature does, thus imparting a faint glow keyed to the actual color of specific forage fishes, squids, and other tidbits of the sea. No game fish has ever told us precisely what he sees in that bright or increasingly twilight environment of the shoals or deeps, so human beings can only study the feeding patterns of various species, ponder the implications of such patterns, experiment, and grope for answers. The old idea that all fishes are color blind has been discredited by angler and biologist alike. If they were monochromatic, there'd be little need for bright camouflage patterns and chameleonlike changes.

Perhaps, more than we know, sound already plays a great part in the success of any artificial lure. Sonic waves are created by the rapid swimming action of a plug or a metal spoon. Obviously, surface poppers bring predators from surprising distances. The Southland's old popping cork and trailing shrimp routine is based on sound waves and commotion, in this case a true decoy operation. Theoretically, the cruising game fish senses commotion, sees or hears it, and immediately assumes that its fellows are feasting on something delectable. The flash of attractor spoons ahead of trolled baits accomplishes the same end result. Both popping cork and attractor spoon are decoys.

We must probe this field and actually build sound effects into artificial lures. So far, attempts have been far from scientific. Chairborne inventors have offered curious baits that buzz like a hive of bees, squeak like mice in a trap, gurgle, bubble, and rattle. They are rather vague about the fish-attracting potential of bees swimming a couple of fathoms under the ripples, or why the squeaks, bubbles, and rattles chosen are calculated to intrigue a hungry predator.

Nonetheless, these innovators pursue a very hot track. Marine biologists have demonstrated that practically all sea creatures emit sound, and declare that it may one day become possible to identify each separate species by the grunts, squeals, clicks, and aquatic rumblings recorded on sophisticated instruments. Moreover, and this is of supreme importance, scientists aver that many fishes boast a considerable range of sound emission, with separate notes indicating well-being, fright, pain, and emotion triggered by pursuit.

A classic example is the southern pigfish used as a decoy to draw sea trout. In this somewhat cruel operation, a pigfish's fins are clipped and the little bait is then tethered on a short line and allowed to swim, bleating its distress. Sea trout vector in to feast on a wounded quarry, and are then taken on various baits or artificials cast by anglers. The technique has been well tested and it works. Perhaps, although deliberate mutilation is never employed, this is another reason for the spectacular success of live-lining, in which a free-swimming forage fish is secured by a hook pinned through the skin ahead of its dorsal fin, or at some other point deemed most effective by the angler. That bait, if it is capable of doing so, must emit sounds indicating fright and impairment of healthy action.

Logically, it should be possible for electronic ears to record the fright talk of any important forage species and for manufacturers to somehow simulate this sound in the construction of a lure. I am convinced that artificials of the future will be so equipped, and that a plug built to resemble, say, a tinker mackerel will broadcast the sonic waves of a mackerel in distress. The sea is a babel of strange voices. We have only to learn the language.

Scent, even in the human animal, is a subtle blend of taste and the olfactory. We know that certain fishes can be vectored in by a chum slick that is watery and contains little of actual substance. Sharks are famed for their ability to zero in on the source of a blood trace. All logic indicates that scent (or call it taste) is a very important attractor in the sea.

Again, lure manufacturers have experimented without ever really succeeding. Artificials fitted with reservoirs of fish oils and patent scents come and go with monotonous regularity. Anise is commonly incorporated in the blending of soft plastic baits, and many feel that it adds a measure of attraction. Sniff that "rubber" eel or sea worm, just out of a plastic packaging bubble, and you will inhale the fragrance of licorice. Are fish partial to licorice? Maybe so, and maybe no. Possibly the rendered-out oils that have failed, or seem mildly effective at best, are far removed from "live" odor. Perhaps it will never be possible to simulate the come-hither smells, but the possibility is fascinating and it will be thoroughly investigated by lure makers of the future. Scent and sound—if they can be utilized by clever designers and field testers—might well make it possible to take dead aim at specific game species and to turn away unwanted varieties. I think it likely that the commercial fishery, with its vested interest in specialized harvests, may be first to successfully utilize sound and scent to reap a given crop. All over our watery world, serious researchers are investigating the enigma.

So far as the evolution of tackle is concerned, we always return to the plebeian hook, an item too often taken for granted although it may well be the weakest link in a weapons system. Very recently *Angling,* the British magazine, discussed an "infallible fly hook," and Chairman Dick Orton of the British Association of Fishing Tackle Makers declared that yes, such a hook could be made—for approximately $50 to $75 apiece!

In Chicago, one humid summer night, under the mellowing influence of certain juices, soft music, and good food, a representative of a famous American hook manufacturer, attending the American Fishing Tackle and Manufacturers' Association trade show, admitted that his firm *could* produce a faultless stainless-steel barb for marine angling, but it would cost about $30, a bit better than the British estimate but still a wild escalation over the present five to ten cents per hook.

The ultimate hooks will arrive, of course, because metallurgists constantly improve alloys and industry forever upgrades equipment. If we now agree that high-carbon steel, plated with nickel and cadmium, remains an all-around best choice, be assured that tomorrow will witness an almost complete switch to stainless steel and hooks that will be finely tempered, bereft of instability in the form of soft spots, brittle bends, and points that fail to hold an edge. It is unlikely that radical new patterns will evolve. Indeed, many of the old faithfuls will phase out because they have been upstaged by the relatively new claws and the time-tested O'Shaughnessy, Siwash, Sobey, and Martu bends.

Accessories and tools will improve quite as rapidly as basic tackle—perhaps more rapidly because they have been neglected. Not so very long ago a saltwater tackle box was a homemade affair, or perhaps a plebeian bucket. Freshwater containers were simply too delicate and too thoroughly cursed with miniature trays for work in the big leagues. Happily, a few makers have now produced practical boxes, tough enough to absorb punishment and with trays that are calibrated to the big lures of the salt chuck. With increasing demand, there will be more and better saltwater tackle boxes, each designed to carry a necessary supply of indispensable gear. They will be tough, roomy, and they will be fitted with foolproof locking devices to prevent accidental opening during transit in airplane baggage compartments.

Today, the gaff and the net are accepted as final answers in devices to beach or boat marine game fish. Both have faults. Unless a gaff is placed in the jaw of a battler, it draws blood and thus injures a quarry destined for release. It is a killer and a maimer in the hands of most anglers.

Nets are fine on small game fish, and sometimes a huge hoop net does well on big Pacific salmon where the lure or bait is fitted with no more than one or two single hooks. Otherwise, barbs foul in the meshes and much valuable fishing time is lost. Where sharp-toothed species are sought, netting becomes more expensive, because the critters will proceed to chop strands.

There will be new developments in landing devices, perhaps some practical variation of the salmon "tailer" that can be applied to a fish of any size, so that it can be landed without injury, tagged, and released. Some such noose arrangement is inevitable, because sport fishermen will increasingly place greater emphasis on the conservation and management of marine resources than in the senseless kill. Anglers (and commercial operators) are beginning to understand that the ocean's largess is not inexhaustible and that it must be protected. Within a few years, mankind will accept the logic of maintaining a renewable resource through management and the reaping of a safe harvest. There is no other alternative.

Make no mistake—as sportsmen we will range all the seas and we will discover great grounds now unknown or screened by distance and a lack of facilities. We will be competitors until the last sunset, yet there will be far less killing for the sake of killing. The meat-fishing tournaments will become memory, denounced by an outraged citizenry, and any fish brought to boat or beach will either be released, retained for a personal dinner table, or, if it is commercially important on an open and legal market, sold. There will be an aversion to waste and a universal revulsion against slaughter for the sake of promotion and area advertising.

Increasingly, angling tournaments will stress the release of game fish, coupled with tagging to further the knowledge of migration and the ecology of those species concerned. Only prizes important enough to be mounted as trophies, or those destined to serve as food, will be harvested. In most cases, the camera will supersede the taxidermist's knife, plastic, and epoxy. As fishermen, we will mature.

The time of transition is—now! Marine anglers, whether they know it or not, have already seen the end of an era. The old wild and woolly days of all-out assault on an environment are receding into history. Like the market hunters of earth, those well-meaning reivers who believed that a given resource was inexhaustible, the wanton fish killers are a vanishing breed. Many of the erstwhile marauders, again like history's ancient market gunners, have become the most ardent of conservationists. Firsthand knowledge is the ultimate teacher.

Fortunately, the modern saltwater sport fisherman courts a bright future. Hopefully, he is halting his all-out depredation at a safe moment in time. He will insist upon intelligent, well-funded research and management to preserve the bounty of the seas, and he will be savage in opposition to industrial pirates and politicians who would still gamble away a world biological ecosystem in pollution of the environment or ill-conceived oil and mineral operations on fragile continental coasts.

John Masefield wrote: "I must go down to the seas again, to the lonely sea and the sky," and billions of future world citizens will echo and applaud. As sportsmen, we go down to the sea because it is the last almost unlimited field of beneficent combat, the earth's last frontier.

BIBLIOGRAPHY

Ackerman, Bill. *Handbook of Fishes of the Atlantic Seaboard*. Washington, D.C.: American, 1951.

Adams, Leon D. *Striped Bass Fishing in California and Oregon*. Palo Alto: Pacific Books, 1953.

Babson, Stanley M. *Bonefishing*. New York: Harper & Row, 1965.

Bates, Joseph D., Jr. *Atlantic Salmon Flies and Fishing*. Harrisburg, Pennsylvania: Stackpole, 1970.

_____. *Streamer Fly Tying and Fishing*. Harrisburg, Pennsylvania: Stackpole, 1950.

Bigelow, Henry B., and Schroeder, William C. *Fishes of the Gulf of Maine*. Washington, D.C.: U.S. Government Printing Office, 1953.

Bird, Esteban A. *Fishing Off Puerto Rico*. New York: Barnes, 1960.

Boyle, Robert H. *The Hudson River*. New York: Norton, 1969.

Brooks, Joe. *Bermuda Fishing*. Harrisburg, Pennsylvania: Stackpole, 1957.

_____. *Complete Book of Fly Casting*. New York: Barnes, 1958.

_____. *Salt Water Game Fishing*. New York: Harper & Row, 1968.

_____. *A World of Fishing*. New York: Van Nostrand, 1964.

Brooks, Win. *The Shining Tides*. New York: William Morrow, 1952.

Butler, Jean Campbell. *Danger Shark!* Boston: Little, Brown, 1964.

Caine, Lou S. *Game Fish of the South*. Boston: Houghton Mifflin, 1935.

Camp, Raymond R. *Fishing the Surf*. Boston: Little, Brown, 1941.

Cannon, Raymond. *How to Fish the Pacific Coast*. Menlo Park, California: Lane, 1962.

_____. and the Sunset Editors. *Fishing the Sea of Cortez*. Menlo Park, California: Lane, 1966.

Cousteau, Jacques-Yves, and Cousteau, Philippe. *The Shark, Splendid Savage of the Sea*. New York: Doubleday, 1970.

Evanoff, Vlad. *How to Fish in Salt Water*. New York: Barnes, 1962.

_____. *Natural Salt Water Fishing Baits*. New York: Barnes, 1953.

_____. *Surf Fishing*. New York: Ronald Press, 1958.

Farrington, S. Kip, Jr. *Fishing the Atlantic*. New York: Coward, McCann, 1949.

_____. *Fishing the Pacific*. New York: Coward, McCann, 1953.

_____. *Fishing with Hemingway and Glassell*. New York: David McKay, 1971.

Francis, Phil. *Salt Water Fishing from Maine to Texas*. New York: Macmillan, 1963.

Gifford, Tom. *Anglers and Muscleheads*. New York: E. P. Dutton, 1960.

314

Goadby, Peter. *Big Fish and Blue Water.* New York: Holt, Rinehart and Winston, 1972.

Goode, G. Brown. *American Fishes.* Boston: W. A. Houghton, 1888.

Grey, Zane. *Adventures in Angling.* Edited by Ed Zern. New York: Harper & Brothers, 1952.

Halstead, Bruce W. *Dangerous Marine Animals.* Cambridge, Maryland: Cornell Maritime Press, 1959.

Haw, Frank, and Buckley, Raymond M. *Salt Water Fishing in Washington.* State of Washington, 1971.

Heilner, Van Campen. *Salt Water Fishing.* New York: Knopf, 1953.

Holm, Don. *Pacific North!* Caldwell, Idaho: Caxton, 1969.

Jansen, Jerry. *Successful Surf Fishing.* New York: E. P. Dutton, 1959.

LaMonte, Francesca. *Marine Game Fishes of the World.* New York: Doubleday, 1952.

Lyman, Henry. *Bluefishing.* Boston: Salt Water Sportsman, 1950.

————. and Woolner, Frank. *The Complete Book of Striped Bass Fishing.* New York: Barnes, 1954.

————. *The Complete Book of Weakfishing.* New York: Barnes, 1959.

————. *Tackle Talk.* New York: Barnes, 1971.

Major, Harlan. *Salt Water Fishing Tackle.* New York: Funk & Wagnalls, 1939.

McClane, Al. *McClane's Standard Fishing Encyclopedia.* New York: Holt, Rinehart & Winston, 1965.

Migdalski, Edward C. *Anglers' Guide to the Salt Water Gamefishes.* New York: Ronald Press, 1958.

Moss, Frank T. *Successful Ocean Game Fishing.* Camden, Maine: International Marine, 1971.

Mundus, Frank, and Wisner, Bill. *Sportfishing for Sharks.* New York: Macmillan, 1971.

Netboy, Anthony. *The Atlantic Salmon.* Boston: Houghton Mifflin, 1968.

Norman, J. R. *A History of Fishes.* London: Ernest Benn, 1958.

Pell, Claiborne. *Challenge of the Seven Seas.* New York: William Morrow, 1966.

Ray, Carleton, and Ciampi, Elgin. *The Underwater Guide to Marine Life.* New York: Barnes, 1956.

Reiger, George. *Zane Grey, Outdoorsman.* Englewood Cliffs, New Jersey: Prentice-Hall, 1972.

Reinfelder, Al. *Bait Tail Fishing.* New York: Barnes, 1969.

Rodman, Oliver H. P. *A Handbook of Salt Water Fishing.* Philadelphia: Lippincott, 1940.

————. *Striped Bass.* New York: Barnes, 1944.

————. *The Salt Water Fisherman's Favorite Four.* New York: William Morrow, 1948.

Roedel, Phil M. *Common Ocean Fishes of the California Coast.* State of California, 1953.

Roman, Erl. *Fishing for Fun in Salty Waters.* New York: David McKay, 1940.

Rosko, Milt. *Fishing from Boats.* New York: Macmillan, 1968.

————. *Secrets of Striped Bass Fishing.* New York: Macmillan, 1966.

Sand, George X. *Salt Water Fly Fishing.* New York: Knopf, 1969.

Scott, Genio C. *Fishing in American Waters.* New York: Harper & Brothers, 1875.

Tinsley, Jim Bob. *The Sailfish.* Gainesville, Florida: University of Florida Press, 1964.

Waterman, Charles F. *Modern Fresh and Salt Water Fly Fishing.* New York: Winchester, 1972.

Westman, James. *Why Fish Bite and Why They Don't Bite.* Englewood Cliffs, New Jersey: Prentice-Hall, 1961.

Wulff, Lee. *The Atlantic Salmon.* New York: Barnes, 1958.

INDEX

INDEX